Built for Speed

The World's Fastest Helicopters

by Glen and Karen Bledsoe

Consultant:
U.S. Army
Special Operations Command

CAPSTONE
HIGH-INTEREST
BOOKS

an imprint of Capstone Press
Mankato, Minnesota

Capstone High-Interest Books are published by Capstone Press
151 Good Counsel Drive, P.O. Box 669, Mankato, Minnesota 56002
http://www.capstone-press.com

Library of Congress Cataloging-in-Publication Data
Bledsoe, Glen.
    The World's fastest helicopters/by Glen and Karen Bledsoe.
    p. cm.—(Built for speed)
    Includes bibliographical references and index.
    Summary: Discusses the history and development of some of the world's fastest
helicopters, describing the specific features and specifications of such aircraft as
the SA 360 Dauphin, Boeing-Sikorsky RAH-66 Comanche, AH-64 Apache, and
V-22 Osprey.
    ISBN 0-7368-1059-5
    1. Helicopters—Juvenile literature. 2. Military helicopters—Juvenile literature.
[1. Helicopters. 2. Military helicopters.] I. Bledsoe, Karen E. II. Title. III. Built for
speed (Mankato, Minn.)
TL716.2 .B58 2002
629.133'352—dc21   2001003440

Editorial Credits

Leah K. Pockrandt, editor; Karen Risch, product planning editor; Timothy Halldin,
    cover designer and illustrator; Katy Kudela, photo researcher

Photo Credits

Boeing Management Company, cover, 24, 27, 31, 39 (top)
Defense Visual Information Center, 28, 37
Digital Vision Ltd., 40
Fotodynamics/Ted Carlson, 18, 21, 32, 39 (bottom)
Hulton Getty/Archive Photos, 7
Intora-Firebird of the United Kingdom, 43
The Military Picture Library/Corbis, 11
Photri-Microstock, 8, 16; Photri-Microstock/B. Howe, 12, 38 (top);
    Photri-Microstock/Glen Jackson, 15
Richard Zellner/Sikorsky Aircraft Corp., 22, 38 (bottom)
William B. Folsom, 4, 35

1 2 3 4 5 6 07 06 05 04 03 02

Table of Contents

Chapter 1

Fast Helicopters

People have been interested in flying for centuries. In 1488, an artist and inventor named Leonardo da Vinci drew a picture of a flying machine. It looked much like a helicopter. Da Vinci's idea may have come from a popular toy called a whirligig.

Da Vinci's drawing was a plan for a rotorcraft. An overhead propeller lifts these flying machines into the air. Da Vinci never built his aircraft. In the 1400s, engines did not exist to power flying machines.

History

In the early 1900s, Henry Berliner created a helicopter. It flew only about 15 feet

Today, Henry Berliner's helicopter is in the College Park Aviation Museum in College Park, Maryland.

(4.6 meters) above the ground for a distance of 100 yards (91 meters). Others also tried to build helicopters. But none of them flew long enough to be practical. No one was successful until Igor Sikorsky.

In 1919, Sikorsky moved to the United States from Russia. In 1923, he formed an aviation company called Sikorsky Aero Engineering Corporation. In 1939, Sikorsky built the VS-300. This aircraft could fly vertically, sideways, and backward. But it could not fly forward. Sikorsky changed the design. On May 6, 1941, he flew the VS-300 for 1 hour, 32 minutes, and 26 seconds.

The VS-300 was the first practical helicopter. It could move in any direction. Today, several types of rotorcraft exist. These aircraft include helicopters, autogyros, and tiltrotors.

Helicopters

A helicopter has one or more motorized overhead rotors. A rotor has two to five blades that spin. The blades allow the pilot to operate the helicopter.

Igor Sikorsky built the first practical helicopter.

Many helicopters have only one large horizontal rotor. This rotor lifts the craft. But it also causes the helicopter to spin in the opposite direction of the blades. Some helicopters have a small vertical tail rotor that faces sideways. This rotor keeps the helicopter from spinning with the force of the overhead rotor. Pilots also use the tail rotor to turn the helicopter.

Some helicopters have two large overhead blades that turn in opposite directions. This

Most helicopters have hinged rotor blades.

movement stops the aircraft from spinning. The blades are either located on top of each other or side by side. Some helicopters also have a blade on the front end and another on the rear.

The rotor blades of most helicopters are hinged. This features allows the blades to tip. The helicopter moves in the direction of the tip.

Autogyros and Tiltrotors

An autogyro looks much like a helicopter. But the two machines work differently. The autogyro has a horizontal overhead blade like a helicopter. But an engine does not rotate the autogyro's blade. A vertical propeller located at the front of the craft pushes the autogyro forward. Air rushes past the horizontal overhead rotor and lifts the autogyro into the air.

Autogyros cannot hover in one spot as helicopters do. But they can make short takeoffs and landings like helicopters.

Tiltrotor aircraft look similar to airplanes. But the wings have propellers attached to them. The rotors tilt horizontally during takeoff like a helicopter's rotors do. The rotors tilt down into a vertical position once the helicopter is in the air. This position pulls the aircraft forward.

Uses of Rotorcraft

Rotorcraft have many advantages over airplanes. They can turn quickly and fly in any direction. They can fly close to the ground. Some can hover. Rotorcraft need little space in which to land and take off. Rotorcraft can fly in strong winds. Rotors have the same ability to lift despite the direction of the wind.

Rotorcraft have many uses. Some people fly small rotorcraft for sport. Some companies offer sight-seeing helicopter rides. People often use helicopters to search for or rescue missing or injured people. Rescuers also use rotorcraft to carry cargo to remote locations and to fight fires.

The U.S. military uses the world's fastest helicopters. The military uses many of these helicopters to rescue wounded soldiers. It uses specially equipped helicopters to spy on enemies. The military also uses some helicopters in combat.

This Westland Lynx is similar to the Lynx that was used to break the speed record.

A specially-designed helicopter set the world speed record in 1986. This helicopter is a Lynx. A British company called Westland makes the Lynx. The record-setting Lynx had high-speed, lightweight rotor blades.

On August 11, 1986, a Lynx reached a speed of 249.09 miles (400.87 kilometers) per hour. It set the record on a 9.3-mile (15-kilometer) course.

The Lynx is an anti-tank helicopter. It is equipped with weapons powerful enough to destroy a tank. The Lynx is powered by two Rolls-Royce Gem 41 engines. The maximum speed of a standard Lynx helicopter is 205 miles (330 kilometers) per hour. A helicopter's range is the distance it can travel without refueling. The Lynx's range is 53 miles (85 kilometers).

Chapter 2

Dauphin and Panther

A company in France called Eurocopter makes several types of helicopters. These include two similar light- to medium-weight helicopters. The SA 360 Dauphin is for civilian use. The AS 565 Panther is for military use.

SA 360 Dauphin
The SA 360 Dauphin is a single-engine helicopter. It was first flown in 1972.

Combat helicopters have landing gear that retracts. The pilot can pull the landing gear safely inside the helicopter. But pilots do not use the Dauphin in combat. It does not need to protect its landing gear. The Dauphin's landing gear is fixed.

The Dauphin's landing gear does not retract.

People use the Dauphin to travel to hard-to-reach places. Pilots can land the Dauphin on boats, rooftops, and other small areas.

Hospitals and rescue services use the Dauphin to carry injured or sick people to hospitals. Some hospital landing pads are on the hospitals' roofs.

Many police and fire departments also use the Dauphin. They use the helicopter to search for lost or injured people. They also use it to transport fire fighters and police officers to areas where they are needed.

The Dauphin is useful as a rescue helicopter because of its speed. The Dauphin can reach a speed of 196 miles (315 kilometers) per hour.

The AS 565 Panther

The AS 565 Panther is the military version of the Dauphin. It first flew in 1973. The tails of the AS 565 and the SA 360 Dauphin are similar. The helicopters are very different in most other ways.

The Panther is used to bring soldiers and cargo to battle sites. The Panther's landing gear retracts to protect it from enemy weapons. The

Many police departments use the Dauphin for search-and-rescue work.

Panther also is used to bring wounded soldiers to hospitals.

The Panther can carry a great deal of weight. Two pilots fly each helicopter. The Panther can carry eight to 10 soldiers. It also can carry weapons, medicine, and supplies.

The AS 565 SB is a Panther that is armed with weapons. The AS 565 SB can be carried

aboard combat ships at sea. Pilots may use it to gather information about an enemy's position. The AS 565 SB also can launch attacks from a ship. It can carry cannons and missiles to destroy aircraft and tanks. It also can carry rockets and torpedoes. These weapons are used to destroy ships and submarines.

The AS 565 SB flies slower than the Dauphin. The weapons add extra weight to the helicopter. The AS 565 SB can reach speeds of 184 miles (296 kilometers) per hour.

The AS 565 and AS 565 SB both have a four-blade rotor on top of the aircraft. The rotor is turned by two turboshaft engines. Each engine produces 749 horsepower. This unit measures the engine's power. The helicopter's range is 506 miles (814 kilometers).

The Panther is used as a military transport and combat helicopter.

Chapter 3

RAH-66 Comanche

The RAH-66 Comanche is a new type of helicopter. Boeing and Sikorsky Aircraft Corporation build this small, fast helicopter. It can reach speeds of 204 miles (328 kilometers) per hour.

The U.S. Army plans to begin using this helicopter in 2006. The Comanche will replace older attack and observation helicopters.

The Comanche's Mission

The Comanche does not carry supplies or troops. It is a reconnaissance helicopter. The U.S. military uses these helicopters to scout out areas and search for enemy soldiers. This information is sent back to support troops. The military has used other helicopters for

The U.S. Army plans to begin using the RAH-66 Comanche in 2006.

reconnaissance. But the Comanche is the first helicopter designed for that purpose only.

The Comanche is equipped with special visual and electronic sensors. These devices help crew members identify and locate enemy weapon systems. The sensors allow the helicopter to operate at night and in bad weather.

The Comanche's Engine

The Comanche has twin turboshaft engines. A turboshaft engine creates hot air to turn the helicopter's five-blade rotor. Each engine produces 1,300 horsepower.

The Comanche's engines are different than other helicopter engines. The engines have a high thrust-to-weight ratio. They produce a great deal of power compared to their weight. Thrust is the force that moves helicopters forward. Thrust is measured in pounds.

Weapons

The Comanche will be armed with weapons. Crew members can attack targets on the ground or direct support troops to enemy targets. The Comanche also can serve as a combat aircraft against other aircraft in the air. Special equipment

The Comanche's twin turboshaft engines each produce 1,300 horsepower.

helps the gunner quickly target an enemy. The gunner targets and fires the Comanche's weapons. The Comanche will be teamed with the AH-64D Apache Longbow. These two attack helicopters can trade electronic information easily.

The Comanche carries a three-barrel General Electric Gatling gun mounted on a turret. This device turns to allow crew members to fire the gun in many directions. A motor powers the turret. Electronic sensors will not allow the gun to fire at targets that are too far away to hit.

The Comanche is loaded with different types of weapons.

The Comanche can carry different types of missiles and rockets. The missiles are mounted on the weapon bay doors. The doors open sideways from the aircraft.

Pilots will wear a special kind of helmet during missions. The helmet is connected to the helicopter's computer system. The helmet visor contains an electronic display screen. The display screen shows information about enemy targets. Sensors inside the helmet tell the computer when the pilot's head turns. The computer can lock onto the targets that the pilot looks at. The helmets will allow pilots to fire weapons very quickly.

The Comanche's Design

The Comanche is hard for enemy soldiers to see, hear, or detect with radar. Radar uses radio waves to find distant aircraft and objects. Machines and people give off heat. Heat rays are called infrared rays. Weapon instruments can detect infrared. The Comanche has shields to hide its infrared rays.

The Comanche will need little maintenance. Pilots can easily replace many of the helicopter parts. This ability is an advantage when pilots are on long-distance missions. The Comanche also uses less fuel than other helicopters. This feature gives the Comanche a longer range than other helicopters. The Comanche has a range of 1,406 miles (2,263 kilometers). To reach this range, the helicopter must be equipped with extra gas tanks.

BIPOLAR DISORDER

A Clinician's Guide
to Biological Treatments

Edited by
LAKSHMI N. YATHAM
VIVEK KUSUMAKAR
STANLEY P. KUTCHER

BRUNNER-ROUTLEDGE
New York • London

Published in 2002 by
Brunner-Routledge
29 West 35th Street
New York, NY 10001

Published in Great Britain by
Brunner-Routledge
27 Church Road
Hove, East Sussex, BN3 2FA

Brunner-Routledge is an imprint of the Taylor & Francis Group.

Printed in the United States of America on acid-free paper.

Cover design: Pearl Chang

10 9 8 7 6 5 4 3 2

Library of Congress Cataloging-in-Publication Data
Bipolar disorder : a clinician's guide to biological treatments / [edited] by Lakshmi N. Yatham,
Vivek Kusumakar, and Stanley P. Kutcher.
    p. ; cm.
  Includes bibliographical references and index.
  ISBN 0–415–93390–0
  1. Manic-depressive illness—Chemotherapy. 2. Depression, Mental—Chemotherapy.
3. Neuropsychopharmacology. 4. Manic-depressive illness—Treatment. I. Yatham,
Lakshmi N. II. Kutcher, Stanley P. III. Kusumakar, Vivek.
  [DNLM: 1. Bipolar Disorder—drug therapy. 2. Tranquilizing Agents—therapeutic use.
WM 207 B6157 2002]
RC516 .B5246 2002
616.89'5061—dc21   2002018282

Contents

106|70

Contributors

Charles L. Bowden, M.D.,
　　Karren Professor and Chairman,
　　Department of Psychiatry,
　　University of Texas Health Science Center,
　　San Antonio, Texas

K. N. Roy Chengappa, M.D.,
　　Associate Professor of Psychiatry,
　　Western Psychiatric Institute & Clinic,
　　University of Pittsburgh Medical Center,
　　Special Studies Center at Mayview State Hospital,
　　Stanley Center for the Innovative Treatment of Bipolar Disorder

William H. Coryell, M.D.,
　　Professor of Psychiatry,
　　Psychiatry Research—MEB,
　　College of Medicine,
　　University of Iowa

A. Eden Evins, M.D.,
　　Instructor in Psychiatry,
　　Harvard Medical School,
　　Co-Director, Schizophrenia Research Program,
　　Massachusetts General Hospital, Boston

Samuel Gershon, M.D.,
　　Professor of Psychiatry,
　　Western Psychiatric Institute & Clinic,
　　University of Pittsburgh Medical Center,
　　Stanley Center for the Innovative Treatment of Bipolar Disorder,
　　Pittsburgh

A. Dooley Goumeniouk, M.D.,
　　Clinical Associate Professor,
　　Department of Psychiatry,
　　The University of British Columbia,
　　Vancouver

Paul E. Keck, Jr., M.D.,
　　Biological Psychiatry Program,
　　Department of Psychiatry,
　　University of Cincinnati College of Medicine,
　　Cincinnati, Ohio

Terence A. Ketter, M.D., F.R.C.P(C),
　　Chief, Bipolar Disorders Clinic,
　　Department of Psychiatry and Behavioral Sciences,
　　Stanford University of Medicine, Stanford, California

Vivek Kusumakar, M.D., F.R.C.P.C.
　　Associate Professor of Psychiatry,
　　Director, Stanley International Centre for the Study of Bipolar Disorder,
　　Dalhousie University, Halifax, Nova Scotia

Stanley P. Kutcher, M.D., F.R.C.P.C.,
　　Professor and Head, Department of Psychiatry,
　　Dalhousie University,
　　Halifax, Nova Scotia

Raymond W. Lam, M.D.,
　　Professor of Psychiatry, University of British Columbia,
　　Medical Director, Mood Disorders Clinic, UBC Hospital
　　Vancouver

Joseph Levine, M.D.,
　　Visiting Faculty,
　　Western Psychiatric Institute & Clinic,
　　University of Pittsburgh Medical Center,
　　Special Studies Center at Mayview State Hospital,
　　Stanley Center for the Innovative Treatment of Bipolar Disorder,
　　Pittsburgh

Xiaohua Li, M.D., Ph,D.,
  Department of Psychiatry and Behavioral Neurobiology,
  University of Alabama at Birmingham
  Frank P. McMaster, Research Associate,
  Mood Disorders Group,
  Dalhousie University,
  The I.W.K. Grace Health Centre,
  Halifax, Nova Scotia

Frank P. MacMaster,
  Research Associate,
  Mood Disorders Group,
  Dalhousie University,
  The I.W.K. Grace Health Centre,
  Halifax, Nova Scotia

Susan L. McElroy, M.D.,
  Professor of Psychiatry,
  Biological Psychiatry Program,
  Department of Psychiatry,
  University of Cincinnati College of Medicine,
  Cincinnati, Ohio

Roy H. Perlis, M.D.,
  Psychopharmacology Chief Resident,
  Massachusetts General Hospital,
  Boston, MA 02115
  Clinical Fellow in Psychiatry,
  Harvard Medical School

Gary S. Sachs, M.D.,
  Assistant Professor of Psychiatry,
  Department of Psychiatry,
  Massachusetts General Hospital, Boston

Karen Saperson, M.B., Ch.B.,
  Assistant Professor of Psychiatry,
  Department of Psychiatry,
  McMaster University,
  Hamilton, Ontario

Kenneth I. Shulman, M.D., S.M.,
Professor of Psychiaty,
Department of Psychiatry,
University of Toronto

Jair C. Soares, M.D.,
Western Psychiatric Institute & Clinic,
University of Pittsburgh Medical Center,
Stanley Center for the Innovative Treatment of Bipolar Disorder,
Pittsburgh

Mauricio F. Tohen, M.D.,
Professor of Psychiatry
Associate Clinical Professor of Psychiatry,
Lilly Research Laboratories,
Indianapolis, Indiana,
Harvard Medical School

Po W. Wang, M.D.,
Department of Psychiatry and Behavioral Sciences,
Stanford University of Medicine,
Stanford, California

Lakshmi N. Yatham, M.B., F.R.C.P.C.
Associate Professor of Psychiatry,
Division of Mood Disorders, University of British Columbia,
Director, Mood Disorders Clinical Research Unit, UBC Hospital,
Vancouver Hospital and Health Sciences Centre

L. Trevor Young, M.D., Ph.D.,
Associate Professor,
McMaster University,
Department of Psychiatry,
Hamilton, Ontario

Carlos A. Zarate, Jr., M.D.,
Chief, Mood Disorders Research Unit,
Assoc. Clinical Director, Laboratory of Molecular Pathophysiology,
Mood and Anxieties Disorders Program,
National Institute of Mental Health,
Bethesda, MD

Anthanasios P. Zis, M.D.,
Professor and Head,
Department of Psychiatry,
The University of British Columbia,
Vancouver

Preface

Bipolar Disorder affects at least 1.6% of the population and is the sixth leading cause of disability. The discovery of lithium offered the hope that this condition could be treated effectively. This has been true for bipolar I, classical, episodic disorder, but as our understanding of the heterogenous manifestations of this disorder have increased, clinicians have realized that lithium is not a panacea for bipolar disorder. The recognition that carbamazepine and, later, valproate, have mood modulating properties opened the door to a new era. This happened even as traditional treatment with neuroleptics of mania continued. With the advent of a new generation of anticonvulsants and atypical neuroleptics, there has been a resurgence of interest in the pharmacological treatment of bipolar disorder, with a continuing search for the ideal mood stabilizer that is effective both in acute phases of a mood disorder and for prophylaxis. Thus, the clinician is faced with making choices from a variety of medications.

This book is intended to provide the clinician with an up-to-date review of the data on efficacy and safety of medications, and practical guidelines with which medication treatment choices can be made for a patient with bipolar disorder. In keeping with these aims, the chapters in this book fall into three main categories: the first four chapters provide clinical guidelines for the treatment of different phases of bipolar disorder; chapters 5 and 6 deal with the management of bipolar disorder in young people, the elderly, those with other psychiatric comorbidity, and in pregnant women. Chapters 7 to 11 review the efficacy of various psychotropic medications and somatic treatments commonly used for treatment of bipolar disorder, and the final chapter reviews the pharmacokinetic interactions, pharmacodynamics, adverse effects, and the authors' management of psychotropic medications. The division of chapters as outlined above necessitated allowing some overlap in content between the chapters.

This book focuses mainly on pharmacotherapy because it is the mainstay of symptomatic treatment of bipolar disorder. Clinicians, however, should be aware that the optimal treatment of bipolar disorder includes a combination of psychoeducation, lifestyle management, psychotherapy, and rehabilitative techniques with medications in the context of an empathic and longitudinal therapeutic relationship to improve symptoms, functioning, and quality of life. Clinicians will need to mold their practice around their bipolar patients' long-term symptomatic and functional needs, and establish a comprehensive illness management strategy, the cornerstone of which will be a collaborative multimodal approach and promotion of treatment adherence.

We sincerely hope that this book will help clinicians to provide rational, evidence-based treatment for patients with bipolar disorder. This book has been made possible by numerous patients suffering from bipolar disorder whose experiences and resolve have been an inspiration for the authors to find safer and more effective treatments. We also thank all the contributors for the thought, time, and energy they have given to this book, and to Gayle Scarrow and Denise Jollymore for their untiring efforts in the final preparation and formating of the manuscripts.

LAKSHMI N. YATHAM
VIVEK KUSUMAKAR
STANLEY P. KUTCHER

Foreword

The bipolar form of manic–depressive disorder is one of the oldest and newest of the major mental illnesses (Baldessarini, 2000; Goodwin & Jamison, 1990). Mania and melancholia have been recognized at least from antiquity, and the occurrence of both mania and melancholia in the same person was recognized by the Alexandria physician Aretæus of Cappadocia as early as 150 AD (Adams, 1856). In the mid-1800s, Parisian alienists Falret (1854) and Baillarger (1854) modernized the concept as insanity of double form or circular insanity, and in Germany Griesinger, recognized mania and melancholia in the same persons over time (Griesinger, 1845). In the United States, Hammond used lithium bromide as a relatively specific treatment for mania in the 1860s (Hammond, 1871). Later, Kahlbaum recognized a broad group of episodic disorders characterized as cyclothymia (Kahlbaum, 1882). In the 1890s, Weygandt recognized that manic and melancholic features of mood, thought, and behavior could co-occur in the same person at the same time in mixed states (Weygant, 1899). Kraepelin is usually credited with formulating the modern entity of manic–depressive insanity at the end of the 19th century, but he denied the importance of bipolar and unipolar forms (Kraepelin, 1899). His broad concept was not again subdivided until the mid-20th century by European investigators including Kleist (1947), Leonhard (1957), Angst (1966), and Perris (1966)—after the introduction of lithium carbonate as a specific antimanic treatment by Cade in Melbourne in 1949.

Our current American Psychiatric Association (DSM-IV) diagnostic system recognizes bipolar disorder with mania (type I) and hypomania (II), with or without depression, as well as a rapid-cycling subtype (American Psychiatric Association). It is increasingly apparent that bipolar disorder is quite common in adolescence, and even found in childhood, when its differentiation from attention and conduct disorders remains problematic. There are also increasingly recognized forms of the illness in geriatric patients, including some primary conditions of late onset (Shulman et al., 1996). There are also secondary forms associated with brain diseases and reactions to mood-elevating medicines at all ages (Krauthammer & Klerman, 1978). Lifetime prevalence of even the most classic, type I form of bipolar disorder involves at least 1.5% of the general population, and the prevalence of bipolar II disorders and secondary mania are probably similar or even greater (Akiskal et al., 2000; Kessler et al., 1994). Accordingly, bipolar disorder, as currently conceived, represents one of the most common major mental illnesses. Moreover, bipolar and unipolar major affective disorders with psychotic features are, by far, the most common idiopathic psychotic disorders, and are found in greater numbers of people than schizophrenia (Kessler et al., 1994).

Bipolar disorder presents major challenges for contemporary clinical practice. The diagnosis is frequently missed or mistaken for simple depressive illness, sometimes with potentially dangerous overuse of antidepressants (Ghaemi, Lenox, & Baldessarini, 2001). Similarly, the condition is commonly misdiagnosed in children and the elderly, often in association with inappropriate use of antidepressants or stimulants (Faedda et al., 1995; Shulman et al., 1996). Management of pregnant women with the disorder is a particularly acute challenge (Viguera et al., 2000). Additional challenges include the high mortality rates in the disorder, owing not only to very high risks of suicide, but also to accidents and medical complications of commonly comorbid substance use disorders, as well as to stress-sensitive general medical disorders (Baldessarini & Jamison, 1999; Baldessarini, Tondo, & Hennen, 2001; Tondo, Hennen, & Baldessarini, 2001). In addition, rates of sustained disability and poor outcome are much more common than formerly suspected (Tohen et al., 2000). Bipolar disorder is both a major public health problem and a large economic burden, costing many tens of billions of dollars per year in the United States alone in direct costs for care as well as indirect costs related to disability and premature death (Wyatt & Henter, 1995).

My expert colleagues, Drs. Lakshmi Yatham, Vivek Kusumaker, and Stanley Kutcher have edited an extraordinarily well-balanced and comprehensive overview of rational and research-informed contemporary clinical practice in the assessment and medical management of patients with bipolar disorder. This book contains chapters on diagnosis and treatment of mania and mixed manic-depressive states by Drs. Bowden, Kusumakar, Yatham, and Mr. MacMaster, on bipolar depression by Drs. Yatham, Kusumakar, and Kutcher, on special problems of rapid cycling by Drs. McElroy and Keck, and on long-term maintenance treatments to prevent bipolar recurrences by Dr. Coryell. The often challenging problems presented by the young and the elderly are covered by Drs. Kusumakar, Kutcher, Shulman, and Mr. MacMaster. The very common problems of psychiatric and substance use comorbidity with bipolar disorder are discussed by Drs. Zarate and Tohen. Use of specific classes of medication is reviewed in several chapters, including one on lithium by Drs. Levine, Soares, Chengappa, and Gershon; the place of antipsychotic agents by Drs. Perlis, Evins, and Sachs; the appropriate use of antidepressants by Drs. Saperson and Young; and the use of mood-altering anticonvulsants by Drs. Yatham and Kusumakar. Additional clinically important pharmacological topics reviewed include drug disposition and interactions by Drs. Ketter, Wang, and Li, and a final chapter provides a comprehensive overview of somatic treatments for the disorder by Drs. Lam, Zis, and Goumeniouk.

This volume offers a particularly well-balanced view of therapeutics, recognizing the continued value of lithium as the only long-term maintenance treatment with substantial research support for benefits in both mania and bipolar depression, as well as against suicide (Baldessarini et al., 2001; Tondo et al., 2001). It also considers the emerging alternatives to lithium, including a growing number of agents initially identified by their anticonvulsant or antipsychotic properties. The particularly difficult challenge of recognizing and safely managing bipolar depressive and mixed dysphoric-agitated states is also met in this text. In short, the book offers a scientifically sound and also very useful and practical guide for practicing primary care physicians as well as psychiatrists and other clinicians who find themselves responsible for the care of persons with one of the most common and potentially devastating psychiatric illnesses.

ROSS J. BALDESSARINI, M.D., D.Sc., FAPA, FACP, FACNP

References

Adams, F. (1856). *The Extant Works of Aretæus the Cappadocian*. London: The Syndenham Society.

Akiskal, H. S., Bourgeois, M. L., Angst, J., Post, R. M., Möller, H.-J., & Hirschfeld, R. M. A. (2000). Re-evaluating the prevalence of and diagnostic composition within the broad clinical spectrum of bipolar disorders. *Journal of Affective Disorder, 59*(Suppl), 5–30.

American Psychiatric Association. (2000). *Diagnostic and statistical manual of mental disorders* (4th ed.). Washington, DC: Author

Angst, J. (1966). Zur Ätiologie und Nosologie Endogener Depressiver Psychosen. *Monographien aus dem Gesamtgebiete der Neurologie und Psychiatrie*. Berlin: Springer Verlag.

Baillarger, J. (1854). De la folie à double-forme. *Annals of Medical Psychology [Paris], 6*, 367–391.

Baldessarini, R. J. (2000). A plea for integrity of the bipolar disorder concept. *Bipolar Disorder, 2*, 7.

Baldessarini, R. J., & Jamison, K. R. (1999). Effects of medical interventions on suicidal behavior: Summary and conclusions. *Journal of Clinical Psychiatry, 60*(Suppl. 2), 117–122.

Baldessarini, R. J., Tondo, L., & Hennen, J. (2001). Reduced suicide risk during long-term treatment with lithium. *Annals of the New York Academy of Sciences, 932*, 24–43.

Cade, J. F. J. (1949). Lithium salts in the treatment of psychotic excitement. *Medical Journal of Australia, 2,* 349–352.

Faedda, G. L., Baldessarini, R. J., Suppes, T., Tondo, L., Becker, I., & Lipschitz, D. (1995). Pediatric-onset bipolar disorder: A neglected clinical and public health problem. *Harvard Reviews of Psychiatry, 3,* 171–195.

Falret, J. (1854). Mémoire sur la folie circulaire, forme de maladie mentale caractérisée par la reproduction successive et régulière de l'état maniaque, de l'état mélancolique, and d'un intervalle lucide plus ou moins prolongé. *Bulletin of the Academy of Medicine [Paris], 19,* 382–415.

Ghaemi, S. N., Lenox, M. S., & Baldessarini, R. J. (2001). Effectiveness and safety of long-term antidepressant treatment in bipolar disorder. *Journal of Clinical Psychiatry, 62,* 565–569.

Griesinger, W. (1845). *Pathologie und Therapie der Psychischen Krankheiten.* Stuttgart: Adolf Krabbe Verlag.

Goodwin, F. K., & Jamison, K. R. (1990). *Manic Depressive Illness.* New York: Oxford University Press.

Hammond, W. A. (1871). The treatment of insanity. In *A treatise on diseases of the nervous system* (pp. 325–384). New York: Appleton and Co.

Kahlbaum, K. (1882). Über cykliches Irresein. *Der Irrenfreund, 10,* 145–157.

Kessler, R. C., McGonagle, K. A., Zhao, S., Nelson, C. B., Hughes, M., Eshleman, S., et al. (1994). Lifetime and 12-month prevalence of DSM-III-R psychiatric disorders in the United States. *Archives of General Psychiatry, 51,* 9–19.

Kleist, K. (1947). *Fortschritte der Psychiatrie.* Frankfurt-am-Main: W Kramer Verlag.

Kraepelin, E. (1899). *Psychiatrie: Ein Kurzes Lehrbuch für Studierende und Ärtze* (6th ed.). Leipzig: von Barth Verlag.

Krauthammer, C., & Klerman, G. L. (1978). Secondary mania: Manic syndromes associated with antecedent physical illness or drugs. *Archives of General Psychiatry, 35,* 1333–1339.

Leonhard, K. (1957). *Aufteilung der Endogenen Psychosen* (Vol. 1). Jena: Akademie Verlag.

Perris, C. (1966). A study of bipolar (manic-depressive) and unipolar recurrent depressive psychoses. *Acta Psychiatrica Scandinavia, 42*(Suppl. 194), 1–188.

Shulman, K. I., Tohen, M., & Kutcher, S. P. (Eds.). (1996). *Mood Disorders Across the Life-Span.* New York: John Wiley-Liss.

Tohen, M., Hennen, J., Zarate, C. A., Jr., Baldessarini, R. J., Strakowski, S. M., & Stoll, A. L. (2000). The McLean first episode project: Two-year syndromal and functional recovery in 219 cases of major affective disorders with psychotic features. *American Journal of Psychiatry, 157,* 220–228.

Tondo, L., Hennen, J., & Baldessarini, R. J. (2001). Reduced suicide risk with long-term lithium treatment in major affective Illness: A meta-analysis. *Acta Psychiatrica Scandinavia, 104,* 163–172.

Viguera, A. C., Nonacs, R., Cohen, L. S., Tondo, L., Murray, A., & Baldessarini, R. J. (2000). Risk of discontinuing lithium maintenance in pregnant vs. nonpregnant women with bipolar disorders. *American Journal of Psychiatry, 157,* 179–184.

Weygant, W. (1899). *Über die Mischzustände des Manisch-depressiven Irreseins.* Munich: JF Lehmann Verlag.

Wyatt, R. J., & Henter, I. (1995). An economic evaluation of manic-depressive illness. *Society for Psychiatry & Psychiatric Epidemiology, 30,* 213–219.

List of Figures

Diagnosis and Treatment of Hypomania and Mania

Charles L. Bowden
Vivek Kusumakar
Frank P. MacMaster
Lakshmi N. Yatham

Hypomania: Diagnostic Issues

Hypomania may occur as part of a bipolar II disorder or as a transitional state from euthymia to mania in patients with bipolar I disorder. Dunner and Day (1993) demonstrated that an expert clinician using a semistructured interview, when compared with a nonphysician trained interviewer who used the Structured Clinical Interview for DSM-III-R (SCID; American Psychiatric Association, 1987), assigned a bipolar II diagnosis much more often than did the less experienced interviewer. This raises the issue that trained interviewers on the SCID may be insensitive to histories of hypomania if they limit probing or if they fail to direct questioning about hypomania to periods immediately before or after depressive episodes. Hence it is important for clinicians to routinely question depressed patients about expanded mood states that may have preceded or followed depressive episodes. Data from ongoing genetic linkage study of bipolar I families suggests that bipolar II disorder may be the most common phenotype or clinical manifestation in both bipolar I and bipolar II families (Simpson et al., 1993).

Thus, there is some support for the clinical impression that bipolar II disorder may be more common than bipolar I disorder. The underrecognition of bipolar II disorder in research and clinical settings in adult patients, and in adolescents, may be attributable to difficulties associated with a diagnosis of hypomania. Individuals with bipolar II disorder may not view hypomanic episodes as pathological, and may even see them as very desirable. However, family members and friends may be perplexed or disturbed by the hypomanic individual's erratic behavior. It is also much more common for those suffering from bipolar II disorder to seek help only during a depressive episode. When they do present in a depressive episode, many patients may not recall or distinguish previous hypomanic episodes from euthymia without collateral information from family members or friends. Hence, it is wise to retain a high index of suspicion for bipolar II disorder in any patient with apparent recurrent unipolar depression (Akiskal et al., 1996). Further, bipolar II disorder often tends to breed true to type: Offspring and relatives of bipolar II probands commonly also have bipolar II disorder (DePaulo, Simpson, Gayle, & Folstein, 1990). Hence, a careful screening for a family history of bipolar II disorder can assist in diagnosis of a given patient. However, the clinician should also be careful not to diagnose bipolar disorder in patients, particularly those with borderline personality disorder, who often have uniphasic mood lability in the depressive to euthymic spectrum, and who may mistakenly describe euthymic states as "highs." It is, however, important to bear in mind that borderline personality disorder can be comorbid with bipolar disorder in up to 30% of patients with bipolar disorder. The clinician is also well advised to be cautious in interviewing patients with somatization disorder with depressive symptoms, because these patients can be highly suggestible, thus resulting in false positive assessments of hypomanic symptoms. Conversely, adolescent and young adult patients with rapid and ultrarapid biphasic mood cycling may be mistakenly diagnosed as having a primary borderline personality disorder. To safeguard against this, prospective mood charting and careful collateral histories and observations from friends and family members can be vital.

A hypomanic episode, as per DSM-IV (American Psychiatric Association, 1994) consists of elevated, expansive, or irritable mood plus at least three (four, if only irritable) additional manic symptoms, lasting for a minimum of 4 days, and observed as a change from baseline by others and without marked impairment, hospitalization, or psychotic features. The criterion that symptoms should last for at least 4 days is arbitrary, and clinically relevant hypomanias may be missed with this criterion because hypomanic symptoms can often last for 1 to 3 days (Wicki & Angst, 1991). Clinicians should note that many patients may simply show a decreased need for sleep and an increased energy and drive, which may all be masked within a socially or occupationally acceptable spectrum, particularly in adolescents, young adults, and those in situations where a "driven" lifestyle may be seen as acceptable or even desirable. By definition, symptoms of hypomania differ quantitatively from those of mania. No clear qualitative differences appear to exist between manic and hypomanic syndromes. Although clear-cut mixed states are classified under mania, hypomanic patients may also suffer from dysphoric symptoms. Bipolar II disorder, on average, has an earlier age of onset than does nonbipolar disorder (Akiskal et al., 1995). This is particularly important because acts of deliberate self-harm in adolescents and young adults warrant an assessment for bipolar II disorder. Bipolar II patients are more likely than nonbipolar major depressive disorder patients to have a history of suicide attempts (Kupfer, Carpenter, & Frank, 1988). Despite the turbulence that hypomania and recurrent depression can cause in bipolar II patients, these patients are less likely to be hospitalized although the psychosocial impairment, risk of suicide, and other functional morbidity may be significant in the bipolar II group as well (Cook, Young, Levitt, Pearce, & Joffe, 1995). Bipolar II patients also have a greater liability to rapid cycling (for a more detailed review of rapid cycling see chapter 3, "Rapid Cycling," in this book).

Mania: Diagnostic Issues

DSM-IV defines a manic episode as a distinct abnormally and persistently elevated, expansive, or irritable mood, lasting at least one week (or shorter if hospitalization is necessary), with three (four if only irritability is present) or more of the following symptoms present to a significant degree: inflated self-esteem or grandiosity; decreased need for sleep; more talkative than usual; flight of ideas or a subjective experience that thoughts are racing; distractibility by unimportant and irrelevant external stimuli; increase in goal directed activity or psychomotor agitation; and an excessive involvement in pleasurable activities that have a high potential for painful or negative consequences. The mood disturbance in mania must be sufficiently severe to cause marked impairment in occupational and social functioning, sometimes requiring hospitalization to prevent harm to self or others, and may be accompanied by psychotic symptoms. Although the DSM-IV definition of manic episode does not include those manias associated with pharmacologically induced states, medical, or neurological conditions, these states are important to recognize because they have significant implications for assessment, investigations, and management.

In their longitudinal analysis of untreated manic episodes, Carlson and Goodwin (1973) described three stages of mania progressing from mild hypomania to delirious psychotic mania. This model is useful in planning clinical management as well. The stages are summarized in the Table 1.1.

Differentiating bipolar disorder from schizophrenia and schizoaffective illness is a diagnostic challenge, particularly in adolescents and young adults who are having their first or early episodes. Cross-sectionally, acute symptoms of irritability, anger, paranoia, catatoniclike excitement are not useful in distinguishing mania from schizophrenia. The clinician should incorporate information about family history of psychiatric illness, premorbid functioning, nature of onset of symptoms, including presence of any prodrome, and previous history of episodes of illness, particularly previous depression or psychotic states when making a diagnosis. The presence of psychotic symptoms, including bizarre or mood incongruent delusions and Schneiderian first rank symptoms, is not inconsistent with a mania so long as there are continuous and substantial mood symptoms as well. However, active or prodromal psychotic symptoms without mood symptoms for periods of 2 weeks or longer should alert the clinician to consider the diagnoses of schizophrenia or schizoaffective disorder. In addition to the mental status examination, the family history of bipolar disorder and a history of episodic illness with good interepisode functioning are often helpful in assisting in the diagnosis of an acute mania.

Mixed states, which can occur in a significant proportion of bipolar

TABLE 1.1
Stages of Mania

	Stage 1	Stage 2	Stage 3
Mood	Labile affect; euphoria predominates; irritable if demands not satisfied	Increased dysphoria and depression; open hostility and anger	Clearly dysphoric; panic-stricken; hopeless
Cognition	Expansivity, grandiosity, overconfidence; thoughts coherent but occasionally tangential; sexual and religious preoccupations; racing thoughts	Flight of ideas; disorganization of cognitive state; delusions	Incoherent, definite loosening of associations; bizarre and idiosyncratic delusions; hallucinations in one-third of patients; disorientation to time and place; occasional ideas of reference
Behavior	Increased psychomotor activity; increased initiation and rate of speech; increased spending, smoking and telephone use	Continued increased psychomotor acceleration; increased pressure of speech; occasional assaultive behavior	Frenzied and frequently bizarre psychomotor activity

patients pose diagnostic challenges. There are varied definitions in different diagnostic systems and these patients can present with a confusing mixture of manic and depressive symptoms. Furthermore, mixed states may not be a distinct category but may lie within a spectrum of bipolar mood states with various degrees of mixture of manic and depressive symptoms depending on the severity of the mania (e.g., stage 3).

Mixed states could represent a severe stage of mania, an intermediate or transitional state between mania and depression, or a distinct state that is a true combination of depressive and manic syndrome. A summary of the diagnostic and clinical implications are summarized by Keck, McElroy, Kmetz, and Sax (1996) and Freeman and McElroy (1999). The definitions of mixed states range from presence of full depressive episode to any depressive symptom in association with a manic episode. DSM-IV defines mixed episode as patients meeting criteria for both depressive and manic episodes (except duration criteria) nearly every day for at least a one-week period. It is increasingly being accepted that the DSM-IV definition of a mixed state is restrictive and arbitrary. The recognition of a wider spectrum of mixed states is not only important diagnostically but also has management implications, as mixed states are often associated with a turbulent course and increased suicidal risk, and a relatively poorer response to lithium and a better response to valproate and carbamazepine (Bowden et al., 1994; McElroy et al., 1992).

McElroy et al. (1992) offer operational criteria which offers compromise between DSM-IV definition and other definitions that are overinclusive. They define dysphoric mania by the presence of two or more specific depressive symptoms such as depressive mood, markedly diminished interest or pleasure in all or almost all activities, substantial weight gain or an increase in appetite, psychomotor retardation, hypersomnia, fatigue or loss of energy, feelings of worthlessness or excessive, inappropriate guilt, feelings of helplessness or hopelessness, recurrent thoughts of death or suicide. Mixed states appear to constitute 30 to 40% of all manic episodes.

The Management of Hypomania and Mania

ASSESSMENT

It is not uncommon for patients experiencing hypomania or mania to have a loss of insight fairly early in the course of the episode, hence self-rating scales are rarely, if ever, useful. Friends and family members can be vital informants in helping provide history and in offering observations of problems with emotional or behavioral dyscontrol. Clinicians should routinely screen for symptoms of depression and more complex mixed states, as well as for psychotic symptoms, suicidality, aggression, and dangerousness with or without homicidality. Observer rating scales have been commonly used in clinical research studies, but are increasingly being used to measure change and response to treatment in ordinary clinical settings. Although rating scales for mania and depression are increasingly used in clinical practice, and provide a standard set of information which can assist in monitoring change, there is little doubt that ratings that include patient reports, informant reports, and clinical staff observations are likely to be the most valid in establishing or ruling out the variety of symptoms that are present in a mania. For a review of a variety of rating scales refer to Goodwin and Jamieson (1990).

INITIAL STEPS, MEDICAL EXAMINATION, AND RELEVANT INVESTIGATIONS

An important and necessary first step is to ascertain if the manic patient is able to consent to treatment. If not, valid consent should be obtained as soon as possible from a person recognized under state law to be able to do so. Although symptomatic management of the mania may have to begin in the emergency room, the clinician is well advised to confirm or rule out, early on in treatment, any reasonable possibility of mania secondary to an underlying medical condition, current or recent substance use, and pharmacologically induced hypomania. A good history of sleep hygiene and sleep deprivation should be obtained, because sleep deprivation is associated with triggering or exacerbating hypomania and mania. Ensuring the safety of the acutely manic patient and those around him or her is a high priority at all stages of treatment. Hence, the initial steps may well involve screening for and managing an overt or covert attempt at suicide or other deliberate self-harm, particularly by overdose. Patients who are aggressive and combative would benefit not only from being in a low-stimulus, comfortable, and nonchallenging environment but also from rapid institution of medications to manage behavior dyscontrol and aggression.

Ideally, a medical evaluation and baseline investigations should be completed before the institution of biological treatment. In certain circumstances, however, because of a very acute clinical situation, treatment may have to begin prior to the completion of a full medical workup. Apart from a thorough medical examination, the following baseline investigations should be completed (Kusumakar et al., 1997): complete blood count including platelets; serum electrolytes; liver enzymes and serum bilirubin; urinanalysis and urine toxicology for substance use; serum creatinine; and, if there is any personal or family history of renal disorder, a 24-hour creatinine clearance; thyroid-stimulating hormone (TSH); electrocardiogram (EKG) in patients over 40 years of age or with a previous history of cardiovascular problems; and a pregnancy test where relevant.

Serum levels of mood stabilizers should be done at the trough point, approximately 12 hours after the last dose of medication, at admission (as many patients are noncompliant with medications in the days or weeks leading up to an acute manic episode), and approximately 5 days after achieving a mood stabilizer dose titration. Two consecutive serum levels within the therapeutic range (0.8–1.1 mmols/l for lithium) or above a minimum target serum level (above 400 mmols/l for valproate) are sufficient during the acute phase. Any additional serum level monitoring is better guided by the clinical need and clinical state of the patient. There is no evidence that blood counts and liver enzymes need to be done more frequently than at baseline, at the end of 4 weeks, and once every 6 months thereafter, unless there is a specific clinical concern. Closer monitoring is, however, required in children and the elderly, in patients being treated with multiple medications, or in any patients where there is legitimate clinical concern about hematological, hepatic, renal, endocrine, cardiovascular, or neurological dysfunction.

RATIONALE IN DESIGNING TREATMENT STRATEGIES IN HYPOMANIA AND MANIA

The reader is advised to refer to the chapters in this book on lithium (chapter 7), anticonvulsants (chapter 10), neuroleptics (chapter 8), somatic treatments including electroconvulsive treatment (ECT; chapter 11), and pharmacokinetics and drug interactions (chapter 12), for up-to-date reviews on the evidence of efficacy, common adverse effects, and dosing strategies with various treatments. These reviews form the basis for the rationale in designing treatment strategies. However, outlined below is a summary of commonly asked questions and issues that underpin the treatment of hypomania and mania, followed by some treatment algorithms.

1. *Is the patient medically stable?* Baseline medical assessment and investigations, and medical stabilization should occur as soon as is clinically feasible. Pregnancy should be considered as a possibility and ruled out whenever clinically relevant.

2. *Is the patient competent to give consent?* If yes, record this. If not, seek the next person who can give valid consent. In most jurisdictions (check this to determine if it is the case in your city or state), patients can be treated

in emergency situations without consent, but consent should be obtained as soon as possible.

3. *Why choose a mood stabilizer plus an atypical antipsychotic as a core first choice treatment over a neuroleptics in mania?* Lithium, valproate, and carbamazepine are all proven to be effective in acute mania, and are the only medication treatments with some (valproate and carbamazepine) or good (lithium) evidence for prophylactic efficacy. Mood stabilizers can be effective against both manic and depressive symptoms, *and* there is no evidence that they provoke depression. Both risperidone and olanzapine have been shown to be efficacious in treating mania when combined with lithium or valproate (Sachs, 2000; Yatham, 2000; and Tohen, 2001). In a clinical situation, the combination of an atypical antipsychotic medication, like risperidone or olanzapine with lithium or valproate is not only likely to result in a relatively earlier onset of action but is also more likely to result in a greater remission rate. Olanzapine and risperidone have been shown to be efficacious in monotherapy in acute mania in placebo controlled studies (Tohen et al., 1999; Tohen et al., 2000), but there is no evidence of the efficacy of atypical antiphsychotics in monotherapy in the prophylaxis of bipolar disorder, although studies are under way. Hence, the use of antipsychotics in monotherapy in bipolar patients cannot yet be recommended. Although typical neuroleptics are effective antimanic agents, they are associated with a significant risk of dystonic reactions and EPS in the short-term, and with tardive dyskinesia in the long-term, particularly in patients with mood disorders. Further, there is a potential risk of inducing or exacerbating depressive symptoms with the use of typical neuroleptics (Kukopulos et al., 1980). Hence, if a neuroleptic is to be used, there is increasing justification for the use of atypical neuroleptics, like risperidone and olanzapine, which have proven antimanic efficacy (Tohen et al., 1999; Sachs, 2000; Yatham, 2000) and have fewer short-term adverse effects than the typical neuroleptics. Although there is very little long-term data on tardive dyskinesia in bipolar patients treated with atypical neuroleptics, data from schizophrenic cohorts with these medications is encouraging.

4. *Does the patient have marked behavioral dyscontrol, or is very aggressive or dangerous to self or others?* The patient may well need valid and ethical chemical or low confrontation and stimulus physical restraint that can be effective in minutes or at most a few hours. Treatment with benzodiazepines or neuroleptics as an adjunctive treatment to mood stabilizers, should be considered. Neuroleptics should be considered especially if there is a previous history of disinhibition being exacerbated by benzodiazepines. Use atypical neuroleptics where possible. Typical neuroleptics may have to be used in the short term if there is known response to a previous medication or if parenteral treatment is indicated. However, parenteral

atypical neuroleptic treatments are being developed at the time of writing this chapter and may well be available in the forseeable future. However, if the patient is not responding to optimal doses of the above, and the mania is escalating rapidly, then electroconvulsive therapy (ECT) needs to be considered as a treatment option.

5. *If typical neuroleptics were used for behavioral control when patient was refusing oral medications, should the patient be switched to an atypical neuroleptic and if so when and how?* As soon as the patient begins to accept treatment orally, consideration should be given to switching the patient to atypical neuroleptic for reasons outlined above. Furthermore, there is evidence from open studies that both risperidone and olanzapine may have prophylactic properties in bipolar patients (Sanger et al., 2001; Vieta et al., 2001). As the dose of atypical neuroleptic is increased, the dose of typical neuroleptic should be cut down. If not already on a mood stabilizer, patients also should be started on it at this point.

6. *Is the patient out of touch with reality due to psychotic thinking and perceptions?* The patient may respond to mood stabilizer treatment alone; however, in the presence of persistent, severe, or chronic mood incongruent psychotic symptoms, atypical neuroleptic treatment may be required in addition to mood stabilizers.

7. *Has the patient had a previous history of response to a particular mood stabilizer medication for mania, or was the patient ever stable in maintenance for bipolar disorder on a particular mood stabilizer medication or combination of medications?* The previously effective medication treatment in monotherapy or combination therapy should be considered, unless newer effective medications with fewer adverse effects are available and are clinically indicated.

8. *Did the patient, historically, not respond effectively to a previous monotherapy or combination treatment or had intolerable side effects to treatment?* Consider a new option of antimanic medication.

9. *Does the patient have a recent or current history of rapid cycling or mixed state? Does the patient suffer from a bipolar disorder secondary to a neurological condition?* Consider valproate or carbamazepine in a mixed state mania, or valproate in a manic episode as part of a recent rapid cycling course of illness. Failure with lithium treatment is associated with mixed state mania and a rapid cycling course. Atypical neuroleptics such as olanzapine can be effective in mixed state mania. Valproate and carbamazepine are effective in secondary mania. Also note that carbamazepine and lithium have significant interactions with other medications used in medical treatment.

10. *Is rapid onset of action of a medication indicated?* Loading dose treatment with valproate 20 to 30 mg per kg per day or risperidone 3 to 6

mg per day or olanzapine 10 to 20 mg per day or zuclopenthixol acetate IM 50 to 150 mg every 72 hours, should be considered.

11. *How often is serum level monitoring of lithium or valproate required?* Obtain trough serum lithium or valproic acid levels after 4 to 5 days after a dose increase. Titrate the dose as required. Two consecutive serum levels within "target" is sufficient. Serum lithium should be between 0.8 and 1.1 mmols/l and serum valproic acid above 400 mmols/l. Acutely manic and agitated patients may well need and tolerate doses producing higher serum levels. Thereafter, the clinical picture should determine the frequency of serum medication level monitoring. Once every 6 months is sufficient during maintenance treatment.

12. *How often does one monitor CBC including platelets in patients being treated with valproate or carbamazepine?* After bloodwork proximal to the initiation of treatment, this needs to be repeated approximately 3 to 4 weeks into treatment, or as indicated by the clinical picture. In patients whose results are within the normal range or are clinically within normal limits, the bloodwork needs to be repeated only once every 6 months during continuation or maintenance treatment.

13. *In what circumstances do patients require an EKG or the 24-hour creatinine clearance test?* Patients with a known risk for cardiovascular disease should have an EKG. Those with a past or family history of renal dysfunction should have a creatinine clearance test. In addition, all patients above 40 years of age and who are being considered for lithium treatment should have an EKG at baseline and as clinically indicated.

14. *If the patient has been treated for 3 weeks and does not show a trend toward improvement, and if you have optimized the medication for at least 2 weeks what are the treatment options?* Consider adding a new antimanic medication, either a second mood stabilizer or an atypical neuroleptic. Combinations of lithium and valproate are reasonably safe, while a combination of valproate and carbamazepine should only be instituted with close serum level monitoring due to pharmacokinetic interaction. Also, if the patient has not responded to treatment up to now, it would be worthwhile, again, to rule out an underlying medical or neurological condition, and treat it if present. If the patient has not responded to the above strategies, combinations of three mood stabilizers or two mood stabilizers and an atypical or typical neuroleptic might be appropriate at this stage. If there is no response with the above options, ECT could be considered. In patients with a history of chronic, severe refractory mania lasting over 3 months, and who do not respond to or are unable to receive ECT, clozapine treatment should be considered.

15. *Is ECT effective in bipolar disorder?* ECT is a highly effective treatment in both mania and bipolar depression. There is no clear consen-

sus if bilateral ECT is superior to unilateral ECT. Treatment with ECT during an acute episode does not protect against recurrence of future episodes, nor does it convert medication nonresponders into responders. However, the cognitive adverse effects of ECT, although clearly present, as evidenced by research, during the hours and days after a treatment, are neither long-term nor permanent.

16. *Should patients with mania be treated only during the manic phase?* Patients who suffer from bipolar disorder have a significant risk of relapse and recurrence. This is particularly so if there is a family history of bipolar disorder and the acute manic episode has been prolonged, turbulent, with psychosis, and difficult to treat to full remission. There is growing concern about patients who exhibit deterioration with each relapse or recurrence. A significant number of patients who experience mania have either gone off their medications or have been underdosed. Both these factors are associated with an increased risk for relapse and recurrence. Patients should be treated and monitored optimally, while providing timely psychoeducation and family support. Patients who have experienced a mania should be automatically considered for prophylactic mood stabilizer treatment in the majority of cases.

17. *How can drug–drug interactions affect patients and management?* Clinicians should bear in mind that drug–drug interactions may alter the metabolism and serum levels of medications. This can result in subtherapeutic serum levels, which can be associated with treatment failure (e.g., failure of risperidone, as carbamazepine can induce hepatic enzymes to increase metabolism of risperidone resulting in low serum risperidone levels) or excessive serum levels, resulting in toxicity (e.g., lithium toxicity due to decreased clearance and increased serum level when used in conjunction with thiazide diuretics). Patients with developmental handicaps, the elderly, and those with medical or neurological problems may not only manifest exaggerated or idiosyncratic reactions to combinations of medications, but also to monotherapy.

TREATMENT ALGORITHMS

Hypomania (Stage 1 Mania)

Hypomania (stage 1 mania) in a patient who suffers from bipolar II disorder, can often be managed with the following strategies. Hypomania can commonly be managed in an ambulatory setting, and, in special circumstances, in a day hospital or day treatment setting.

- The current dose of mood stabilizer or other current antimanic medication should be optimized.
- Good sleep hygiene should be encouraged.
- Antidepressants should be discontinued.
- Lorazepam or clonazepam, 1 to 6 mg per day as clinically indicated should be initiated or added. Patients who have a recent history of alcoholism and substance abuse, and those who have a history of benzodiazepine-induced disinhibition are unlikely to respond well to benzodiazepines alone. In such patients, small doses of atypical neuroleptic such as olanzapine or risperidone might be appropriate.
- Mood stabilizer treatment should be initiated (lithium, divalproex, or carbamazepine) in patients who are not on mood stabilizers.
- Where there is a previous history of rapid escalation into stage 2 or 3 mania, and this hypomania is clinically deemed to be a transitional phase into mania, or there is a previous or recent history of rapid response to neuroleptics, treatment with atypical neuroleptics may have to be commenced or recommenced; for example, risperidone 0.5 to 2 mg per day or olanzapine 2.5 to 5 mg per day, initially at low dose and titrated upwards as required. Consideration should be given for inpatient admission for such patients.

Manic (Stage 2 and 3)

Patients with stage 2 or 3 mania, especially with significant agitation, risk of gross occupational, social, financial, and interpersonal misjudgments, deliberate self-harm, destructiveness, aggression, dangerousness, or homicidality will commonly need the specialized observation and treatment that only a psychiatric inpatient unit can offer.

The following treatment strategies can be effective in *severely agitated and manic patients with or without psychosis:*

- Admission into an intensive care psychiatric observation and treatment unit.
- Close observation for deliberate self-harm, destructiveness, and aggression.
- If rapid behavioral control is desired for safety, use zuclopenthixol acetate intramuscular injection 50 to 150 mg once every 72 hours or haloperidol oral or intramuscular 2 to 10 mg/day with or without adjunctive lorazepam oral or intramuscular 2 to 12 mg/day, or a trial of a typical neuroleptic (e.g., loxapine 30–150 mg/day), can be considered. Institute a mood stabilizer as soon as patient is able to take oral medication.

- In patients where there is a need to deal rapidly with agitation and manic symptoms:

    Optimize the dose of currently prescribed mood stabilizer or initiate mood stabilizer (e.g., lithium, valproate, or carbamazepine) *with or without adjunctive* lorazepam oral or intramuscular 2 to 12 mg/day, or risperidone 1 to 6 mg per day or olanzapine 10 to 20 mg per day. Note that to achieve efficacy, serum lithium should be at least >0.8 mmols/l, and serum valproate at least >400 mmols/l. Patients may well tolerate and need doses higher than they would tolerate when stabilized.

    Or valproate 20 to 30 mg/kg/day loading dose with or without adjunctive Lorazepam oral or intramuscular 2 to 12 mg/day or intramuscular 2 to 12 mg/day, or Risperidone 3 to 6 mg per day or Olanzapine 10 to 20 mg per day.

    Or ECT if the patient worsens rapidly or is excessively aggressive or does not respond to other strategies within a reasonable period or has a previous history of response to only ECT in a severely manic situation.

    Or a combination of valproate and lithium (safer than a valproate–carbamazepine combination) if monotherapy with one mood stabilizer has not yielded desired clinical benefit within 3 weeks.
- In manic patients with a history of only a partial or a nonresponse to combination of two or three mood stabilizers, or mood stabilizer and typical or atypical neuroleptic combinations, a trial of the newer anticonvulsant topiramate, from 25 to 500 mg/day can be considered because there is preliminary data suggesting its efficacy in mania.
- In patients who have a history of nonresponse to optimal use of the above strategies, or where there is severe chronic mania that is persistent, clozapine 50 to 900 mg/day (serum level 200 to 350 ng/ml) should be considered.

Manic Patients

In manic patients with significant psychotic symptoms without significant aggression or behavior dyscontrol use the following strategies:

- Restart or optimize previous treatment, or initiate a mood stabilizer (e.g., lithium, valproate, or carbamazepine) with the option of adjunctive lorazepam. If the above strategy does not begin to diminish psychotic symptoms within 1 week, then add an atypical neuroleptic (e.g., risperidone 2 to 6 mg/day or olanzapine 5 to 15 mg/day) to the mood stabilizer.

Or restart, optimize, or initiate a mood stabilizer (e.g., lithium, valproate, or carbamazepine) with an adjunctive atypical neuroleptic (e.g., risperidone or olanzapine) from day 1 if there is a history of significant, persistent, and bizarre psychotic symptoms.

- If a patient does not respond to the above treatment within 3 weeks, consider combining valproate and lithium (safer than a valproate–carbamazepine combination), with or without an atypical neuroleptic.
- If a patient does not respond to the above regime within 4 weeks of optimal dosing, a trial with newer agents such as topiramate or ECT should be considered.
- If there is a history of nonresponse to the above regimes, or if the psychotic mania does not respond to any of the above strategies in a timely manner, then clozapine 50 to 900 mg/day (serum level 200–350 ng/ml) should be considered.

Pure Mania without Psychotic Symptoms and with No Significant Behavioral Dyscontrol

The following strategy should be considered for patients with pure mania without psychotic symptoms, and with no significant behavioral dyscontrol:

- Monotherapy with lithium (0.8 to 1.2 mmols/l), valproate (>400 mmols/l) or carbamazepine in monotherapy may be sufficient for the core manic symptoms. However, in order to regulate sleep, lorazepam (1 to 4 mg/day) over the first 7 to 10 days may be necessary.
- If a rapid onset of action in needed, a combination of lithium (0.8–1.2 mmols/l) or valproate (>400 µmols/l) and risperidone (1 to 6 mg/day) or olanzapine (10 to 20 mg/day) can be used.
- If there is poor or no response to the above regime within 3 weeks, consider the following: Combine lithium and valproate (safer than a valproate–carbamazepine combination) or the addition of an atypical neuroleptic (e.g., risperidone 2–6 mg/day of olanzapine 5–20 mg/day.
- Failure to respond to the above strategies would necessitate the consideration of a trial with a typical neuroleptic, topiramate, or ECT.

Patients in a Mixed State

The following strategy should be considered for patients in a mixed state:

- Valproate (serum level > 400 mmols/l) or carbamazepine would be the first medications of choice. Mixed states are associated with failure to respond to lithium.
- Lorazepam 1 to 12 mg/day can be used for mild, moderate, or severe behavior dyscontrol without a history of benzodiazepine induced disinhibition.
- Risperidone 2 to 6 mg/day or olanzapine 5 to 20 mg/day can be useful adjuncts in the presence of excessive agitation, hostility, or psychotic symptoms.
- Electroconvulsive treatment should be considered if the above strategies, even when optimized, are ineffective.
- Clozapine 50 to 900 mg/day (serum level 200–350 mg/ml) should be considered if the above strategies fail after an adequate trial.

References

Akiskal, H. S. (1996). The prevalent clinical spectrum of bipolar disorders: Beyond DSM-IV. *Journal of Clinical Psychopharmacology, 16,* 2S–14S.

Akiskal, H. S., Maser, J. E., Zeller, P. F., Endicott, J., Coryell, W., Keller, M., et al. (1995). Switching from unipolar to bipolar II: An eleven year prospective study of clinical and temperamental predictors in 559 patients. *Archives of General Psychiatry, 52,* 114–123.

American Psychiatric Association. (1987). *Diagnostic and statistical manual of mental disorders* (3rd ed. rev.). Washington, DC: Author.

American Psychiatric Association. (1996). *Diagnostic and statistical manual of mental disorders* (4th ed.). Washington, DC: Author.

Bowden, C. P., Brugger, A. M., Swann, A. C., Calabrese, J. R., Janicak, P. G., Petty, F., et al. (1994). Efficacy of divalproex vs. lithium and placebo in the treatment of mania. *Journal of the American Medical Association, 271,* 918–924.

Carlson, G. A., & Goodwin, F. K. (1973). The stages of mania: A longitudinal analysis of the manic episode. *Archives of General Psychiatry, 28,* 221–228.

Cooke, R. G., Young, L. T., Levitt, A. J., Pearce, M. M., & Joffe, R. T. (1995). Bipolar II: Not so different when co-morbidity is excluded. *Depression, 3,* 154–156.

DePaulo, J. R., Jr., Simpson, S. G., Gayle, J. O., & Folstein, S. E. (1990). Bipolar II disorder in six sisters. *Journal of Affective Disorders, 19,* 259–264.

Dunner, D. L., & Day, L. K. (1993). Diagnostic reliability of the history of hypomania in bipolar II patients and patients with major depression. *Comprehensive Psychiatry, 34,* 303–307.

Freeman, M. P., & McElroy, S. L. (1999). Clinical picture and etiologic models of mixed states. In A. S. Akiskal (Ed.), *The Psychiatric Clinics of North America. Bipolarity: Vol. 22. Beyond classic mania* (pp. 535–546). Philadelphia, PA: Saunders.

Goodwin, F. K., & Jamieson, K. R. (1990). Assessment of manic and depressive states. In F. K. Goodwin & K. R. Jamieson (Eds.), *Manic depressive illness* (pp. 318–331). New York: Oxford University Press.

Keck, P. E., McElroy, S. L., Kmetz, G. F., & Sax, K. W. (1996). Clinical features of mania in adulthood. In K. I. Shulman, M. Tohen, & S. P. Kutcher (Eds.), *Mood disorders across the life span* (pp. 272–274). New York: Wiley-Liss.

Kukopulos, A,. Reginaldi, D., Laddomada, P., Floris, G., Serra, G., & Tondo, L. (1980). Course of manic depressive cycle and changes caused by treatments. *Pharmacopsychiatry and Neuropsychopharmacology, 13,* 156–167.

Kupfer, D. J., Carpenter, L. L., & Frank, E. (1988). Is bipolar II a unique disorder? *Comprehensive Psychiatry, 29,* 228–236.

Kusumakar, V., Yatham, L. N., Haslam, D. R. S., Parikh, S. V., Matte, R., Silverstone, P. H., et al. (1997). Treatment of mania, mixed state and rapid cycling. *Canadian Journal of Psychiatry.* (Suppl 2), 79S–86S.

McElroy, S. L., Keck, P. E., Pope, H. G., Hudson, J. I., Faedda, G. L., & Swann, A. C. (1992). Clinical and research implications of the diagnosis of dysphoric or mixed mania or hypomania. *American Journal of Psychiatry, 149,* 1633–1644.

Sachs, G. S. (2000). Safety and efficacy of risperidone versus placebo in combination with lithium or valproate in the manic phase of bipolar disorder [Abstract]. *International Journal of Neuropsychopharmacology, 3* (Suppl. 1), S143.

Sanger, T. M., Grundy, S. L., Gibson, P. J., Namjsh, M. A., Greaney, M. G., & Tohen, M. F. (2001). Long term olanzapine therapy in the treatment of bipolar I disorder: An open label continuation phase study. *Journal of Clinical Psychiatry, 62*(4), 273–281.

Simpson, S. G., Folstein, S. E., Meyers, D. A., McMahon, F. J., Brusco, D. M., & DePaulo, J. R., Jr. (1993). Bipolar II. The most common phenotype? *American Journal of Psychiatry, 150,* 901–903.

Tohen, M., Jacobs, T. G., Grundy, S. L., McElroy, S. L., Banov, M. C., Janicak, P. G. et al. (2000). Efficacy of olanzapine in acute bipolar mania: A double-blind, placebo-controlled study. The Olanzapine HGGW Study Group. *Archives of General Psychiatry, 57*(9) 841–849.

Tohen, M., Chengappa, K. N. R., Suppes, T., Baker, R. W., Risser, R. C., Evans, A. R., et al. (2001). Olanzapine combined with lithium or valproate in prevention of recurrence in bipolar disorder: An 18-month study. *Paper presented at the American College of Neuropsychopharmacology Meeting,* Hawaii, USA.

Tohen, M., Sanger, T. M., McElroy, S. L., Tollefson, G. D., Chengappa, K. N. R., Daniel, D. G., et al. (1999). Olanzapine versus placebo in the treatment of acute mania. *American Journal of Psychiatry, 156,* 702–709.

Vieta, E., Goikolea, J. M., Corbella, B., Benabarre, A., Reinares M., Martínez, G., et al. (2001). Risperidone safety and efficacy in the treatment of bipolar and schizoaffective disorders: results from a six-month, multicentre, open study. *Journal of Clinical Psychiatry, 62*(10), 818–825.

Wicki, W., & Angst J. (1991). The Zurich study: Hypomania in a 28–30 year old cohort. *European Archives of Psychiatry and Clinical Neurosciences, 240,* 339–348.

Yatham, L. N. (2000). Safety and efficacy of risperidone as combination therapy for the manic phase of bipolar disorder: preliminary findings of a randomised, double-blind study (RIS-Int-46) [Abstract]. *International Journal of Neuropsychopharmacology, 3*: S142.

CHAPTER 2

Treatment
of Bipolar Depression

Lakshmi N. Yatham
Vivek Kusumakar
Stanley P. Kutcher

A diagnosis of bipolar depression should be considered in any patient presenting with depressive symptoms that meet DSM-IV criteria for a major depressive episode (American Psychiatric Association, 1994). A history of a previous manic episode in such patient suggests a diagnosis of bipolar I depression, whereas a history of hypomania would indicate a diagnosis of bipolar II depression. Hypomanic episodes often go undetected; hence careful attention should be paid in eliciting symptoms of hypomania. Decreased need for sleep, increased energy, and racing thoughts are the most commonly reported symptoms by hypomanic patients; absence of a history of elated mood does not rule out hypomania. A depressive episode is the first mood episode in more than 50% of patients with a diagnosis of bipolar disorder (Roy-Byrne, Post, Uhde, Porcu, & Davis, 1985), more so in those with childhood or adolescent onset (Lish, Dime-Meehan, Whybrow, Price, & Hirschfield, 1994).

Hence in a patient presenting with depressive symptoms who has not yet had a manic or hypomanic episode, one should carefully look for clinical features that might predict a bipolar course. These features include a family history of bipolar disorder, psychotic symptoms during a depressive episode, younger age at onset, reverse vegetative symptoms such as hypersomnia and hyperphagia, chronicity of index episode, and pharmacological hypomania (Akiskal et al., 1983; Coryell et al., 1995). The first two features seem to have the highest predictive power. Patients who have these features are considered to have "pseudounipolar depression" or "prebipolar depression," and should be monitored closely for emergence of manic or hypomanic symptoms.

Pharmacological Treatment of Bipolar Depression

A review of the efficacy of lithium, antidepressants, and anticonvulsants in the treatment of bipolar depression can be found in chapters 7, 9, and 10, respectively in this book. The focus of this chapter, therefore, is to provide clinicians with rational and pragmatic approaches for treating patients with bipolar depression.

As can be seen from data in the chapters that reviewed the efficacy of various medications, few controlled trials have rigorously examined pharmacological treatment of bipolar depression. Most clinical trials of antidepressant medications, for example, systematically excluded bipolar depressed patients due to concerns about inducing a manic switch, or because the use of concomitant treatment with mood stabilizers such as lithium might confound the interpretation of clinical efficacy of antidepressants. Therefore, most data that is currently available on treatment of depression was derived from studies in unipolar patients. There are concerns about whether this data could be generalizable for treatment of bipolar depressed patients as there is evidence to indicate that bipolar patients differ from unipolar patients in symptoms (Brockington, Altman, Hillcer, Meltzer, & Nand, 1982; Katz, Robins, Croughar, Secunda, & Swan, 1982; Kupfer et al., 1974), course of illness (Angst, 1986; Coryell, Andreason, Endicott, & Keller, 1987; Egeland, Blumental, Nee, Sharpe, & Endicott, 1987; Winokur, Coryell, Keller, Endicott, & Akiskal, 1983), and response to treatment (Baumhachl et al., 1989; Calabrese et al., 1999; Goodwin, Murphy, Dunner, & Bunney, 1972; Himmelhoch, Thase, Mallinger, & Houck, 1991; Noyes, Dempsey, Blum, & Cavanaugh, 1974; Post, Uhde, Roy-Byrne, & Joffe, 1986; Sachs et al., 1994; Young, Joffe, Robb, McQueen, & Marriott, 2000). Recent long-term studies examining the course and outcome provided further support for the unipolar-bipolar distinction (Coryell et al., 1995; Goldberg, Harrow, & Grossman, 1995).

Therefore, although the available data is very limited, the recommendations formulated in this chapter for treatment of bipolar depression were based mainly on the treatment studies of bipolar depressed patients. The questions that will be addressed here include: What is the first line treatment for bipolar depression? What is refractory bipolar depression? What are the treatment strategies for refractory bipolar depression? And finally, we will provide clinical guidelines for treating bipolar depressed patients.

WHAT IS THE FIRST LINE OF TREATMENT FOR BIPOLAR DEPRESSION?

This decision will hinge on four factors: (1) Has the drug been shown to be effective in double-blind, controlled trials for bipolar depression? (2) Does it have a propensity to induce a manic switch? (3) Can it induce and maintain rapid cycling? (4) Does it have any prophylactic properties in preventing further manic and depressive episodes? The goal of treatment would be to relieve depressive symptoms while minimizing the chances of patients switching into a manic–hypomanic episode or rapid-cycling course. The medications that are commonly used in treatment of bipolar depression include lithium, antidepressants, and anticonvulsants.

Although the sample sizes were small, double-blind, placebo, crossover trials have shown that response rates to lithium vary from 64 to 100%. The relapse of depressive symptoms occurred in 38 to 70% with placebo substitution thus suggesting that lithium is effective in treating bipolar depression (see Srisurapanont, Yatham, & Zis, 1995 for review; Yatham et al., 1997). There have not been any reports of lithium inducing a manic switch or rapid cycling in bipolar depressed patients. There is evidence indicating that lithium is useful in prophylaxis of bipolar disorder (see chapter 4 in this book for review).

Although antidepressants have been reported to be effective in treating bipolar depression, they have also been reported to induce manic switch and rapid cycling (see chapter 9 in this book; Srisurapanont et al., 1995; Yatham et al., 1997; Zornberg & Pope 1994, for reviews). The data is particularly strong for tricyclic antidepressants and monoamine oxidase inhibitors; these groups of medications seem to have the highest propensity to induce manic switch in bipolar depressed patients. There are also reports of serotonin reuptake inhibitors (SSRIs) and newer antidepressant such as bupropion inducing a manic switch but no long-term data are available on the propensity of these agents to induce rapid cycling (see chapter 9 in this book).

Three small double-blind trials reported efficacy for the anticonvulsant carbamazepine in bipolar depression, although small sample sizes make the results less than robust. The data for valproate in bipolar depression come mainly from open studies and case series; results are not very supportive of efficacy. Recent double-blind trials (Sachs et al., 2001) showed numerical but not statistically significant superiority of valproate over placebo in the treatment of bipolar disorder. However, neither of these medications has been reported to induce a manic switch or rapid cycling. Double-blind studies suggest prophylactic efficacy for carbamazepine. Post hoc analysis of the data also suggests prophylactic efficacy for divalproex sodium in bipolar disorder. Gabapentin and topiramate have also been reported in open studies to be useful in treating bipolar depression as an augmentation to mood stabilizer; however, there are reports of the former inducing a manic switch in some patients. The only anticonvulsant that has been rigorously tested for its efficacy in a large, double-blind, parallel group study design is lamotrigine. In the first study (Calabrese et al., 1999), lamotrigine monotherapy at a dose of 200 mg daily ($n = 63$) was shown to be superior to placebo ($n = 66$) with 51% of bipolar I depressed patients showing much or very much improvement on CGI compared to the 26% of patients in the placebo group. Lamotrigine 50 mg daily was also numerically superior to placebo in treating depressive symptoms on various scales. In the second study, the efficacy of lamotrigine ($n = 103$) was compared with placebo ($n = 103$) in a 10-week, double-blind parallel study in bipolar I and bipolar II depression (Bowden et al., 2000). Overall, no significant differences were noted on either HAM-D or MADRS using LOCF but a subgroup analysis revealed results favoring lamotrigine group on both measures in bipolar I but not in bipolar II depressed patients. The results of this study may have been confounded by higher placebo response rates and the potential possibility of inclusion of some unipolar patients due to diagnostic difficulties with bipolar II patients. Although there are case reports of manic switch with lamotrigine, switch rates into mania were not higher in the lamotrigine groups (5.4% in the first study and 1% in the second study) compared with switch rates in the placebo groups (4.6% in the first study and 1% in the second study) in these double-blind studies. This would suggest that the manic switches noted in patients on lamotrigine in this study were likely part of the natural course of bipolar illness. Two recent double-blind trials (Bowden, Calabrese, Sachs, et al., 2001; Bowden, Calabrese, DeVeaugh-Geiss, et al., 2001) reported that lamotrigine was significantly superior to placebo in time to intervention for a mood episode in bipolar I patients recruited after stabilization in mood from a manic or a depressive episode. A sub-analysis showed that lamotrigine was superior to placebo in time to intervention for a depressive episode but not for a manic episode. (See chapter 10 on anticonvulsants for details of anticonvulsant efficacy.)

Based on the above, it is clear that lithium is probably the only medication that meets all the criteria proposed for determining the first line treatment for bipolar depression. Lamotigine, however, also comes very close to meeting the criteria proposed with the exception that it has not proven effective for preventing manic episodes. We, therefore, recommend that lithium should be the first line agent for treatment of bipolar depression.

Electroconvulsive therapy (ECT) has consistently been shown to have effectiveness in bipolar depression (Abrams & Taylor, 1974; Bratfos & Haug, 1965; Homan, Lachenbruch, Winokur, & Clayton, 1982; Stromgren 1973). The consensus is that ECT is likely the most potent treatment at a clinician's disposal for a patient, particularly those experiencing severe bipolar depression with marked suicidality or psychotic depression. Hence, ECT may be considered a first-line treatment in bipolar depression in some circumstances. It should be noted, however, that there are no double-blind controlled data nor any long-term systematic data about prophylactic efficacy of ECT for bipolar depression.

WHAT IS REFRACTORY BIPOLAR DEPRESSION?

There is some consensus in the literature as to what constitutes refractory *uni*polar depression. This has been defined as a depression without significant response to two adequate trials of antidepressants from different classes. A literature review failed, however, to find any systematic attempts to define refractory bipolar depression. In fact, the only definition that exists is the one provided by Sachs (1996) who defined refractory bipolar depression as depression without remission despite two adequate trials of standard classes of antidepressant agents (6 weeks each) with or without augmentation strategies. The problem with this definition is that antidepressants are not likely to be used as first-line agents for bipolar depression. Hence, any definition of refractory bipolar depression should take into account what agent patients are most likely to be prescribed as the first and second line.

Based on the criteria proposed above, we recommend that lithium should be the first line agent for bipolar depression. If an adequate trial with lithium fails, the next agent that could be tried may include: (1) lamotrigine as monotherapy or as an additional agent; (2) addition of an antidepressant such as bupropion or an SSRI (avoid tricyclic antidepressants); or (3) the addition of a mood stabilizing drug such as carbamazepine or valproate. Which of these options is most appropriate will vary depending upon the severity of depression, whether it is bipolar I or II depression, whether the patient is willing to accept the risk of a hypomanic or manic switch, or risk of rash.

Therefore, the only step in the treatment of bipolar depression for which there likely will be a relatively wide consensus is treatment with lithium. Hence, from a pragmatic point of view, it might make more sense to define refractory bipolar depression as depression that failed to respond to a trial with lithium at serum levels of 0.8 mmol/L and above for 6 weeks.

Treatment Strategies for Refractory Bipolar Depression

The following strategies should be considered: (1) optimization, (2) combination, (3) augmentation, and (4) substitution. We will discuss each of these strategies below.

OPTIMIZATION

If the patient has been on lithium for treatment of depression, the first step should be to optimize lithium treatment before considering other options. Optimization involves ensuring that the patient has been compliant with lithium and that his or her serum levels have been in the therapeutic range of not less than 0.8 mmol/L. It is also important at this stage to look again for any comorbid psychiatric or medical conditions that might be contributing to treatment refractoriness; if present, these should be treated. It would also be important to look for psychosocial stressors and significant personality issues that might be contributing to treatment refractoriness. These latter factors may be best dealt with by lifestyle changes, interpersonal conflict resolution or reduction, and cognitive behavior therapy (CBT).

COMBINATION

The term combination implies that two or more active treatments are combined to treat depressive symptoms. Therefore, this option involves adding a new treatment to the existing treatment and should be considered if optimization of lithium fails to improve symptoms. The options here would include: (1) lamotrigine; (2) carbamazepine or valproate; (3) antidepressants such as bupropion or an SSRI; or (4) compounds with relatively lesser evidence of efficacy, such as gabapentin, topiramate, or one of the atypical neuropleptics.

Addition of Lamotrigine

Double-blind data indicate that lamotrigine monotherapy is effective in treating bipolar depression (Bowden et al., 2000; Calabrese et al., 1999). The risk of manic switch appears to be very low with this medication, and there is evidence that it may also be useful for rapid cycling bipolar patients, particularly those with bipolar II disorder. The main problem with lamotrigine therapy is the risk of rash, which occurs in 10% of patients; in

1% of patients, it can lead to Steven-Johnson syndrome. The risk of rash can be reduced by using low starting doses such as 12.5 mg/day, and slow up-titration of dose by 12.5 to 25 mg/week. Particular care should be taken in patients who are also on valproate (which can double serum lamotrigine levels); and in those with a history of significant dermatological problems or blood dyscrasias. Patients who have difficulty in self-monitoring for rash or in adherence to treatment advice should not be prescribed lamotrigine.

Addition of Carbamazepine or Valproate

Although addition of a second mood stabilizer is a common clinical practice in treating bipolar depression, only two studies to date examined the effectiveness of combining two mood stabilizers in bipolar depression. Young et al. (2000) reported that addition of a second mood stabilizer (i.e., valproate in patients on lithium and vice versa) was as effective as adding paroxetine to a mood stabilizer in treating depressive symptoms in bipolar patients. In the second study, 6 out of 13 bipolar depressed patients who had not responded to carbamazepine improved when lithium was added (Kramlinger & Post, 1989).

Although the data for combining two mood stabilizers is limited, it nevertheless suggests efficacy that is comparable to adding an antidepressant. Since this strategy does not carry a risk of inducing manic switch or rapid cycling, it should be considered as a second-line option (lamotrigine addition being the first line for such patients) for bipolar patients who have a previous history of severe or treatment refractory manic episodes, because the goal in these patients would be to relieve depressive symptoms while avoiding any risk of manic switch.

Addition of an Antidepressant

Fluoxetine (Cohn, Collins, Ashbrook, & Wernicke, 1989), paroxetine (Young, Joffe, Robb, McQueen, & Marriott, 2000; Nemeroff et al., 2001), bupropion (Sachs et al., 1994), tranylcypromine (Himmelhoch, Fuchs, & Symons, 1982; Himmelhoch, 1991; Thase, Mallinger, McKnight, & Himmelhoch, 1992), moclobemide (Baumhachl et al., 1989), and imipramine (Baumhachl et al., 1989; Cohn et al., 1989; Himmelhoch et al., 1991; Thase et al., 1992) have been studied and found to be effective in treating bipolar depression. It is likely that the other antidepressants may also be effective although they have not been assessed systematically in clinical trials.

The issue of antidepressant induced manic switch and rapid cycling is covered in detail in chapter 9 in this book. Although the issue continues to be controversial, our view is that it is a significant problem, particularly with tricyclic antidepressants, because they appear to have the highest propensity to induce a manic switch (Himmelhoch, Thase, et al., 1991; Peet 1994; Thase et al., 1992; also please see chapter 9 for further details) and rapid cycling (Kukopulos, 1980) in bipolar patients. Similarly, the risk with monoamine oxidase inhibitors (MAOIs) also appears to be higher, although the data are not as strong as for tricyclics. The risk with bupropion and SSRIs appears to be lower and hence, if this option is warranted, we would recommend considering addition of bupropion or an SSRI rather than a tricyclic. If trials with these fail, addition of tranylcypromine may be appropriate, as there are some data that suggest an MAOI induced switch is more in the mild to moderate hypomanic range rather than the severe or manic range. The strategy of adding an antidepressant, therefore, should be considered as an option mainly for bipolar depressed patients refractory to lithium who have a previous history of hypomania or mild, uncomplicated mania.

Clinicians commonly believe that using an antidepressant in combination with a mood stabilizer prevents the induction of an antidepressant induced manic switch. However, studies have shown that the incidence of manic episodes and rapid cycling in patients on antidepressant mood stabilizer combinations is higher than in patients who receive mood stabilizers alone (Prien, Klett, & Caffey, 1973; Kukopulos et al., 1980; Quitkin, McGrath, Liebowitz, Stewart, & Howard, 1981; Sachs et al., 1994; Wehr & Goodwin 1979a, 1979b). Therefore, clinicians should note that using antidepressants under the cover of a mood stabilizer may not offer full protection from antidepressant induced manic switch. If antidepressants are used, attempts should be made to begin tapering the antidepressant within 4 to 6 weeks after remission of depressive symptoms.

Addition of Topiramate or Gabapentin

Open data supports the efficacy of gabapentin (Young, Robb, Patelis-Siotis, Macdonald, & Joffe, 1997) and topiramate (Hussain, 1999). Although a single-blind trial supported the efficacy of topiramate in bipolar depression (McIntyre et al., 2000), a small, double-blind trial that compared gabapentin with placebo and lamotrigine did not find that gabapentin was better than placebo in treating depressive symptoms (Frye et al., 1998). Reports of gabapentin induced hypomanic–manic symptoms have also appeared in the literature (Short & Cooke, 1995; Ghaemi, Kutzow, Desai, & Goodwin, 1998).

Addition of a Novel Antipsychotic

Risperidone has been reported to improve depressive symptoms in schizo-phrenia, schizoaffective depression, refractory depression, and psychotic depression (Dwight, Keck, Stanton, Strakowski, & McElroy, 1994; Hillert, Maier, Wetzel, & Benkert, 1992; Keck et al., 1995; Lane & Chang, 1998; Lane, Chiu, & Chang, 1999; Muller-Seicheneder et al., 1998; O'Connor & Silver, 1998; Ostroff & Nelson, 1999). Similarly, olanzapine also has been noted to improve depressive symptoms in schizophrenia (Tollefson, Sanger, Lu, & Thieme, 1998; Tran et al., 1997), schizoaffective depression (Tollefson et al., 1997), psychotic depression (Rothschild, 1996; Rothschild, Bates, Boehringer, & Syed, 1999), and treatment refractory depression (Shelton et al., 2001; Weisler, Ahearn, Davidson, & Wallace, 1997). However, no con-trolled trials have examined the efficacy of these agents in bipolar depres-sion to date. Both risperidone and olanzapine have been reported to induce manic symptoms (Dwight et al., 1994; Fitz-Gerald, Pinkofsky, Brannon, Dandridge, & Calhoun, 1999) but larger controlled studies which exam-ined these agents in mania reported efficacy and no worsening of manic symptoms (Sachs, 1999; Tohen et al., 1999; Yatham, 2000).

The standard treatment for psychotic depression is either electrocon-vulsive therapy (ECT) or a combination of an antidepressant and antipsy-chotic. Since both risperidone and olanzapine have been reported to improve both depressive and psychotic symptoms, it is worthwhile considering one of these agents in combination with mood stabilizers to treat psychotic bi-polar depressed patients, although there are no systematic, controlled stud-ies of these agents in psychotic depressed patients.

SUBSTITUTION

This strategy involves substitution of a failed agent with another agent. For example, this could involve replacing lithium with a novel anticonvulsant lamotrigine or another mood stabilizer such as carbamazepine or valproate, or replacing an antidepressant with another antidepressant (e.g., replacing paroxetine with bupropion or vice versa) or with a novel anticonvulsant such as topiramate.

Bipolar depressed patients refractory to tricyclic antidepressants (Himmelhoch, Detre, Kupfer, Swartzburg, & Byck, 1972; Thase et al., 1992) or bupropion (Price, Charney, & Heninger, 1985) have been reported to respond when they were switched to tranylcypromine. Similarly patients refractory to various antidepressant medications were observed to respond when they were switched to bupropion (Fogelson, Bustritsky, & Pasnau,

1992; Haykal & Akiskal, 1990) or paroxetine (Baldessano, Sachs, Stoll, Lafer, & Truman, 1995).

Similarly, patients who were refractory to a combination of two mood stabilizers or a mood stabilizer and an antidepressant, responded when lamotrigine was substituted for a mood stabilizer or an antidepressant (Kusumakar & Yatham, 1997).

AUGMENTATION

Augmentation usually involves adding an agent that does not have antidepressant properties by itself but which has the capacity to augment the antidepressant properties of another drug; some examples include pindolol, tryptophan, methylphenidate, or thyroid hormone (T3). All these agents have been reported to augment antidepressants in unipolar depressed patients (Aronson, Offman, Joffe, & Naylor, 1996; Coppen, Shaw, & Farrel, 1963; Fawcett, Kravitz, & Zajecka, 1991; Perez, Gilaberte, Faries, Alvarez, & Artigas, 1997; Stoll, Pillay, Diamond, Workum, & Cole, 1996; Tome, Isaac, Harte, & Holland, 1997; Wharton, Perel, Dayton, & Malitz, 1971).

Pindolol has been reported to augment antidepressants in bipolar depression (Yatham et al., 1999). Methylphenidate has also been reported to be useful in treating bipolar depressed patients (Kraus, McEachran, & Persad, 1997). Sleep deprivation has been used successfully in the treatment of refractory bipolar depression (Szuba, Baxter, Fairbanks, Luzek, & Schwartz, 1991; Wehr & Goodwin, 1979a, 1979b). There are also reports of the effectiveness of light therapy (Deltito, Moline, Pollak, Martin, & Maremmani, 1991).

Role of ECT

As stated earlier, the consensus is that ECT is one of the most potent treatments for bipolar depression. Several open prospective trials and a number of retrospective studies have reported the efficacy rate of ECT in bipolar depression to be at least 50% and as high as 100% (see Srisurapanont et al., 1995 for a review). Bilateral ECT is commonly believed to be more effective than unilateral ECT in bipolar disorder, although bilateral ECT is associated with more severe transient cognitive side effects. ECT should be actively considered as a treatment option in severely suicidal, agitated, or psychotic depressed patients, and in those suffering from refractory bipolar depression.

Clinical Recommendations

A patient with bipolar depression presenting for treatment may or may not already be on a mood stabilizer. If the patient has not been on a mood stabilizer, we recommend that treatment with lithium be initiated after appropriate medical screening and bloodwork. This would include a thorough systems review, physical examination, EKG, and bloodwork for CBC, electrolytes, serum creatinine and urea, aspartate transferase (AST), alanine transferase (ALT), gamaglutamyl transferase (GGT), and thyroid stimulating hormone (TSH). An attempt should be made to bring serum lithium levels to above 0.8 mmol/L and maintained between 0.8 to 1.2 mmol/L. An adequate trial with lithium will consist of maintaining serum levels at this range for 4 to 6 weeks. This is not always possible, particularly when the patient is worsening or becoming suicidal, or when there is no sign of improvement in symptoms by the end of 3 weeks. In such situations, addition or substitution of a second agent is appropriate before the end of 6 weeks. If the patient has already been on a mood stabilizer, this should be optimized regardless of whether it was lithium, valproate, or carbamazepine.

If there is no response with mood stabilizer alone, the next step would involve a combination strategy. This would vary depending upon whether the patient has a previous history of severe mania or hypomania. If the patient has a previous history of severe and difficult to treat mania, we recommend addition of lamotrigine or a second mood stabilizer. If these options fail, addition of an antidepressant such as bupropion or an SSRI would be appropriate. Tricyclics should be avoided in such patients. In a patient with a previous history of mild mania or hypomania, addition of lamotrigine or an antidepressant such as bupropion or an SSRI can be the first alternative; if this fails, substitution with another antidepressant would be appropriate. In these patients, if addition of an antidepressant fails, augmentation with pindolol or thyroid hormone 3 (T3) could be considered.

If the patient has psychotic symptoms, a trial with an atypical antipsychotic such as risperidone or olanzapine in combination with a mood stabilizer would be appropriate. ECT should be considered for bipolar depressed patients with severe suicidal ideation or plans, and in those with psychotic features that have not responded to an atypical antipsychotic, mood stabilizer, and an antidepressant combination.

Since the risk of manic switch likely increases with the duration of antidepressant therapy (Boerlin, Gitlin, Zoellner, & Hammen, 1998; Prien et al., 1984; Sachs et al., 1994; Wehr & Goodwin, 1987), we recommend that antidepressant tapering should begin within 4 to 6 weeks of remission of depressive symptoms. If repeated attempts to taper lead to relapse of depressive symptoms, antidepressants may be continued for a longer period of time, particularly in bipolar II patients with depressive episodes as the predominant presentation.

References

Abrams, R., & Taylor, M. A. (1974). Unipolar and bipolar depressive illness: Phenomenology and response to electroconvulsive therapy. *Archives of General Psychiatry, 30,* 320–321.

Akiskal, H. S., Walker, P., Puzantian, V. R., King, D., Rosenthal, T. L., & Dranon, M. (1983). Bipolar outcome in the course of depressive illness: Phenomenalogic, familial, and pharmacological predictors. *Journal of Affective Disorders, 5,* 115–128.

American Psychiatric Association. (1994). *Diagnostic and statistical manual of mental disorders* (4th ed.). Washington, DC: Author.

Angst, J. (1986). The course of affective disorders. *Psychopathology, 19*(Suppl. 2), 47S–52S.

Aronson, R., Offman, H. J., Joffe, T., & Naylor, C. D. (1996). Triiodothyronine augmentation in the treatment of refractory depression: A meta-analysis. *Archives of General Psychiatry, 53*(9), 842–848.

Baldessano, C. F., Sach, G. S., Stoll, A. L., Lafer, B., & Truman, C. J. (1995). Paroxetine for bipolar depression: outcome in patients failing prior antidepressant trials. *Depression, 3*(4), 182–186.

Baumhachl, U., Biziere, K., Fischbach, R., Geretsegger, C., Hebenstreit, G., Radmayr, E., et al. (1989). Efficacy and tolerability of moclobemide compared with imipramine in depressive disorder (DSM-III): An Austrian double-blind multicentre study. *British Journal of Psychiatry, 155*(Suppl. 6), 78S–83S

Boerlin, H. L., Gitlin, M. J., Zoellner, L. A., & Hammen, C. L. (1998, July). Bipolar depression and antidepressant-induced mania: A naturalistic study. *Journal of Clinical Psychiatry, 59*(7), 374–379.

Bowden, C. L., Calabrese, J. R., Ascher, J., DeVeaugh-Geiss, J., Earl, N., Evoniuk, G., et al. (2000). *Spectrum of efficacy of lamotrigine in bipolar disorder: Overview of double-blind, placebo-controlled studies.* Poster session presented at the American College of Neuropsychopharmacology Meeting, Puerto Rico.

Bowden, C. L., Calabrese, J. R., DeVeaugh-Geiss, J., Leadbetter, R., Paska, W., & Sachs, G. (2001). *Lamotrigine demonstrates long-term mood stabilization in bipolar I depression.* Poster session presented at the American College of Neuropsychopharmacology Meeting, American College of Neuropsychopharmacology Meeting, Hawaii.

Bowden, C. L., Calabrese, J. R., Sachs, G. S., Yatham, L. N., Asghar, S. A., Hompland, M., et al. (2001). A placebo-controlled 18-month trial of lamotrigine and lithium maintenance treatment in recently manic or hypomanic patients with bipolar I disorder. Manuscript submitted for publication.

Bratfos, O., & Haug, J. O. (1965). Electroconvulsive therapy and antidepressant drugs in manic-depressive disease. *Acta Psychiatrica Scandinavia, 41,* 588–596.

Brockington, I. F., Altman, E., Hillier, V., Meltzer, H. Y., & Nand, S. (1982). The clinical picture of bipolar affective disorder in its depressed phase: A report from London and Chicago. *British Journal of Psychiatry, 141,* 558–562.

Calabrese, J. R., Bowdes, C. L., Sachs, G. S., Ascher, J. A., Monaghan, E., & Rudd, E. D. (1999). A double-blind placebo-controlled study of Lamotrigine monotherapy in outpatients with bipolar I depression. Lamictal 602 study group. *Journal of Clinical Psychiatry, 60*(2),79–88.

Cohn, J. B., Collins, G., Ashbrook, E., & Wernicke, J. F. (1989). A comparison of fluoxetine, imipramine and placebo in patients with bipolar depressive disorder. *International Clinical Psychopharmacology, 4,* 313–322.

Coppen, A., Shaw, D. M., & Farrel, J. P. (1963). Potentiation of the antidepressant effect of monoamine oxidase inhibitors by tryptophan. *Lancet, i,* 79–81.

Coryell, W., Andreasen, N. C., Endicott, J., & Keller, M. (1987). The significance of past mania or hypomania in the course and outcome of major depression. *American Journal of Psychiatry, 144,* 309–315.

Coryell, W., Endicott, J., Maser, J. D., Keller, M. B., Leon, A. C., & Akiskal, H. S. (1995). Long-term stability of polarity distinctions in the affective disorders. *American Journal of Psychiatry, 152,* 385–390.

Deltito, J. A., Moline, M., Pollak, C., Martin, L. Y., & Maremmani, I. (1991). Effects of photo-therapy on non-seasonal unipolar and bipolar depressive spectrum disorders. *Journal of Affective Disorders, 23,* 231–237.

Dwight, M. M., Keck, P. E., Jr., Stanton, S. P., Strakowski, S. M., & McElroy, S. L. (1994). Antidepressant activity and mania associated with risperidone treatment of schizoaffective disorder. *Lancet, 344,* 554–555.

Egeland, J. A., Blumenthal, R. L., Nee, J., Sharpe, L., & Endicott, J. (1987). Reliability and relationship of various ages of onset criteria for major affective disorder. *Journal of Affective Disorders, 12,*159–165.

Fawcett, J., Kravitz, H. M., & Zajecka, M. R. (1991). CNS stimulant potentiation of monoamine oxidase inhibitors in treatment-refractory depression. *Journal of Clinical Psychopharmacology, 11,* 127–132.

Fitz-Gerald, M. J., Pinkofsky, H. B., Brannon, G., Dandridge, E., & Calhoun A. (1999). Olanzapine-induced mania. *American Journal of Psychiatry, 156*(7), 1114.

Fogelson, D. L., Bystritsky, A., & Pasnau, R. (1992). Bupropion in the treatment of bipolar disorders the same old story. *Journal of Clinical Psychiatry, 53,* 443–446.

Frye, M. A., Ketter, T. A., Osuch, E. A., Timbrell, T. A., Speer, A. M., Dunn, R. M., et al. (1998). Gabapentin and lamotrigine monotherapy in mood disorders. *Annual Meeting of the American Psychiatric Association,* Toronto, Canada. Abstract 77D:150.

Ghaemi, S. N., Katzow, J. J., Desai, S. P., & Goodwin, F. K. (1998). Gabapentin treatment of mood disorders: a preliminary study. *Journal of Clinical Psychiatry, 59*(8), 426–429.

Goldberg, J. F., Harrow, M., & Grossman, L. S. (1995). Course and outcome in bipolar affective disorder: a longitudinal follow up study. *American Journal of Psychiatry, 152,* 379–84.

Goodwin, F. K., Murphy, D. L., Dunner, D. L., & Bunney, W. E., Jr. (1972). Lithium response in unipolar versus bipolar depression. *American Journal of Psychiatry, 15,* 187–193.

Haykal, R. F., & Akiskal, H. S. (1990). Bupropion as a promising approach to rapid cycling bipolar II patients. *Journal of Clinical Psychiatry, 51,* 450–455.

Hillert, A., Maier, W., Wetzel, H., & Benkert, O. (1992). Risperidone in the treatment of disorders with combined psychotic and depressive syndrome: a functional approach. *Pharmacopsychiatry, 25,* 213–217.

Himmelhoch, J. M., Detre, T., Kupfer, D. J., Swartzburg, M., & Byck, R. (1972). Treatment of previously intractable depressions with tranylcypromine and lithium. *Journal of Nervous and Mental Disorders, 155,* 216–220.

Himmelhoch, J. M., Fuchs, C. Z., & Symons, B. J. (1982). A double-blind study of tranylcypromine treatment of major anergic depression. *Journal of Nervous and Mental Disorders, 170,* 628–634.

Himmelhoch, J. M., Thase, M. E., Mallinger, A. G., & Houck, P. (1991). Tranylcypromine versus imipramine in anergic bipolar depression. *American Journal of Psychiatry, 148,* 910–916.

Homan, S., Lachenbruch, P. A., Winokur, G., & Clayton, P. (1982). An efficacy study of electroconvulsive therapy and antidepressants in the treatment of primary depression. *Psychological Medicine, 12,* 615–624.

Hussain, M. (1999, December). *Treatment of bipolar depression with topiramate.* Paper presented at the American College of Neuropsychopharmacology 38th Annual Meeting,

Acapulco, Mexico. Scientific Abstracts:231.

Katz, M. M., Robins, E., Croughan, J., Secunda, S., & Swann, A. (1982). Behavioural measurement and drug response characteristics of unipolar and bipolar depression. *Psychological Medicine, 12,* 25–36.

Keck, P. E., Jr., Wilson, D. R., Strakowski, S. M., McElroy, S. L., Kizer, D., Balistreri, T. M., et al. (1995). Clinical predictors of acute risperidone response in schizophrenia, schizoaffective disorder, and psychotic mood disorders. *Journal of Clinical Psychiatry, 56,* 466–470.

Kramlinger, K. G., & Post, R. M. (1989). The Addition of lithium to carbamazepine: antidepressant efficacy in treatment-resistant depression. *Archives of General Psychiatry, 46,* 794–800.

Kraus, R., McEachran, A., & Persad, E. (1997, September). *Open study of methylphenidate augmentation of mood stabilizer treatment in patients suffering from bipolar affective disorder, depressed episode, with atypical vegetative symptoms.* Paper presented at the 47th Annual Meeting of the Canadian Psychiatric Association Calgary, Canada. Book of Abstracts: 79–81.

Kukopulos, A., Reginaldi, D., Laddomada, P., Floris, G., Serra, G., & Tondo, L. (1980). Course of manic depressive cycle and changes caused by treatments. *Pharmokopsychiatry and Neuropsychopharmacology, 13,* 156–167.

Kupfer, D. J., Weiss, B. L., Foster, F. G., Detre, T. P., Delgado, J., & McPartland, R. (1974). Psychomotor activity in affective states. *Archives of General Psychiatry, 30,* 765–768.

Kusumakar, V., & Yatham, L. N. (1997). An open study of lamotrigine in refractory bipolar depression. *Psychiatry Resident, 72*(2), 145–148.

Lane, H. Y., & Chang, W. H. (1998). Risperidone monotherapy for psychotic depression unresponsive to other treatments. *Journal of Clinical Psychiatry, 59*(11), 624.

Lane, H. Y., Chiu, W. C., & Chang, W. H. (1999). Risperidone monotherapy for mania and depression. *American Journal of Psychiatry, 156*(7), 1115.

Lish, J. D., Dime-Meenan, S., Whybrow, P. C., Price, R. A., & Hirschfield, R. M. (1994). The National Depressive and Manic Depressive Association (DMDA) survey of bipolar members. *Journal of Affect Disorders, 31,* 281–294.

McIntyre, R. S., Manlini, D., McCann, S., Srinivasan, J., Sagman, D., & Kennedy, S. (2000, December). *Randomized, single-blind comparison of topiramate and bupropion SR as add-on therapy in bipolar depression.* Poster presentation at the Annual Meeting of the American College of Neuropsychopharmacology, San Juan, Puerto Rico.

Muller-Siecheneder, F., Muller, M. J., Hillert, A., Szegedi, A., Wetzel, H., & Benkert, O. (1998). Risperidone versus haloperidol and amitriptyline in the treatment of patients with a combined psychotic and depressive syndrome. *Journal of Clinical Psychiatry, 18*(2),111–120.

Nemeroff, C. B., Evans, D. L., Gyulai, L., Sachs, G. S., Bowden, C. L., Gergel, I. P., et al. (2001). Double-blind, placebo-controlled comparison of imipramine and paraxetine in the treatment of bipolar depression. *American Journal of Psychiatry, 158*(6), 906–912.

Noyes, R., Dempsey, G. M., Blum, A., & Cavanaugh, G. L. (1974). Lithium treatment of depression. *Comprehensive Psychiatry, 15,*187–193.

O'Connor, M., & Silver, H. (1998). Adding risperidone to selective serotonin reuptake inhibitor improves chronic depression [Letter to the editor]. *Journal of Clinical Psychopharmacology, 18,* 89–91.

Ostroff, R. B., & Nelson, J. C. (1999). Risperidone augmentation of selective serotonin reuptake inhibitors in major depression. *Journal of Clinical Psychiatry, 60*(4), 256–259.

Peet, M. (1994). Induction of mania with selective serotonin re-uptake inhibitors and tricyclic antidepressants. *British Journal of Psychiatry, 164,* 549–550.

Perez, V., Gilaberte, I., Faries, D, Alvarez, E., & Artigas, F. (1997). Randomized, double-blind, placebo-controlled trial of pindolol in combination with fluoxetine antidepressant treatment. *Lancet, 349,* 1594–1597.

Post, R. M., Uhde, T. W., Ballenger, J. C., Chatterji, D. C., Greene, R. F., & Bunney, W. E., Jr. (1983). Carbamazepine and its −10, 11-epoxide metabolite in plasma and CSF: Relationship to antidepressant response. *Archives of General Psychiatry, 40,* 673–676.

Post, R. M., Uhde, T. W., Roy-Byrne, P. P., & Joffe, R. T. (1986). Antidepressant effects of carbamazepine. *American Journal of Psychiatry, 143,* 29–34.

Price, L. H., Charney, D. S., & Heninger, G. R. (1985). Efficacy of lithium-tranylcypromine treatment in refractory depression. *American Journal of Psychiatry, 142,* 619–623.

Prien, R. F., Klett, C. J., & Caffey, E. M. (1973). Lithium carbonate and imipramine in prevention of affective episodes. *Archives of General Psychiatry, 29,* 420–425.

Prien, R. F., Kupfer, D. J., Mansky, P. A., Small, J. G., Tuason, V. B., Voss, C. B., et al. (1984). Drug therapy in the prevention of recurrences in unipolar and bipolar affective disorders. *Archives of General Psychiatry, 41,* 1096–1104.

Quitkin, F. M., McGrath, P., Liebowitz, M. R., Stewart, J., & Howard, A. (1981). Monoamine oxidase inhibitors in bipolar endogenous depressives. *Journal of Clinical Psychopharmacology, 1,* 70–73.

Rothschild, A. J. (1996). Management of psychotic, treatment-resistant depression. *Psychiatric Clinics of North America, 19*(2), 237–252.

Rothschild, A. J., Bates, K. S., Boehringer, K., & Syed, A. (1999, February). Olanzapine response in psychotic depression. *Journal of Clinical Psychiatry, 60*(2), 116–118.

Roy-Byrne, P., Post, R. M., Uhde, T. W., Porcu, T., & Davis, D. (1985). The longitudinal course of recurrent affective illness: Life chart data from research patients at the NIMH. *Acta Psychiatrica Scandinavia, 71*(Suppl. 317), 1–34

Sachs, G. S., Lafer, B., Stoll, A., Banov, M., Thibault, A. B., Tohen, M., et al. (1994). A double-blind trial of bupropion versus desipramine for bipolar depression. *Journal of Clinical Psychiatry, 55,* 391–393.

Sachs, G. S. (1996). Treatment-resistant bipolar depression. *Psychiatric clinics of North America, 19*(2), 215–235.

Sachs, G. S. (1999, December). *Safety and efficacy of risperidone vs. placebo vs. haloperidol as add-on therapy to mood stabilizers in the treatment of manic phase of bipolar disorder.* Paper presented at the American College of Neuropsychopharmacology 38th Annual Meeting Acapulco, Mexico. (Scientific Abstract No. 175).

Sachs, G., Altshuler, L., Ketter, T., Suppes, T., Rasgon, N., Frye, M., et al. (2001, December). *Divalproex versus placebo for the treatment of bipolar depression.* Poster presentation. American College of Neuropsychopharmacology, Hawaii.

Shelton, R., Tollefson, G., Tohen, M., Stahl, S., Gannon, K. S., Jacobs, T. G., et al. (2001). A novel augmentation strategy for treating resistant major depression. *American Journal of Psychiatry, 158*(1), 131–134.

Short, C., & Cooke, L. (1995). Hypomania induced by gabapentin. *British Journal of Psychiatry, 166,* 679–680.

Srisurapanont, M., Yatham, L. N., & Zis, A. P. (1995). Treatment of acute bipolar depression: a review of the literature. *Canadian Journal of Psychiatry, 40,* 533–544.

Stoll, A. L., Pillay, S. S., Diamond, L., Workum, S. B., & Cole, J. O. (1996). Methylphenidate augmentation of serotonin selective reuptake inhibitors: a case series. *Journal Clinical Psychiatry, 57,* 72–76.

Stromgren, L. S. (1973). Unilateral versus bilateral electroconvulsive therapy: Investigations into the therapeutic effect in endogenous depression. *Acta Psychiatrica Scandinavia* (Suppl. 240), 7S–65S.

Szuba, M. P., Baxter, L. R., Fairbanks, L. A., Guze, B. H., & Schwartz, J. M. (1991). Effects of partial sleep deprivation on the diurnal variation of mood and motor activity in major depression. *Biological Psychiatry, 30,* 817–829.

Thase, M. E., Mallinger, A. G., McKnight, D., & Himmeloch, J. M. (1992). Treatment of imipramine-resistant recurrent depression, IV: A double blind crossover study of tranylcypromine for anergic bipolar depression. *American Journal of Psychiatry, 149,* 195–198.

Tohen, M., Sanger T., McElroy, S., Tollefson, G., Chengappa, R., Daniel, D., et al. (1999). Olanzapine versus placebo in the treatment of acute mania. *American Journal of Psychiatry, 156,* 702–709.

Tollefson, G. D., Sanger, T. M., Lu, Y., & Thieme, M. E. (1998). Depressive signs and symptoms in schizophrenia. A prospective blinded trial of olanzapine and haloperidol. *Archives General Psychiatry, 55,* 250–258.

Tollefson, G. S., Beasley, C. M., Tran, P. V., Street, J. S., Krueger, J. A., Tamura, R. N., et al. (1997). Olanzapine versus haloperidol in the treatment of schizophrenia, schizoaffective and schizophreniform disorders: results of an international collaborative trial. *American Journal of Psychiatry, 154,* 457–465.

Tome, M. B., Isaac, M. T., Harte, R., & Holland, C. (1997). Paroxetine and pindolol: A randomized trial of serotonergic autoreceptor blockade in the reduction of antidepressant latency. *International Clinical Psychopharmacology, 12,* 81–89.

Tran, P. V., Hamilton, S. H., Kuntz, A. J., Potvin, J. H., Andersen, S. W., Beasley, C., Jr., et al. (1997). Double-blind comparison of olanzapine versus risperidone in the treatment of schizophrenia and other psychotic disorders. *Journal of Clinical Psychopharmacology, 17,* 407–418.

Weisler, R. H., Ahearn, E. P., Davidson, J. R. & Wallace, C. D. (1997). Adjunctive use of olanzapine in mood disorders: five case reports. *Annals of Clinical Psychiatry, 9,* 259–262.

Wehr, T. A., & Goodwin, F. K. (1979a). Rapid cycling in manic-depressives induced by tricyclic antidepressants. *Archives of General Psychiatry, 36,* 555–559.

Wehr, T. Z., & Goodwin, F. K. (1979b). Rapid cycling between mania and depression caused by maintenance tricyclics. *Psychopharmacology Bulletin, 15,* 17–19.

Wehr, T. A., & Goodwin, F. K. (1987). Can antidepressants cause mania and worsen the course of affective illness? *American Journal of Psychiatry, 144,* 1403–1411.

Wharton, R., Perel, J., Dayton, P., & Malitz, S. (1971). A potential clinical use for methylphenidate with tricyclic antidepressants. *American Journal of Psychiatry, 127,* 1619–1625.

Winokur, G., Coryell, W., Keller, M., Endicott, J., & Akiskal, H. (1983). A prospective follow-up of patients with bipolar and primary unipolar affective disorder. *Archives of General Psychiatry, 50,* 457–465.

Yatham, L. N. (2000). Safety and efficacy of risperidone as combination therapy for the manic phase of bipolar disorder: Preliminary findings of a randomised, double-blind study (RIS-INT-46) [Abstract]. *International Journal of Neuropsychopharmacology, 3*(Suppl. 1), S142.

Yatham, L. N., Kusumakar, V., Parikh, S. V., Haslam, D. R. S., Matte, R., Sharma, V., et al. (1997). Bipolar depression: Treatment options. *Canadian Journal of Psychiatry, 42,* (Suppl. 2), 87S–91S.

Yatham, L. N., Lint, D., Lam, R. W., & Zis, A. P. (1999). Adverse effects of pindolol augmentation in patients with bipolar depression. *Journal of Clinical Psychopharmacology, 19*(4), 383–384.

Young, L. T., Robb, J. C., Patelis-Siotis, I., Macdonald, C., & Joffe, R. T. (1997). Acute treatment of bipolar depression with gabapentin. *Biological Psychiatry, 42,* 851–853.

Young, L. T., Joffe, R. T., Robb, J., MacQueen, G., & Marriot, M. (2000). A double blind comparison of the addition of a second stabilizer versus an antidepressant to an initial mood stabilizer for treatment of patients with bipolar depression. *American Journal of Psychiatry, 157,* 124–126.

Zornberg, G. L., & Pope, H. G. (1994). Treatment of depressive bipolar disorder: New directives for research. *Journal of Clinical Psychopharmocology, 13,* 397–408.

CHAPTER 3

Diagnosis and Treatment of Rapid Cycling States in Bipolar Disorder

Susan L. McElroy
Paul E. Keck, Jr.

Although the recurrent nature of bipolar disorder was well documented by many early authorities (Kraeplin, 1921/1989; Sedler, 1983), it was not until 1974 that rapid cycling was clearly defined by Dunner and Fieve (1974). In an attempt to identify factors associated with poor response of bipolar disorder to lithium prophylaxis, Dunner and Fieve (1974) found that poor outcome was primarily associated with an increased frequency of mood episodes prior to initiation of treatment. In particular, patients experiencing four or more mood episodes per year were disproportionately represented in the prophylaxis-failure group. Dunner and Fieve (1974) introduced the term *rapid cycling* to describe these patients. Specifically, of 55 bipolar patients studied, 9 (82%) of 11 rapid cyclers failed lithium prophylaxis compared with 18 (41%) of 44 nonrapid cyclers.

Based on subsequent data suggesting that rapid cycling bipolar disorder may in fact be distinct from the nonrapid form regarding differences in sex distribution, outcome, treatment response, and possibly other factors (as discussed in this chapter), DSM-IV (American Psychiatric Association,

Supported by a grant from the Theodore and Vada Stanley Foundation.

1994) has included rapid cycling as a course specifier for bipolar disorder (Bauer et al., 1994; Coryell, Endicott, & Keller, 1992; Maj, Magliano, Pirozzi, Marasco, & Guarneri, 1994; Maj, Pirozzi, Formicola, & Tortorella, 1999). Consistent with Dunner and Fieve's original definition, DSM-IV has defined rapid cycling as the occurrence of at least four major depressive, manic, hypomanic, or mixed episodes during the previous year. Unlike Dunner and Fieve's definition, however, DSM-IV has specified that the mood episodes be demarcated either by a remission of at least 2 months duration or by a switch to an episode of opposite polarity. In addition, duration criteria for mood episodes must be met; each major depressive episode must be at least 2 weeks, each manic or mixed episode at least 1 week, and each hypomanic episode at least 4 days.

It is therefore important to note that rapid cycling has been defined in various ways that differ from that of DSM-IV (Bauer et al., 1994; Maj, Pirozzi, Formicola, & Tortorella, 1999). These include requirement of a continuous circular course of mood episodes (i.e., hypomanias or manias alternating with depressions without an intervening euthymic interval) at some time during the illness (Kukopulos et al., 1980; Wehr, Sack, Rosenthal, & Cowdry, 1988), and lack of specified criteria for demarcation of episodes (Bauer, Whybrow, & Winokur, 1990; Wehr et al., 1988). Also, recognizing that extremely rapid forms of cycling can occur, including cycling that occurs within weeks to days (ultrarapid cycling), as well as within a day (ultradian cycling), some definitions have suspended episode duration criteria, requiring that mood episodes meet only severity criteria (Coryell et al., 1992; Maj, Pirozzi, Formicola, & Tortorella, 1999).

Rapid cycling is an important clinical phenomenon for several reasons. First, it is associated with a high degree of morbidity and possibly an increased risk of suicide. Fawcett and colleagues (1987) found that affective cycling within a mood episode was associated with suicide in patients with major mood disorders. Second, rapid cycling is difficult to treat. Not only do afflicted patients respond poorly to lithium and possibly other mood stabilizers, but evidence suggests that other standard treatments for bipolar disorder, in particular antidepressants, may actually induce or exacerbate the phenomenon (Altshuler et al., 1995; Wehr & Goodwin, 1979). Third, rapid cycling presents in a variety of ways that often go unrecognized or misdiagnosed. Fourth, the disorder may be more prevalent than is currently recognized.

Epidemiology and Clinical Characteristics

Rapid cycling is presumed to be uncommon. However, a recent review of 10 studies of 2,057 patients with rapid and nonrapid cycling bipolar disorder found that 24% of the patients had rapid cycling courses, with prevalence estimates ranging from 13% (Dunner, Vijayalakshmy, & Fieve, 1977) to 56% (Cowdry, Wehr, Zis, & Goodwin, 1983) among the cohorts evaluated (Tondo & Baldessarini, 1998). Some investigators have argued that these rates may overestimate the true prevalence of the disorder, since they are usually derived from tertiary referral centers, which presumably attract higher proportions of treatment resistant patients (Wehr & Goodwin, 1979). However, it has also been argued that rapid cycling may be underdiagnosed. Patients often do not report hypomanic symptoms or episodes, and their rapid mood shifts may go unrecognized or misdiagnosed. Moreover, some data suggest that rapid cycling may be increasing in prevalence (Kukopulos et al., 1983; Wolpert, Goldberg, & Harrow, 1990).

Many studies (Bauer, Whybrow, & Winokur, 1990; Bowden et al., 1999; Calabrese & Delucchi, 1990; Coryell et al., 1992; Dunner & Fieve, 1974; Dunner et al., 1977; Kukopulos, Caliari, et al., 1983; Nurnberger, Guroff, Hamovit, Berrettini, W., & Gershon, E., 1988; Wehr et al., 1988; Tondo & Baldessarini, 1998), but not all (Joffe, Kutcher, & McDonald, 1988; Maj, Magliano, et al., 1994), have reported that rapid cycling is more common among females than males, with proportions of females ranging from 41% (Joffe et al., 1988) to 92% (Wehr & Goodwin, 1979). Indeed, in a recent review of 10 studies of 2,057 bipolar patients, proportions of women and men among rapid cycling cases averaged 72 and 28%, respectively (Tondo & Baldessarini, 1998). However, women and men with rapid cycling had similar cycling rates both before and during lithium maintenance treatment.

Beyond differences in episode frequency, resistance to lithium prophylaxis, and female preponderance, rapid cyclers have also been reported to differ from nonrapid cyclers with respect to having higher rates of thyroid abnormalities (Kleiner, Altschuler, Hendrick, & Hershman, 1999), comorbid panic disorder (Coryell et al., 1992), and resistance to treatment with carbamazepine (Denicoff et al., 1997; Okuma, 1993) and clozapine (Calabrese, et al., 1996). These findings, however, are either less consistent (thyroid abnormalities, carbamazepine response) or based on only a few studies (panic disorder comorbidity, clozapine response), and thus, in need of further study.

Indeed, rapid cyclers have been found to be similar to nonrapid cyclers with respect to many other features. These include age of onset of illness, frequency of life events prior to illness onset, duration of illness, variability in the course of illness, incidence of psychotic symptoms during mania, and family history of mood disorder (Bauer et al., 1994; Coryell et al., 1992; Dunner et al., 1977; Nurnberger et al., 1988; Roy-Byrne, Joffe, Uhde, & Post, 1984). Studies differ, however, regarding reported rates of bipolar I relative to bipolar II disorder among rapid cyclers. Most studies have found that approximately one half of rapid cyclers exhibit bipolar I Disorder, with full manic episodes alternating with major depressive episodes, and the other half bipolar II disorder, with hypomanic episodes alternating with major depressive episodes (Bauer et al., 1994; Calabrese & Delucchi 1990; Dunner et al., 1977; Kukopulos et al., 1983; Maj, Magliano, et al., 1994; Nurnberger et al., 1988; Wehr et al., 1988). However, several studies have found higher rates of bipolar II relative to bipolar I disorder (Coryell et al., 1992; Kukopulos et al., 1980).

As with nonrapid cycling bipolar disorder, the onset of the first mood episode of bipolar disorder associated with rapid cycling typically occurs in late adolescence through the third decade of life, with reported mean ages of onset ranging from 19 to 40 years (Dunner et al., 1977; Kukopulos, Caliari et al., 1983). Unlike nonrapid cyclers, however, the majority of rapid cyclers (79 to 98%) begin their illness with a depressive episode (Kukopulos, Reginaldi et al., 1980; Wehr et al., 1988). Additionally, many patients display subclinical mood symptoms prior to the onset of full mood episodes.

The onset of rapid cycling relative to the onset of bipolar illness is variable. Although some patients (23 to 37%) exhibit rapid cycling at the onset of their mood disorder, most (63 to 77%) develop rapid cycling some time after its onset (Kukopulos et al., 1980; Wehr et al., 1988). In some patients, the onset of rapid cycling may be associated with pharmacological factors, especially treatment with antidepressants (as discussed later in this chapter).

The course of rapid cycling bipolar disorder displays many different patterns. Some patients show an increasing frequency and severity of mood episodes over time, others display nonrapid cycling phases, and some others develop spontaneous protracted remissions (Coryell et al., 1992). Some patients display circular courses with manic or hypomanic periods alternating with depressions without intervening euthymic intervals, whereas others exhibit irregular patterns of cycling. Indeed, some data has suggested that chaotic, rather than cyclic, behavior may characterize the mood pattern over time in rapid cycling bipolar patients as compared to controls (Bauer & Whybrow 1993; Gottschalk, Bauer, & Whybrow, 1990).

As indicated earlier, a wide range of episode frequencies has been reported in rapid cyclers, with some patients experiencing 20 to 50 episodes per year or episodes so frequent that they cannot be reliably counted (Bauer, Whybrow, & Winokur, 1990; Calabrese & Delucchi, 1990). In these extreme forms, patients may display continuous cycling without interepisodic euthymic periods, or ultrafast rapid cycling—the experience of full manic and depressive syndromes within 48- or even 24-hour intervals (Bauer, Whybrow, & Winokur, 1990, Paschalis, Pavlou, & Papactimitriou, 1980). It is currently unclear whether continual or ultrafast forms of rapid cycling are substantially different from "classic" rapid cycling (with cycles lasting weeks to months), or whether they represent ends of a clinical spectrum.

The relationship of rapid cycling—particularly ultrafast and ultradian rapid cycling—to mixed states and dysphoric mania is also currently unclear. Three studies systematically assessing rapid cycling among patients with mixed states have suggested that the two conditions may not be related. Himmelhoch et al. (1979) reported that patients with mixed and nonmixed mania showed similar rates of "mood circularity" (defined as episodes of mania and depression not separated by periods longer than 2 months). Post and colleagues (1989) reported that 22 patients with "dysphoric mania" were significantly less likely to exhibit rapid cycling in the year before their index admissions than were 26 patients with pure mania. Also, although both rapid and nonrapid cycling patients showed equal peak manic severity at their index episodes, rapid cycling patients showed significantly less dysphoria, anxiety, and psychosis during their manias. More recently, Perugi and colleagues (1999) found that the rates of rapid cycling were similar between 143 bipolar patients with broadly defined mixed states and 118 patients with DSM-III-R manic episodes.

Patients with rapid cycling, however, have been reported to experience frequent mixed episodes (Bowden et al., 1999; Calabrese & Delucchi, 1990; Himmelhoch, 1979). Of 75 treatment refractory bipolar patients receiving a prospective lamotrigine trial, 51% of 41 rapid cycling patients had more than 10 lifetime mixed episodes, compared with 7% of 34 nonrapid cycling patients (Bowden et al., 1999). As well, mixed states and rapid cycling may share a greater prevalence among females and of thyroid abnormalities, poorer response to lithium, induction and/or exacerbation by antidepressants, and a possibly better response to valproate (Chang et al., 1998). Further, the rapid mood shifts displayed by patients with mixed mania (Himmelhoch, 1979; Post et al., 1989) resembles the 24-hour mood alterations described by some bipolar patients with ultrarapid cycling (Bauer, Whybrow, & Winokur, 1990).

Indeed, in patients with mixed symptoms, it is often difficult to assess whether manic and depressive symptoms occur simultaneously, alternate rapidly, or both. If manic and depressive symptoms alternate rapidly, it is often difficult to determine how rapidly they do so (e.g., within minutes, hours, or days). This suggests that not only can mania be associated with varying degrees of depression along a dimension, but that the temporal relationship between manic and depressive symptoms may also vary dimensionally (McElroy et al., 1995). In other words, there may be independent or related dimensions of mixity and cyclicity which, because of ultrarapid cycling, are either pathophysiologically distinct but clinically indistinguishable or pathophysiologically similar (e.g., ultrarapid cyclicity may progress into mixity). It is therefore conceivable that rapid cyclers might be more likely to experience mixed states, either as a transitional state between mania or depression, as extremely severe forms of rapid cycling, or as advanced forms of the illness.

In short, the relationship between mixed states and rapid cycling remains unclear. For practical purposes, however, it must be recognized that mixed states (including dysphoric mania) may occur in some rapid cyclers, and that the presence of rapid cycling should be evaluated in any patient who presents with a mixed state.

Associated Conditions

Although the etiology of rapid cycling is unknown, it has been associated with a variety of factors. These include female sex; either an equal distribution of bipolar I and II disorder or a preponderance of bipolar II disorder rather than a preponderance of bipolar I disorder; psychiatric comorbidity; endocrine abnormalities and changes, including overt and subclinical hypothyroidism; various neurological insults and abnormalities including mental retardation, head trauma, stroke, and multiple sclerosis; and exposure to pharmacological agents, especially antidepressants and substances of abuse (Alarcon, 1985; Altshuler et al., 1995; Roy-Byrne et al., 1984; Wehr & Goodwin, 1979).

A variety of psychiatric conditions have been reported to commonly occur in rapid cycling bipolar patients. These include panic disorder, alcohol and substance abuse, eating disorders, and premenstrual syndrome (Coryell et al., 1992). In some patients, these comorbidities appear to be "state dependent," as treatment resulting in mood stabilization is associated with their relief (Calabrese & Delucchi, 1990; Shapira, Goldsmith, & McElroy, 2000).

Regarding thyroid function, several studies have found increased rates of overt hypothyroidism, ranging from 23 to 51% in rapid cycling bipolar patients compared with unselected bipolar patients, ranging from 4 to 15 percent, even when increased preponderance of females and treatment with lithium are controlled for (Bauer, Whybrow, & Winokur, 1990; Kleiner et al., 1999). Rates of thyroid abnormalities increase substantially if subclinical forms are also included. Other studies, however, have not found an association between rapid cycling and thyroid abnormalities in bipolar patients (Bartalena et al., 1990; Joffe, Kutcher, & MacDonald, 1987; Maj, Magliano, et al., 1994). Indeed, since most rapid cyclers do not display serum thyroxine (T_4) deficiencies, the precise role thyroid function plays in rapid cycling, if any, remains unclear. Bauer, Whybrow, and Winokur (1990) have nonetheless hypothesized that some rapid cycling patients may have relative thyroid hormone deficiencies within the central nervous system.

Of the pharmacological agents associated with the induction of rapid cycling, tricyclic antidepressants have been most commonly reported. Virtually all other antidepressants, however, have been implicated. These include tetracyclics, bupropion, monoamine oxidase inhibitors (MAOIs), mianserin, nomifensine, serotonin reuptake inhibitors, and even lithium (Srisurapanont, Yatham, & Zis, 1995; Zornberg & Pope, 1993). Additionally, electroconvulsive therapy (ECT), buspirone, tricyclic withdrawal, dopamine agonists (l-dopa, piribedil), cypropheptadine, and conjugated estrogens have also been associated with rapid cycling (Alarcon, 1985; Roy-Byrne et al., 1984).

The precise frequency of antidepressant induced rapid cycling is unknown, but reported rates have ranged from 26% to 60% of antidepressant treated bipolar patients (Altshuler et al., 1995; Kukopulos, Reginaldi, et al., 1980; Kukopulos et al., 1983; Wehr et al., 1988). It is currently impossible to predict which bipolar patients will develop rapid cycling with antidepressant treatment. Indeed, some investigators remain skeptical about whether or not antidepressants can truly induce rapid cycling (Coryell et al., 1992). However, Wehr and Goodwin's prospective, double-blind, placebo-controlled studies demonstrating reversible induction of rapid cycling in response to antidepressant treatment in bipolar patients (Goodwin & Jamison, 1990; Wehr & Goodwin, 1979; Wehr et al., 1988) and the apparent historical increase in the prevalence of rapid cycling coincident with the advent of antidepressant agents (Wolpert et al., 1990), support the ability of these agents to induce rapid cycling.

Differential Diagnosis

A variety of neuropsychiatric and medical conditions may be characterized by affective lability or rapid mood swings and, thus, may resemble rapid cycling bipolar disorder and should be included in its differential diagnosis. These include cyclothymia, impulsive personality disorders, psychoactive substance use disorders, premenstrual mood changes or late luteal phase dysphoric disorder, temporal lobe epilepsy, and metabolic disorders.

Some of these distinctions may be particularly difficult to make. The affective lability of borderline personality disorder, however, can often be distinguished from that of rapid cycling bipolar disorder by the absence of other co-occurring signs and symptoms of mania and depression, as well as the association with clear-cut interpersonal stressors. Substance induced affective instability may be phenomenologically identical to bipolar rapid cycling, but, unlike substance induced depression, should resolve relatively quickly upon discontinuation of the substance (e.g., within 1 to 2 weeks). If cycling persists, substance triggered bipolar cycling should be considered. Indeed, bipolar rapid cycling is often comorbid with many of the conditions from which it needs to be distinguished.

Studies of Medical Treatment of Rapid Cyclers

To date, there is only one published double-blind, placebo-controlled treatment study of a cohort of patients with rapid cycling bipolar disorder. This trial suggests that lamotrigine may have maintenance mood stabilizing effects in bipolar II (but not bipolar I) rapid cycling disorder. In addition, a growing amount of clinical data along with a small number of controlled studies suggest that a variety of treatments—in particular lithium, some antiepileptics in addition to lamotrigine, standard and atypical antipsychotics, thyroid augmentation, and various antidepressants, often used in various combinations—may be at least partially effective in some patients.

LITHIUM

Recent reports support Dunner and Fieve's (1974) original observation that many rapid cyclers do not respond adequately to prophylactic treatment with lithium. In an analysis of five studies of course and response to lithium prophylaxis involving 576 bipolar patients, Faedda, Baldessarini, Tohen, Strakowski, & Waternaux (1991) found that rapid cycles without euthymic intervals was associated with the lowest response rate (18%), as compared to long cycles without euthymic intervals (55%), a sequence of mania or hypomania followed by depression and then a ≥ 1-month euthymic interval (72%), a sequence of depression followed by mania or hypomania, and then ≥ 1 month euthymic interval (39%), and an irregular course (62%). Okuma (1993) found that of 108 bipolar patients treated with lithium for at least 2 years, lithium was moderately or markedly effective in 11(25%) of the rapid cyclers compared with 38(59%) of the nonrapid cyclers. More recently, Denicoff and colleagues (1991) reported that only 28% of a group of rapid cycling patients responded to up to one year of lithium prophylaxis. Indeed, individuals in whom rapid cycling appeared to be precipitated or exacerbated by lithium treatment have been described (Cowdrey et al., 1983; Roy-Byrne et al., 1984).

A substantial number of rapid cycling patients may, however, show some degree of response to lithium treatment (Dunner et al., 1977; Kukopulos et al., 1980; Paschalis et al., 1980). This improvement may be evident only when the patient is observed on lithium therapy over extended periods of time or when concomitantly administered antidepressants are discontinued. For example, Dunner and Fieve (1974) reported that of 29 rapid cycling patients treated with lithium for at least one year, all displayed a greater percentage of time spent euthymic (due to a decrease in the percentage of time spent hypomanic or depressed) in their last year of lithium treatment as compared to their prelithium baseline. Kukopulos and colleagues (1980) reported that 15 (72%) of 21 rapid cyclers receiving lithium prophylaxis who were persuaded to avoid antidepressant treatment when depressed displayed complete mood stabilization. Thus, although many rapid cyclers may not respond completely to lithium, a substantial number may demonstrate some degrees of response, especially when lithium is administered over extended periods of time with/or without antidepressants. Moreover, increasing clinical reports suggest lithium's mood stabilizing properties in rapid cycling bipolar disorder may be augmented by the coadministration of carbamazepine, valproate, standard or atypical antipsychotics, thyroid hormone, and possibly some of the new antiepileptic agents (Denicoff et al., 1997).

VALPROATE

Valproate continues to hold promise as an agent for rapid cycling bipolar disorder (Calabrese & Woyshville, 1995). In a retrospective review of the short-term effectiveness of valproate in 37 acutely manic bipolar patients, all five rapid cyclers responded favorably, compared to 19 (59%) of 32 nonrapid cyclers (McElroy et al., 1988). In a follow-up study, six consecutive rapid cyclers (including the five in the original report) displayed responses to valproate over extended periods of time ranging from 3 to 25 months. Two patients received valproate alone, one required supplemental haloperidol during hypomanic periods, two required concomitant maintenance lithium, and one required concomitant maintenance lithium with a standard antipsychotic. Five of these patients had failed previous treatment with carbamazepine.

In an open-label, prospective, 7.8-month study of the acute and prophylactic effectiveness of valproate in manic, depressed, and mixed episodes in 55 patients with rapid cycling bipolar disorder, valproate appeared particularly effective in the acute and long-term treatment of manic and mixed states, but less effective in the acute and long-term treatment of depression (Calabrese & Delucchi, 1990). Specifically, 31 (91%) of 34 and

48 (94%) of 51 patients displayed a moderate or marked acute and prophylactic antimanic response, respectively, and 12 (86%) of 14 and 13 (93%)
of 14 patients displayed an acute and prophylactic antimixed state response,
respectively. By contrast, 16 (47%) of 41 and 39 (77%) of 51 patients, respectively, displayed an acute and prophylactic antidepressant response.
Twenty (36%) patients received valproate monotherapy and 35 (64%) received valproate in combination with other agents, including lithium,
carbamazepine, and antidepressants. Thirty-five (64%) patients had been
resistant to treatment with lithium or carbamazepine.

Controlled studies also suggest valproate may be effective for rapid
cyclers. In the first parallel-group, double-blind, placebo-controlled study
of valproate in acute bipolar mania, valproate proved superior to placebo in
reducing manic symptoms and improving overall level of function (Pope et
al., 1991). When the 12 responders were compared to the five nonresponders,
the presence of rapid cycling did not affect valproate response (McElroy,
Keck, Pope, Hudson, & Morris, 1991). Similarly, in a double-blind, placebo-controlled comparison of valproate versus lithium in 179 bipolar I
inpatients with acute mania, the proportion of responders was comparable
for divalproex (48%) and lithium (49%) and superior to placebo (25%;
Bowden et al., 1994). All patients with rapid cycling ($n = 8$) were randomly
assigned to valproate; four (50%) displayed at least 50% improvement on
the Mania Rating scale of the SADS-C, which was comparable to the overall degree of response of the valproate treated group. However, it remains
unclear whether rapid and nonrapid cyclers respond differentially to
valproate.

CARBAMAZEPINE

Initial reports suggested carbamazepine might be an effective alternative to
lithium for rapid cycling bipolar disorder (Calabrese & Woyshville, 1995;
Joyce, 1988). In a double-blind, placebo-controlled study of carbamazepine
in 19 acutely manic patients, for example, Post, Uhde, Roy-Byrne, and Joffe
(1987) found that a history of rapid cycling was associated with a favorable
acute antimanic response. However, subsequent clinical reports have suggested that many rapid cycling patients respond inadequately to
carbamazepine. Wehr et al. (1988) reported that only two (7%) of 27 lithium
resistant rapid cyclers responded to open label carbamazepine, which was
usually administered in conjunction with lithium or other drugs (e.g., tranylcypromine and thioridazine). Similarly, Okuma (1993) found that of 101
bipolar patients treated with carbamazepine for at least 2 years,
carbamazepine was moderately (33%) or markedly (6%) effective in 39%

of the nonrapid cyclers, compared with 78% (44 and 34%, respectively) of the nonrapid cyclers. More recently, Denicoff and colleagues (1997) reported that 19% of 35 rapid cyclers receiving carbamazepine for up to 1 year displayed at least moderate improvement compared with 33% of the entire group. Of note, this study also showed that response of rapid cycling to carbamazepine could be augmented by lithium: 56% of the rapid cyclers responded to the combination of carbamazepine and lithium.

GABAPENTIN

A growing number of open reports have described bipolar patients with acute manic, mixed, and depressed symptoms, including those with rapid cycling, who have responded favorably to gabapentin—both as monotherapy (Stanton, Keck, & McElroy, 1997) and in combination with other agents (Altshuler et al., 1999; McElroy, Soutullo, Keck, & Kmetz, 1997; Schaffer & Schaffer, 1997).

However, the two controlled studies that have evaluated the response of acute bipolar manic symptoms to treatment with gabapentin are both negative. In the first, 117 outpatients with bipolar I disorder who displayed a total of $\geq$ 12 on the Young Mania Rating scale (YMRS) despite ongoing therapy with lithium, valproate, or the combination were randomized to the addition of gabapentin ($n = 55$) (600–3600 mg/day) or placebo ($n = 59$) for up to 10 weeks (Pande, Crockatt, Janney, & Werth, 2000). Patients randomized to placebo displayed statistically superior improvement on the YMRS compared with patients randomized to gabapentin. In the second study, 28 patients with bipolar I ($n = 13$) or bipolar II ($n = 15$) disorder were evaluated in a double-blind, randomized, crossover series of three 6-week monotherapy trials of gabapentin, lamotrigine, and placebo using the Clinical Global Impression-Bipolar Version (CGI-BP) as the primary efficacy measure (Frye et al., 2000). Twenty-three percent of patients were rapid cyclers. The rate of CGI-BP response for manic symptoms did not differ among the three groups: gabapentin 20%, lamotrigine 44%, and placebo 32%. This study was limited by the extremely low mean ± SD YMRS scores at the beginning of all three treatment phases (4.4 ± 4.1 for gabapentin, 5.5 ± 4.6 for lamotrigine, and 6.1 ± 4.8 for placebo), reflecting minimal or subclinical manic symptomatology.

Of note, gabapentin's anxiolytic properties may prove useful in the treatment of rapid cycling bipolar disorder accompanied by anxiety symptoms or syndromes. Specifically, gabapentin has been demonstrated to have anxiolytic effects in various animal models predictive of anxiolysis (Singh et al., 1996), to decrease ratings of anxiety and depression in patients with epilepsy (Harden et al., 1999), and to be superior to placebo in the treatment of social phobia in one controlled trial (Pande, Crockatt, Janney, Werth, & Tsaroucha, 2000).

LAMOTRIGINE

Several open studies have suggested that lamotrigine may have antimanic, antidepressant, and long-term mood-stabilizing properties in rapid cycling bipolar patients (Calabrese et al., 1999; Fatemi, Rapport, Calabrese, & Thuras, 1997; Kusumakar & Yatham, 1997; Sporn & Sachs, 1997). In one report, 75 patients with treatment refractory bipolar disorder received an open label, prospective, 48-week trial of lamotrigine—either as adjunctive treatment ($n = 60$) or as monotherapy ($n = 15$; Calabrese, Bowden, McElroy, et al., 1999). Of these patients, 41 met DSM-IV criteria for rapid cycling. Of the 31 patients who received lamotrigine while manic, hypomanic, or mixed, 84% exhibited moderate (3%) or marked (81%) improvement. Of the 41 depressed patients who received lamotrigine, 68% showed moderate (20%) or marked (40%) improvement. When patients with and without rapid cycling were compared, improvement in depressive symptomatology was equivalent for patients presenting in a depressive episode (48% vs. 47%, respectively; Bowden et al., 1999). By contrast, among patients beginning lamotrigine in a manic, mixed or hypomanic episode, rapid cyclers displayed less improvement in manic symptomatology (58%) than those without rapid cycling (99%; $p = 0.01$).

In the only prospective, double-blind, placebo controlled, parallel design study of any medication in rapid cycling bipolar disorder, patients with rapid cycling bipolar I or bipolar II disorder received open-label lamotrigine for 8 to 12 weeks while concomitant psychotropies were gradually withdrawn. Respondents were then randomized to lamotrigine ($n = 90$; dose 100–500 mg/day) or placebo ($n = 87$) for a further 26 weeks of treatment. In a general survival analysis using time to intervention for a mood episode (TIME) or premature discontinuation as end-points, lamotrigine treated patients were significantly ($p = 0.044$) more likely to remain well for a longer period than placebo treated patients. However, this statistically significant difference was only observed in rapid cycling bipolar II patients ($n = 24$ vs. placebo $n = 28$) and not in rapid cycling bipolar I patients. Lamotrigine treated patients in the bipolar II subset of this study were also more likely to complete the study without additional psychotropic treatment. Finally, lamotrigine treatment was not associated with induction of mania (Calabrese et al., 2000).

TOPIRAMATE

Although there are no published controlled trials of topiramate in the treatment of bipolar disorder, open studies suggest the drug may have mood stabilizing, as well as beneficial weight loss and antibinge eating properties, in some bipolar patients, including those with rapid cycling (Calabrese et al., 1998; McElroy et al., 2000; Shapira et al., 2000). For example, in one report, topiramate was given as monotherapy or adjunctive therapy to 44 patients with rapid cycling bipolar disorder; 52% were described as displaying moderate or marked improvement after a mean duration of treatment of 16 weeks with a mean (range) dosage of 200 (25–400) mg/day (Marcotte, 1998). In another study, topiramate was added to existing medication regimens in 27 female outpatients with rapid cycling bipolar disorder and psychotropic-induced weight gain (Kusumaker, Yatham, O'Donovan, & Kutcher, 1999). Fifteen patients displayed significant improvement in mood and nine experienced a weight loss of more than 5%. In another report, 20 patients with bipolar ($n = 18$) or schizoaffective ($n = 2$) disorder with manic, hypomanic, mixed, or rapid cycling symptoms received adjunctive topiramate from 100 to 300 mg/day (Chengappa et al., 1999). By five weeks, 12 (60%) of the patients were responders, defined as a $\geq 50\%$ reduction in YMRS score and a CGI-BP rating of much or very much improved. In addition, all patients lost weight, losing a mean of 9.4 pounds by five weeks.

TIAGABINE

Tiagabine is a selective gaba reuptake inhibitor approved by the FDA for the treatment of partial seizures. There are isolated case reports of successful tiagabine augmentation of refractory bipolar I rapid cycling (Schaffer & Schaffer, 1999). In these cases, tiagabine was used in small doses, ranging from 1 mg to 4 mg/day. However, tiagabine has also been reported to be ineffective in a 2-week, open-label trial in eight hospitalized patients with bipolar I mania (Grunze et al., 1999). In this trial, high doses of tiagabine were rapidly achieved, specifically 20 to 40 mg/day within 4 days. Of note, none of the patients had previously displayed rapid cycling.

OTHER ANTIEPILEPTICS

There are case reports describing the use of other antiepileptics, in particular clonazepam and phenytoin, in the treatment of rapid cyclers (Keck &

McElroy, 1988). Of two patients receiving clonazepam, both displayed some degree of response. One patient receiving phenytoin under double-blind, placebo-controlled conditions, however, did not respond.

Antipsychotics

Growing data suggests that typical and particularly atypical antipsychotics may be effective in rapid cycling bipolar disorder. Case reports and case series have described the successful treatment of rapid cycling bipolar disorder with standard antipsychotics, including depot formulations (Lowe & Batchelor, 1986). Case reports, case series, and open prospective studies have reported the successful use of clozapine (Calabrese et al., 1996; Calabrese et al., 1991; Suppes, Phillips, & Judd, 1994; Suppes et al., 1999; Zarate, Tohen, & Baldessarini, 1995), olanzapine (McElroy et al., 1998), and risperidone (Vieta et al., 1998) in patients with treatment resistant rapid cycling. Moreover, in a double-blind, controlled monotherapy study which demonstrated olanzapine superior to placebo in the treatment of acute bipolar mania in 139 inpatients (32% of whom had DSM-IV rapid cycling), a subgroup analysis showed that the rapid cyclers treated with olanzapine showed superior improvement compared with placebo-treated patients (Tohen et al., 1999). These positive reports, however, must be tempered with clinical observations that standard antipsychotics may exacerbate post manic depressions (Kukopulos et al., 1980) and atypical antipsychotics may induce or exacerbate manic symptoms (McElroy & Keck, 2000).

ANTIDEPRESSANTS

Although most classes of antidepressants efficacious in unipolar depression—tricyclics, serotonin reuptake inhibitors, bupropion, and monoamine oxidase inhibitors—have also been shown to be effective in bipolar depression, there are no controlled antidepressant treatment studies in rapid cycling bipolar disorder (Srisurapanont et al., 1995; Zornberg & Pope, 1993). Indeed, since these agents have been reported to induce or exacerbate rapid cycling, even in controlled trials, and their discontinuation has been associated with cessation of rapid cycling (Altshuler et al., 1995; Wehr & Goodwin, 1979), pharmacologic treatment studies of bipolar depression have often excluded rapid cycling patients (Calabrese et al., 1999a; Young et al., 2000).

However, rapid cyclers often experience depressive symptoms and episodes resistant to mood stabilizer therapy, and hence, require treatment with antidepressant agents. Preliminary data suggest that serotonin reuptake inhibitors (Peet, 1994) and bupropion (Sachs et al., 1994) may be less likely than tricyclics to induce mania in nonrapid cycling patients, and hence, may be less likely to induce rapid cycling in rapid cycling patients. Clinical data suggest that serotonin reuptake inhibitors, bupropion, monoamine oxidase inhibitors, and even tricyclics may successfully treat persistent depressive symptoms and episodes without reinduction of cycling in rapid cycling patients who are on optimized mood stabilizer regimens (Calabrese & Woyshville, 1995; Haykal & Akiskal, 1990; Potter, Murphy, Wehr, Linnoila, & Goodwin, 1982). We have also observed that light therapy given in conjunction with mood stabilizers, usually only during depressed phases, may be effective in treating depression without the induction of cycling. However, controlled data are needed to support these largely clinical observations.

THYROID HORMONE

Case reports and open studies, but no controlled data, suggest that thyroid hormone augmentation may exert mood stabilizing effects in some rapid cycling bipolar patients, regardless of the patient's baseline thyroid state. Both levothyroxine (T_4) and triiodothyronine (T_3) have been used successfully, almost always in conjunction with mood stabilizers or antidepressants (especially lithium, carbamazepine, and tricyclics). Although doses standard for replacement therapy in hypothyroidism (e.g., 0.15–0.2 mg/day for T_4 and 0.25–0.5 mg/day for T_3) have been reported to be effective, many patients have responded only when supraphysiologic or hypermatabolic doses (e.g., 0.3 to 0.6 mg/day of T_4) were administered and/or the free thyroxine index was increased to approximately 1.5 times the upper limit of the normal range. Stancer and Persad (1982) described five (63%) of eight rapid cycling bipolar patients who displayed complete or near complete remissions for periods of 9 months to 9 years when treated with hypermetabolic doses of T_4 or T_3. Two other patients displayed partial remissions. Bauer and Whybrow (1990) reported that 10 (92%) of 11 rapid cyclers refractory to standard regimens (typically combinations of lithium, carbamazepine, and replacement doses of T_4) displayed reduced depressive symptoms in response to the open label addition of hypermetabolic doses of T_4 (0.15–0.4 mg/day). Five (71%) of the seven patients with manic symptoms displayed an antimanic response. Treatment response was not dependent on baseline thyroid status, and in 9 of the 10 responders, supraphysiologic serum concentrations of T_4 were necessary for response.

Of interest, the successful treatment of intractable nonrapid cycling bipolar disorder (Baumgartner, Bauer, & Hellweg, 1994) and bipolar depression (Bauer, Hellweg, Graf, & Baumgarten, 1998) with high doses of T_4 has also been described. By contrast, emergence of mania has been reported with T_3 augmentation of antidepressant-resistant bipolar depression (Evans et al., 1986).

ELECTROCONVULSIVE THERAPY (ECT)

Electroconvulsive therapy (ECT) is a highly effective treatment for acute bipolar mania, depression, and mixed states (Mukherjee, Sackheim, & Schnur, 1994). Although there are no controlled or systematic studies of ECT in rapid cycling bipolar disorder, and ECT has occasionally been reported to induce mania (particularly hypomania), there are case reports of ECT successfully treating intractable rapid cycling (Berman & Wolpert, 1987). Indeed, our group and others have witnessed ECT to be highly effective in some rapid cycling bipolar patients both acutely and over the long term, including in those refractory to many pharmacotherapies (Kusumakar et al., 1997).

OMEGA 3 FATTY ACIDS

Stoll, Severus, Freeman, Rueter, Zboyan, and Diamond (1999) conducted a 4-month, double-blind, placebo-controlled study evaluating omega 3 fatty acids versus placebo (olive oil) in 30 patients with bipolar disorder, 40% of whom had rapid cycling. Survival analysis of the group showed that the omega 3 fatty acid treated group had a significantly longer period of remission than the placebo treated group ($p = 0.002$; Mantel-Cox). Moreover, although the numbers in each group were small, the presence of rapid cycling did not affect response to omega 3 fatty acids.

OTHER SOMATIC TREATMENTS

Other medical treatments that have been reported effective in rapid cycling bipolar disorder in case reports or small case series include calcium channel blockers (e.g., nimodipine), estrogen replacement, and sleep deprivation (Roy-Byrne et al., 1984).

PSYCHOSOCIAL TREATMENTS

There are no systematic studies of psychosocial treatment of rapid cycler bipolar disorder. However, supportive psychotherapy, focusing on education about bipolar disorder in general and rapid cycling in particular, are useful in developing and maintaining a therapeutic alliance, enhancing adherence to often complex medication regimens, and in reducing the patient's sense of isolation. Participation in self-help organizations such as the National Depressive and Manic–Depressive Association (NDMDA) and National Alliance for the Mentally Ill (NAMI) are also helpful.

General Clinical Guidelines

The first step in the successful treatment of rapid cycling bipolar disorder is recognition and accurate diagnosis. Rapid cycling can present in a variety of ways. These include prominent irritability, hostility, dysphoria, anxiety, or depression, and behavioral dysregulation (e.g., impulsive aggression, suicidality, substance abuse), as well as clear-cut, recurrent mood swings or discrete mood episodes. In most cases, a significant other should be interviewed as patients may have difficulty accurately reporting their symptoms, often not recognizing hypomanic episodes or misinterpreting ultrarapid or ultradian cycling or mixed states as pure depression. Constructing a life chart of the patient's mood episodes, along with their concurrent pharmacological treatments, medical conditions, and psychosocial stressors, is a particularly useful way of illustrating his or her course of illness over time, thereby helping to establish whether or not rapid cycling is occurring as well as identifying potential precipitants (e.g., development of hypothyroidism or exposure to antidepressant agents or drugs of abuse) and evaluating whether any treatments have been helpful or harmful over the long term.

Once rapid cycling is established, a thorough medical and psychiatric evaluation should be done, with particular attention to thyroid and neurological status and possible psychiatric comorbidities. The primary goal of treatment is mood stabilization. If possible, at least in the initial stages of pharmacotherapy, use of antidepressants should be avoided or minimized and treatment restricted to mood stabilizing agents (e.g., valproate, lithium, carbamazepine, atypical antipsychotics, new antiepileptics, thyroid hormone augmentation). Thus, if the patient is receiving antidepressants or other potential cycle-inducing agents, these agents should be discontinued or at least reduced in dose, and the subsequent course of illness reevaluated. If cycling persists, treatment with a mood stabilizer should be initiated or maximized, and response over time (preferably for at least one to two cycle lengths) carefully reevaluated. Patients may display several patterns of response: unabated persistence of cycling; reduced frequency and/or intensity of mood swings but with residual cycling; cessation of hypomanic or manic episodes but persistent depression; amelioration of depression but persistent hypomania or mania; and complete cessation of cycling. With persistent cycling, hypomanic, manic, or mixed symptoms, a second and sometimes a third mood stabilizer can be added to or substituted for the first. If manic symptoms are ameliorated but depression persists, antidepressants may be indicated. Fortunately, increasing clinical experience indicates that antidepressants can often be successfully added to optimized mood stabilizer regimens without inducing or exacerbating cycling as long as manic and cycling symptoms (including ultradian cycling) are suppressed and the antidepressant is administered carefully. Thus, the antidepressant should typically be started at a subtherapeutic dose and increased gradually, observing carefully for reemergence of manic or cycling symptoms, and decreased in dose promptly if such symptoms occur. If depression continues to persist, another mood stabilizer, thyroid hormone, or lamotrigine may be substituted or added. As well, ECT is always an option for the severely ill or treatment-resistant patient, whether they are cycling, manic, or depressed.

TREATMENT ALGORITHM FOR RAPID CYCLING

Based on the research reviewed in this chapter, and on previous algorithms proposed by other experts (Bauer et al., 1999; Calabrese & Woyshville, 1995; Kusumakar et al., 1997), we present below a preliminary treatment algorithm for rapid cycling bipolar disorder (Figure 3.1). In general, unless there is a family history of response to another mood stabilizer or a medical contraindication, our group generally considers valproate to be the first-line agent for the treatment naive patient with bipolar rapid cycling. Patients who respond well are maintained on valproate as prophylactic treatment. For patients who respond partially or who do not respond at all, a second mood stabilizer—usually lithium, an atypical antipsychotic other than clozapine, carbamazepine, or topiramate—is added to (or substituted for) valproate. For patients who continue to cycle on two mood stabilizers, a third mood stabilizer is added to (or substituted for one of) the first two mood stabilizers. In patients who become persistently depressed, a nontricyclic antidepressant (generally a serotonin reuptake inhibitor or bupropion) or lamotrigine is carefully added to the mood stabilizer regi-

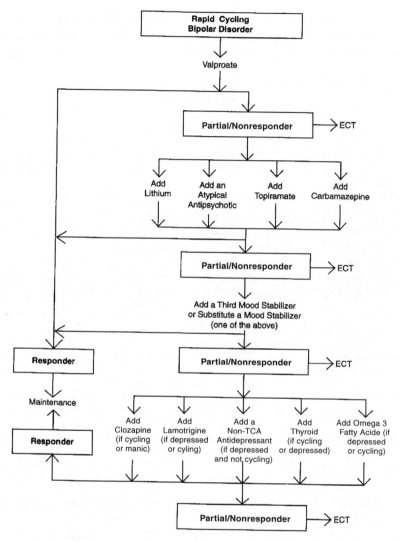

FIGURE 3.1. Treatment Algorithm for Rapid Cycling Disorder

men. For patients with refractory cycling, our group considers clozapine, thyroid augmentation, and lamotrigine; for refractory depression, we consider treatment with monoamine oxidase inhibitors, lamotrigine, and thyroid augmentation. ECT is an option for severely ill or treatment resistant patients at any point in the algorithm.

In conclusion, although rapid cycling bipolar disorder is often difficult to treat, heightened awareness of the phenomenon and an increased number of available treatment options provide afflicted patients with enhanced chances of achieving substantial degrees of mood stabilization.

References

Alarcon, R. D. (1985). Rapid cycling affective disorders: a clinical review. *Comprehensive Psychiatry, 26,* 522–540.

Altshuler, L. L., Keck, P. E., Jr., McElroy, S. L., Suppes, T., Brown, E. S., Denicoff, K., et al. (1999). Gabapentin in the acute treatment of refractory bipolar disorder. *Bipolar Disorders, 1,* 61–65.

Altshuler, L. L., Post, R. M., Leverich, G. S., Mikalauskas, K., Rosoff, A., & Ackerman, L. (1995). Antidepressant-induced mania and cycle acceleration: A controversy revisited. *American Journal of Psychiatry, 152,* 1130–1138.

American Psychiatric Association. (1994). *Diagnostic and statistical manual of mental disorders* (4th ed.). Washington, DC: American Psychiatric Association.

Anand, A., Oren, D. A., Berman, R. M., Cappiello, A., & Charney, D. S. (1999). Lamotrigine treatment of lithium failure outpatient mania: a double-blind, placebo-controlled trial. In J. C. Soares & S. Gershon (Eds.), *Abstract Book on 3rd International Conference on Bipolar Disorder* (p. 23). Pittsburgh, PA. Copenhagen: Munksgaard.

Bartalena, L., Pellegrini, L., Meschi, M., Antonangeli, L., Bogazzi, F., Dell'Osso, L., et al. (1990). Evaluation of thyroid function in patients with rapid-cycling and non-rapid cycling bipolar disorder. *Psychiatry Research, 34,* 13–17.

Bauer, M. S., Calbrese, J., Dunner, D. L., Post, R., Whybrow, P. C., Gyulai, L, et al. (1994). Multisite data reanalysis of the validity of rapid cycling as a course modifier for bipolar disorder in DSM-IV. *American Journal of Psychiatry, 151,* 506–515.

Bauer, M. S., Callahan, A. M., Jampala, C., Petty, F., Sajatovic, M., Schaefer, V., et al. (1999). Clinical practice guidelines for bipolar disorder from the department of veterans affairs. *Journal of Clinical Psychiatry, 60,* 9–21.

Bauer, M., Hellweg, R., Graf, K-J, & Baumgartner, A. (1998). Treatment of refractory depression with high dose thyroxine. *Neuropsychopharmacology, 18,* 444–455.

Bauer, M. S., & Whybrow, P. C. (1990). Rapid cycling bipolar affective disorder. II. Treatment of refractory rapid cycling with high-dose levothyroxine: A preliminary study. *Archives of General Psychiatry, 47,* 435–440.

Bauer, M. S., & Whybrow, P. C. (1993). Validity of rapid cycling as a modifier for bipolar disorder in DSM-IV. *Depression, 1,* 11–19.

Bauer, M. S., Whybrow, P. C., & Winokur, A. (1990). Rapid cycling bipolar affective disorder. I. Association with grade I hypothyroidism. *Archives of General Psychiatry, 47,* 427–432.

Baumgartner, A., Bauer, M., & Hellweg, R. (1994). Treatment of intractable nonrapid cycling bipolar affective disorder with high dose thyroxine: an open clinical trial. *Neuropsychopharmacology, 10,* 183–189.

Berman, E., & Wolpert, E. A. (1987, April). Intractable manic-depressive psychosis with rapid cycling in an 18-year-old woman successfully treated with electroconvulsive therapy. *Journal of Nervous and Mental Disease, 174*(4), 236–239.

Bowden, C. L., Brugger, A. M., Swann, A. C., Calabrese, J. R., Janicak, P. G., Petty, F., et al., (1994). Efficacy of divalproex versus lithium and placebo in the treatment of mania. *Journal of the American Medical Association, 271,* 918–924.

Bowden, C. L., Calabrese, J. R., McElroy, S. L., Rhodes, L. J., Keck, P. E., Cookson, J., et al.,

(1999): The efficacy of lamotrigine in rapid cycling and non-rapid cycling patients with bipolar disorder. *Biological Psychiatry, 45,* 953–958.

Calabrese, J. R., Bowden, C. L., McElroy, S. L., Cookson, J., Andersen, J., Keck, P. E., Jr., et al. (1999a). Spectrum of activity of lamotrigine in treatment-refractory bipolar disorder. *American Journal of Psychiatry, 156,* 1019–1023.

Calabrese, J. R., Bowden, C. L., Sachs, G. S., Ascher, J. A., Monaghan, E., Rudd, G. D., et al. (1999b). A double-blind placebo-controlled study of lamotrigine monotherapy in outpatients with bipolar I depression. *Journal of Clinical Psychiatry, 60,* 79–88.

Calabrese, J. R., & Delucchi, G. A. (1990). Spectrum of efficacy of valproate in 55 patients with rapid-cycling bipolar disorder. *American Journal of Psychiatry, 147,* 431–434.

Calabrese, J. R., Keck, P. E., Jr., McElroy, S. L., & Werkner, J. E. (1998). Topiramate in severe treatment-refractory mania). *American Psychiatric Association Annual Meeting,* Toronto, Canada (Abstract New Research *202,* 121–122).

Calabrese, J. R., Kimmel, S. E., Woyshville, M. J., Rapport, D. J., Faust, C. J., Thompson, P. A., et al. (1996). Clozapine for treatment-refractory mania. *American Journal of Psychiatry, 153,* 759–764.

Calabrese, J. R., Meltzer, H. Y., & Markovitz, P. J. (1991). Clozapine prophylaxis in rapid-cycling bipolar disorder (letter). *Journal of Clinical Psychopharmacology, 11,* 396–397.

Calabrese, J. R., Suppes, T., Bowden, C. L., Sachs, G. S., Swann, A. C., McElroy, S. L., et al. (2000, November). A double-blind, placebo-controlled, prophylaxis of lamotrigne in rapid-cycling bipolar disorder. *Journal of Clinical Psychiatry, 61*(11), 841–850.

Calabrese, J. R., & Woyshville, M. J. (1995). A medication algorithm for treatment of bipolar rapid cycling? *Journal of Clinical Psychiatry, 56* (Suppl. 3), 11–18.

Chang, K. D., Keck, P. E., Jr., Stanton, S. P., McElroy, S. L., Strakowski, S. M., & Geracioti, T. D., Jr. (1998). Differences in thyroid function between bipolar manic and mixed states. *Biology Psychiatry, 43,* 730–733.

Chengappa, R. K. N., Rathmore, D., Levine, J., Atzert, R., Solai, L., Parepally, H., et al. (1999). Topiramate as add-on treatment for patients with bipolar mania. *Bipolar Disorders, 1,* 42–53.

Coryell, W., Endicott, J., & Keller, M. (1992). Rapidly cycling affective disorder. Demographics, diagnosis, family history, and course. *Archives of General Psychiatry, 49,* 126–131.

Cowdry, R. W., Wehr, T. A., Zis, A. P., & Goodwin, F. K. (1983). Thyroid abnormalities associated with rapid cycling bipolar illness. *Archives of General Psychiatry, 40,* 414–420.

Denicoff, K. D., Smith-Jackson, E. E., Disney, E. R., Ali, S. O., Leverich, G. S., & Post, R. M. (1997). Comparative prophylactic efficacy of lithium, carbamazepine, and the combination in bipolar disorder. *Journal of Clinical Psychiatry, 58,* 470–478.

Dunner, D. L., & Fieve, R. R. (1974). Clinical factors in lithium carbonate prophylaxis failure. *Archives of General Psychiatry, 30,* 229–233.

Dunner, D. L., Vijayalakshmy, P., & Fieve, R. R. (1977). Rapid cycling manic depressive patients. *Comprehensive Psychiatry, 18,* 561–566.

Evans, D. L., Strawn, S. K., Haggerty, J. J., Garbutt, J. C., Burnett, G. B., & Pedersen, C. A. (1986). Appearance of mania in drug-resistant bipolar depressed patients after treatment with L-triiodothyronine. *Journal of Clinical Psychiatry, 47,* 521–522.

Faedda, G. L., Baldessarini, R. J., Tohen, M., Strakowski, S. M., & Waternaux, C. (1991). Episode sequence in bipolar disorder and response to lithium treatment. *American Journal of Psychiatry, 148,* 1237–1239.

Fatemi, S. H., Rapport, D. J., Calabrese, J. R., & Thuras, P. (1997). Lamotrigine in rapid-cycling bipolar disorder. *Journal of Clinical Psychiatry, 58*(12), 522–527.

Fawcett, J., Scheftner, W. A., Clark, D. C., Hedeker, D., Gibbons, R. D., & Coryell, W. (1987). Clinical predictors of suicide in patients with major affective disorders: a controlled prospective study. *American Journal of Psychiatry, 144,* 35–40.

Frye, M. A., Ketter, T. A., Kimbrell, T. A., Dunn, R. M., Speer, A. M., Osuch, E. A., et al. (2000, December). A placebo controlled study of lamotrigine and gabapentin monotherapy in refractory mood disorders. *Journal of Clinical Psychopharmacology, 20*(6), 607–614.

Goodwin, F. K., & Jamison, K. R. (1990). *Manic-depressive illness.* New York: Oxford University Press.

Gottschalk, A., Bauer, M., & Whybrow, P. C. (1990). A chaotic form of affective illness. *Biological Psychiatry, 27,* 99A.

Grunze, H., Erfurth, A., Marcuse, A., Amann, B., Normann, C., & Walden, J. (1999). Tiagabine appears not to be efficacious in the treatment of acute mania. *Journal of Clinical Psychiatry, 60,* 759–762.

Harden, C. L., Lazar, L. M., Pick, L. H., Nikolov, B., Goldstein, M. A., Carson, D., et al. (1999). A beneficial effect on mood in partial epilepsy patients treated with gabapentin. *Epilepsia, 40*(8), 1129–1134.

Haykal, R. F., & Akiskal, H. S. (1990). Bupropion as a promising approach to rapid cycling bipolar II patients. *Journal of Clinical Psychiatry, 51,* 450–455.

Himmelhoch, J. (1979). Mixed states, manic-depressive illness, and the nature of mood. *Psychiatric Clinics of North America, 2,* 449–459.

Joffe, R., Kutcheer, S., & MacDonald, C. (1987). Thyroid function and bipolar affective disorder. *Psychiatry Research, 21,*117–121.

Joyce, P. R. (1988). Carbamazepine in rapid cycling bipolar affective disorder. *International Clinical Psychopharmacology, 3,* 123–129.

Keck, P. E., Jr., & McElroy, S. L. (1988). Anticonvulsants in the treatment of rapid-cycling bipolar disorder. In S. L. McElroy, H. G. Pope, Jr. (Eds.), *Use of anticonvulsants in psychiatry: Recent advances* (pp. 115–125). Clifton, NJ: Oxford Health.

Kleiner, J., Altshuler, L., Hendrick, V., & Hershman, J. M. (1999). Lithium-induced subclinical hypothyroidism: Review of the literature and guidelines for treatment. *Journal of Clinical Psychiatry, 60,* 249–255.

Kraeplin, E (1921). *Manic-depressive insanity and paranoia* (E. T. Carlson, Editor). Edinburgh: Livingstone. (Original work published 1921)

Kukopulos, A., Caliari, B., Tundo, A., Minnai, G., Floris, G., Reginaldi, D., et al. (1983). Rapid cyclers, temperament, and antidepressants. *Comprehensive Psychiatry, 24,* 249–258.

Kukopulos, A., Reginaldi, D., Laddomada, P., Floris, G., Serra, G., & Tondo, L. (1980). Course of the manic-depressive cycle and changes caused by treatments. *Pharmakopsychiatrica, 13,* 156–167.

Kusumakar V., & Yatham, L. N. (1997). Lamotrigine treatment of rapid cycling bipolar disorder [Letter to the editor]. *American Journal of Psychiatry, 154*(8), 1171–1172.

Kusumakar, V., Yatham, L. N., Haslam, D. R., Parikh, S. V., Matte, R., Silverstone, P. H., et al. (1997). Treatment of mania, mixed state, and rapid cycling. *Canadian Journal of Psychiatry, 42* (Suppl. 2), 79S–86S.

Kusumakar, V., Yatham, L., O'Donovan, C., & Kutcher, S. (1999). *Topiramate in women with refractory rapid cycling bipolar disorder.* Paper presented at American College of Neuropsychopharmacology Meeting, Acapulco, Mexico, pp. 166.

Lowe, M. R., & Batchelor, D. H. (1986). Depot neuroleptics and manic depressive psychosis. *International Clinical Psychopharmacology, 1*(Suppl. 1), 53–62.

Maj, M., Magliano, L., Pirozzi, R., Marasco, C., & Guarneri, M. (1994). Validity of rapid cycling as a course specifier for bipolar disorder. *American Journal of Psychiatry, 151,* 1015–1019.

Maj, M., Pirozzi, R., Formicola, A. M. R., & Tortorella, A. (1999). Reliability and validity of four alternative definitions of rapid-cycling bipolar disorder. *American Journal of Psychiatry, 156,* 421–1424.

Marcotte, D. (1998). Use of topiramate, a new antiepileptic as a mood stabilizer. *Journal of Affective Disorders, 50,* 245–251.

McElroy, S. L., & Keck, P. E., Jr. (2000, September). Pharmacologic agents for the treatment of acute bipolar mania. *Biological Psychiatry, 48*(6), 539–557.

McElroy, S. L., Keck, P. E., Jr., Pope, H. G., Jr., & Hudson, J. I. (1988). Valproate in primary psychiatric disorders: literature review and clinical experience in a private psychiatric hospital. In S. L. McElroy & H. G. Pope, Jr. (Eds.), *Use of anticonvulsants in psychiatry: Recent advances* (pp 25-41). Clifton NJ: Oxford Health Care.

McElroy, S. L., Keck, P. E., Jr., Pope, H. G., Jr., Hudson, J. I., & Morris, D. (1991). Correlates of antimanic response to valproate. *Psychopharmacology Bulletin, 27,* 127–133.

McElroy, S. L., Soutullo, C. A., Keck, P. E., Jr., & Kmetz, G. F. (1997). A pilot trial of adjunctive gabapentin in the treatment of bipolar disorder. *Annals of Clinical Psychiatry, 9,* 99–103

McElroy, S. L., Frye, M., Denicoff, K., Altshuler, L., Nolen, W., Kupka, R., et al. (1998). Olanzapine in treatment-resistant bipolar disorder. *Journal of Affective Disorders, 49,* 119–122.

McElroy, S. L., Strakowski, S. M., Keck, P. E., Jr., Tugrul, K. L., West, S. A., & Lonezak, H. S. (1995, May–June). Differences and similarities in mixed and pure mania. *Comprehensive Psychiatry, 36*(3), 187–194.

McElroy, S. L., Suppes, T., Keck, P. E., Jr., Frye, M. A., Denicoff, K. D., Altshuler, L. L., et al. (2000). Open-label adjunctive topiramate in the treatment of bipolar disorders. *Biology & Psychiatry.*

Mukherjee, S., Sackheim, H. A., & Schnur, D. B. (1994). Electroconvulsive therapy of acute manic episodes: a review of 50 years' experience. *American Journal of Psychiatry, 151,* 169–176.

Nurnberger, J., Guroff, J. J., Hamovit, J., Berrettini, W., & Gershon, E. (1988). A family study of rapid-cycling bipolar illness. *Journal of Affective Disorders, 15,* 87–91.

Okuma, T. (1993). Effects of carbamazepine and lithium on affective disorders. *Neuropsychobiology, 27,* 138–145.

Pande, A. C., Crockatt, J. G., Janney, C. A., Werth, J. L., & Tsaroucha, G. (2000, September). Gabapentin in bipolar disorder: A placebo-controlled trial of adjunctive therapy. Gabapentin Bipolar Disorder Study Group. *Bipolar Disorders, 2*(3 Pt. 2), 249–255.

Paschalis, C., Pavlou, A., & Papadimitriou, A. (1980). A stepped forty-eight hour manic-depressive cycle. *British Journal of Psychiatry, 137,* 332–336.

Peet, M. (1994). Induction of mania with serotonin selective re-uptake inhibitors and tricyclic antidepressants. *British Journal of Psychiatry, 164,* 549–550.

Perugi, G., Akiskal, H. S., Romacciotti, S., Nassini, S., Toni, C., Milanfranchi, A., et al. (1999). Depressive comorbidity of panic, social phobia, and obsessive compulsive disorders reexamined: Is there a bipolar connection? *Journal of Psychiatric Research, 33,* 53–61.

Pope, H. G., Jr., McElroy, S. L., Keck, P. E., Jr., & Hudson, J. I. (1991). Valproate in the treatment of acute mania: a placebo-controlled study. *Archives of General Psychiatry, 48,* 62–68.

Post, R. M., Rubinow, D. R., Uhde, T. W., Roy-Byrne, P. P., Linnoila, M., Rosoff, A., et al. (1989): Dysphoric mania: Clinical and biological correlates. *Archives of General Psychiatry, 46,* 353–358.

Post, R. M., Uhde, T. W., Roy-Byrne, P. P., & Joffe, R. T. (1987). Correlates of antimanic response to carbamazepine. *Psychiatry Research, 21,* 71–83.

Potter, W. Z., Murphy, D. L., Wehr, T. A., Linnoila, M., & Goodwin, F. K. (1982). Clorgyline. A new treatment for patients with refractory rapid-cycling disorder. *Archives of General Psychiatry, 39,* 505–510.

Roy-Byrne, P. P., Joffe, R. T., Uhde, T. W., & Post, R. M. (1984). Approaches to the evaluation and treatment of rapid cycling affective illness. *British Journal of Psychiatry, 145,* 543–550.

Sachs, G. S., Lafer, B., Stoll, A. L., Banov, M., Thibault, A. B., Tohen, M., et al. (1994). A double-blind trial of bupropion versus desipramine for bipolar depression. *Journal of Clinical Psychiatry, 55,* 391–393.

Schaffer, C. B., & Schaffer, L. C. (1997). Gabapentin in the treatment of bipolar disorder. *American Journal Psychiatry, 154,* 291–292.

Schaffer, L. C., Schaffer, C. B. (1999). Tiagabine and the treatment of refractory bipolar disorder (letter). *American Journal of Psychiatry, 156,* 2014–2015.

Sedler, M. J. (1983). Falret's discovery: The origin of the concept of bipolar affective illness. *American Journal of Psychiatry, 140,* 1127–1133.

Shapira, N. A., Goldsmith, T. D., & McElroy, S. L. (2000, May). Treatment of binge-eating disorder with topiramate: A clinical case series. *Journal of Clinical Psychiatry, 61*(5), 368–372.

Singh, L., Field, M. J., Ferris, P., Hunter, J. C., Oless, R. J., Williams, R. G., et al. (1996). The antiepileptic agent gabapentin (Neurontin) possesses anxiolytic-like and antinociceptive actions that are reversed by D-serine. *Psychopharmacol (Berlin), 127,* 1–9.

Sporn, J., & Sachs, G. (1997). The anticonvulsant lamotrigine in treatment-resistant manic depressive illness. *Journal of Clinical Psychopharmacology, 17,* 185–189.

Srisurapanont, M., Yatham, L. N., & Zis, A. P. (1995). Treatment of acute bipolar depression: a review of the literature. *Canadian Journal of Psychiatry, 40,* 533–544.

Stancer, H. C., & Persad, E. (1982). Treatment of intractable rapid-cycling manic-depressive disorder with levothyroxine. *Archives of General Psychiatry, 39,* 311–312.

Stanton, S. P., Keck, P. E., Jr., & McElroy, S. L. (1997). Treatment of acute mania with gabapentin [Letter to the editor]. *American Journal of Psychiatry, 154,* 287.

Stoll, A. L., Severus, W. E., Freeman, M. P., Rueter, S., Zboyan, H. A., Diamond, E., et al. (1999, May). Omega 3 fatty acids in bipolar disorder: A preliminary double-blind, placebo-controlled trial. *Archives of General Psychiatry, 56*(5), 407–412.

Suppes, T., Phillips, K. A., & Judd, C. R. (1994). Clozapine treatment of nonpsychotic rapid cycling bipolar disorder: A report of three cases. *Biology Psychiatry, 36,* 338–340.

Suppes, T., Webb, A., Paul, B., Carmody, T., Kraemer, H., & Rush, A. J. (1999). Clinical outcome in a randomized 1-year trial of clozapine versus treatment as usual for patients with treatment-resistant illness and a history of mania. *American Journal of Psychiatry, 156,* 1164–1169.

Tohen, M., Sanger, T. M., McElroy, S. L., Tollefson, G. D., Chengappa, K. N. R., Daniel, D. G., et al. (1999). Olanzapine versus placebo in the treatment of acute mania. *American Journal of Psychiatry, 156,* 702–709.

Tondo, L., & Baldessarini, R. J. (1998). Rapid cycling in women and men with bipolar manic–depressive disorders. *American Journal of Psychiatry, 155,* 1434–1436.

Vieta, E., Gasto, C., Colom, F., Martinez, A., Otero, A., & Vallejo, J. (1998). Treatment of refractory rapid cycling bipolar disorder with risperidone. *Journal of Clinical Psychopharmacology, 18,* 172–174.

Wehr, T. A., & Goodwin, F. K. (1979). Rapid cycling in manic depressives induced by tricylic antidepressants. *Archives of General Psychiatry, 36,* 555–559.

Wehr, T. A., Sack, D. A., Rosenthal, N. E., & Cowdry, R. W. (1988). Rapid cycling affective disorder: Contributing factors and treatment responses in 51 patients. *American Journal of Psychiatry, 145,* 179–184.

Wolpert, E. A., Goldberg, J. F., & Harrow, M. (1990). Rapid cycling in unipolar and bipolar affective disorders. *American Journal of Psychiatry, 147,* 725–728.

Young, L. T., Joffe, R. T., Robb, J. C., MacQueen, G. M., Marriott, M., & Patelis-Siotis, I. (2000). Blind comparison of addition of a second mood stabilizer versus an antidepressant to initial mood stabilizer for treatment of patients with bipolar depression. *American Journal of Psychiatry, 157,* 124–126.

Zarate, C. A., Jr., Tohen, M., & Baldessarini, R. J. (1995). Clozapine in severe mood disorders. *Journal of Clinical Psychiatry, 56,* 411–417.

Zornberg, G. L., & Pope, H. G. (1994). Treatment of depressive bipolar disorder: new directives for research. *Journal of Clinical Psychopharmocology, 13,* 397–408.

CHAPTER 4

Maintenance Therapies in Bipolar Affective Disorder

William H. Coryell

Four broad questions underlie the topic of maintenance therapies in bipolar affective disorder. Is prophylaxis necessary for a given patient? If so, when might it be stopped? Which medications should be considered as first-, second- and third-line treatments? Finally, what additional interventions may optimize outcome?

Need for Maintenance Treatment

To answer the first of these questions, the clinician must balance the risks for recurrences in the absence of treatment, and the likely consequences of such recurrences, against the expense, inconvenience, and risks of treatment. Some patients with bipolar II disorder describe hypomanic episodes which consistently result in little or no impairment, or even in an enhancement of functioning. Because less than one in six patients with bipolar II disorder eventually experience a full manic syndrome (Coryell et al., 1995) thymoleptics are probably not warranted for patients with nonproblematic hypomanias unless the thymoleptic is targeting recurrent depressive episodes. Family study data indicate that bipolar II and bipolar I disorder may differ at a fundament level (Coryell et al., 1989; DePaulo, Simpson, Gayle,

& Folstein, 1990), therefore it cannot be assumed that the results of therapeutic trials in bipolar I patients generalize to patients with bipolar II illness. Notably, the prophylactic efficacy of lithium in bipolar II disorder has not been clearly established (Dunner, Stallone & Fieve, 1976, 1982; Fieve, Kumberaci, & Dunner, 1976).

By definition, manic episodes result in marked impairment and the decision to employ prophylaxis in bipolar I disorder therefore rests solely on the likelihood of recurrence.

The risk is highest during the year following recovery, falls during the next 2 years, and ranges from 20 to 30% each year thereafter (Coryell et al., 1995). With the exception of episode recency (Coryell et al., 1995), no demographic or clinical variable dependably predicts recurrence in bipolar affective disorder.

The lack of prior episodes, in particular, does not seem to lessen the risk of future episodes (Winkour, Coryell, Keller, Endicott, & Akiskal, 1993). Though clinicians commonly consider the presence or absence of previous episodes in the decision to begin maintenance treatment (Frances, Docherty, & Kahn, 1996) this practice has little empirical support (Grof, Angst, Karasek, & Keitner, 1979). Thus, prophylaxis is advisable for any patient recently recovered from an episode of bipolar I disorder.

Length of Maintenance Therapy

The persistently high risk for recurrence that characterizes bipolar affective disorder would seem to indicate that prophylactic treatment should be continued indefinitely. This presumes that thymoleptics continue to prevent episodes long past the most recent episode. Though widely held, this presumption has not been clearly established. There is sound evidence that lithium is beneficial within the first year following an episode but studies have not been designed to show whether benefits persist for those patients who have been symptom-free for a year or longer (Coryell et al., 1997). Very few reports have provided data directly pertinent to this issue and the topic is a controversial one (Kleindienst, Griel, Ruger, & Moller, 1999).

The question of whether to continue maintenance treatment at a given point in time involves other considerations as well. Patients vary greatly as to the side-effects they experience and, in many cases, difficulties persist despite dose adjustments. Also important to this decision is the characteristic severity of a patient's manic episodes, the usual level of insight during episodes, the typical acuteness of onset, and the likely repercussions of a new episode given the patient's circumstances.

It is now clear that lithium discontinuation, if indicated, should be undertaken gradually. Two studies (Faeddea, Tondo, Baldessarini, Suppes, & Tohen, 1993; Baldessarini, Tondo, Floris, & Rudas, 1997) have shown that a discontinuation completed in less then 2 weeks was much more likely to be followed by relapse then one completed in 2 to 4 weeks. Concerns that interruptions in lithium treatment may render patients unresponsive to later lithium trials appear to be unfounded (Coryell et al., 1998).

Selection of Thymoleptic: First-Line Treatment

The question of which thymoleptic to use as first-line treatment for acute mania is a matter of controversy, but it is particularly important because this selection naturally determines what is likely to be used, at least initially, for maintenance. In the United States, lithium and valproate are currently the two agents most often chosen for acute mania. The choice between them should involve several considerations.

The first of these is the fact that prophylactic efficacy has been clearly shown only for lithium (Table 4.1). The literature contains eight placebo-controlled, parallel-design studies of lithium prophylaxis, and, in all but one of these, those taking placebo experienced more morbidity. There are only two such studies of anticonvulsant prophylaxis (Okuma et al., 1981; Bowden et al., 2000). The results of the first (Okuma et al., 1981) favored carbamazepine over placebo, but the numbers enrolled were small and the group differences were not statistically significant.

Valproate has come into wide use largely on the strength of two parallel-design placebo-controlled studies showing its effectiveness in acute mania (Bowden, Brugger, et al., 1994; Pope, McElroy, Keck, & Hudson, 1991). A more recent effort to demonstrate prophylactic efficacy of valproate (Bowden et al., 2000) is notable in several respects. First, though several secondary outcome measures significantly favored valproate over placebo, the primary outcome measures did not. Second, in contrast to seven studies completed several decades ago, none of the outcome measures significantly favored lithium over placebo. Such results imply that bipolar patients responsive to lithium, or perhaps to any monotherapy used for prophylaxis, are much less available to controlled treatment studies now than they once were.

The second consideration concerns clinical features that may justify the selection of an anticonvulsant over lithium. The presence of rapid cycling, the occurrence of four or more episodes in a given year, is now widely considered to be one such indicator (Calabrese, Fatemi, Kujana, & Woyshville, 1996). This view derives from a series of reports in which a history of rapid cycling predicted breakthroughs during lithium prophy-

TABLE 4.1
Placebo-Controlled Studies of Prophylaxis in Bipolar I Affective Disorder

	Numbers In Trial	Trial Duration	Outcome
Lithium			
Baastrup et al. (1970)			
Lithium	28	5 months	0% developed recurrence
Placebo	34		55% developed recurrence
Coppen et al. (1971)			
Lithium	15	2 years	17% of time in episodes
Placebo	22		57% of time in episodes
Cundall, Brooks, & Murray (1972)			
Lithium	12		8% had manic recurrence
		1 year	25% had depressive recurrence
Placebo	12		75% had manic recurrence
			42% had depressive recurrence
Hullinn, McDonald, & Allsop (1972)[1]			
Lithium	18	40 months	6% readmitted
Placebo	18		33% readmitted
Prien, Caffey, & Klett (1973)			
Lithium	101		17% had manic relapse
		2 years	10% had depressive relapse
Placebo	104		61% had manic relapse
			16% had depressive relapse
Prien, Klett, & Caffey (1974b)			
Lithium	18	2 years	28% had relapse
Placebo	13		77% had relapse
Stallone et al. (1973)			
Lithium	25		0.11 manic episodes/pt.-yr.
		2 years	0.44 depressive episodes/pt.-yr.
Placebo	27		0.86 manic episodes/pt.-yr.
			0.70 depressive episodes/pt.-yr.
Carbamazepine			
Okuma et al. (1981)			
Carbamazepine	10		60% moderately or markedly
		1 year	improved
Placebo	9		22% moderately or markedly
			improved
			Median Weeks to 50% Survival
Valproate			
Bowden et al. (2000)			
Valproate	187		40
Lithium	91	1 year	24
Placebo	94		28

[1]Includes unspecified proportion with unipolar illness

laxis (Dunner & Fieve, 1974; Kukopulos et al., 1980), together with others in which anticonvulsants appeared to benefit rapid cycling patients (Calabrese & Delucchi, 1990; Joyce, 1988; Okuma, Kishimoto, Inoue, Matsumoto, & Ogura, 1973; Post & Uhde, 1985, Post, Uhde, Roy-Byrne, & Joffe, 1987). Such cross-study comparisons are quite liable to the effects of cohort and ascertainment differences, though. More meaningful is the testing of response predictors within the same study. Okuma (1993) conducted such a study and found that rapid cycling predicted prophylactic failure to both lithium and carbamazepine to equal degrees. Another study likewise showed that rapid cyclers randomly assigned to carbamazepine were as likely as those assigned to lithium to have poor prophylactic outcomes (Denicoff et al., 1997).

Only two reports have described placebo-controlled trials of lithium prophylaxis in patients with rapid cycling. In one, none of the rapid cycling patients, whether assigned to lithium ($n = 9$) or placebo ($n = 6$) remained episode free in the 2 years of observation but other measures of efficacy were not provided (Prien, Caffey, & Klett, 1974a). The other report described patients with bipolar II disorder and included a small number of rapid cycling patients assigned to lithium ($n = 2$) or placebo ($n = 4$) (Dunner et al., 1976). With these small numbers no differences were statistically significant, however, the two taking lithium remained in the study much longer than did the four given placebo, and the authors concluded that results supported the use of lithium in rapid cycling illness (Dunner et al., 1976).

Dysphoric mania and mixed states are now also widely viewed as indications for valproate as first-line treatment in bipolar affective disorder (Frances et al., 1996). Two studies with random treatment assignment have addressed the differential response of patients with mixed states to lithium versus valproate (Freeman, Clothier, Pazzaglia, Lesem, & Swann, 1992; Swann et al., 1997). In the first (Freeman et al., 1992) lithium was significantly superior to valproate in nonmixed states and, in the second, valproate was significantly superior to lithium in mixed states (Swann et al., 1997).

A third consideration is the relative tolerability of lithium, carbamazepine, and valproate. Because side-effect rates are highly sensitive to ascertainment methods, the direct comparison of agents within the same study is necessary. Few of the trials comparing thymoleptics have systematically listed side effects, though. Descriptions of lithium and valproate used acutely (Bowden et al., 1994) and prophylactically (Bowden et al., 2000) have reported higher rates of fever, sedation, infection and tinnitus among those who received valproate and more polyuria and thirst among those who received lithium. Placidi, Lenzi, Lazzerini, Cassano, and Akiskal (1986) found weight gain to be more common with lithium than with those given carbamazepine. Finally, a pharmacoepidemiological study of 2,228 patients exposed to either divalproex, carbamazepine, or a tricyclic antidepressant, found that carbamazepine entailed risks for blood dyscrasias that were sevenfold higher than those for valproate and sixfold higher than those for tricyclic antidepressants (Tohen et al., 1995).

The simple listing of side effects does not reflect their severity. A more meaningful measure of relative tolerability derives from the proportions of patients who left randomized trials because of adverse effects. Table 4.2 shows two things in this regard. First, there are too few direct comparisons of lithium with valproate to draw conclusions about relative tolerability. Second, though most individual comparisons of lithium and carbamazepine have not yielded significant differences, a pooling of the data suggests that lithium is the better tolerated.

TABLE 4.2
Direct Comparisons of Lithium and Anticonvulsants: Discontinuations Due to
Adverse Effects (A = acute, P = prophylaxis)

	Lithium vs. Carbamazepine		Lithium vs. Valproate	
Bowden et al. (1994) (A)				
n			36	69
% discontinuation			11	6
Coxhead, Silverstone, & Cookson (1992) (P)				
n	16	15		
% discontinuation	0	13		
Denicoff et al. (1997) (P)				
n	50	46		
% discontinuation[1]	4	22		
Lerer et al. (1987) (A)				
n	19	15		
% discontinuation	10	7		
Placidi et al. (1986) (P)				
n	27	29		
% discontinuation	7	14		
Simhandl, Denke, & Thaw (1993) (P)				
n	26	58		
% discontinuation	0	0		
Watkins et al. (1987) (P)				
n	18	19		
% discontinued	11	0		
Greil et al. (1997) (P)				
n	74	70		
% discontinued	5	13		
	12/230 =	26/252 =		
	5.2%	10.3%	$X^2 = 4.3$, dv = 1, $p < 0.05$	

[1]Lithium vs. carbamazepine: $X^2 = 9.3$, df = 1, $p < 0.005$.

There are differences between lithium and the anticonvulsants which will be relevant for individual patients. Lithium's effects on the kidneys make its use more problematic than the anticonvulsants for patients with renal impairment. Valproate, unlike lithium, is highly protein-bound and its displacement of other drugs may result in significant toxicity. In the case of carbamazepine, it induces hepatic enzymes that are likely to have a contrary effect on the plasma levels of other drugs, making some of them clinically ineffective.

In summary, when selecting first-line treatment for bipolar affective disorder, clinicians must compare agents by the overall weight of evidence for prophylactic efficacy, by whether certain clinical features favor one agent over the other, and by expected tolerability as predicted by the patient's medical condition. The accumulated evidence for prophylactic efficacy is clearly most substantial for lithium. Though widely held, the view that rapid cycling indicates the use of valproate over lithium is not adequately supported by the data. There is better evidence that the presence or absence of a mixed state is useful in this selection. Thus, with the exception of patients who have significant renal impairment and those with clearly mixed states, the literature does not yet justify displacement of lithium as first-line treatment for patients with bipolar I disorder.

Selection of Thymoleptic: Second Line

Clinicians usually consider a change in thymoleptic regimen when the existing drug is insufficiently effective or poorly tolerated. In the first instance, possibilities include both addition and substitution; in the latter, only substitution is indicated. Given the limited array of demonstratively effective thymolytics, clinicians should be particularly circumspect before taking either step. The premature abandonment of a specific thymolytic substantially decreases future options.

The apparent ineffectiveness of prophylaxis should raise a series of questions. The first of these is whether the patient has been compliant. Noncompliance may precede, or follow, the reappearance of manic symptoms, and input from family members may be necessary to determine whether either sequence was at play. If discontinuation occurred first, the reasons for noncompliance should be sought from the patient and from informants. In some cases the patient is simply averse to taking medication generally, but in others he or she has grown weary of certain side effects. If so, these may improve with the careful titration of dose against plasma levels and clinical stability. Other approaches to improving tolerability will be listed below under "Optimizing Maintenance."

Erratic compliance may indicate substance abuse (Keck et al., 1998; Prien et al., 1974; Vestergaard et al., 1998). Among the mental disorders, the likelihood of coexisting substance abuse is particularly high for bipolar affective disorder (Regier et al., 1999). Again, input from family members may be necessary to determine the extent of such problems and the need for focused intervention.

The second question concerns trial adequacy. Was an apparently failed acute trial of sufficient duration and did the patient achieve appropriate plasma levels? In the only comparison of both lithium and valproate against placebo for acute mania (Bowden et al., 1994), differences favoring either active drug over placebo were significant at day 10 but not at day 5. Contemporary pressures to limit hospital stays are considerable and may lead the clinician to a hasty abandonment of an antimanic trial. This should be actively resisted because the loss of a potentially effective option is likely to result in greater long-term morbidity and, consequently, greater medical costs.

The third question is whether an apparently unsuccessful prophylactic trial has, in fact, shown the drug to be ineffective. The failure of a drug to prevent all recurrences does not necessarily indicate the absence of benefit. If possible, the clinician should determine whether recurrences during prophylaxis are less frequent or less severe than they were without prophylaxis. This determination may be difficult or, in first episode cases, impossible, but is particularly important for patients prone to cycling. For these, a readiness to switch agents will quickly exhaust reasonable options.

Different questions are necessary to determine whether side effects or adverse events necessitate a drug change. One is whether patient complaints or changes in laboratory measures are being correctly attributed. The management of bipolar affective disorder with two or more medications is now quite common and identification of the drug responsible for a given adverse event is correspondingly difficult. This is one of the chief disadvantages of multiple drug regiments and one of the principle reasons they should be simplified when possible.

A frequent opportunity for such simplification arises with the use of adjunct antipsychotics to hasten symptom control in acute mania. Often antipsychotics are then continued at discharge though there exists no controlled clinical trial showing that this enhances prophylaxis. On the contrary, the results of at least one large, naturalistic follow-up suggested that the long-term use of conventional antipsychotics leads to greater depressive morbidity (Kukopulos et al., 1980). In the absence of residual psychotic features, or of a history which clearly demonstrates the necessity of antipsychotic maintenance treatment, adjunct antipsychotics should be carefully tapered and discontinued.

Manifestations of occult medical illnesses may also be misinterpreted as drug side effects. The recognition, investigation, and management of underlying medical illness will vary greatly from case to case. When possibly transient disorders occur, particularly gastrointestinal disturbances and flulike syndromes, a temporary lowering of dose may prevent the unnecessary abandonment of effective treatment.

If it is determined, after all, that a given patient does not benefit from a specific thymoleptic, the clinician must next decide whether to substitute, or to simply add, a new agent. This decision could be best informed by a study in which patients resistant to one agent are randomly assigned either to the addition or to the substitution of another agent. No such study has been published but existing studies allow some inferences.

There is limited evidence from randomized trials that a prior history of poor lithium response does not portend a poor response to anticonvulsants in acute mania. This has been shown both for divalproex (Bowden et al., 1994) and for carbamazepine (Lerer, Moore, Meyerdorff, Cho, & Gershon, 1987), and supports the use of anticonvulsant monotherapy after lithium has proven ineffective.

Only one study of prophylaxis has directly compared lithium monotherapy with combination treatment (Solomon et al., 1997). Patients receiving lithium together with valproate were significantly less likely to experience relapse than were those receiving lithium alone. Another group (Denicoff et al., 1987) described prophylaxis during an initial year on lithium, during a subsequent year on carbamazepine, and during a year with the two drugs combined. In comparison to the year preceding the trial, improvement was greatest in the final year, indicating that combination therapy was superior to treatment with either lithium or carbamazepine monotherapy. This was particularly so among rapid cycling patients. While both of the above studies found that combination therapy offered greater protection than did monotherapy, both also showed that this was at a cost of significantly more side effects.

Thus, the clinician must weigh the prospects of an adequate response against the likelihood of reduced tolerability in deciding whether to substitute or to add an alternative thymoleptic. The characteristics of a given case will often determine this decision. If the first drug resulted in few side effects and if, as is usual, pressures exist to minimize the time to improvement, the addition of an alternative agent is justified. This may be followed, after clinical stability, by the cautious withdrawal of the first agent.

No study has compared carbamazepine to valproate among lithium resistant patients and there is no clear theoretical reason to select one over the other. In some cases the tendency of carbamazepine to induce hepatic enzymes, and of valproate to displace other drugs from protein binding, will determine this choice.

For patients unresponsive to monotherapy with either carbamazepine or valproate, alternative monotherapy may lie either in another anticonvulsant or in lithium. The choice of lithium is more readily justified, for the reasons listed previously, and for the intuitive reason that lithium is likely to work through mechanisms which differ from those of the anticonvulsants. An additional anticonvulsant may, of course, be added and several case series have suggested that the combination of carbamazepine and valproate may have synergistic benefits (Keck, McElroy, Vuckovic, & Friedman, 1992; Ketter, Pazzaglia, & Post, 1992; Tohen et al., 1994). However, the pharmacodynamic properties of these two drugs make their combined use difficult and potentially hazardous (Kondo, Otani, Hirano, Kaneko, & Fukushima, 1990). Carbamazepine is likely to induce the metabolism of valproate rendering blood levels inadequate and valproate may displace carbamazepine from protein binding and result in toxicity (Onady & Calabrese, 1989; Sovner 1988; Tohen et al., 1994).

Selection of Thymoleptic: Third Line

Medications now attracting the most attention as alternatives to lithium, carbamazepine, and valproate fall into two groups: the atypical antipsychotics and the newer anticonvulsants, lamotrigine and gabapentin. At present, the relevant literature does not clearly favor one group over the other.

A number of open trials have suggested that both gabapentin (Cabras, Hardoy, Hardoy, & Carta, 1999; Letterman & Markowitz, 1999; Perugi et al., 1999; Sokolski, Green, Maris, & DeMet, 1999) and lamotrigine (Calabrese, Bowden, McElroy, et al., 1999; Kusumaker & Yatham, 1997a, 1997b) are effective in some patients who are refractory to the more conventional thymoleptics. However, one placebo-controlled trial found lamotrigine, but not gabapentin, to be more effective than placebo (Frye et al., 2000). Another placebo-controlled trial of gabapentin as adjunctive therapy yielded results favoring placebo (Pande et al., 2000). Moreover, lamotrigine produced significantly more stability than placebo in the only controlled study which has targeted bipolar patients with a rapid cycling pattern (Calabrese et al., 2000). This effect was entirely confined to the bipolar II subgroup, though.

Likewise, various open trials (Calabrese et al., 1996; McElroy et al., 1998; Vieta et al., 1998), but only one placebo-controlled one, has tested the value of atypical antipsychotics in bipolar affective disorder. Tohen et al. (1999) conducted a multicenter comparison of olanzapine and placebo, both given as monotherapy, to inpatients with acute mania. Response was twice as likely among those given olanzapine. No patient discontinued due to adverse events and olanzapine was as effective for those with a rapid cycling pattern or with a mixed state as for those without these conditions.

Several other trials of atypical antipsychotics used prospective, random assignment to a comparison treatment but did not include a placebo cell. Suppes and colleagues (1999) assigned patients with a history of treatment resistance or intolerance to either the addition of clozaril or to "treatment as usual." Ratings over the ensuing year favored clozaril on five of six outcome scales. Segal, Berk, and Brook (1998) randomly assigned patients with manic disorder to risperidone, lithium, or haloperidol and the three groups had similar outcomes. Likewise, Berk (1999) compared acutely manic patients given lamotrigine, olanzapine, or lithium and found no differences over a 4-week trial. Finally, Janicak and colleagues (2001) randomly assigned 62 patients with schizoaffective disorder, many of whom where bipolar, to risperidone or haloperidol given as monotherapy. While the two drugs produced similar improvements in manic symptoms, the former was better tolerated and produced a greater reduction in depressive symptoms.

This is currently an area of very active research, largely driven by pharmaceutical companies, and a number of new findings are likely in the near future. In the meantime, placebo-controlled studies support the use of olanzapine in acute mania, and lamotrigine in bipolar depression and in rapid cycling bipolar II disorder. The only study of clozaril (Suppes et al., 1999), targeted treatment resistant patients, but its comparison group receiving treatment as usual, may not have received the same attention from therapists and therefore may have been less compliant. Pending further reports, then, the selection of third-line strategies will be largely matters of trial and error.

Optimizing Maintenance

RECOGNITION OF PRODROMAL SYMPTOMS

Perry, Tarrier, Morris, McCarthy, and Limb (1999) randomly assigned outpatients undergoing routine treatment for bipolar disorder to experimental or control groups. The former underwent training designed to identify symptoms that had reliably preceded past manic or depressive episodes so that the individual would promptly seek medical attention at the earliest sign of recurrence. Those who received this training developed significantly fewer manic symptoms during the eighteen months of follow-up. Though the intervention had no affect on depressive symptoms, it was associated with significant improvements in social functioning and in employment.

THYMOLEPTIC DOSE ADJUSTMENT

The therapeutic serum level range for lithium falls between 0.4 and 1.4 mol/l. Within this range, higher levels are associated both with improved prophylactic efficacy and with increasing side effects. Both side effects and the emergence of manic or hypomanic symptoms will adversely affect compliance. It is critical, therefore, that a serum level is established for each patient that optimally balances side effects with efficacy.

A small number of carefully designed studies have attempted to identify the serum level range which, on average, provides the best balance between beneficial and adverse effects. Three studies randomly assigned patients to prophylaxis with high or low serum level ranges. One found no group difference in recurrence rates or side-effects (Vestergaard et al., 1998). The other two found a higher recurrence rate among patients in the lower range (0.4 meq/l to 0.6 meq/l or 0.4 meq/l to 0.8 meq/l) in comparison to those assigned to the high doses (0.8 meq/l-1.4 meq/l or 0.8 meq/l-1.0 meq/l) (Gelenberg et al., 1989; Waters et al., 1982). In the latter two studies, patients who received the higher doses were more likely to discontinue treatment due to side effects.

Maj, Starace, Nolfe, and Kemali (1986) increased precision by assigning patients to four groups (Table 4.3). Results suggested little advantage to maintaining patients above 0.75. Indeed, higher levels may have adverse effects of which the patient is unaware. Squire, Judd, Janowsky, and Huey (1980), in a carefully designed placebo-controlled, crossover trial, showed that, while 2 weeks of lithium did not produce complaints of cognitive impairment, performance was significantly impaired on several tests in comparison to placebo and this impairment correlated with lithium levels. Clinicians must treat individuals, though. Trial and error is often necessary

TABLE 4.3
Lithium Serum Level Ranges, Morbidity, and Side Effect Scores during
Prophylaxis (Maj et al., 1986)

Range, meq/l	n	Morbidity Score Mania[1]	Depression[2]	Side-Effect Score[3]
A. 0.30–0.45	17	1.5	2.5	0.8
B. 0.46–0.60	17	0.7	1.5	1.4
C. 0.61–0.75	18	0.6	1.0	2.0
D. 0.76–0.90	17	0.4	1.1	2.2

[1]A > B, C, D, $p < 0.05$
[2]A > C, D, $p < 0.05$
[3]A< C, D; B < D, $p < 0.05$

to find the level which best balances tolerability and protection.

Much less attention has been directed at the relationships between anticonvulsant plasma levels and therapeutic response. The plasma level range of carbamazepine used for seizure control (4 to 12 mcg/l) has been adopted for use in bipolar disorder although no study has validated this convention. Efforts to identify plasma level/response relationships must employ fixed doses. The only study of carbamazepine prophylaxis to do so found no difference in efficacy between doses targeting a range of 3.5 to 5.9 mcg/ml and those targeting a higher range of 6.6 to 9.5 mcg/ml (Simhamdl, Denk, & Thau, 1993). Bowden et al. (1996) assessed valproate serum levels and antimanic responses and determined a lower limit of 46.2 to 49.8 mcg/ml. Free valproate levels increased nonlinearly beyond 100 mcg/ml, accounting for the substantially higher rates of side effects noted at these levels.

The frequency of plasma level monitoring will depend on the agent used, the time since initiation of treatment, the presence of coexisting medical conditions, and the degree of plasma level stability to date. The timing of lithium plasma level assessment is particularly important in the initial dose finding phase. Lithium reaches steady state in approximately 5 days. Dose changes based on levels drawn at smaller intervals may seriously overshoot the target. Because carbamazepine often autoinduces its own metabolism after 2 to 3 weeks of treatment, plasma levels should be checked at that point to determine the need for dose adjustment.

BREAKTHROUGH EPISODES

As noted earlier, the reappearance of manic symptoms during prophylaxis does not necessarily show the agent being used to be without benefit. A given thymoleptic may reduce episode frequency and severity but fail to eliminate all breakthroughs. To avoid a precipitous progression through the limited array of thymoleptics available, the clinician may, depending on clinical circumstances, attempt to abort an episode with the temporary use of antipsychotics. Because the atypical antipsychotics are better tolerated than the traditional agents, and are probably less likely to promote depressive symptoms, these are preferred unless the relative cost is prohibitive.

MANAGEMENT OF DEPRESSIVE EPISODES—ANTIDEPRESSANTS

Many patients develop depressive episodes after an acute mania has resolved and maintenance treatment has begun. Such symptoms may range from severe major depressive episodes with incapacitation with/or without psychotic features to levels which, though subsyndromal, may cause substantial psychosocial impairment (Judd et al., 1998). This confronts the clinician with several questions. Are antidepressants effective in bipolar affective disorder and, if so, are some more so than others? Should antidepressants be used prophylactically? Do they increase risks for manic breakthroughs or for rapid cycling patterns?

There are two placebo-controlled, parallel-design studies of antidepressants in the acute treatment of bipolar depression. The first (Cohn, Collins, Ashbrook, & Wernicke, 1989) described a significantly higher response rate for depressed patients given fluoxetine than for those given either imipramine or placebo. The other (Nemeroff et al., 2001) found no overall outcome difference between placebo and the two active drugs, imipramine and paroxetine. However, both active drugs were associated with superior outcomes among those who maintained lithium levels of less than 0.8 MEQ/ML. Other studies have used random assignments to compare a tricyclic antidepressant (TCA) with another class of antidepressant and, in one, tranylcypromine proved superior to imipramine (Himmelhoch, Thase, Mallinger, & Houck, 1991). When those who failed to respond were then crossed to the alternative drug, patients switched from imipramine to tranylcypromine were much more likely to respond than were those switched from tranylcypromine to imipramine (Thase, Mallinger, McKnight, & Himmelhoch, 1992). In another comparison, Sachs and colleagues (1994) found no difference between desipramine and bupropion in antidepressant response. Finally, Altshuler and colleagues (2001) described the subsequent course bipolar patients who had responded to antidepressant treatment. Those who subsequently discontinued their antidepressants were much more likely to experience a depressive relapse in the coming year than those who continued treatment. Only 3 of the twenty-five who continued antidepressant therapy took a tricyclic antidepressant, though.

Evidence from a large placebo-controlled, parallel design study (Calabrese, 1999b) shows that the anticonvulsive lamotrigine has antidepressant effects in bipolar depression. Significant differences favoring both 50 mg and 200 mg daily doses over placebo emerged at week 3 of the 7-week trial.

Thus, a small body of evidence supports the use of SSRIs, MAIOs, and lamotrigine in the management of bipolar depressive disorder. Evidence from other controlled studies, presented later, support a number of nonpharmacological approaches to bipolar depression, as well.

Two placebo-controlled studies of prophylaxis have considered whether imipramine enhances the prophylactic effects of lithium (Prien et al., 1984;

Quitkin, Kane, Rifkin, Ramos-Lorenzi, & Nayak, 1981). In both, the likelihood of depressive episodes was somewhat lower among patients who took both lithium and imipramine than among those who took lithium alone; in neither was the difference significant, though. No such study has tested the MAOIs or the newer antidepressants in this way. The limited findings favoring serotonin reuptake inhibitors (SSRIs) and monoamine oxydase inhibitors (MAOIs) over TCAs in the acute treatment of bipolar depression suggests that such a study would support the routine use of such drugs for the prevention of depressive morbidity in bipolar affective disorder.

Nearly all psychotherapeutic drugs and, in particular, antidepressants have been alleged to promote manic episodes. It is likely that many of these perceptions reflect the presumption of causal relationships between sequential events, the prescribing of an antidepressant and the development of a mania. As such sequences were known to be quite common before the advent of antidepressants (Kraepelin, 1921/1989) only controlled studies can quantify the risks that antidepressants provoke manias. The meta-analysis presented by Peet (1994) is therefore quite relevant (Table 4.4). Notably, patients who received SSRIs for the treatment of bipolar depression were no more likely then those who received placebo to develop manic episodes. A trend does emerge across relevant studies to indicate that the TCAs may incur more risks for manic episodes then either placebo or other antidepressants. Only the comparison described by Peet (1994) reached statistical significance, though.

The use of antidepressants has also been implicated in the development and continuation of rapid-cycling patterns (Kukopulos et al., 1980; Wehr, Sack, Rosenthal, & Cowdry, 1988). These observations derive from naturalistic studies in which the development of a rapid-cycling pattern was temporally associated with antidepressant use. In both reports, a subset of patients ceased to show this pattern when antidepressants were stopped. Due to the fact that their designs were naturalistic, neither study could dismiss the possibility that depressive episodes increased the likelihood of both antidepressant use and a subsequent rapid cycling pattern. Analyses from another, large naturalistic study, in fact, clearly supported this interpretation (Coryell, Endicott, & Keller, 1992; Coryell, 1993).

The fear that antidepressant use may provoke a malignant course in bipolar illness is a prevalent one, though, and comprises a paradox for clinicians as they manage patients with bipolar depression. This further justifies a large scale, controlled study of antidepressant prophylaxis in bipolar affective disorder. In the meantime, clinicians are justified in using antidepressants, particularly SSRI and MAOI agents, to treat bipolar depression.

TABLE 4.4

Manic Episodes during Acute and Prophylactic Treatment with Antidepressants: Controlled Trials

Acute Treatment	n	% Developing Manía/Hypomania
Cohn et al. (1989)		
Fluoxetine	30	0.0
Imipramine	30	6.7
Placebo	29	3.4
Peet (1994)[1]		
SSRIs	242	3.7
TCAs	125	11.2
Placebo	48	4.2
Himmelhoch et al. (1991)		
Tranylcypromine	26	11.5
Imipramine	21	23.8
Sachs et al. (1984)		
Bupropion	9	11.1
Desipramine	10	50.0
Prophylaxis		
Quitkin et al. (1981)		
Lithium + Imipramine	37	24.3
Lithium	38	10.5
Prien, Klett, & Caffey (1973)		
Lithium	17	11.8
Imipramine	9	66.7
Placebo	9	33.3
Prien et al. (1984)		
Lithium + Imipramine	36	27.8
Lithium	42	26.2
Nemeroff et al. (2001)		
Lithium + Imipramine	39	7.7
Lithium + Paroxetine	35	0.0
Lithium + Placebo	43	2.3

[1]SSRI vs. TCA, $x^2 = 6.7$, df = 1, p = 0.01

Hormonal Replacement

The thyroid axis is relevant to the maintenance treatment of bipolar illness for a variety of reasons. Lithium produces hypothyroidism in a substantial proportion of cases and this may mediate the adverse effects of lithium on cognitive performance (Honig et al., 1999; Prohaska, Stern, Nevels, et al., 1996; Tremont & Stern 1997). At least one placebo-controlled study has shown that thyroid replacement significantly improves processing and motor speed in patients undergoing lithium treatment (Prohaska, Stern, Mason, et al., 1995). Moreover, the association between hypothyroidism and depressive symptoms is well known. An inverse correlation between affective morbidity and free T_4 levels has recently been noted among patients undergoing lithium prophylaxis (Frye et al., 1999) and elevated TSH values have been associated with antidepressant resistance among patients with unipolar depression (Joffe & Levitt, 1992). Controlled studies of patients with refractory depressive disorders have shown that the addition of T_3 at 37.5 meq/day produces substantially more improvement than either placebo (Joffe, Singer, Levitt, & MacDonald, 1993) or the addition of T_4 at 150 meq/day (Joffe & Singer, 1990). Together, these findings indicate that patients on lithium who complain of cognitive slowing, or who have persistent depressive symptoms, may benefit from thyroid replacement, particularly if subclinical hypothyroidism is present. Likewise, the correction of hypothyroidism in patients treated with other thymoleptics may be helpful.

MANAGEMENT OF DEPRESSIVE EPISODES— NONPHARMACOLOGICAL STRATEGIES

In their review of 61 papers describing over 1,700 patients, Wu and Bunney (1990) concluded that the majority of patients with depressive disorders experience marked improvement on the day after total or partial sleep deprivation (SD). The fact that four in five unmedicated patients relapse after a subsequent night of sleep has limited the practical value of this procedure. Accumulating evidence, though, indicates that sleep deprivation has more sustained benefits for medicated patients and that this may be of particular relevance to patients with bipolar affective disorder.

One of these studies used a single SD before clomipramine treatment began (Elsenga & van den Hoofdakker, 1982–1983), and another used three SDs given during the second week of fluoxetine treatment (Benedetti et al., 1997). In both, SD appeared to significantly shorten time to recovery but the advantage conferred by SD was no longer apparent in the third and fourth week in these 4-week trials.

Four controlled studies have assessed the antidepressant effects of SD when added to lithium and all four found significant benefits extending beyond the day following the procedure. Two of these studies observed patients for less then a week (Baxter et al., 1986; Grube & Hartwich, 1990) but the other two showed that improvement was sustained for at least one (Szuba et al., 1994) or three (Benedetti et al., 1999) months. Pindolol has also been shown to prime patients with bipolar depression for a sustained response to a combination of sleep deprivation and lithium (Smeraldi, Benedetti, Barbini, Campori, & Colombo, 1999).

The study showing the clearest synergism between SD and lithium confined its sample to patients with bipolar I disorder (Benedetti et al., 1999). Though a number of studies have not found that the unipolar–bipolar distinction predicted response to SD, none has found better responses among unipolar patients then among bipolar patients, while at least three have found significantly better responses among bipolar patients (Barbini et al., 1998; Fahndrich, 1981; Szuba et al., 1991). This, and the apparent interaction of SD with lithium treatment, invite further investigation into the management of bipolar depression, particularly that which develops during lithium prophylaxis. The use of SD may be most effective during hospitalization in that patients can be assisted in procedure compliance. Evidence so far suggests that the hospital stay may be shortened considerably as a consequence.

As with all other treatments used to manage depression, sleep deprivation has been associated with switches into mania. Colombo, Benedetti, Barbini, Campori, and Smeraldi (1999) recently pooled their sample of 206 inpatients who had been given SD as treatment for bipolar depression and found that 4.8% had developed mania, a figure not dissimilar to the 4.2% given by Peet (1994) as the proportion of bipolar patients who had developed mania while taking placebo in controlled trials.

As an adjunct to lithium therapy in the treatment of bipolar depression, the use of SD now has more support from controlled studies then does the use of antidepressants. Sleep deprivation has the added advantage of being inexpensive and free of side effects other than drowsiness. Moreover, a trial takes 24 hours rather than the 2 weeks generally considered the minimum for antidepressants. When undergoing total SD, patients remain awake from one morning to the next evening for a total of 36 hours. Partial SD requires wakefulness only from 2:00 a.m. to the next evening. Both have been studied extensively and appear to be equivalent in their benefits (Kuhs and Tolle, 1991). Many patients will find the prospect of partial SD the more acceptable of the two approaches.

Phototherapy is another benign somatotherapy potentially useful for bipolar depression. Though most of the research into phototherapy has focused on seasonal disorders, controlled trials have indicated that it is equally effective for nonseasonal depression (Kripke, Mullaney, Klauber, Risch, & Gillin, 1992; Kripke, 1998). At least one has shown that, among patients with nonseasonal depression, those with bipolar disorders have significantly better responses to phototherapy then do unipolar patients (Deltito, Moline, Pollack, Martin, & Maremmani, 1991). In addition, phototherapy may sustain the effects of SD. Neumeister et al. (1996) described 20 inpatients who had failed to respond to 3 weeks of antidepressant treatment. All underwent one night of partial SD and were randomly assigned to receive phototherapy with bright or with dim (placebo) light. Those in the former group were significantly more likely to sustain the benefit they derived from SD then were those who received dim light.

It has long been appreciated that adverse life events often precede new episodes of affective disorder. Researchers have recently focused on the particular importance to bipolar affective disorder of those events which effect the sleep–wake cycle. Such "social rhythm disruptions" seem especially likely to precede the onset of manic episodes (Malkoff-Schwartz et al., 1998) and efforts are underway to determine whether treatment designed to decrease the likelihood of such events might improve the course of bipolar affective disorder (Frank et al., 1997). Preliminary results show this approach to be a promising one (Frank, Swartz, & Kupfer, 2000).

Such nonpharmacological approaches as sleep deprivation, phototherapy, and social rhythm therapy may eventually prove of considerable benefit to patients but with few side effects and little monetary costs. Given the relative influence of marketing on clinical practice, these tools will come into wide use much more slowly then will new pharmaceutical options. Clinicians who track the literature faithfully will therefore be better prepared to manage the many bipolar patients who continue to experience symptoms despite pharmacological management.

References

Altshuler, L., Kiriakos, L., Calcagno, J., Goodman, R., Gitlin, M., Frye, M., et al. (2001). The impact of antidepressant discontinuation versus antidepressant continuation on the 1-year risk for relapse of bipolar depression: A retrospective chart review. *Journal of Clinical Psychiatry, 62,* 612–616.

Baastrup, P. C., Poulsen, J. C., Schou, M., Thomsen, K., & Amidsen, A. (1970). Prophylactic lithium: Double-blind discontinuation in manic-depressive and recurrent-depressive disorders. *Lance, 2,* 326–330.

Baldessarini, R. J., Tondo, L., Floris, G., & Rudas, N. (1997). Reduced morbidity after gradual discontinuation of lithium treatment for bipolar I and II disorders: A replication study. *American Journal of Psychiatry, 154*(4), 551–553.

Barbini, B., Colombo, C., Benedetti, F., Campori, E., Bellodi, & Smeraldi, E. (1998). The unipolar-bipolar dichotomy and the response to sleep deprivation. *Psychiatry Res*earch, 79, 43–50.

Baxter, L. R., Liston, E. H., Schwartz, J. M., Altshuler, L. L., Wilkins, J. N., Rucheimer, S., et al. (1986). Prolongation of the antidepressant response to partial sleep deprivation by lithium. *Psychiatry Research, 19,* 17–23.

Benedetti, F., Barbini, B., Lucca, A., Campori, E., Colombo, C., & Smeraldi, E. (1997). Sleep deprivation hastens the antidepressant action of fluoxetine. *European Archives of Psychiatry & Clinical Neuroscience, 247,* 100–103.

Benedetti, F., Colombo, C., Barbini, B., Campori, E., & Smeradi, E. (1999). Ongoing lithium treatment prevents relapse after total sleep deprivation. *Journal of Clinical Psychopharmacology, 19,* 240–245.

Berk, M. (1999). Lamotrigine and the treatment of mania in bipolar disorder. *European Neuropsychopharmacology, 9*(Suppl. 4), 119–123.

Bowden, C. L., Calabrese, J. R., McElroy, S. L., Gyulai, L., Wassef, A, Petty, F., et al. (2000, May). A randomized, placebo-controlled 12-month trial of divalproex and lithium in treatment of outpatients with bipolar I disorder. Divalproex Maintenance Study Group. *Archives of General Psychiatry, 57*(5), 481–489.

Bowden, C. L., Brugger, A. M., Swann, A. C., Calabrese, J. R., Janicak, P. G., Petty, F., et al. (1994). Efficacy of divalproex vs. lithium and placebo in the treatment of mania. *Journal of the American Medical Association, 271,* 918–924.

Bowden, C. L., Janicak, P. G., Orsulak, P., Swann, A. C., Davis, J. M., Calabrese, J. R., et al. (1996). Relation of serum valproate concentration to response in mania. *American Journal of Psychiatry, 153,* 765–770.

Cabras, P. L., Hardoy, M. J., Hardoy, M. C., & Carta, M. G. (1999). Clinical experience with gabapentin in patients with bipolar or schizoaffective disorder: Results of an open labeled study. *Journal of Clinical Psychiatry, 60,* 245–248.

Calabrese, J. R., Bowden, C. L., McElroy, S. L., Cookson, J., Andersen, J., Keck, P. E., Jr., et al. (1999a). Spectrum of activity of lamotrigine in treatment refractory bipolar disorder. *American Journal of Psychiatry, 156,* 1019–1023.

Calabrese, J. R., Bowden, C. L., Sachs, G. S., Ascher, J. A., Monaghan, E., & Rudd, G. D. (1999b). A double-blind placebo-controlled study of the lamotrigine monotherapy in outpatients with bipolar I depression. *Journal of Clinical Psychiatry, 60,* 79–88.

Calabrese, J. R., & Delucchi, G. A. (1990). Spectrum of efficacy of valproate in 55 patients with rapid cycling bipolar disorder. *American Journal of Psychiatry, 147,* 431–434.

Calabrese, J. R., Fatemi, S. H., Kujawa, M., & Woyshville, M. J. (1999, April). Predictors of response to mood stabilizers. *Journal of Clinical Psychopharmacology, 16*(2 Suppl. 1), 25S–31S.

Calabrese, J. R., Kimmel, S. E., Woyshville, M. J., Rapport, D. J., Faust, C. J., & Thompson, P. A. (1996). Clozapine for treatment refractory mania. *American Journal of Psychiatry, 153,* 759–764.

Calabrese, J. R., Suppes, T., Bowden, C. L. Sachs, G. S., Swann, A. C., McElroy, S. L., et al. (2000). A double-blind placebo control prophylaxis study of lamotrigine and rapid cycling bipolar disorder. *Journal of Clinical Psychiatry, 61,* 841–850.

Cohn, J. B., Collins, G., Ashbrook, E., & Wernicke, J. F. (1989). A comparison of fluoxetine, imipramine and placebo in patients with bipolar depressive disorder. *International Clinical Psychopharmacology, 4,* 313–322.

Colombo, C., Benedetti, F., Barbini, B., Campori, E., & Smeraldi, E. (1999). Rate of switch from depression into mania after therapeutic sleep deprivation in bipolar depression. *Psychiatry Research, 86,* 267–270.

Coppen, A., Nogvera, R., Bailey, J., Burns, B. H., Swani, M. S., Hare, E. H., et al. (1971). Prophylactic lithium in affective disorders. *Lancet, 2,* 275–279.

Coryell, W. (1993). Can antidepressants induce rapid cycling? *Archives of General Psychiatry, 50,* 497–498.

Coryell, W., Endicott, J., & Keller, M. (1992). Rapidly cycling affective disorder: demographics, diagnosis, family history, and course. *Archives of General Psychiatry, 49,* 126–131.

Coryell, W., Endicott, J., Maser, J. D., Keller, M. B., Leon, A. C., Akiskal, H. S. (1995). Long-term stability of polarity distinctions in the affective disorders. *Journal of Affective Disorders, 152,* 385–390.

Coryell, W., Endicott, J., Maser, J. D., Mueller, T., Lavori, P., Keller, M. (1995). The likelihood of recurrence in bipolar affective disorder: the importance of episode recency. *Journal of Affective Disorders, 33,* 201–206.

Coryell, W., Keller, M., Endicott, J., Andreasen, N., Clayton, P., & Hirschfeld, R. (1989). Bipolar II illness: Course and outcome over a five-year period. *Psychological Medicine, 19,* 129–141.

Coryell, W., Winokur, G., Solomon, D., Shea, T., Leon, A., & Keller, M. (1997). Lithium and recurrence in a long-term follow-up of bipolar affective disorder. *Psychological Medicine, 27,* 281–290.

Coryell, W., Solomon, D., Leon, A. C., Akiskal, H. S., Keller, M. B., Scheftner, W. A., et al. (1998). Lithium discontinuation and subsequent effectiveness. *American Journal of Psychiatry, 155,* 895–898.

Coxhead, N., Silverstone, T., & Cookson, J. (1992). Carbamazepine vs. lithium in the prophylaxis of bipolar affective disorder. *Acta Psychiatrica Scandinavia, 85,* 114–118.

Cundall, R. L., Brooks, P. W., & Murray, L. G. (1972). A controlled evaluation of lithium prophylaxis in affective disorders. *Psychological Medicine, 2,* 308–311.

Deltito, J. A., Moline, M., Pollak, C., Martin, L. Y., & Maremmani, I. (1991). Effects of phototherapy on nonseasonal unipolar and bipolar depressive spectrum disorders. *Journal of Affective Disorders, 23,* 231–237.

Denicoff, K. D., Smith-Jackson, E. E., Disney, E. R., Ali, S. O., Leverich, G. S., & Post, R. M. (1997). Comparative prophylactic efficacy of lithium, carbamazepine, and the combination in bipolar disorder. *Journal Clinical Psychiatry, 58,* 470–478.

DePaulo, J. R., Simpson, S. G., Gayle, J. O., & Folstein, S. E. (1990). Bipolar II disorder in six sisters. *Journal of Affective Disorders, 19,* 259–264.

Dunner, D. L., & Fieve, R. R. (1974). Clinical factors in lithium carbonate prophylaxis failure. *Archives of General Psychiatry, 30,* 229–233.

Dunner, D. L., Stallone, F., & Fieve, R. R. (1982). Prophylaxis with lithium carbonate: An update. *Archives of General Psychiatry, 39,* 1344–1345.

Dunner, D. L., Stallone, F., & Fieve, R. R. (1976). Lithium carbonate and affective disorders V: A double-blind study of prophylaxis of depression in bipolar illness. *Archives of General Psychiatry, 33,* 117–120.

Elsenga, S., & van den Hoofdakker, R. H. (1982–1983). Clinical effects of sleep deprivation and clomipramine in endogenous depression. *Journal of Psychiatric Research, 17,* 361–374.

Faedda, G. L., Tondo, L., Baldessarini, R. J., Suppes, T., & Tohen. M. (1993). Outcome after rapid versus gradual discontinuation of lithium treatment in bipolar disorders. *Archives of General Psychiatry, 50,* 448–455.

Fahndrich, E. (1981). Effects of sleep deprivation on depressed patients of different nosological groups. *Psychiatry Research, 5,* 277–285.

Fieve, R. R., Kumberaci, T., & Dunner, D. L. (1976). Lithium prophylaxis of depression in bipolar I and bipolar II and unipolar patients. *American Journal of Psychiatry, 133,* 925–929.

Frances, A., Docherty, J. P., & Kahn, D. A. (1996). Treatment of bipolar disorder. *Journal of Clinical Psychiatry, 57*(Suppl. 12A), 1–88.

Frank, E., Halastala, S., Ritenour, A., Houck, P., Tu, X. M., & Monk, T. H. (1997). Inducing lifestyle regularity in recovering bipolar disorder patients: Results from the maintenance therapies in bipolar disorder protocol. *Biological Psychiatry, 41,* 1165–1173.

Frank, E., Swartz, H. A., & Kupfer, D. J. (2000). Interpersonal and social rhythm therapy: Managing the chaos of bipolar disorder. *Biological Psychiatry, 48,* 593–604.

Freeman, T. W., Clothier, J. L., Pazzaglia, P., Lesem, M. D., & Swann, A. C. (1992). A double-blind comparison of valproate and lithium in the treatment of acute mania. *American Journal of Psychiatry, 149,* 108–111.

Frye, M. A., Ketter, T. A., Kimbrell, T. A., Dunn, R. T., Speer, A. M., Osuch, E. A., et al. (2000). A placebo controlled study of lamotrigine and gabapentin monotherapy in refractory mood disorders. *Journal of Clinical Psychopharmacology, 20,* 607–614.

Frye, M. A., Denicoff, K. D., Bryan, A. L., Smith-Jackson, E. E., Ali, S. O., Luckenbaugh, D., et al. (1999). Association between lower serum-free T_4 and greater mood instability and depression in lithium-maintained bipolar patients. *American Journal of Psychiatry, 156*, 1909–1914.

Gelenberg, A. J., Kane, J. M., Keller, M. B., Lavori, P., Rosenbaum, J. F., Cole, K., et al. (1989). Comparison of standard and low serum levels of lithium for maintenance treatment of bipolar disorder. *New England Journal of Medicine, 321*, 1489–1493.

Greil, W., Ludwig-Mayerhofer, W., Erazo, N., Schochlin, C., Schmidt, S., Engel, R. R., et al. (1997). Lithium vs carbamazepine in the maintenance treatment of bipolar disorders—A randomized study. *Journal of Affective Disorders, 43*, 151–161.

Grof, P., Angst, J., Karasek, M., & Keitner, G. (1979). Patient selection for long-term lithium treatment in clinical practice. *Archives of General Psychiatry, 36*, 894–897.

Grube, M., & Harwich, P. (1990). Maintenance of antidepressant effect of sleep deprivation with the help of lithium. *European Archives of Psychiatry and Clinical Neuroscience, 240*, 60–61.

Himmelhoch, J. M., Thase, M. E., Mallinger, A. G., & Houch, P. (1991). Tranylcypromie versus imipramine in anergic bipolar depression. *American Journal of Psychiatry, 148*, 910–916.

Honig, A., Arts, B. M. G., Ponds, R. W., & Riedel, W. J. (1999). Lithium induced cognitive side-effects in bipolar disorder: A qualitative analysis and implications for daily practice. *International Clinical Psychopharmacology, 14*, 167–171.

Hullin, R. P., McDonald, R., & Allsopp, M. N. E. (1972). Prophylactic lithium in recurrent affective disorders. *Lancet, 1*, 1044–1046.

Janicak, P. G., Keck, P. E., Jr., Davis, J. M., Kasckow, J. W., Tugrul, K., Dowd, S. M., et al. (2001, August). A double-blind, randomized, prospective evaluation of the efficacy and safety of risperidone versus haloperidol in the treatment of schizoaffective disorder. *Journal of Clinical Psychopharmacology, 21*(4), 360–368.

Joffe, R. T., & Levitt, A. J. (1992). Major depression and subclinical (grade 2) hypothyroidism. *Psychoneuroendocrinology, 17*, 215–221.

Joffe, R. T., & Singer, W. (1990). A comparison of triiodothyronine and thyroxin in the potentiation of tricyclic antidepressants. *Psychiatry Research, 32*, 241–251.

Joffe, R. T., Singer, W., Levitt, A. J., & MacDonald, C. (1993). A placebo-controlled comparison of lithium and triiodothyronine augmentation of tricyclic antidepressants in unipolar refractory depression. *Archives of General Psychiatry, 50*, 387–393.

Joyce, P. R. (1988). Carbamazepine in rapid-cycling bipolar affective disorder. *International Clinical Psychopharmacology, 3*, 123–129.

Judd, L. L., Akiskal, H. S., Maser, J. D., Zeller, P. J., Endicott, J., Coryell, W., et al. (1998). A prospective 12-year study of subsyndromal and syndromal depressive symptomatology in unipolar major depressive disorders. *Archives of General Psychiatry, 55*, 694–700.

Keck, P. E., McElroy, S. L., Strakowski, S. M., West, S. A., Sax, K. W., Hawkins, J. M., et al. (1998). 12 month outcome of patients with bipolar disorder following hospitalization for a manic or mixed episode. *American Journal of Psychiatry, 155*, 646–652.

Keck, P. E., McElroy, S. L., Vuckovic, A., & Friedman, L. M. (1992). Combined valproate and carbamazepine treatment of bipolar disorder. *Journal of Neuropsychiatry Clinical Neuroscience, 4*, 319–322.

Ketter, T. A., Pazzaglia, P. J., & Post, R. M. (1992). Synergy of carbamazepine and valproic acid in affective illness: Case report and review of the literature. *Journal of Clinical Psychopharmacology, 12*, 276–281.

Kleindienst, N., Greil, W., Ruger, B., Moller, H. J. (1999). The prophylactic efficacy of lithium—Transient or persistent. *European Archives of Psychiatry & Clinical Neuroscience, 249*, 144–149.

Kondo, T., Otani, K., Hirano, T., Kaneko, S., & Fukushima, Y. (1990). The effects of phenytoin and carbamazepine on serum concentrations of mono-unsaturated metabolites of valproic acid. *British Journal of Clinical Pharmacology, 29,* 116–119.

Kraepelin, E. (1921). *Manic-depressive insanity and paranoia* (E. T. Carlson, Editor). Edinburg, Scotland: Livingstone. (Original work published 1921)

Kripke, D. F. (1998). Light treatment for a non-seasonal depression: Speed, efficacy and combined treatment. *Journal of Affective Disorders, 49,* 109–117.

Kripke, D. F., Mullaney, D. J., Klauber, M. R., Risch, S. C., & Gillin, J. C. (1992). Controlled trial of bright light for non-seasonal major depressive disorders. *Biology & Psychiatry, 31,* 119–134.

Kuhs, H., & Tolle, R. (1991). Sleep deprivation therapy. *Biology & Psychiatry, 29,* 1129–1148.

Kukopulos, A., Reginaldi, D., Laddomada, P., Floris, G., Serra, G., & Tondo, L. (1980). Course of the manic depressive cycle and changes caused by treatment. *Pharmakopsychiatrie Neuropsychopharmakologie, 13,* 156–167.

Kusumaker, V., & Yatham, L. N. (1997a). An open study of lamotrigine in refractory bipolar depression. *Psychiatry Research, 72,* 145–148.

Kusumaker, V., & Yatham, L. N. (1997b). Lamotrigine treatment of rapid cycling bipolar disorder. *American Journal of Psychiatry, 154,* 1171–1172.

Lerer, B., Moore, N., Meyendorff, E., Cho, S. R., & Gershon, S. (1987). Carbamazepine vs. lithium in mania: A double-blind study. *Journal of Clinical Psychiatry, 48,* 89–93.

Letterman, L., & Markowitz, J. S. (1999). Gabapentin: A review of published experience in the treatment of bipolar disorder and other psychiatric conditions. *Pharmacotherapy, 19,* 565–572.

Maj, M., Strace, F., Nolfe, G., & Kemali, D. (1986). Minimum plasma lithium levels required for affective prophylaxis in DSM-III Bipolar Disorder: A prospective study. *Pharmacopsychiatry, 19,* 420–423.

Malkoff-Schwartz, S., Frank, E., Anderson, B., Sherrill, J. T., Siegel, L., Patterson, D., et al. (1998). Stressful life events and social rhythm disruption in the onset of manic and depressive bipolar episodes. *Archives of General Psychiatry, 55,* 702–707.

McElroy, S. L., Frye, M., Denicoff, K., Altshuler, L., Nolen, W., Kupka, R., et al. (1998). Olanzapine in treatment resistant bipolar disorder. *Journal of Affective Disorders, 49,* 119–122.

Nemeroff, C. B., Evans, D. L., Gyulai, L., Sachs, G. S., Bowden, C. L., Gergel, I. P., et al. (2001). Double-blind, placebo-controlled comparison of imipramine and paroxetine in the treatment of bipolar depression. *American Journal of Psychiatry, 158*(6), 906–912.

Neumeister, A., Goesslar, R., Lucht, M., Kapitany, T., Bamas, C., & Kasper, S. (1996). Bright light therapy stabilizes the antidepressant effect of partial sleep deprivation. *Biology & Psychiatry, 39,* 16–21.

Okuma, T. (1993). Effects of carbamazepine and lithium on affective disorders. *Neuropsychobiology, 27,* 138–145.

Okuma, T., Kishimoto, A., Inue, K., Matsumoto, H., & Ogura, A. (1973). Anti-manic and prophylactic effects of carbamazepine (Tegretol) on manic depressive psychosis. *Folia Psychiatrica at Neurologica Japonica, 27,* 283–297.

Okuma, T., Inanaga, K., Otsuki, S., Sarai, K., Takahashi, R., Hazama, H., et al. (1981). A preliminary double-blind study on the efficacy of carbamazepine in prophylaxis of manic depressive illness. *Psychopharmacology, 73,* 95–96.

Onady, A. A., & Calabrese, J. R. (1989). Carbamazepine auto- and hetero-induction complicating clinical care. *Journal of Clinical Psychopharmacology, 9,* 387–388.

Pande, A. C., Crockett, J. G., Janney, C. A., Werth, J. L., & Tsaroucha, G. (2000). Gabapentin in bipolar disorder: A placebo-controlled trial of adjunctive therapy. Gabapentin Bipolar Study Group. *Bipolar Disorder, 2*(3 pt. 2), 249–255.

Peet, M. (1994). Induction of mania with selective serotonin re-uptake inhibitors and tricyclic antidepressants. *British Journal of Psychiatry, 164,* 549–550.

Perry, A., Tarrier, N., Morris, R., McCarthy, E, & Limb, K. (1999). Randomized controlled trial of efficacy of teaching patients with bipolar disorder to identify early symptoms of relapse and obtain treatment. *British Medical Journal, 318,* 149–153.

Perugi, G., Toni, C., Ruffolo, G., Sartini, S., Simonini, E., & Akiskal, H. (1999, July). Clinical experience using adjunctive gabapentin in treatment-resistant bipolar mixed states. *Pharmacopsychiatry, 32*(4), 136–141.

Placidi, G. F., Lenzi, A., Lazzerini, F., Cassano, G. B., & Akiskal, H. S. (1986). The comparative efficacy and safety of carbamazepine vs lithium: A randomized double-blind 3-year trial in 83 patients. *Journal of Clinical Psychiatry, 47,* 490–494.

Pope, H. G., McElroy, S. L., Keck, P. E., & Hudson, J. I. (1991). Valproate in the treatment of acute mania. *Archives of General Psychiatry, 48,* 62–68.

Post, R. M., & Uhde, T. W. (1985). Carbamazepine in bipolar illness. *Psychopharmacology Bulletin, 21,* 10–17.

Post, R. M., Uhde, T. W., Roy-Byrne, P. P., & Joffe, R. T. (1987). Correlates of antimanic response to carbamazepine. *Psychiatry Research, 21,* 71–83.

Prien, R. F., Caffey, E. M., & Klett, C. J. (1973). Prophylactic efficacy of lithium carbonate in manic depressive illness. *Archives of General Psychiatry, 28,* 337–341.

Prien, R. F., Caffey, E. M., & Klett, J. (1974a). Factors associated with treatment success on lithium carbonate prophylaxis. *Archives of General Psychiatry, 31,* 189–192.

Prien, R. F., Klett, J., & Caffey, E. M. (1974b). Lithium prophylaxis in recurrent affective illness. *American Journal of Psychiatry, 131,* 198–203.

Prien, R. F., Klett, J., & Caffey, E. M. (1973). Lithium carbonate and imipramine in prevention of affective episodes. *Archives of General Psychiatry, 29,* 420–425.

Prien, R. F., Kupfer, D. J., Mansky, P. A., Small, J. G., Tuason, V. B., Voss, C. B., et al. (1984). Drug therapy in the prevention of recurrences in unipolar and bipolar affective disorders. *Archives of General Psychiatry, 41,* 1096–1104.

Prohaska, M. L., Stern, R. A., Mason, G. A., Nevels, C. T., & Prange, A. J. (1995). Thyroid hormones and lithium-related neuropsychological deficits: A preliminary test of the lithium-thyroid interactive hypothesis. *Journal of the International Neuropsychological Society, 1,* 134.

Prohaska, M. L., Stern, R. A., Nevels, C. T., Mason, G. A., & Prange, A. J. (1996). The relationship between thyroid status and neuropsychological performance in psychiatric outpatients maintained on lithium. *Neuropsychiatry, Neuropsychology, and Behavioral Neurology, 9,* 30–34.

Quitkin, F. M., Kane, J., Rifkin, A., Ramos-Lorenzi, J. R., & Nayak, D. V. (1981). Prophylactic lithium carbonate with and without imipramine for bipolar I patients. *Archives of General Psychiatry, 35,* 902–907.

Regier, D. A., Farmer, M. E., Rae, D. S., Locke, B. Z., Keith, S. J., Judd, L. L., et al. (1990). Comorbidity of mental disorders with alcohol and other drug abuse. *Journal of the American Medical Association, 264,* 2511–2518.

Sachs, G. S., Lafer, B., Stroll, A. L., Banov, M., Thibault, A. B., Tohen, M., et al. (1994). A double-blind trial of bupropion versus desipramine for bipolar depression. *Journal of Clinical Psychiatry, 55,* 391–393.

Segal, J., Berk, M., Brook, S. (1998, May–June). Risperidone compared with both lithium and haloperidol in mania: A double-blind randomized controlled trial. *Clinical Neuropharmacology, 21*(3), 176–180.

Simhandl, C., Denk, E., & Thau, K. (1993). The comparative efficacy of carbamazepine low and high serum level and lithium carbonate in the prophylaxis of affective disorders. *Journal of Affective Disorders, 28,* 221–231.

Smeraldi, E., Benedetti, F., Barbini, B., Campori, E., & Colombo, C. (1999). Sustained antidepressant effect of sleep deprivation combined with pindolol in bipolar depression. *Neuropsychopharmacology, 20,* 380–385.

Sokolski, K. N., Green, C., Maris, D. E., & DeMet, E. M. (1999). Gabapentin as an adjunct to standard mood stabilizers in outpatients with mixed bipolar symptomatology. *Annals of Clinical Psychiatry, 2,* 217–222.

Solomon, D. A., Ryan, C. E., Keithner, G. I., Miller, I. W., Shea, M. T., Kazim, A., et al. (1997). A pilot study of lithium carbonate plus divalproex sodium for the continuation and maintenance treatment of patients with bipolar I disorder. *Journal of Clinical Psychiatry, 58,* 95–99.

Sovner, R. (1988). A clinically significant interaction between carbamazepine and valproic acid. *Journal of Clinical Psychopharmacology* [Letter to Editor], *8,* 448–449.

Squire, L. R., Judd, L. L., Janowsky, D. S., & Huey, L. Y. (1980). Effects of lithium carbonate on memory and other cognitive functions. *American Journal of Psychiatry, 137,* 1042–1046.

Stallone, F., Shelley, E., Mendlewica, J., & Fieve, R. R. (1973). The use of lithium in affective disorder III: A double-blind study of prophylaxis in bipolar illness. *American Journal of Psychiatry, 130*(9) 1006–1010.

Suppes, T., Webb, A., Paul, B., Carmody, T., Kraemer, H., Rush, A. J. (1999). Clinical outcome in a randomized one year trial of clozapine vs treatment as usual for patients with treatment resistant illness and a history of mania. *American Journal of Psychiatry, 156,* 1164–1169.

Swann, A. C., Bowden, C. L., Morris, D., Calabrese, J. R., Petty, F., Small, J., et al. (1997). Depression during mania. *Archives of General Psychiatry, 54,* 37–42.

Szuba, M. P., Baxter, L. R., Altshuler, L. L., Allen, E. M., Guze, B. H., & Schwartz, J. M., et al., (1994): Lithium sustains the acute antidepressant of sleep deprivation: Preliminary findings from a controlled study. *Psychiatry Res* 51: 283-295.

Szuba, M. P., Baxter, L. R., Fairbanks, L. A., Guze, B. H., & Schwartz, J. M. (1991). Effects of partial sleep deprivation on the diurnal variation of mood and motor activity in major depression. *Biological Psychiatry, 30,* 817–829.

Thase, M. E., Mallinger, A. G., McKnight, D., & Himmelhoch, J. M. (1992). Treatment of imipramine resistant recurrent depression, IV: A double-blind crossover study of tranylcypromine for anergic depression. *American Journal of Psychiatry, 149,* 195–198.

Tohen, M., Castillo, J., Baldessarini, R. J., Zarate, C., Jr., & Kando, J. C. (1995). Blood dyscrasias with carbamazepine and valproate: A pharmacoepidemiological study of 2,228 patients at risk. *American Journal of Psychiatry, 152,* 413–418.

Tohen, N., Castillo, J., Pope, H. G., & Herbstein, J. (1994, February). Concomitant use of valproate and carbamazepine in bipolar and schizoaffective disorders. *Journal of Clinical Psychopharmacology, 14,* 67–70.

Tohen, M., Sanger, T. M., McElroy, S. L., Tollefson, G. D., Chengappa, K. N., Daniel, D. G., et al. (1999). Olanzapine vs placebo in the treatment of acute mania. *American Journal of Psychiatry, 156,* 702–709.

Tremont, G., & Stern, R. A. (1997). Use of thyroid hormone to diminish the cognitive side-effects of psychiatric treatment. *Psychopharmacology Bulletin, 33,* 273–280.

Vestergaard, P., Licht, R. W., Bordersen, A., Rasmussen, N. A., Christensen, H., Arngrim, T., et al. (1998). Outcome of lithium prophylaxis: A prospective follow-up of affect disorder patients assigned to high and low serum lithium levels. *Acta Psychiatrica Scandinavia, 98*(4), 310–315.

Vieta, E., Gasto, C., Colom, F., Martinez, A., Otero, A., & Vallejo, J. (1998). Treatment of refractory rapid cycling bipolar disorder with risperidone. [Letter to the editor]. *Journal of Clinical Psychopharmacology, 18,* 172–174.

Waters, B., Lapierre, Y., Gagnon, A., Cahudhry, R., Tremblay, A., Sarantidis, D., et al. (1982). Determination of the optimal concentration of lithium for the prophylaxis of manic-depressive disorder. *Biology & Psychiatry, 17,* 1323–1329.

Watkins, S. E., Callender, K., & Thomas, D. R. (1987). The effect of carbamazepine and lithium on remission from affective illness. *British Journal of Psychiatry, 150,* 180–182.

Wehr, T., Sack, D., Rosenthal, N., & Cowdry, R. W. (1988). Rapid cycling affective disorder: Contributing factors and treatment responses in fifty-one patients. *American Journal of Psychiatry, 145,* 179–184.

Winokur, G., Coryell, W., Keller, M., Endicott, J., & Akiskal, H. (1993). A prospective follow-up of patients with bipolar and primary unipolar affective disorder. *Archives of General Psychiatry, 50,* 457–465.

Wu, J. C., & Bunney, W. E. (1990). The biological basis of antidepressant response to sleep deprivation and relapse: Review and hypothesis. *American Journal of Psychiatry, 147,* 14–21.

CHAPTER 5

Bipolar Disorder in Young People, the Elderly, and Pregnant Women

Vivek Kusumakar
Frank P. MacMaster
Stanley P. Kutcher
Kenneth I. Shulman

Bipolar Disorder in Young People

EPIDEMIOLOGY

North American studies estimate the point prevalence of bipolar disorder at 0.2 to 0.4% for the prepubertal population and about 1.0% in adolescents (Lewinsohn, Klein, & Seeley, 1995; Zarate & Tohen, 1996). There has been no identified gender difference in prevalence. The age of onset for bipolar disorder is earlier (17.1–29.0 years) than major depression (24.8–29.7 years; Bland, 1997). Over 60% of patients with bipolar disorder report onset of mood disorder with depressive symptoms in adolescence and young adulthood.

PHENOMENOLOGY AND DIFFERENTIAL DIAGNOSIS

A number of developmental issues complicate the diagnosis of a mood disorder in children and adolescents. Underdeveloped verbal communication skills in the younger child hinder the interviewing process; hence the clinician's utilization of the observations of collateral informants becomes critical. During adolescence, normal developmental mood shifts complicate the diagnosis of mood disorders (Golombeck & Kutcher, 1990). DSM-IV does not differentiate between criteria for adults and young people in the diagnosis of hypomania and mania (American Psychatric Association, 1994). There are, however, minor modifications for the criteria of a major depressive episode, and the duration of symptoms for cyclothymia and dysthymia.

The most common presentation in children and adolescents is not the classic picture seen in adults. Peripubertally and in adolescence, the course is characterized by mixed episodes, rapid and ultrarapid cycling (Geller et al., 1995; Kutcher, 1993), often presenting as dysphoric behavioral storms. Hence, the alternating episodes of depression and mania or hypomania are not easily identified, and may be mistakenly diagnosed as attention deficit hyperactivity disorder (ADHD) or another disruptive behavior disorder (Kutcher, 1994).

Chaotic biphasic mood dysregulation may be present without meeting diagnostic criteria for either depression, mania, or hypomania and may manifest for months to years through adolescence before the episodes become more clinically distinguishable. Quiescent interepisode periods, episodic disruptive, depressive and obsessive–compulsive or other anxiety symptom clusters, significant alcohol and substance abuse before the age of 14 years, mood congruent psychotic symptoms and subthreshold hypomanic symptoms in the presence of a family history of bipolar disorder should alert the clinician to an emerging or evolving bipolar disorder. Whereas it has become fashionable to conceptualize in terms of comorbid or coexistent conditions, one should also recognize the possibility that many of the phenomena attributed to comorbid conditions may in fact be "symptoms in evolution" of a bipolar disorder.

The major differential psychiatric diagnoses to consider are ADHD, conduct disorder, borderline personality disorder, schizophrenia, and substance abuse (Weller, & Fristall, 1995).

In the majority of adolescent-onset bipolar disorder cases, the initial episode is one of major depression (Kutcher & Robertson, 1994). Hypomania or mania may manifest in a discrete manner later in adolescence or early adulthood. Kutcher et al. (personal communication, 1999) in a sample of adolescent onset subjects report that 75% experienced depression as the first affective episode with a mean age of onset 15.8 years. Interestingly, the mean age of onset for the first manic episode was 16.7 years. The majority of this sample presented with either mixed (74%) mania or a rapid cycling (76%) course of biphasic mood dysregulation at the first manic episode. Comorbidity may also be a more common feature in the early onset versus adult onset population. This further complicates the clinical presentation and diagnosis because the clinician has to decipher the overlap of symptomatology between the primary and secondary conditions.

Although not well studied as yet, initial reports do indicate some differences in presentation noted between prepubertal children, adolescents, and adults (Weller, Weller, & Fristad, 1995). Prepubertal manic children more commonly present with irritability and lability of mood, whereas adolescents are more likely to present with euphoric, grandiose, and paranoid features. Prepubertal manic children with psychosis are more likely than adults to exhibit hallucinations, usually visual (70%) rather than auditory (50%).

Bowring and Kovacs (1992) present four reasons for the difficulty in diagnosing bipolar disorder in the child and adolescent population. They are as follows: (1) the low incidence rate in this population means that the more common disorders, such as ADHD, may be preferentially diagnosed in a child presenting with psychomotor overactivity or irritability; (2) there is considerable variance in presentation, both cross-sectionally and longitudinally; (3) the influence of developmental factors on clinical presentation, as "excessive involvement in pleasurable activities that have a high potential for painful consequences" will differ in meaning or presentation between an 8-year-old, 15-year-old, and 30-year-old and the definition of grandiosity will be in flux for these ages, given that the definition for developmentally appropriate play and fantasizing differs throughout the lifespan; and (4) the commonality of symptoms associated with a variety of childhood disorders confuses the diagnostic process.

Attention deficit and other disruptive behavior disorders are commonly recognized comorbid problems in juvenile bipolar disorder. A family history of disruptive behavior disorders, chronic rather than episodic sleep difficulties, preschool onset attentional problems and hyperactivity, and a chronic course without biphasic mood dysregulation are the hallmarks of ADHD. Children with conduct disorder are more hurtful and vindictive, with little or no guilt or remorse. Flight of ideas, pressured speech, and psychosis are not present, although some young people may demonstrate suspiciousness, but it is usually related to fear of getting caught as opposed to persecutory delusions. However, Biederman et al. (1995), suggest that the nosological picture may be similar in borderline and ADHD in early onset disorder.

Increasingly, generalized anxiety, social phobia, panic, and obsessive–compulsive symptoms are being recognized as commonly coexisting with juvenile bipolar disorder. In fact, in our unpublished data, anxiety disorders are even more common than disruptive behavior problems or substance abuse (Kusumakar, personal observation, 1999). These coexisting symptomatologies often do not meet criteria for a separate comorbid disorder, but nevertheless have major adverse effects on medication efficacy, scholastic or work performance, and interpersonal and other social functioning.

Personality disorders have a comorbidity rate of between 22 and 68% with bipolar disorder (Hirschfeld, 1999). Borderline personality disorder has a prevalence rate of between 21 and 30% in bipolar subjects (Barbato & Hafner, 1998; O'Connell, Mayo, & Sciutto, 1991). The affective aspects of borderline personality disorder include labile affect, irritability, instability of mood, stress, and low mood (dysphoria). The impulsive aspects of borderline personality disorder include tendency to overdose, self-mutilation, suicidal behavior, food or alcohol binges, promiscuity, and assaultive or other antisocial acts. However, the mood fluctuations in borderline personality disorder are classically from depression to euthymia. Biphasic mood dysregulation, from depression to hypomania or mania, is a hallmark of bipolar disorder. Ultrarapid cycling bipolar disorder in adolescence and early adulthood may underlie some borderline personality functioning seen in this age group in some instances.

It has long been an "accepted," but mistaken notion that schizophrenia has an earlier age of onset than borderline, that the latter is rare in adolescents, and virtually unknown in childhood. This notion may explain why children and adolescents presenting with psychotic symptoms are commonly diagnosed with schizophrenia. Months or years later, the biphasic mood changes become apparent in many and they are rediagnosed with borderline. Carlson, Fennig, and Bromet (1994), in their sample of 231 hospitalized psychotic patients (15 to 60 years old), found that more than 50% of the young borderline cases were initially misdiagnosed. Akiskal (1996) described the common reasons for misdiagnosis of borderline as schizophrenia and they are as follows: (1) there is overreliance on cross-sectional instead of longitudinal presentation; (2) incomplete interepisode recovery is equated with schizophrenia; (3) psychotic symptoms are equated with schizophrenia; (4) clinicians presume irritability to be due to paranoid delusion; (5) clinicians attribute depressive symptoms and apathy to negative schizophrenia symptomatology; (6) flight of ideas are misperceived as loosening of associations; and (7) there is the presumption that Schneiderian symptoms are diagnostic of schizophrenia psychosis, although they can also be present in manic psychosis.

Problem substance abuse can coexist with early onset bipolar disorder and may even cloud the clinical picture for many years. However, episodic substance abuse, substance abuse temporally related to affective episodes, presence of biphasic mood symptoms in the absence of substance abuse, and a family history of bipolar disorder can help the clinician in the diagnosis of bipolar disorder.

TREATMENT

Foundations of Effective Management

As bipolar disorder is a recurrent, relapsing, and, in a proportion of young people, chronic condition, a longitudinal therapeutic relationship between the young person and family, and the treatment team is the cornerstone of effective treatment (Kusumakar, Yatham, Haslam, Parikh, Matte, Sharma, et al., 1997). The goals of the therapeutic relationship should be to recognize symptoms and dysfunction early so that support and early effective interventions can be instituted to control symptoms, prevent deterioration, promote healthy development, and achieve reasonable functioning.

It is essential to promote family involvement in understanding the illness and the scope and limitations of treatment interventions. Families need support and help to cope with the burden of illness not only because bipolar disorder in a young person can pose many challenges to the family's emotional, energy, and financial reserves but also because it is not uncommon for more than one family member to be affected by a psychiatric disorder. Families can play a major role in the promotion of treatment adherence in the young person, early detection of symptoms or dysfunction, and support of healthy functioning. Getting various family members to work in concordance is most helpful as discordant family relationships with high expressed negative emotions and attitudes can jeopardize healthy supports for the young person, decrease treatment adherence, and also increase stress in an already vulnerable young person.

It may take many months, if not years, and many episodes before the young person and the clinical team develop a robust and effective relationship. As illness and treatment can challenge the quest for autonomy, the young person may, from time to time, experience the clinical team as restrictive. The clinician should be prepared to contain and deal with passive and deferential attitudes or oppositional and defiant stances on the part of the young person at different stages in the therapeutic encounter. Some of this may be part of the young person coming to an "accommodation" with his or her illness and treatment.

While instilling hope, the clinician and team also need to help the young

person, family and significant others to understand the recurrent and fluc-
tuating nature of bipolar disorder, the associated morbidity and mortality,
and the opportunities presented by implementation of effective treatment.
The effective and empathic management of feelings of denial, guilt, self-
blame, and hostility can significantly improve the potential for a collaborative and individualized treatment plan.

It is also very important to assist the young person and family to identify a supportive network of people who will, in an effective yet
nonstigmatizing manner, help the young person seek or continue in treatment. They may also often require active assistance to maintain and not
jeopardize key relationships and school or work situations.

Although pharmacotherapy is an effective and potent treatment for
bipolar disorder, one cannot underestimate the value of psychoeducation
and psychotherapy as an adjunct to medication. Many young people have
experienced subsyndromal dysfunction in emotions and behavior, and may
also have suffered a decline in scholastic and relationship functioning. It is
not uncommon for there having been months, if not years, of different diagnoses being considered and unsuccessful attempts with treatment interventions before a diagnosis of bipolar disorder is considered and appropriate
treatment initiated. During this protracted pathway into appropriate care
young people and families often experience considerable frustration, loss
of hope, and inappropriate labeling of their problems.

Medical Management and Investigations

As with adults, it is essential to conduct a full medical examination to rule
out any underlying medical problem, and treat any problem that may exist.
There is little empirical evidence for the need for extensive laboratory investigations in the absence of findings on a good history and physical examination. However, most clinics would do a complete blood count including
platelets, serum electrolytes, liver enzymes, TSH, serum creatinine,
urinanalysis, and urine toxicology for substance use (Kusumakar, Yatham,
Haslam, Parikh, Matte, Silverstone, et al., 1997). A serum pregnancy test
should be done as clinically indicated. There is no evidence, from published literature in adult bipolar disorder and epilepsy, that serum medication levels, blood counts, and liver functions need to be done frequently.
After two consecutive serum levels have been confirmed to be in the target
range in the acute phase of treatment, serum levels need to be repeated after
4 weeks and once every 6 months thereafter. Similarly, other investigations
need be done at baseline, 4 weeks into treatment and once every 6 months.
Serum levels or investigations may be repeated more frequently if clini-

cally indicated (Kusumakar, Yatham, Haslam, Parikh, Matte, Silverstone, et al., 1997).

Mood Stabilizers

There is no published double-blind placebo controlled study of the antimanic effects of mood stabilizers in mania in young people (Papatheodorou & Kutcher, 1996). However, there are currently studies under way with both lithium and divalproex in adolescent mania. Strober and colleagues (Strober et al., 1988 and Strober et al., 1995) studied two cohorts of adolescents who were treated with lithium begun during acute mania. About 68% responded well to this medication, while preadolescent mania was less responsive. However, Geller and colleagues (1998), in a prospective study of young people with borderline and comorbid substance dependency, demonstrated that lithium was superior to placebo.

Whereas lithium can be effective in pure adolescent mania (Geller et al., 1998; McKnew et al., 1981) it has a narrow therapeutic range, with reduced efficacy below 0.8 mmols/L, increased adverse effects, particularly cognitive, above 1.1 mmols/L and can be lethal in overdose. Lithium likely has a shorter half-life in children than in adults due to more efficient renal clearance in children (Vitiello et al., 1988). The onset of action of lithium can be from seven to 14 days, and patients do not tolerate well oral loading doses of lithium. Thus it can take days to weeks to achieve therapeutic levels with lithium. Kusumakar and colleagues (Kusumakar, Yatham, Haslam, Parikh, Matte, Silverstone, et al., 1997), summarized the predictors of lithium response to include pure mania, family history of response to lithium, and mania as the first mood disorder episode. The predictors of lithium nonresponse included mixed states, rapid cycling, and depression as the first mood disorder episode. Further, because of the narrow safety range of lithium, it is not a drug of choice in impulsive, actively suicidal young people, and in chaotic families where monitoring of serum levels and side effects can be elusive.

Acne, tremor, weight gain, and cognitive side effects ("fog in the head") are commonly reported side effects of lithium by young people. Cognitive impairment due to lithium treatment has been well documented in two separate studies in children with aggression and depression respectively (Geller, Fox, & Clark, 1994; Silva et al., 1992). Long-term use is associated with hypothyroidism, and there is an increased risk of renal dysfunction in patients who have a history of overdose on lithium, or family or personal history of renal disease.

Divalproex sodium has been shown to be effective in open studies with adolescents (Papatheodorou & Kutcher, 1993). There is very robust data in adult mania showing that divalproex and lithium are equal in efficacy and superior to placebo (Bowden et al., 1994). Divalproex has the advantage of being well tolerated in loading doses of 20 to 30 mg/kg per day in mania in adults as well as in adolescents (McElroy et al., 1996). Although there is no therapeutic range per se for DVP, Bowden and colleagues (1996) have shown that it is less effective when serum levels are below 45 mg/ml (approximately 330 mmols/L) and is associated with increased adverse effects when serum levels exceed 125 mg/ml (approximately 800 μmols/L). Data from adult studies suggests that divalproex is efficacious in pure mania, mixed states, and rapid cycling bipolar disorder (Kusumakar, Yatham, Haslam, Parikh, Matte, Silverstone, et al., 1997).

Divalproex is generally better tolerated by adolescents than lithium, and this is also reflected in better compliance with divalproex compared with lithium; weight gain is reported in monotherapy with both medications. The reports of hepatic failure with divalproex are primarily in preadolescents on polytherapy. Blood dyscrasias with divalproex are as rare as with tricyclic antidepressants (TCAs). Transient thrombocytopenia is a well-recognized phenomenon associated with divalproex treatment. It needs active treatment and discontinuation of medication only if it is persistent, severe or clinically relevant. Isojarvi, Laatikainen, Pakarinen, et al. (1993) and Isojarvi, Laatikainen, Knip et al. (1996) reported that young females receiving valproic acid for epilepsy were significantly more likely to develop obesity and polycystic ovary syndrome when compared with those not being treated with divalproex. The relationship between bipolar disorder, treatment with divalproex, obesity, and polycystic ovary syndrome warrants further study; hence young female patients should be carefully monitored.

Although there is published data with adult manics treated with carbamazepine, there is only limited data of its efficacy in adolescents with bipolar disorder. There is no specific study in mania as such, although there is a published report of the efficacy of carbamazepine in lithium resistant adolescents (Himmelhoch & Garfinkel, 1986). There is no proven serum therapeutic level for carbamazepine. Moderate and severe blood dyscrasias have been noted in up to 2.1% of psychiatric patients treated with carbamazepine (Tohen, Castillo, Baldessarini, Zarate, & Kando, 1995). Dermatological complications can be a significant problem and can be heralded by a delayed onset rash.

There is consensus that, for a patient on maintenance treatment, the emergence of severe insomnia or hypomanic symptoms can herald a full-blown mania, and that the use of benzodiazepines, both to help with sleep and "nip mania in the bud," is a reasonable intervention. In mild cases, advice on sleep hygiene and stoppage of any substances that interfere with sleep may be sufficient treatment.

Neuroleptics

There is no controlled study with neuroleptics in juvenile mania. Although there is growing evidence for the efficacy of the newer generation of neuroleptics, such as olanzapine (Tohen, Sanger, et al., 1999) and risperidone (Segal, Beric, & Brook, 1998; Yatham, 2000) in acute mania with or without psychotic symptoms in adults, many young people find the dramatic weight gain, more with olanzapine than risperidone, and galactorhhea with risperidone, as unacceptable, thus affecting compliance. Typical neuroleptics offer the advantage of being able to be administered parenterally (e.g., haloperidol or zuclopenthixol) but carry the risk of acute dystonic reactions, provocation of depression and tardive dyskinesia, and hence should be used only for brief periods and only if absolutely needed.

Other Medication Treatments

In an open study of lamotrigine augmentation of divalproex treatment in bipolar depression, it was reported that this combination was effective even in adolescents within this sample (Kusumakar & Yatham, 1997). Lamotrigine has to be used with great caution, particularly in younger adolescents, in view of the danger of a rash progressing to Steven-Johnson's syndrome. The risk of rash with lamotrigine is increased with rapid up-titration of the dose or combination with medications like divalproex, which nearly double the serum levels of lamotrigine.

There is little data on young people that would allow the recommendation, at this point in time, of the value of combining lithium with either divalproex or carbamazepine. However, these combinations are not uncommon in clinical practice with young people with refractory bipolar depression.

If selective serotonin reuptake inhibitor (SSRI) antidepressants are to be used in adolescent bipolar depression they are better restricted to the acute phase and used under the cover of a mood stabilizer, which reduces but does not totally eliminate the risk of manic switch and induction of accelerated cycling. It is common practice to reduce and gradually discontinue the antidepressants starting 4 to 6 weeks after euthymia has been achieved. However, there will always be patients who relapse when discontinuation of antidepressants is attempted, and who require antidepressants with mood stabilizers over the longer term. Tricyclic antidepressants should be avoided because they cause switch and accelerated cycling, without being effective in many young people (Geller, Fox, & Fletcher, 1993).

Light Therapy

Light therapy, twice daily at 10,000 lux for 2 weeks, added to ongoing thymoleptic treatment has been demonstrated, in an open study (Papatheodorou & Kutcher, 1995), to effectively treat bipolar depressive symptoms. Clinically, this treatment seems most useful if applied early on in the onset of the depressive episode (Kutcher, personal communication, 1998).

Electroconvulsive Therapy (ECT)

Electroconvulsive therapy (ECT) is known to be effective in adolescent depression (Kutcher, 1994), although there are no specific studies in bipolar depression. The efficacy and relative safety of ECT have been reasonably established in adolescent depression (Kutcher & Marton, 1996). However, there is considerable negative mythology about ECT particularly in adolescents, leading to this treatment being not considered even where there are obvious clinical indications for its use. From published literature (Yatham et al., 1997) related to adults with bipolar depression, ECT is one of the most effective treatments in both the depressive and manic phases of bipolar illness. Hence, ECT should be considered as an option at least in adolescents with refractory or chronic bipolar depression, bipolar depression with chronic and significant suicidal or homicidal risk, and where there is a clinical picture of severe psychomotor retardation or agitation.

Prophylaxis

Unfortunately, there is no published data from double-blind placebo controlled trials of the value of mood stabilizers in maintenance treatment in young people. Strober, Morrell, et al. (1990), Stroker, Schmidt-Lackner, et al. (1995) recommend keeping adolescents on mood stabilizer treatment throughout the teenage years. Their data, albeit from an open study, is supportive of maintenance lithium treatment for adolescents with bipolar disorder based on the findings that 63% remained well on lithium compared only 8% of whom discontinued lithium. Strober et al (personal communication, 1999) in a case control comparison of lithium and valproate in adolescents with mixed mania found both medications effective in the acute phase. However, the probability of remaining well by the third year of follow up was approximately 80% for valproate compared with 50% for lithium, thus representing a two-fold increase in the hazard of relapse in lithium treated subjects.

We have analyzed data from a case control open study of early onset ($n = 38$) and adult onset ($n = 38$) bipolar subjects matched for gender and duration of illness, and who were compliant with maintenance treatment over 3 years with lithium or divalproex sodium. We found that adolescents with bipolar disorder responded significantly better to divalproex, with 60% of young people having adequate episode suppression compared with 27% in the lithium treated group (Kusumakar, personal observation, 2000). Serum levels of valproic acid were over 500 mmols/L and lithium were between 0.8 to 1.1 mmols/L. However, over 60% of the young people in this study suffered from rapid cycling or mixed states, predictors of lithium nonresponse. Further, over 80% of both groups of young people continued to exhibit subthreshold symptoms and considerable dysfunction at the end of 3 years, even in "responders." These findings emphasize both the need to recognize the recurrent, relapsing, and even chronic nature of the symptoms and dysfunction in juvenile bipolar disorder, and to also strive to identify newer and more efficacious treatments for prophylaxis.

Bipolar Disorder in the Elderly

BACKGROUND

Considerable confusion pervades the diagnosis and classification of manic syndromes in old age. Many manic syndromes in the elderly are present in the context of medical conditions and medical treatment. In these situations it is difficult, if not impossible, to differentiate between a mania that is a direct consequence of a medical condition or its treatment (secondary bipolar disorder) and when it is a truly comorbid condition. Given that only a few elderly patients with serious medical and neurologic conditions present with manic symptoms, it would be risky to conclude that mania is a direct consequence of a medical condition. Borderline is a chronic illness (Angst & Weis, 1967; Zis & Goodman, 1979), so many cases that originate in youth and adulthood persist into old age. Although it may be misdiagnosed or not recognized, the late primary onset of borderline in community samples is infrequent, but present, in seniors. Whereas the dichotomy between primary and secondary mania in the elderly may have some value in the presence of a treatable underlying medical condition, symptomatic treatment of the mania may still be warranted in the majority of cases.

EPIDEMIOLOGY, ONSET, COURSE, AND OUTCOME

The Epidemiological Catchment Area (ECA) study (Weissman et al., 1996) showed a decreasing prevalence with age from a high of 1.4% in young adults to less than 0.1% in those above the age of 65 years. Goodwin and Jamison (1990) estimated that between 1 and 3% of borderline patients experience the onset over 60 years of age. However, this may be due to inadequate–inaccurate histories being taken as a depressive episode may occur many years prior to a manic episode (Shulman & Post, 1980). In a study of borderline patients diagnosed for the first time after age 60, 42% had had a prior depressive or manic episode (Stone, 1989). Relatively high treated prevalence rates (4–18% percent) are reported on inpatient psychogeriatric units (Post et al., 1982; Yassa, Nair, Nasyase, Camille, & Belzile, 1988), while incidence of first admission rates for mania increase with age (Spicer, Hare, & Slater, 1973; Eagles & Whalley, 1985). The earlier the age of onset, the more likely there is a positive family history of bipolar disorder (Stone, 1989).

Almost 20% of all first admission rates for mania occurred after the age of 60 in a Finnish study (Rasanen, Tiihonen, & Hakkp, 1998). About half of elderly manic inpatients have experienced depression as the first mood disorder episode (Broadhead, Blazer, George, & Tse, 1990; Shulman, Tohen, Satlin, Mallya, & Kalunian, 1992). There is often a long latency period, averaging 15 years, before mania becomes manifest. A small subgroup may pursue a course of unipolar mania (Shulman & Tohen, 1994). The prognosis of mania in old age appears to have improved across studies (Dhingra & Rabins, 1991). Seventy-two percent of patients who were still alive were symptom free and often living independently. There is a high mortality rate in elderly bipolar patients, with approximately one third to one half of the original cohort having died in the 5- to 7-year follow-up period (Shulman, Tohen, Satlin, et al., 1992). Berrios and Bakshi (1991) reported mania was less likely to respond to regular treatment than depression in the elderly, and that cognitive dysfunction was prevalent in association with cerebrovascular disease.

CLINICAL ASPECTS

Presentation is heterogeneous, with more agitation than florid mania, delusions, poor treatment response and outcome (Baldessarini, 1984). Anecdotally, there are reports of increased risk of mixed states in the elderly (Post et al., 1982). Cognitive dysfunction has been consistently identified in association with manic syndromes in late life (Shulman, 1997). Increased comorbid neurological conditions and general medical disorders are found in elderly populations. However, there is still no consensus whether irreversible dementia is more common in the presence of mania. Right sided lesions are more common in mania of old age, and more specific involvement of orbitofrontal and basal temporal cortices have been postulated (Cummings, 1993; Starkstein, Chemerinski, et al., 1997; Starkstein, Mayberg, et al., 1990). Lesions associated with secondary mania are, however, heterogenous and are linked with head injuries, chronic alcoholism, tumors, endocrine disorders, AIDS, and multiple sclerosis. Hence, polypharmacy and complex treatment strategies are common in this age group. The consideration of other medical conditions is paramount in the case of elderly patients (Sargenti, Rizos, & Jeste, 1988). As organic brain syndrome is common in 15% of borderline patients and even more so in elderly borderline patients (23%), it is important to rule this out as a causative factor for the symptom presentation (Goodwin & Jamison, 1990). Many other neurological conditions present with manic or depressive symptoms and diligent assessment is required. The reverse is also true, with some neurological conditions being mistaken for borderline, such as Alzheimer's disease. Presentation may also be interpreted as schizophrenia or schizoaffective disorders if an accurate history is not uncovered (Goodwin & Jamison, 1990).

TREATMENT

There are no published controlled treatment trials in bipolar disorder in the elderly (Shulman & Herrmann, 1999). Age associated increased risk of severity of side effects experienced by the elderly (Smith & Helms, 1982) is well documented. This is probably due to age and illness related changes to the brain, liver, kidney, and other organ systems, and to polypharmacy. Seniors have a more pronounced sensitivity to the neurotoxic effects of antimanic agents (Strayhorn & Nash, 1977). The clinician must differentiate these from the normal deficits associated with aging. The elderly are also more vulnerable to tardive dyskinesia secondary to neuroleptic treatment. With the above limitations in mind, ECT is used commonly in this age group (Fink, 1997). However, the mix of psychotic features/agitation results in the clinician utilizing combinations of antipsychotics and mood stabilizers. These combinations increase the possibility of untoward effects and delirium in the elderly than in younger populations (Sargenti et al., 1988).

Lithium and valproate have been used as first-line treatment in acute mania. However, in the presence of a mixed manic state, valproate is associated with better effectiveness. With regard to the gold standard, a review of findings of uncontrolled trials suggest a response rate of 70% for lithium, which is comparable to efficacy in younger (adult and pediatric) patients. A positive initial response to treatment has been reported to be sustained in follow up examinations (Abou-Saleh & Coppen, 1989). However, whether lithium response diminishes with age is still a controversial topic. Some investigators have noted a loss of efficacy, while others have doubted this (Hewick, Newbury, Hopwood, Naylor, & Moody, 1977; Murray, Hopwood, Balfour, Ogston, & Hewick, 1983). Benzodiazepines and neuroleptics, preferably atypical neuroleptics, are often used for insomnia, psychotic symptoms, agitation, or hostility. These adjunctive medications should be tapered down and discontinued about 6 to 12 weeks after stabilization. Substituting or adding a second mood stabilizer can be a useful strategy in patients who do not respond adequately in 2 to 3 weeks. For more details of a treatment algorithm see the chapter on treatment of mania (chapter 1).

The major confound with regard to lithium, however, is that while some senior subjects benefit and tolerate therapy, others suffer adverse effects. Neurotoxic effects have been seen in elderly patients with serum lithium concentrations commonly tolerated by young patients (0.75–1.00 mmol/L). Negative effects seem to correlate proportionately with dose or blood concentration of lithium (Chacko, Marsh, Marmion, Dworkin, & Telschow, 1987). Oral–facial dyskinesias, confusion, delirium, and a marked worsening of Parkinson's disease have been noted (Chacko et al., 1987; Himmelhoch, Neil, et al., 1980; Post et al., 1982; Roose, Bone, Haidorfer, Dunner, & Fieve, 1979; Shukla, Cook, Hoff, & Aronson, 1988; Smith & Helms, 1982; Strayhorn & Nash, 1977). The typically observed effects such as thirst and polyuria/nocturia, are just as common as in younger patients. Aside from toxicity, intolerance to lithium may also confound any possible benefits. Patients with comorbid neurological or psychiatric illness may not respond as well to lithium treatment (Black, Winokur, Bell, Nasrallah, & Hulbert, 1988), nor will patients with psychotic symptoms (Johnson et al., 1971; Young & Klerman, 1992). Unfortunately, as noted earlier, the elderly borderline patient is commonly afflicted with comorbidity. As renal clearance is diminished in the elderly, dosages for adults should be halved to enhance tolerance and safety.

Studies of other treatments are even fewer in number. For example, neuroleptics are commonly used in geriatric borderline patients despite limited controlled study of efficacy and more importantly, safety. This is especially curious because the elderly are particularly prone to developing Parkinsonism and tardive dyskinesia (Baldessarini, 1985). Even the low potency neuroleptics carry the possibility of inducing confusion or delirium (Frankenburg & Zanarini, 1994). There are only scant case reports regarding valproate, carbamazepine and verapamil, but valproate was noted to be fairly well tolerated in the elderly (McFarland, Miller, & Straumfjord, 1990; Shulman & Herrman, 1999).

The treatment of bipolar depression is the same as in younger patients (see chapter 2), with mood stabilizers and ECT being mainstays of treatment. Antidepressants, especially trycyclic antidepressants (TCAs), should be used with caution, particularly because they may produce switch or accelerate cycling. Ensuring normal or stable thyroid functioning is essential. ECT is a relatively safe, effective treatment in the acute phases of both mania and depression and can often be administered to patients on multiple medications.

Lithium and valproate can be used in the prophylactic treatment of bipolar disorder in the elderly. Carbamazepine is an inducer of cytochrome P250-2D6 and because it is highly protein bound, it has the significant potential for drug interactions (Shulman & Herrmann, 1999). Due to concerns of neurotoxicity in old age, low serum levels are recommended, less than 9 mg/ml. Gabapentin, in anxious patients, and lamotrigine in depressed patients or with rapid cycling, may be useful adjunctive medications when added to lithium or valproate. However, only case reports in the elderly are available.

Bipolar Disorder during Pregnancy and Postpartum

INTRODUCTION

Historically, there have been changing views regarding the advice given to women about the management of mood disorders and pregnancy. In the 1950s and 1960s, women had a significant chance of being advised by physicians to avoid pregnancy because of the perceived likelihood of passing on a genetically transmitted disease for which there was limited effective treatment. In the early 1970s, the prophylactic value of lithium was recognized and there was concern about its teratogenic effects, so women were routinely advised to avoid lithium during the first trimester of pregnancy. Pregnancy is often seen as a period of quiescence for psychiatric illness;

however, more recent data suggests that pregnancy neither increases nor decreases the risk of psychiatric illness (Lier, Kastrup, & Rafaelson, 1989 Viguera et al., 2000). The postpartum period has been increasingly recognized as a period of high risk for the first onset, recurrence, or exacerbation of serious psychiatric disorders (Brockington, Cernik, et al., 1981; Dean, Williams, & Brockington, 1989; Kendell, Chalmers, & Platz, 1987; Reich & Winokur, 1970).

Epidemiology, Clinical Aspects, and Hypotheses

Pregnancy is reported to be associated with relatively low incidence of psychiatric disorders, reported to be 7.1 per 10,000 woman years when compared with 35 per 10,000 woman years in nonchildbearing years (Paffenbarger, 1982). Marzuk and colleagues (1997) reported from a population based study that pregnant women of childbearing age were at significantly lower risk of suicide compared with women who were not pregnant. Sharma and Persad (1995) and Sharma (1997) have observed that pregnancy is likely associated with greater periods of euthymia in some women with bipolar disorder when compared with the course of their illness prepregnancy. Groff et al. (personal communication, 2000) have also observed that women with classical bipolar I disorder, who did not take lithium during pregnancy, remained well in most cases during their pregnancies. Groff and colleagues (2000) studied data gathered during the first pregnancy in 28 women from Canada and Europe with bipolar I disorder who were considered to be lithium responders. The subjects were drawn from the International Group for the Study of Lithium-treated-patients (IGSLI) database, which is noted for diagnostic and follow-up data integrity. The women experienced only one-fourth the expected number of episodes and one eighth the expected length of episodes compared with their prepregnancy course of illness. Their illness course prior to pregnancy was not different from the course of childless women with illness of similar duration. Findings that pregnancy may be a period of relative quiescence during the course of a psychiatric disorder are often contested mainly because psychiatric disorders have, historically, not been studied adequately (Brockington et al., 1981; Brockington, 1988; Leibenluft, 1996). There are also contradictory reports of depression and schizophrenia worsening during pregnancy (Altshuler & Szuba, 1994; Kitamura, Sugawara, Sugawara, Toda, & Shima, 1996; Kumar & Robson, 1984; Spielvogel & Wile, 1986, 1992). Furthermore, recent data suggests that pregnancy is risk neutral for bipolar disorder, that is, it does not increase or decrease the risk of bipolar disorder (Lier et al., 1989; Viguera et al., 2000).

There is growing interest in the observation that there may be an increased risk for prepartum recurrence or exacerbation of psychiatric illness in the 4 to 6 weeks before delivery (Brockington, Oates, & Rose, 1990; Grof et al., 2000; Paffenberger & McCabe, 1966).

There is overwhelming consensus in the literature that there is a high incidence (10%) of postpartum depression (Kendell et al., 1987; Parry, 1989). Although postpartum illnesses often begin within 1 to 3 weeks after childbirth, there may, in some instances, be a delayed onset of 6 weeks to 3 to 4 months after delivery. The risk for postpartum psychosis is one in 1,000, and occurs in about 50% of women with previous episodes of bipolar disorder (Cohen, Sichel, Robertson, Heckscher, & Rosenbaum, 1995; Stewart, Klompenhouwer, Kendell, & van Hulst, 1991). Grof et al.'s (in press) study from the IGSLI database showed that 25% of women with bipolar I disorder experienced postpartum mood dysfunction. British, German, and Dutch studies have demonstrated that most episodes of postpartum psychosis start abruptly between 3 to 14 days into the postpartum period (Dean & Kendell, 1981; Klompenhouwer & van Hulst 1991; Rohde & Marneros, 1993; Schopf & Rust, 1994). These episodes tend to be severe, and are mainly made up of depressive, manic, dysphoric manic, psychotic, and confusional symptoms. When psychotic thoughts predominate, risk for deliberate self-harm, infanticide, and homicide is significant. There may be periods of lucidity in the midst of frightening psychosis even during periods of high risk (Spinelli, 1999).

Interestingly, pregnancy and childbirth may have adverse consequences in the spouses of women with bipolar disorder, with up to 50% of them experiencing mood disorder symptoms (Davenport & Adland, 1982).

There have been many theories put forward to explain the increased risk of psychiatric disorder in the postpartum period, and in some women, even in the 4 to 6 weeks prepartum. Research is increasing focusing on corticotropin releasing hormone (CRH), which may have a potential effect on mood regulation in the central nervous system (Modell et al., 1998; Tsigos & Chrousos, 1994). CRH, which is produced both by the placenta and the hypothalamus, has been observed to be low in women with postpartum mood changes, raising the possibility that the hypothalamus adjusts poorly to the dramatic drop in CRH after delivery when placental CRH is no longer available (Chrousas, 1995; Dorn & Chrousas, 1997). The production of placental hormones normally increases during pregnancy, but it occasionally decreases during the final weeks before delivery (Smith et al., 1990). This phenomenon may be linked to prepartum mood disorders occurring in the 4- to 6-week period before delivery.

Although the clinician is well advised to consider bipolar disorder as a possibility in any florid psychiatric illness postpartum, she or he should also consider the following differential diagnoses: schizophrenia, schizoaffective illness, autoimmune thyroiditis, vitamin B^{12} deficiency, central nervous system infections, cerebral embolism, seizure disorder and anoxia, and concomitant alcohol and substance abuse.

MANAGEMENT AND TREATMENT DURING PREGNANCY AND POSTPARTUM

In the event of a planned pregnancy, the woman with bipolar disorder, and key family members with her consent, should be involved in receiving information and support to make appropriate choices. The foci should include: (1) Development of a collaborative management plan; (2) likely course of bipolar disorder during pregnancy and postpartum, and level of risk thereof to the mother, fetus, and newborn; (3) risks and benefits of therapy and treatment during the different stages of pregnancy and postpartum.

Foundations for Effective Management

The primary foundation will be to establish a collaborative plan between the patient, family, key friends, obstetric and psychiatric teams, family practitioner, and other helping professionals or agencies, throughout the course of the pregnancy and postpartum period. In addition, the treatment team should have ready access to a summary that includes the episodicity and course of the bipolar illness prepregnancy, history of deliberate self-harm, impulsive and destructive stimulus seeking behaviors, comorbidity including alcohol and substance abuse, previous treatment response and adherence to treatment plans. This would allow for credible risk–benefit analyses at different time points.

Bipolar Disorder during Pregnancy and Postpartum, and Level of Risk Thereof to the Mother, Fetus, and Newborn

Many mothers and their families are interested in knowing about the risk to the child of inheriting bipolar disorder. The lifetime risk of the offspring of a mother with bipolar I disorder developing a bipolar disorder has been variously estimated at between 12 and 20% (Gershon, 1990). The risk is increased if there is a multigenerational history of bipolar disorder, if the father has bipolar disorder too, and the mother has had a younger age of onset of illness herself. This information needs to be provided in a humane and nonalarmist manner with the caveat that the predictive value of the above is not foolproof.

If the mother remains psychiatrically well during pregnancy and post-partum, she is not an alcohol or drug user, and she is medically well, the fetus and newborn will not be at any significant additional risk of immediate problems. However, episodes of mood disorder, psychosis, alcohol or substance abuse, or an unstable medical condition in the mother will increase risk for the fetus and the newborn through increased risk of impulsive, destructive, and unhealthy lifestyle, and risk of deliberate self-harm, abuse and neglect, and infanticide.

Teratogenic Risks from and Secretion in Breast Milk of Psychotropic Medications

The primary risk period for the developing embryo and fetus from psychotropic medications is in the first trimester of pregnancy. Medications may also interact with other drugs administered during delivery, produce immediate toxic effects in the newborn if they are continued through childbirth, and are invariably secreted in the breast milk.

Contrary to previous estimates, the risk of teratogenicity with fetal exposure to mood stabilizers is lower with lithium than with valproate or carbamazapine. The incidence of neural tube defects is about 1% with carbamazapine and 1 or 2% with valproate (American Academy of Pediatrics Committee on drugs report 2000 for a review; (2000). Both carbamazapine and valproate have also been reported to be associated with higher than expected rates of fetal craniofacial defects, fingernail hypoplasia, and developmental delay. The rate of spina bifida in fetuses exposed to valproate is much higher than the risk of lithium induced Ebstein's cardiac anomaly (Altshuler et al., 1996). Altshuler and colleagues (1996) have noted that, although there is less of a risk for Ebstein's anomaly through exposure to lithium in the first trimester than previously feared, it is still 20 times higher (1:1000) in the lithium exposed group when compared with incidence in the general population (1:20,000 births). Lithium is known to cause a hypotonia and a floppy babylike syndrome, and even toxicity in the newborn if continued through childbirth.

Haloperidol is not associated with teratogenicity, unlike aliphatic phenothiazines (AAPC, 2000). Fetal cardiac function problems are associated with low potency antipsychotic medications that have anticholinergic effects (AAPC, 2000). Many typical neuroleptics may also cause muscle spasm, tremor, and sedation in the newborn if used in the mother through childbirth. There is no systematic data about the teratogenic effects of the atypical neuroleptics, like risperidone and olanzapine. However, there is growing clinical consensus that these agents are likely associated with lower teratogenic risk. All antipsychotic medications are secreted through the breast milk.

Tricyclic antidepressants (TCAs) appear to have little potential for teratogenecity (AAPC, 2000; Pies, 1998). Pastuszak et al. (1993) found no evidence of teratogenecity in 128 women who took fluoxetine in the first trimester of pregnancy when compared with matched control subjects. This study found that there was a trend toward higher miscarriage rates in the fluoxetine group, but Chambers et al. (1996) in a separate study did not find this to be true. It should be borne in mind that depression itself increases the risk for miscarriage. Nulman et al. (1997) found that in utero exposure to either TCAs or fluoxetine does not affect global IQ, language development, or behavior development in preschoolers. There is only sparse data on antidepressants other than desipramine, nortriptyline, and fluoxetine. Clomipramine and other antidepressants associated with anticholinergic effects carry the risk of inducing fetal arrhythmias, urinary retention, and intestinal obstruction (Pies, 1998). All antidepressants are secreted in the breast milk.

Benzodiazepines are associated with a small (less than 1%) but higher (than in the general population) (0.06%) risk for cleft lip and cleft palate when used in the first trimester of pregnancy. These medications are also secreted in the breast milk.

Management during the First Trimester of Pregnancy

Although, ideally, the pregnant woman should be managed without medication in the first trimester, there are two instances in which women will receive psychotropic medications during this period. First, women who conceive without planning for it will likely be on medications during crucial stages of the first trimester before they know they are pregnant. Second, in women who have a high risk of relapse, predicted by serious relapses on previous discontinuations of medication or previous history of psychiatric illness even through the first trimester of pregnancy, the risk to themselves and the fetus thereof, cannot justify discontinuation of medications. If patients are already on a mood stabilizer, or a mood stabilizer is seen as the best clinical choice, the patient should have appropriate and timely monitoring, amniocentesis and cell studies (for neural tube defects), and ultrasound examinations between weeks 18 to 20 (for cardiac or other anomalies). In the event that fetal malformations or defects are confirmed, the mother and family will need considerable support to make choices, including a termination of pregnancy. If elective treatment is planned in the first trimester for a mood disorder, mania, or psychosis, the medications of choice are a selective serotonin reuptake inhibitor (SSRI) (for depression) and haloperidol or fluphenazine (for mania or psychosis). As previously stated, although systematic data is not available for risperidone or olanzapine, clinical experience suggests that these may also carry lower risk and should be considered for those patients who cannot tolerate the side effects of haloperidol or fluphenazine. Excessive weight gain, commonly associated with atypical neuroleptics, can itself produce complications during pregnancy, and hence should be used with care. Electroconvulsive therapy (ECT) is an effective and safe treatment with rapid onset of action in the first trimester of pregnancy.

Management during the Second and Third Trimesters of Pregnancy

It is not unsafe to begin psychotropic medication treatment, including mood stabilizers, in the second and third trimesters of pregnancy when clinically indicated. However, with increased body fluid volume and alterations in hepatic functioning and protein binding of medications, a close monitoring of doses and serum levels is needed. Again, florid or rapidly deteriorating mania, depression, and psychosis may be best treated with ECT. Patients should be monitored carefully for prepartum onset/exacerbation of illness and this should be treated robustly.

Mild to moderate depression during pregnancy has been treated successfully in a case series reported by Spinelli (1997). In these women, it is reported that beneficial and "preventative" effects were noted even up to 6 months postpartum.

There is no clear consensus as to when psychotropic medications should be tapered down and discontinued, or if they should be at all, before delivery. However, it is common practice, in those women receiving medications, to begin the down titration of medications about 4 to 5 weeks before delivery and to have them off all medications about 4 to 7 days before childbirth, unless they continue to have florid symptoms.

POSTPARTUM MANAGEMENT

As previously stated, the postpartum period is a very high risk period for recurrence of bipolar disorder. One in two (50%) women with a history of bipolar disorder will experience a mood episode during this period. Therefore, pregnant women with bipolar disorder should be informed of the high risk for relapse during the postpartum period and the value of timely and optimal treatment immediately post partum. Cohen and colleagues (1995) followed up 27 women with bipolar I disorder through pregnancy and found a significantly lower relapse rate after 3 months in those women who received prophylactic mood stabilizers (7%) from within 48 hours after delivery when compared with those who received no prophylactic treatment (62%).

Most psychotropic medications are secreted in breast milk. The concentration of lithium in breast milk is approximately 40% of the mother's serum levels (see Chaudron & Jefferson, 2000, for review) and infant serum levels are generally equal to those in breast milk. Since the infant's excretory system is not well developed, particularly within the first few days, there are concerns about the adverse effects of lithium in the neonate which include cardiac arrhythmias, sedation, gastrointestinal problems, and nephrotoxicity. The American Academy of Pediatrics Committee on drugs (AAPC, 1994) states that lithium is contraindicated during breast feeding. Although valproate is also secreted in breast milk, the concentrations in breast milk and infant serum is lower, and range from 1 to 10% of maternal serum levels. The AAPC on drugs (1994) recommends that treatment with valproate and carbamazapine is compatible with breast-feeding. This is despite the fact that the infant serum to maternal serum ratio of carbamazapine levels is 0.31 which is only slightly lower than the ratio for lithium. Treatment with carbamazapine and valproate could lead to hepatic, hematological, or central nervous system dysfunction in infants, although such risk is very low. It should be noted that, at the current time, we do not have adequate data about long-term "behavioral toxicity" in the child from being exposed to psychotropic medications through breast milk during the neonatal and infancy periods.

Therefore, the decision to start prophylactic treatment should include consideration of the risk of relapse of bipolar disorder and its consequences (e.g., infanticide in a psychotic state), risk of breast-feeding with mood stabilizer treatment, and consequences of not breast-feeding, as breast-feeding has been reported to confer many benefits to both mother and infant.

Prophylaxis with a mood stabilizer beginning immediately after delivery should be strongly recommended, particularly for those with a history of more severe forms of bipolar disorder. The choice of mood stabilizer will depend on the patient's symptoms profile, history of previous response or nonresponse to a particular mood stabilizer, and side-effect profile. Mothers should receive timely information about the risks to the infant from breast-feeding while taking psychotropic medication, and symptoms to watch out for in the infant. Where the mother is determined to feed the baby while also wishing to take psychotropic medication for bipolar disorder, risk of toxicity to the neonate could be reduced by "pumping and dumping"

(i.e., collecting and not using the breast milk collected at the anticipated peak breast milk level of the medication), while feeding the baby with breast milk at the anticipated trough breast milk level of the medication. If toxicity is suspected, infant and maternal serum levels should be obtained and breast-feeding suspended temporarily. Treatment should also include encouraging good sleep hygiene and offering short-term sedative hypnotics to facilitate sleep if necessary.

References

Abou-Saleh, M. T., & Coppen, A. (1989). The efficacy of low-dose lithium: Clinical, psychological and biological correlates. *Journal of Psychiatric Research, 23,* 157–162.

Akiskal, H. (1996, April). The prevalent clinical spectrum of bipolar disorders: Beyond DSM-IV. *Journal of Clinical Psychopharmacology, 16,* 4S–14S.

Altshuler, L. L., Cohen, L., Szuba, M., Burt, V. K, Gitlin, M., & Mintz, J. (1996). Pharmacologic management of psychiatric illness during pregnancy: Dilemmas and guidelines. *American Journal of Psychiatry, 153,* 592–606.

Altshuler, L. L., & Szuba, M. P. (1994). Course of psychiatric disorders in pregnancy: Dilemmas in pharmacologic management. *Neurologic Consultant, 12,* 613–635.

American Academy of Pediatrics Committee (AAPC) on Drugs. (1994). The transfer of drugs and other chemicals into human milk. *Pediatrics, 93,* 137–150

American Academy of Pediatrics Committee (AAPC) on Drugs. (2000). Use of psychoactive medication during pregnancy and possible effects on the fetus and newborn. *Pediatrics, 105*(4), 880–887.

American Psychiatric Association. (1994). *Diagnostic and statistical manual of mental disorders* (4th ed.). Washington, DC: Author.

Angst, J., & Weis, P. (1967). Peridicity of depressive psychosis. In H. Brill, J. Cole, P. Deniker, H. Hippus, & P. Bradley (Eds.), *Neuropsychopharmacotherapy* (pp. 703–710). Amsterdam: Experta Medica.

Baldessarini, R. J. (1984). Risk rates for depression [Letter to the editor]. *Archives of General Psychiatry, 41,* 103–106.

Baldessarini, R. J. (1985). Clinical and epidemiologic aspects of tardive dyskinesia. *Journal of Clinical Psychiatry, 46,* 8–13.

Barbato, N., & Hafner, R. J. (1998). Comorbidity of bipolar and personality disorder. *Australian & New Zealand Journal of Psychiatry, 32*(2), 276–280.

Berrios, G. E., & Bakshi, N. (1991). Manic and depressive symptoms in the elderly: Their relationships to treatment outcome, cognition and motor symptoms. *Psychopathology, 24*(1), 31–38.

Biederman, J., Wozniak, J., Kiely, K., Ablon, S., Faraone, S., Mick, E., et al. (1995). CBCL clinical scales discriminate prepubertal children with structured interview-derived diagnosis of mania from those with ADHD. *Journal of the American Academy of Child & Adolescent Psychiatry, 34,* 464–471.

Black, D. W., Winokur, G., Bell, S., Nasrallah, A., & Hulbert, J. (1988). Complicated mania. Comorbidity and immediate outcome in the treatment of mania. *Archives of General Psychiatry, 45,* 232–236.

Bland, R. (1997). Epidemiology of affective disorders: A review. *Canadian Journal Psychiatry, 42,* 367–377.

Bowden, C. L., Brugger, A., Swann, A. C., Calabrese, J. R., Janicak, P. G., Petty, F., et al. (1994). Efficacy of divalproex vs. lithium and placebo in the treatment of mania. The Depakote Mania Study Group. *Journal of the American Medical Association, 271,* 918–924.

Bowden, C. L., Janicak, P. G., Orsulak, P., Swann, A. C., Davis, J. M., Calabrese, J. R., et al. (1996). Relation of serum valproate concentration to response in mania. *American Journal of Psychiatry, 153,* 765–770.

Bowring, M., & Kovacs, M. (1992). Difficulties in diagnosing manic disorders among children and adolescents. *Journal of the American Academy of Child & Adolescent Psychiatry, 31,* 611–614.

Broadhead, W. E., Blazer, D. G., George, L. K., Tse, C. K. (1990). Depression, disability days, and days lost from work in a prospective epidemiologic survey. *Journal of the American Medical Association, 264,* 2524–2528.

Brockington, I. F. (1988). Maternity blues and post-partum euphoria. *British Journal of Psychiatry, 152,* 433–434.

Brockington, I. F., Cernik, K. F., Schofield, E. M. (1981). Puerperal psychosis: Phenomena and diagnosis. *Archives of General Psychiatry, 33,* 829–833.

Brockington, I. F., Oates, M., & Rose, G. (1990). Prepartum psychosis. *Journal of Affective Disorders, 19,* 31–35.

Carlson, G. A., Fennig, S., & Bromet, E. J. (1994). The confusion between bipolar disorder and schizophrenia in youth: where does it stand in the 1990s? *Journal of the American Academy of Child & Adolescent Psychiatry, 33,* 453–460.

Chacko, R. C., Marsh, B. J., Marmion, J., Dworkin, R. J., & Telschow, R. (1987). Lithium side effects in elderly bipolar outpatients. *Hillside Journal of Clinical Psychiatry, 9,* 79–88.

Chambers, C. D., Johnson, K. A., Dick, L. M., Felix, R. J., & Jones, K. L. (1996). Birth outcomes in pregnant women taking fluoxetine. *New England Journal of Medicine, 335*(14), 1010–1015.

Chaudron, L. H., & Jefferson, J. W. (2000). Mood mtabilizers during breastfeeding: A review. *Journal of Clinical Psychiatry, 61*(2), 79–90.

Chrousos, G. P. (1995). The hypothalamic-pituitary-adrenal axis and immune-mediated inflammation [Review]. *New England Journal of Medicine, 332*(20), 1351–1362.

Cohen, L., Sichel, D., Robertson, L., Heckscher, E., & Rosenbaum, J. F. (1995). Postpartum prophylaxis for women with bipolar disorder. *American Journal of Psychiatry, 152,* 1641–1642.

Cummings, J. (1993). Frontal-subcortical circuits and human behavior. *Archives of Neurology, 50,* 873–880.

Davenport, Y. B., & Adland, M. L. (1982). Postpartum psychoses in female and male bipolar manic-depressive patients. *American Journal of Orthopsychiatry, 52,* 288–297.

Dean, C., & Kendell, R. E. (1981). The symptomatology of puerperal illness. *British Journal of Psychiatry, 139,* 128–133.

Dean, C., Williams, R. J., & Brockington, I. F. (1989). Is puerperal psychosis the same as bipolar manic-depressive disorder? A family study. *Psychological Medicine, 19,* 637–647.

Dhingra, U., & Rabins, P. V. (1991). Mania in the elderly: A 5–7 year follow-up. *Journal of the American Geriatric Society, 39*(6), 581–583.

Dorn, L. D., & Chrousos, G. P. (1997). The neurobiology of stress: Understanding regulation of affect during female biological transitions. [Review] *Seminars in Reproductive Endocrinology, 15*(1), 19–35.

Eagles, J. M., & Whalley, L. J. (1985). Ageing and affective disorders: The age at first onset of affective disorders in Scotland, 1969–1978. *British Journal of Psychiatry, 147,* 180–187.

Fink, M. (1997). The decision to use ECT: For whom? When? *Modern Problems in Pharmacopsychiatry, 25,* 203–214.

Frankenburg, F. R., & Zanarini, M. C. (1994). Uses of clozapine in nonschizophrenic patients. *Harvard Review of Psychiatry, 2,* 142–150.

Geller, B., Fox, L., & Fletcher, M. (1993). Effect of tricyclic antidepressants on switching to mania and on the onset of bipolarity in depressed 6- to 12-year-olds. *Journal of the American Academy of Child & Adolescent Psychiatry, 32,* 43–50.

Geller, B., Cooper, T., Sun, K., Zimerman, B., Frazier, J., Williams, M., et al. (1998). Double-blind and placebo-controlled study of lithium for adolescent bipolar disorders with secondary substance dependency. *Journal of the American Academy of Child & Adolescent Psychiatry, 37,* 171–178.

Geller, B., Fox, L., & Clark, K. (1994). Rate and predictors of prepubertal bipolarity during follow-up of 6 to 12 year old depressed children. *Journal of the American Academy of Child & Adolescent Psychiatry, 33,* 461–468.

Geller, B., Sun, K., Zimmerman, B., Luby, J., Frazier, J., & Williams, M. (1995). Complex and rapid-cycling in bipolar children and adolescents: A preliminary study. *Journal of Affective Disorders, 34,* 259–298.

Gershon, E. S. (1990). Genetics. In F. K. Goodwin & K. R. Jamison (Eds.), *Manic-depressive illness* (pp. 373–399). New York: Oxford University Press.

Golombek, H., & Kutcher, S. (1990). Feeling states during adolescence. *Psychiatric Clinics of North America, 13,* 443–454.

Goodwin, F. K., & Jamison, K. R. (1990). *Manic depressive illness.* New York: Oxford University Press.

Grof, P., Robbins, W., Alda, M., Berghoefer, A., Vojtechovsky, M., Nilsson, A., et al. (2000, December). Protective effect of pregnancy in women with lithium-responsive bipolar disorder. *Journal of Affective Disorders, 61*(1–2), 31–39.

Hewick, D. S., Newbury, P., Hopwood, S., Naylor, G., & Moody, J. (1977). Age as a factor affecting lithium therapy. *British Journal of Clinical Pharmacology, 4*(2), 201–205.

Himmelhoch, J. M., & Garfinkel, M. (1986). Sources of lithium resistance in mixed mania. *Psychopharmacology Bulletin, 22,* 613–620.

Himmelhoch, J. M., Neil, J. F., May, S. J., Fuchs, C. Z., & Lacata, S. M. (1980). Age, dementia, dyskinesias, and lithium response. *American Journal of Psychiatry, 137,* 941–945.

Hirschfeld, R. M. A. (1999, June). *Personality disorder or bipolar illness: New thoughts.* Paper presented at the Third International Conference on Bipolar Disorder, Pittsburgh, PA.

Isojarvi, J., Laatikainen, T., Pakarinen, A. J., Juntunen, K. T., & Myllyla, V. V. (1993). Polycystic ovaries and hyperandrogenism in women taking valproate for epilepsy. *New England Journal of Medicine, 329,* 1383–1388.

Isojarvi, J., Laatikainen, T., Knip, M., Pakarinen, A. J., Juntunen, K. T., & Myllyla, V. V. (1996). Obesity and endocrine disorders in women taking valproate for epilepsy. *Annals of Neurology, 39,* 579–584.

Johnson, G., Gershon, S., Burdock, E. I., Floyd, A., & Hekimian, L. (1971). Comparative effects of lithium and chlorpromazine in the treatment of acute manic states. *British Journal of Psychiatry, 119,* 267–276.

Kendell, R., Chalmers, J., & Platz, C. (1987). Epidemiology of puerperal psychoses. *British Journal of Psychiatry, 150,* 662–673.

Kitamura, T., Sugawara, M., Sugawara, K., Toda, M. A., & Shima, S. (1996). Psychosocial study of depression in early pregnancy. *British Journal of Psychiatry, 168,* 732–738.

Klompenhouwer, J. L., & van Hulst, A. M. (1991). Classification of postpartum psychosis: A study of 250 mother and baby admissions in the Netherlands. *Acta Psychiatrica Scandavia, 84,* 255–261.

Kumar, R., & Robson, K. M. (1984). A prospective study of emotional disorders in childbearing women. *British Journal of Psychiatry, 144,* 35–47.

Kusumakar, V., & Yatham, L. N. (1997). Lamotrigine treatment of rapid cycling bipolar disorder [letter; comment]. *American Journal of Psychiatry, 154,* 1171–1172.

Kusumakar, V., Yatham, L. N., Haslam, D. R., Parikh, S. V., Matte, R., Sharma, V., et al. (1997). The foundations of effective management of bipolar disorder. *Canadian Journal of Psychiatry, 42* (Suppl. 2), 69S–73S.

Kusumakar, V., Yatham, L. N., Haslam, D. R., Parikh, S. V., Matte, R., Silverstone, P. H., et al. (1997). Treatment of mania, mixed state, and rapid cycling. *Canadian Journal of Psychiatry, 42* (Suppl. 2), 79S–86S.

Kutcher, S. (1994, May). *Bipolar disorder in adolescence: Mania through the life cycle.* American Psychiatric Association Annual Meeting. Philadelphia, PA.

Kutcher, S., & Marton, P. (1996). Treatment of adolescent depression. In K. Shulman, M. Tohen, S. Kutcher (Eds.), *Mood disorders across the lifespan* (pp. 101–126). New York: John Wiley.

Kutcher, S., & Robertson, H. (1994, June). *ECT treatment in adolescents: A review of the Sunnybrook experience.* Paper presented at the 13th Annual Child & Adolescent Depression Consortium Meeting. Providence, RI.

Leibenluft, E. (1996). Women with bipolar illness: Clinical and research issues. *American Journal of Psychiatry, 153,* 163–173.

Lewinsohn, P., Klein, D., & Seeley, J. (1995). Bipolar disorders in a community sample of older adolescents: Prevalence, phenomenology, comorbidity, and course. *Journal of the American Academy of Child & Adolescent Psychiatry, 34,* 454–463.

Lier, L., Kastrup, M., & Rafaelsen, O. J. (1989). Psychiatric illness in relation to pregnancy and childbirth. II: Diagnostic profiles, psychosocial and perinatal aspects. *Nordic Psykiatrisk Tidsskrift, 43,* 535–542.

McElroy, S., Keck, P., Stanton, S., Tugrul, K. C., Bennett, J. A., & Strakowski, S. M. (1996). A randomized comparison of divalproex oral loading versus haloperidol in the initial treatment of acute psychotic mania. *Journal of Clinical Psychiatry, 57,* 142–146.

McFarland, B. H., Miller, M. R., & Straumfjord, A. A. (1990). Valproate use in the older manic patient. *Journal of Clinical Psychiatry,* 51, 479–481.

McKnew, D. H., Cytryn, L., Buchsbaum, M. S., Hamovit, J., Lamur, M., Rapoport, J. L., et al. (1981). Lithium in children of Lithium responding parents. *Psychiatry Research, 4,* 171–180.

Marzuk, P. M., Tardiff, K., Leon, A. C., Hirsch, C. S., Portera, L. Hartwell, N., et al. (1997). Lower risk of suicide during pregnancy. *American Journal of Psychiatry, 154,* 122–123.

Modell, S., Lauer, C. J., Schreiber, W., Huber, J., Krieg, J. C., & Holsboer, F. (1998). Hormonal response pattern in the combined DEX-CRH test is stable over time in subjects at high familial risk for affective disorders. *Neuropsychopharmacology, 18*(4), 253–262.

Murray, N., Hopwood, S., Balfour, D. J., Ogston, S., Hewick, D. S. (1983). The influence of age on lithium efficacy and side-effects in out-patients. *Psychological Medicine,* 13, 53–60.

Nulman, I., Rovet, J., Stewart, D. E., Wolpin, J., Gardner, H. A., & Theis, J. G. (1997). Neurodevelopment of children exposed in utero to antidepressant drugs. *New England Journal of Medicine, 336*(4), 258–262.

O'Connell, R. A., Mayo, J. A., & Sciutto, M. S. (1991). PDQ-R personality disorders in bipolar patients. *Journal of Affective Disorders, 23*(4), 217–221.

Paffenburger, R. S. (1982). Epidemiological aspects of mental illness associated with childbearing. In I. F. Brockington & R. Kumar (Eds.), *Motherhood and mental illness* (pp. 21-36). New York: Grune & Stratton.

Paffenburger, R. S., & McCabe, L. J. (1966). The effects of obstetric and perinatal events on risk of mental illness in women of childbearing age. *American Journal of Public Health, 56,* 400–407

Papatheodorou, G., & Kutcher, S. (1993). Divalproex sodium treatment in late adolescent and young adult acute mania. *Psychopharmacology Bulletin,* 29, 213–219.

Papatheodorou, G., & Kutcher, S. (1995). The effect of adjunctive light therapy on ameliorating breakthrough depressive symptoms in adolescent-onset bipolar disorder. *Journal of Psychiatry & Neuroscience, 20,* 226–232.

Parry, B. L. (1989, March). Reproductive factors affecting the course of affective illness in women. *Psychiatric Clinic of North America, 12,* 207–220

Pastuszak, A., Schick-Boschetto, B., Zuber, C., Feldkamp, M., Pinelli, M., Sihn, S., et al. (1993). Pregnancy outcome following first-trimester exposure to fluoxetine (Prozac). *Journal of the American Medical Association, 269,* 2246–2248.

Pies, W. P. (1998). Antidepressants. In W. P. Pies (Ed.), *Handbook of essential psychopharmacology.* Washington, DC: American Psychiatric Press.

Post, R. M., Ballenger, J. C., Uhde, T. W., Smith, C., Rubinow, D. R., & Bunney, W. E., Jr. (1982). Effect of carbamazepine on cyclic nucleotides in CSF of patients with affective illness. *Biology & Psychiatry, 17,* 1037–1045.

Rasanen, P., Tiihonen, J., & Hakko, H. (1998). The incidence and onset-age of hospitalized bipolar affective disorder in Finland. *Journal of Affective Disorders, 48,* 63–68.

Reich, T., & Winokur, G. (1970). Postpartum psychoses in patients with manic depressive disease. *Journal of Nervous & Mental Disorders, 151,* 60–68.

Rohde, A., & Marneros, A. (1993). Psychoses in puerperium: Symptoms, course and long-term prognosis. [German] *Geburtshilfe und Frauenheilkunde, 53*(11), 800–810.

Roose, S. P., Bone, S., Haidorfer, C., Dunner, D. L., & Fieve, R. R. (1979). Lithium treatment in older patients. *American Journal of Psychiatry, 136,* 843–844.

Sargenti, C. J., Rizos, A. L., Jeste, D. V. (1988). Psychotropic drug interactions in the patient with late-onset psychosis and mood disorder. Part 1. *Psychiatric Clinics of North America, 11,* 235–252.

Schopf, J., & Rust, B. (1994). Follow-up and family study of postpartum psychoses. Part II: Early versus late onset postpartum psychoses. *European Archives of Psychiatry & Clinical Neuroscience, 244*(3), 135–137.

Segal, J., Berk, M., & Brook, S. (1998). Risperidone compared with both lithium and haloperidol in mania: A double-blind randomized controlled trial. *Clinical Neuropharmacology, 21,* 176–180.

Sharma, V. (1997). Effects of pregnancy on suicidal behaviour. *American Journal of Psychiatry, 154,* 1479–1480.

Sharma, V., & Persad, E. (1995). Effect of pregnancy on three patients with bipolar disorder. *Annals of Clinical Psychiatry, 7,* 39–42.

Shukla, S., Cook, B. L., Hoff, A. L., & Aronson, T. A. (1988) Failure to detect organic factors in mania. *Journal of Affective Disorders, 15,* 17–20.

Shulman, K. I. (1997). Disinhibition syndromes, secondary mania and bipolar disorder in old age. *Journal of Affective Disorders, 46*(3), 175–178.

Shulman, K. I., & Post, F. (1980). Bipolar affective disorder in old age. *British Journal of Psychiatry, 136,* 26–32.

Shulman, K. I., Tohen, M., Satlin, A., Mally, G., & Kalunian, D. (1992). Mania compared with unipolar depression in old age. *American Journal of Psychiatry, 149*(3), 341–345.

Shulman, K. I., & Tohen, M. (1994). Unipolar mania reconsidered: Evidence from an elderly cohort. *British Journal of Psychiatry, 164*(4), 547–549.

Shulman, K. I., & Herrmann, N. (1999). The nature and management of mania in old age. *Psychiatric Clinics of North America, 22,* 649–665.

Silva, R., Campbell, M., Golden, R., Small, A., Pataki, C., & Rosenberg, C. (1992). Side effects associated with lithium and placebo administration in aggressive children. *Psychopharmacological Bulletin, 28,* 319–326.

Smith, R., Cubis, J., Brinsmead, M., Lewin, T., Singh, B., Ownes, P., et al. (1990). Mood changes, obstetric experience and alterations in plasma cortisol, beta-endorphin and corticotrophin releasing hormone during pregnancy and puerperium. *Journal of Psychosomatic Research, 34*(1), 53–69.

Smith, R. E., & Helms, P. M. (1982). Adverse effects of lithium therapy in the acutely ill elderly patient. *Journal of Clinical Psychiatry, 43,* 94–99.

Spicer, C. C., Hare, E. H., & Slater, E. (1973). Neurotic and psychotic forms of depressive illness: Evidence from age-incidence in a national sample. *British Journal of Psychiatry, 123,* 535–541.

Spielvogel, A., & Wile, J. (1986). Treatment of the psychotic pregnant patient. *Psychosomatics, 27*(7), 487–492.

Spielvogel, A., & Wile, J. (1992). Treatment and outcomes of psychotic patients during pregnancy and childbirth. *Birth, 19,* 131–137.

Spinelli, M. G. (1997). Interpersonal psychotherapy for depressed antepartum women: A pilot study. *American Journal of Psychiatry, 154,* 1028–1030.

Starkstein, S. E., Mayberg, H. S., Berthier, M. L., Federoff, P., Price, T. R., Dannals, R. F., et al. (1990). Mania after brain injury: Neuroradiological and metabolic findings. *Annals of Neurology, 27,* 652–659.

Starkstein, S. E., Chemerinski, E., Sabe, L., et al. (1997). Prospective longitudinal study of depression and anosognosia in Alzheimer's disease. *British Journal of Psychiatry, 171,* 47–52.

Stewart, D. E., Klompenhouwer, J. L., Kendell, R. E., & van Hulst, A. M. (1991). Prophylactic lithium in puerperal psychosis: The experience of three centers. *British Journal of Psychiatry, 158,* 393–397.

Stone, K. (1989). Mania in the elderly. *British Journal of Psychiatry, 155,* 220–224.

Stowe, Z. N., & Nemeroff, C. B. (1995). Women at risk for postpartum-onset major depression. *American Journal of Obstetrics and Gynecology, 173,* 639–645.

Strayhorn, J. M., Jr., & Nash, J. L. (1977). Severe neurotoxicity despite "therapeutic" serum lithium levels. *Diseases of the Nervous System, 38,* 107–111.

Strober, M., Morrell, W., Burroughs, J., Lampert, C., Danforth, H., & Freeman, R. (1988). A family study of bipolar I disorder in adolescence. Early onset of symptoms linked to increased familial loading and lithium resistance. *Journal of Affective Disorders, 15,* 255–268.

Strober, M., Schmidt-Lackner, S., Freeman, R., Bower, S., Lampert, C., & DeAntonio (1995). Recovery and relapse in adolescents with bipolar affective illness: A five-year naturalistic, prospective follow-up. *Journal of the American Academy of Child & Adolescent Psychiatry, 34,* 724–731.

Tohen, M., Castillo, J., Baldessarini, R., Zarate, C., Jr., & Kando, J. C. (1995). Blood dyscrasias with carbamazepine and valproate: A pharmacoepidemiological study of 2,228 patients at risk. *American Journal of Psychiatry, 152,* 413–418.

Tohen, M., Sanger, T., McElroy, S., Tollefson, G. D., Chengappa, K. N., Daniel, D. G., et al. (1999). Olanzapine versus placebo in the treatment of acute mania. Olanzapine HGEH Study Group. *American Journal of Psychiatry, 156,* 702–709.

Tsigos, C., & Chrousos, G. P. (1994). Physiology of the hypothalamic-pituitary-adrenal axis in health and dysregulation in psychiatric and autoimmune disorders. [Review] *Endocrinology & Metabolism Clinics of North America, 23*(3), 451–466.

Viguera, A. C., Nonacs, R., Cohen, L. S., Tondo, L., Murray, A., & Baldessarini, R. J. (2000). Risk of recurrence of bipolar disorder in pregnant and nonpregnant women after discontinuing lithium maintenance. *American Journal of Psychiatry, 157,* 179–184.

Vitiello, B., Behar, D., Malone, R., Delaney, M. A., Ryan, P. J., & Simpson, G. M. (1988). Pharmacokinetics of lithium carbonate in children. *Journal of Clinical Psychopharmacology, 8,* 355–359.

Weissman, M. M., Bland, R. C., Canino, G. J., Faravelli, C., Greenwald, S., Hwu, H. G., et al. (1996). Cross-national epidemiology of major depression and bipolar disorder. *Journal of the American Medical Association, 276,* 293–299.

Weller, E. B., Weller, R. A., & Fristad, M. A. (1995). Bipolar disorder in children: Misdiagnosis, underdiagnosis, and future directions. *Journal of the American Academy of Child & Adolescent Psychiatry, 34,* 709–714.

Yassa, R., Nair, V., Nastase, C., Camille, Y., & Belzile, L. (1988). Prevalence of bipolar disorder in a psychogeriatric population. *Journal of Affective Disorders, 14,* 197–201.

Yatham, L. N. (2000). Safety and efficacy of risperidone as combination therapy for the manic phase of bipolar disorder: Preliminary findings of a randomized, double-blind study (RIS-INT-46) [Abstract]. *International Journal of Neuropsychopharmacology, 3:*S12.

Yatham, L. N., Kusumakar, V., Parikh, S. V., Haslam, D. R., Matte, R., Sharma, V., et al. (1997). Bipolar depression: Treatment options. *Canadian Journal of Psychiatry, 42* (Suppl. 2), 87S–91S.

Young, R. C., & Klerman, G. L. (1992). Mania in late life: Focus on age at onset. *American Journal of Psychiatry, 149,* 867–876.

Zarate C., & Tohen, M. (1996). Epidemiology of mood disorders throughout the life cycle. In K. Shulman, M. Tohen, & S. Kutcher (Eds.), *Mood disorders across the life span* (pp. 17–34). New York: Wiley.

Zis, A. P., & Goodwin, F. K. (1979). Major affective disorder as a recurrent illness: A critical review. *Archives of General Psychiatry, 36,* 835–839.

CHAPTER 6

Bipolar Disorder and Comorbid Axis I Disorders: Diagnosis and Management

Charles A. Zarate, Jr.
Mauricio F. Tohen

Introduction

Bipolar disorder, a chronic and recurring condition, is a major public health problem, affecting close to 2% of the population (Kessler et al., 1994; Tohen & Goodwin, 1995). The co-occurrence of axis I disorders with other psychiatric disorders or symptoms has been widely recognized (Regier et al., 1990). Patients with bipolar disorder and with other axis I disorders, commonly referred to as "dual diagnoses," can be a challenge to the clinician. These situations may pose a diagnostic dilemma and therapeutic challenge; first-line treatments may not be sufficiently effective (M. F. Sheehan, 1993).

Definition of Comorbidity

The term *comorbidity* has been used in medicine for many years to refer to the presence of two or more disorders that occur simultaneously over a long period of time (Maser & Cloninger, 1990). Comorbidity in bipolar disorder has been described as the co-occurrence of nonaffective DSM-III-

R Axis I disorders, or serious medical illnesses in patients (Black, Winokur, Hulbert, & Nasrallah, 1988). Strakowski and colleagues' definition of comorbidity in mania is the presence of antecedent or concurrent psychiatric syndrome in addition to the principal diagnosis (Strakowski, Tohen, Stoll, Faedda, & Goodwin, 1992).

Prevalence of Comorbidity of Bipolar Disorder with Other Comorbid Axis I Disorders

Approximately 30–50% of bipolar patients are considered refractory to lithium treatment and those with a comorbid disorder also frequently fail to respond to lithium and other conventional treatments. Almost all axis I and/ or axis II disorders may co-occur with bipolar disorder. The most common are substance use disorders (SUD), panic disorder, obsessive–compulsive disorder (OCD), and borderline personality disorder. The frequencies with which these different comorbid conditions co-occur are listed in Table 6.1. There has been increasing recognition that these comorbid conditions are common and are often difficult to diagnose and treat, but with the possible exception of comorbid alcoholism, the literature provides relatively little

TABLE 6.1
Prevalence Rates of Axis I Disorders in Patients with Bipolar Disorder

Study	Manic Subjects N(%)[1]	Substance Use Disorders (%)	Panic (%)	OCD (%)	Eating Disorder (%)	ICD (%)	ADD (%)
Black et al. (1988) Black, Winokur, Hulbert, & Nasrallah (1988) Black et al. (1989)	438 (13)	8	—	—	2	—	—
Strakowski et al. (1992, 1993)	60 (42)	—	7	8	7	—	—
Strakowski et al. (1992)	39 (74)	—	15[2]	13	15	23	—
Keck et al. (1995)	71 (66)	—	16[2]	10	9	13	—
Kruger, Shugar, & Cooke (1995)	61 (ns)	—	—	—	13	13	—
West et al. (1995)	14 (ns)	—	—	—	—	—	57
Tohen et al. (1996)	123 (ns)	17	—	—	—	—	—
Keck et al. (1998)	134	33	—	—	—	—	—

OCD = obsessive-compulsive disorder; ICD = impulse control disorder; ADD = attention deficit disorder; ns = not specified.
[1]% refers to rate of comorbidity in all patients with mania.
[2]% includes patients with anxiety disorders (panic disorder, agoraphobia, simple and social phobias) in general.
Source: Adapted from Strakowski et al. 1994.

guidance for the clinician on how to diagnose and treat these co-occurring conditions. Among axis I disorders, substance use and anxiety disorders are the most commonly cooccurring comorbid disorders. The lifetime prevalence of comorbid substance use disorders in bipolar I disorder patients in the community has been estimated to be between 60.7 and 48.1% for Bipolar I and II Disorders respectively (Regier et al., 1990). The lifetime prevalence of SUD in patients with mania presenting for treatment varies from 17 to 33%, followed by panic disorder in 7 to 16% and obsessive–compulsive disorder in 8 to 13% (Table 6.1). Panic disorder and OCD generally require long-term treatment with antipanic and antiobsessional agents that generally include the selective serotonin reuptake inhibitors (D. V. Sheehan, 1999). While these agents may help with panic disorder and OCD, they may potentially destabilize the primary mood disorder because the long-term use of antidepressants in bipolar disorder has been associated with higher switch rates and an accelerated course of cycling of illness (Ananth, Wohl, Ranganath, & Beshay, 1993; Goodwin & Jamison, 1990).

Diagnostic Difficulties in Patients with Bipolar Disorder and Comorbid Axis I Disorders

The most robust diagnosis of bipolar disorder is made on a longitudinal basis, taking into account not only clusters of symptoms but also the course of illness. There is inherent difficulty in diagnosing bipolar affective disorder on a purely cross-sectional basis in the face of comorbid psychiatric and medical conditions because substantial overlap exists between the symptoms of bipolar disorder and those of other psychiatric disorders at a given point (Blacker & Tsuang, 1992). This is particularly true of bipolar disorder and stimulant abuse. For example, stimulant intoxication can produce a syndrome indistinguishable from mania. In addition, the phenomenological overlap between bipolar disorder and attention deficit hyperactivity disorder is significant, which often makes it difficult to distinguish between these two syndromes, particularly in the younger patient (Blacker & Tsuang, 1992). Core symptoms of both conditions include impaired attention, distractibility, racing thoughts, and hyperactivity. Ultrarapid cycling bipolar disorder, and other atypical presentations of bipolar disorder, in patients with a history of attachment difficulties and abuse can pose considerable difficulties in distinguishing this from a borderline personality disorder (Akiskal & Pinto, 1999; Perugi, Toni, & Akiskal 1999). To date the temporal relationship of these comorbid diagnoses occurring with bipolar disorder remains unclear. Strakowski et al. (1998), in order to clarify this relationship among bipolar and other Axis I disorders, examined the course of syndromes cooccurring with bipolar disorder for 12 months after their first psychiatric hospitalization. The authors found that obsessive–compulsive disorder had an episodic or waxing and waning course that frequently mirrored that found in bipolar disorder. In addition, they found that the chronic course of primary posttraumatic stress disorder (PTSD) and primary substance abuse syndromes were often distinct from that of bipolar disorder. The distinction and overlap between bipolar disorder on the one hand and substance use disorders, attention deficit hyperactivity disorder, anxiety disorders, PTSD, and borderline personality disorder on the other can only be understood by a careful longitudinal examination of family history, chronology of onset of the different conditions, symptoms, and functioning between mood disorder episodes, course of illness, and response to treatment.

Mania and Comorbidity

Krauthammer and Klerman (1978), who reported 21 cases of mania associated with medical conditions or prescribed medication use, first introduced the concept of comorbidity in mania. Cummings (1986) and Krauthammer and Klerman (1978) also reported manic syndromes occurring in the context of antecedent or coexistent psychiatric disorders. The McLean First-Episode Mania Project reported that 42% of 60 bipolar patients treated for their first lifetime hospitalization for a manic episode had a comorbid disorder. In addition, women were three times more likely than men to have a comorbid diagnosis (Strakowski et al., 1992; Tohen et al., 1992). The University of Cincinnati Mania Project (Keck et al., 1995; Strakowski et al., 1995) reported a much higher rate of psychiatric comorbidity than the previous study—66% (47/71) of bipolar patients. In addition, they compared the comorbidity rates between first and multiple-episode manic patients, finding no differences (71 vs. 62%, respectively) (Keck et al., 1995). In summary, comorbidity is present in a significant number of manic patients even early on in the course of their illness and appears to increase in frequency the longer the duration of illness.

COMORBID SUBSTANCE USE DISORDERS (SUD)

One of the most common comorbid disorders are SUD, especially abuse of alcohol, stimulants such as cocaine and amphetamines, marijuana, and on occasion psychedelic compounds such as PCP and LSD. The National Comorbidity Study (NCS) examined the lifetime cooccurrence of DSM-

III-R alcohol abuse and dependence with other psychiatric disorders (Kessler et al., 1997). Amongst all axis I disorders, bipolar disorder was by far the psychiatric disorder most likely to be associated with comorbid SUD (Kessler et al., 1997). The lifetime prevalence of substance dependence and abuse in the Epidemiologic Catchment Area (ECA) study for patients with mood disorder was estimated to be 60.7% for bipolar I disorder, 48.1% for bipolar II disorder, and 27% for major depression (Regier et al., 1990). The only other psychiatric disorder with a higher lifetime prevalence for SUD was antisocial personality disorder. Indeed, the ECA study (Regier et al., 1990) found that the likelihood of an individual with bipolar disorder having a SUD was six times greater than that of the general population and twice as common as an individual with unipolar depression.

The importance of comorbid SUD is clear. Several studies have shown that patients with bipolar disorder who meet criteria for concurrent substance abuse have a worse outcome compared with those patients without comorbid alcohol or other substance abuse. There is also evidence that patients with a comorbid bipolar disorder and SUD will have a fulminant course of illness. Studies suggest that the presence of SUD in bipolar patients is associated with higher rates of mixed states (Himmelhoch, Mulla, Neil, Detre, & Kupfer, 1976; Keller et al., 1986), rapid cycling (Mayfield & Coleman, 1968), suicide (Feiman & Dunner, 1996; Goldberg et al., 1999; Morrison, 1974), rehospitalizations (Brady, Casto, Lydiard, Malcolm, & Arana, 1991; Reich, Davies, & Himmelhoch, 1974, Sonne, Brady, & Morton, 1994) and nonadherence to treatment (Goldberg et al., 1999; Keck et al., 1997; Keck et al., 1998; Maarbjerg, Aagaurd, & Vestergaaurd, 1988; Strakowski et al., 1998; Weiss et al., 1998a). In addition, the presence of SUD has been reported to be associated with a shorter time to relapse, poor psychosocial outcome (Tohen, Waternaux, Tsnang, & Hunt, 1990) and longer time to remission from mania (Goldberg, Garno, Leon, Kocsis, & Portern, 1999). As well, bipolar patients who abuse stimulants could also be at increased risk for anxiety, insomnia, or switching into mania.

MANAGEMENT OF SUD IN BIPOLAR DISORDER

The patient with bipolar disorder may present for treatment during any phase of their illness (i.e., classic mania, mixed episode, or major depression). In this chapter the manic phase is chosen as the starting point for our treatment decision tree. When a manic patient presents in an acute state, it is incumbent on the clinician to adequately assess and investigate the patient to rule out any major medical illnesses. In addition, it is also important to determine what led to the recent decompensation. The most common rea-

TABLE 6.2
Factors Associated with Acute Manic Decompensation in Bipolar Disorder Patients

• Noncompliance	• Incorrect diagnosis
• Side effects	• Comorbid Axis I disorders
• Psychosocial stressors	• Comorbid Axis II disorders
• Lack of psychosocial support system	• Comorbid medical conditions
• Unusual pharmacokinetics	• Failure to understand how to take the
• Presence of psychotic symptoms	medications correctly
• Presence of residual depressive symptoms	• Mixed episodes, rapid cycling course of illness

sons for decompensation are listed in Table 6.2. The clinician should address these factors accordingly and concurrently with the treatment of mania.

Figure 6.1 provides an algorithm for the diagnosis and management of bipolar and comorbid disorders. Comorbidity generally requires the consideration of different or adjunctive treatments. The comorbid disorders associated with bipolar disorder are presented from top to bottom in Figure 6.2, based on their prevalence. The first step is to exclude medical symptoms or illnesses likely to interfere with the response to treatment. Also, certain medical illnesses may mimic psychiatric symptoms or syndromes. It is beyond the scope of this chapter to review the diagnosis and treatment of medical conditions that may present. Once medical illnesses have been ruled out (as the major cause of the recent decompensation), the clinician should determine if the patient is abusing psychoactive substances. Although substance use disorders is one of the most frequent comorbid diagnoses, it is often overlooked because of either denial or concealment on the part of the patient.

Initial steps include performing a detailed physical examination, obtaining laboratory tests, and reviewing past medical records. Laboratory tests, including urine and blood screens, mean corpuscular volume, and liver function tests, may be helpful in detecting drug or alcohol use (Brady, Casto, et al., 1991). Obtaining additional information from treating clinicians, family members, and friends is essential. Establishing a time-line of a patient's bipolar disorder and substance related problems will help to distinguish the chronology of onset to establish which problem is primary, and its course, thus helping the clinician understand distinct and overlapping issues of both conditions.

Figure 6.2 outlines the recommended steps involved in making the diagnosis and lists the different therapies available for the bipolar patient who abuses substances. The treatment approach to the bipolar disorder pa-

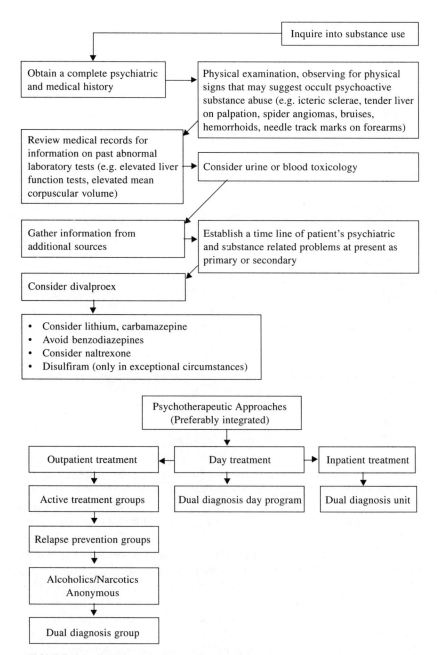

FIGURE 6.1. Diagnosis and management of bipolar disorder with comorbid psychoactive substance abuse.

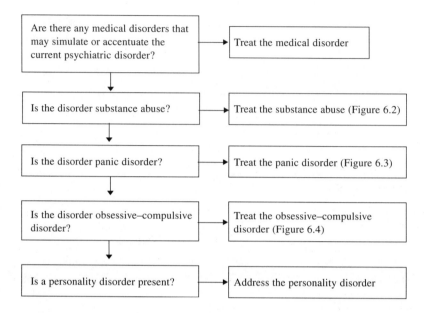

FIGURE 6.2. Relationship between bipolar disorder and other comorbid disorders.

tient with comorbid SUD generally involves both psychotherapy and medications.

PSYCHOTHERAPIES

Many different types of psychotherapy for either bipolar disorder or SUD have been utilized (Miklowitz, 1996; Najavits & Weiss, 1994). However, few studies have examined what psychotherapies should be used in bipolar disorder patients with both conditions (Weiss, Najavits, & Greenfield, 1998). Treatment of comorbid disorders may occur sequentially (i.e., the patient is treated first for SUD and then for the psychiatric disorder) or in parallel (i.e., the patient is treated simultaneously for each disorder; usually treatment is delivered at different sites in unrelated clinical programs). However, since these forms of treatment and treatment delivery have not produced favorable outcomes, recent research has focused on integrated treatment (Weiss et al., 1999). This integrated treatment consists of a 20-session relapse prevention group therapy for patients with coexisting bipolar disorder and substance use disorder. The treatment uses an integrated approach by discussing topics that are relevant to both disorders and by highlighting common aspects of recovery from and relapse to each disorder. Group sessions focus on such topics as identifying and addressing triggers, managing symptoms of bipolar disorder without abusing substances, recognizing early warning signs for both disorders, and taking medications as prescribed.

PHARMACOTHERAPIES

Lithium

In naturalistic outcome studies, SUD has been reported to affect response to lithium in bipolar disorder patients (Albanese, Bartel, & Bruno, 1994; Bowden 1995; O'Connell, Mayo, Flatlow, Cuthbertson, & O'Brien, 1991; Tohen et al., 1990). Two open label studies with lithium show mixed results in bipolar spectrum disorder patients with comorbid cocaine abuse (Gawin & Kleber, 1984; Nunes, McGrath, Wager, & Quiticin, 1990). Gawin and Kleber (1984), in an open label study with lithium carbonate, found it to be effective in cocaine abusers with cyclothymia. In contrast, Nunes and co-workers (1990) failed to find any benefit of lithium in 10 cocaine abusers with bipolar spectrum disorders. More recently, lithium was found to be superior to placebo in the treatment of adolescent bipolar I and II disorder with comorbid substance use disorder in a randomized controlled trial (Geller et al., 1998).

Anticonvulsants: Valproate and Carbamazepine

Weiss, Greenfield, et al, (1998) reported that compliance with mood stabilizer treatment was significantly higher among bipolar patients with SUD when valproate, rather than lithium, was the primary pharmacotherapy. Brady and colleagues (Brady, Sonne, Anton, & Ballenger, 1995) in an open nlabel study with valproate found it to be safe and effective in nine mixed manic bipolar patients with concurrent substance dependence, who had a history of either intolerance or lack of response to lithium. In addition, this study did not show any significant changes in liver transaminases at the end of the study compared to baseline values. Goldberg and colleagues (1999) found in a retrospective medical chart review, that bipolar I inpatients with substance abuse histories who received divalproex or carbamazepine remitted during hospitalization more often than those who had received lithium as the sole mood stabilizer.

Naltrexone

The opiate antagonist drug naltrexone has recently been shown to increase control over alcohol urges and improve cognitive resistance to thoughts about drinking (Anton et al., 1999). However, it remains unknown whether naltrexone will be effective in reducing alcohol urges in bipolar disorder patients. Further studies with this drug are warranted.

COMORBID ANXIETY DISORDERS

After addressing SUD, the decision tree prompts the clinician to consider if comorbid anxiety exists. There has been little attention paid to the relationship between panic attacks or panic disorder and bipolar disorder. It is often difficult during the manic phase of the illness to adequately screen for and confirm comorbid anxiety disorders. The euphoric, elated, and irritable patient's mental state and behavior can mask anxiety or distract the clinical team from recognizing anxiety. Nevertheless, it is recommended that initial steps be taken to determine if other anxiety disorders and or other comorbidity are present. Nonresponse to treatment and atypical courses of bipolar illness should alert the clinical team to assess for comorbidity.

PANIC DISORDER

Comorbid panic disorder in patients with bipolar disorder has been recognized for over a decade (DiNardo & Barlow, 1990). The lifetime prevalence of panic disorder in mania in the ECA study was found to be 1.6% (Eaton, Dryman, & Weismann, 1991). Subsequent analysis of this database at three of the participating ECA sites found that the prevalence of panic disorder was higher than originally estimated and higher than that of the population estimates (Boyd et al., 1984). The reanalysis found that the lifetime prevalence of panic disorder among subjects with bipolar disorder was 21% compared to 10% among subjects with unipolar depression and 0.8% among comparison subjects (Chen & Dilsaver, 1995). The odds ratio for meeting criteria for panic disorder was 19.0 among subjects with bipolar disorder compared with comparison subjects and 10.8 in subjects with unipolar depression compared to comparison subjects (Chen & Dilsaver, 1995). Other studies (estimates based on bipolar patients in treatment rather than on community surveys) have found that the lifetime prevalence rates of panic disorder in mania range from 7 to 16% (McElroy, Strakowski, et al., 1995, Table 1; Strakowski, Keck, et al., 1995; Strakowski et al., 1992, 1993).

In patients with panic disorder, comorbidity of bipolar spectrum disorders appears to be high. In a longitudinal comorbidity study of 140 DSM-III-R panic disorder patients, the authors found that 2% had concurrent mania, 5% had hypomania, and 6% had cyclothymia. An additional 34% of panic disorder patients ultimately met the criteria for hyperthymic temperament (Savino et al., 1993).

The main differential diagnosis of bipolar and panic disorder includes mixed states of bipolar disorder, hyperthyroidism, hypoxia, attention deficit disorder, SUD (especially intoxication and withdrawal symptoms), and other anxiety disorders (e.g., OCD, posttraumatic stress disorder, social phobia), and agitated bipolar depression.

OBSESSIVE–COMPULSIVE DISORDER (OCD)

Few studies estimated the prevalence of OCD in bipolar disorder. Initial case reports and treatment trials suggested that OCD might be comorbid (Baer, Minchiello, & Jenike, 1985; Keck, Lipinski, & White, 1986) in patients with bipolar disorder. In community surveys, OCD was found to be much more prevalent in bipolar disorder patients than in the general population (Boyd et al., 1984). Studies examining the lifetime prevalence of OCD in bipolar patients presenting for treatment found rates ranging from 8 to 13% (Keck et al., 1995, Table 1; McElroy, Strakowski, et al., 1995; Strakowski et al., 1992, 1993; Strakowski, Keck, et al., 1995). Another study of 149 inpatients with DSM-III major affective disorder found that the frequency of OCD syndrome was not significantly different between subjects with unipolar major depression and bipolar disorder (Jefferson, Greist, Perse, & Rosenfeld, 1991). The McLean First-Episode Mania Project reported similar rates of comorbid OCD in first episode manic patients and patients with new onset DSM-III-R schizophrenia (Strakowski et al., 1992, 1993; Tohen et al., 1992). One study found no difference in the lifetime prevalence rates of OCD in first versus multiple episode manic patients (Keck et al., 1995). With regard to whether there are differences in the rates of OCD in the different subtypes of bipolar disorder, one study reported that DSM-III-R bipolar mixed patients compared to pure manic patients were more likely to have a secondary diagnosis of OCD (21% versus 4%, respectively; McElroy et al., 1995). Some studies of antidepressant clinical trials in OCD have reported rates of switches into mania as high as 20% (higher than that of some studies of unipolar depression) thus suggesting that a possible relationship with bipolar disorder may exist (Insel et al., 1983; Jefferson et al., 1991). In another study of patients with body dysmorphic disorder (considered by some authors to be a variant of an obsessive-compulsive spectrum), up to 22% of patients also met criteria for bipolar disorder (McElroy, Phillips, Keck, Hudson, & Pope, 1993). Another syndrome that is believed to belong to the OCD spectrum diagnosis is Tourette's disorder. Kerbeshian, Burd, and Klug (1995) reported that 15 of 205 patients with Tourette's had comorbid bipolar disorder, a rate which far exceeds, by more than four times, the level that would be expected by chance.

In summary, the relationship between bipolar and obsessive–compulsive spectrum disorders is a complex one and deserves further study to clarify their relationship. Before OCD is diagnosed in patients with bipolar disorder, other conditions should be ruled out including eating disorders, sexual paraphilias, gambling, SUD, major depression (especially with ruminations or obsessive brooding), movement disorders secondary to antipsychotic drugs (e.g., Tardive Tourette's), and Tourette's disorder.

MANAGEMENT OF BIPOLAR DISORDER WITH COMORBID PANIC DISORDER OR OCD

The important distinction here is whether the patient has two psychiatric disorders, that is, bipolar disorder and a comorbid anxiety disorder, or whether the anxiety symptoms are simply one manifestation within the bipolar symptom complex. In general, it is recommended to have ongoing mood stabilizer therapy to target the mood disorder. The clinician may wish to begin first with cognitive behavior therapy (CBT) that has proven effective in patients with anxiety disorder (D. V. Sheehan, 1999) before the use of antidepressants. Patients with bipolar disorder who have a rapid cycling course of illness or who have a mixed manic state bipolar disorder, may present with panic attacks as the primary manifestation of bipolar disorder. In this case the patient frequently has symptoms of anxiety, restlessness, insomnia, and agitation secondary to the mood disorder. Treating such patients with a selective serotonin reuptake inhibitor (SSRI) or tricyclic antidepressant for the "panic attacks" may induce rapid cycling and worsen the anxiety symptoms and course of illness of bipolar disorder (Ananth, Wohl, Ranganath, & Beshay, 1993). The treatment in such a case would be to use a mood stabilizer (e.g., divalproex sodium or carbamazepine) or augmentation of the mood stabilizer with lamotrigine or gabapentin.

The pharmacological treatment of patients with OCD and panic disorder commonly includes the use of antidepressants such as the SSRIs. In general, these agents should be used more cautiously in the management of OCD and panic disorder in patients with bipolar disorder than in patients without bipolar disorder because of complications that may occur. Complications of antidepressant therapy in bipolar disorder include switching into hypomania or mania and cycle acceleration (Ananth et al., 1993; Goodwin & Jamison, 1990). Both OCD and panic disorder as well as other anxiety disorders (e.g. social anxiety disorder) are chronic conditions that may require long-term treatment with antidepressants (Allgulander, 1999; Liebowitz, 1999; D. V. Sheehan 1999). While the SSRIs are helpful for both OCD and panic disorder, they may destabilize the underlying affective disorder when used on a long-term basis. When using antidepressants in OCD, panic disorder, and other anxiety disorders, the same guidelines apply as in OCD. The dose should be titrated to high maximum doses of the antidepressant (SSRI) for at least 4 to 6 weeks for panic disorder and up to 10 weeks in OCD to obtain the best results. For panic disorder, in order to minimize the "amphetamine reaction" secondary to SSRIs, the initial starting dose should generally be half that used in unipolar depression. The titration process should also be much slower than in patients with major depression, however, final maximum doses need not be different. Recently, there have been some reports suggesting that divalproex may have antipanic properties (Baetz & Bowen, 1998; Woodman & Noyes, 1994). Therefore, in view of the risk of complications with the use of antidepressants (described above), consideration should be given to using divalproex first, especially because this drug can be used as a primary mood stabilizer. Gabapentin has been suggested in open label and controlled studies to have significant anxiolytic effects and may be a treatment alternative in patients with social anxiety disorder and panic disorder (D. V. Sheehan, 1999; Pande et al., 1999, 2000a). Initial reports suggested that gabapentin may have thymoleptic properties (Letterman & Markowitz, 1999); however, recent controlled studies question its efficacy in bipolar disorder (Frye et al., 2000; Pande et al., 2000b). Therefore, before considering the use of SSRIs or tricyclic antidepressants, the clinician may wish to consider utilizing gabapentin as an adjunct only to a primary mood stabilizer, preferably divalproex sodium, because of its questionable primary mood stabilizing properties. Another option in the treatment of panic disorder is to consider the use of anxiolytics some of which have been shown to have antipanic properties (D. V. Sheehan, 1999). However, their use will need to be carefully monitored in patients with bipolar disorder because of the high lifetime prevalence (60%) of comorbid substance use disorders found to be associated with this diagnosis and the increased risk of dependence with the use of anxiolytic agents in the benzodiazepine family. The clinician may wish to consider using the other agents described above before using anxiolytic agents as the primary treatment for panic disorder. Lamotrigine has been reported by manic authors both in open label and controlled mania studies to be effective in acute bipolar depression, rapid-cyclers, and treatment refractory bipolar patients (Calabrese & Delucchi, 1990; Calabrese,

Bowden, McElroy, et al., 1999; Calabrese, Bowden, Sachs, et al., 1999). Kusumakar and Yatham (1997) reported that lamotrigine, when given in combination with divalproex sodium for 6 weeks, was effective in 16 of 22 treatment refractory depressed bipolar patients. In addition, Kusumakar and Yatham (1999) reported that 6 out of twelve patients who responded to lamotrigine add-on had comorbid obsessive compulsive symptoms or disorders. This raises the intriguing possibility that perhaps lamotrigine may have a major role in the treatment of bipolar disorder and comorbid OCD thus avoiding the use of antidepressants and their associated complications with their use. Figures 6.3 and 6.4 provide a general outline on how to manage comorbid panic disorder and OCD in patients with bipolar disorder.

COMORBID BULIMIA NERVOSA

The relationship between bipolar disorder and eating disorders has received little attention. Some studies have observed high rates of bipolar disorder in patients with bulimia nervosa and their relatives (Kassett et al., 1989). The lifetime prevalence of comorbid bulimia in bipolar disorder patients presenting for treatment has been reported to range between 2 and 15% (Black, Winokur, Bell, Nasrallah, & Hulbert, 1988; Black, Winokur, Hulbert, Nasrallah, 1988; McElroy, Strakowski, et al., 1995, Table 1; Strakowski, Tohen, et al., 1992, 1993; Strakowski, Keck, et al., 1995). Kruger et al. (1996) studied 61 patients meeting DSM-III-R criteria for bipolar disorder and found that eight subjects (13%) met criteria for binge-eating disorder and 15 (25%) met criteria for partial binge eating syndrome. One study found that patients with mixed rather than pure mania were more likely to have a comorbid bulimia diagnosis.

Conversely, studies on the relationship of the comorbidity of bipolar spectrum disorder in patients with eating disorder have been few (Shobe & Brion, 1971). One study found that there was an increased rate of bipolar disorder, especially bipolar II disorder in patients with bulimia nervosa (Mury, Verdoux, & Bourgeois, 1995).

MANAGEMENT OF BIPOLAR DISORDER WITH COMORBID EATING DISORDERS

Very little data exists on the pharmacological treatment of eating disorders in bipolar disorder patients. In general, the same principles for the management of eating disorder apply in bipolar disorder patients. At times it may

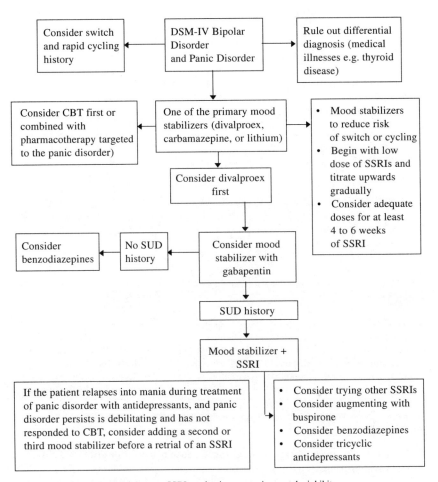

CBT = cognitive behavioral therapy; SSRI = selective serotonin reuptake inhibitor

FIGURE 6.3. Pharmacotherapy of the co-occurrence of bipolar disorder and panic disorder.

be necessary to enlist the support of centers that specialize in the management of eating disorders. Hallmark characteristics of bulimia nervosa include a prodromal period of dissatisfaction with body shape and a fear of becoming overweight, followed by marked dietary restriction. This period is generally followed by episodes of binge eating and, ultimately, self-induced vomiting may occur. Difficulties that may arise in the management of bipolar disorder patients with comorbid bulimia include: (1) the mood stabilizers valproate and lithium as well as other agents commonly used in

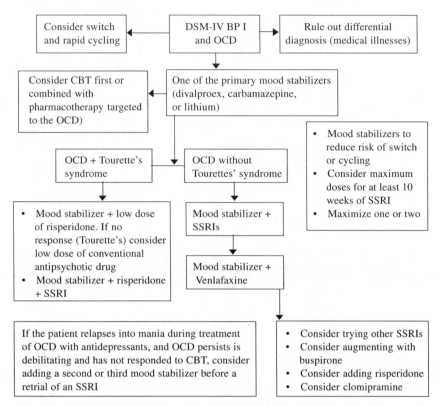

CBT = cognitive behavioral therapy; OCD = obsessive-compulsive disorder; SSRI = selective serotonin reuptake inhibitor

FIGURE 6.4. Pharmacotherapy of the co-occurrence of bipolar disorder and obsessive–compulsive disorder.

the treatment of bipolar disorder (e.g., atypical antipsychotic drugs) are associated with weight gain, (2) self-induced vomiting may lead to electrolyte disturbances and may result in serious complications for patients treated with lithium or adjunctive bupropion; and (3) the SSRIs, while they may prove useful for the treatment of eating disorders (Fluoxetine Bulimia Nervosa Collaborative Study Group, 1992; Mayer & Walsh, 1998), may destabilize the underlying mood disorder. In general, it is recommended to have ongoing mood stabilizer therapy to target the mood disorder and the clinician may wish to begin first with cognitive–behavior therapy that has proven effective in eating disorders (Fairburn, Jones, Peveler, Hope, & O'Connor, 1993) before the use of antidepressants. Recently, the anticonvulsant topiramate has been suggested by some to have thymoleptic properties (Chengappa et al., 1999); however, its efficacy in bipolar disorder remains to be proven in a controlled study. In addition, topiramate has been associated with significant weight loss in some bipolar patients treated with this drug. Recent reports suggest that topiramate may have a role in eating disorders (Colom et al., 2001; Appolinario, Coutinho, & Fontenelle, 2001; Shapira, Goldsmith, & McElroy, 2000); however this awaits confirmation in a systematic way. In addition, topiramate is associated with some worrisome side effects, including paresthesias (15%), psychomotor slowing, word finding problems, and kidney stones (2%). Extreme caution should be exercised when using topiramate before further data about its efficacy and safety is available in patients with comorbid eating disorders. At the present time it is recommended only to use topiramate as an adjunctive treatment in combination with one of the primary mood stabilizers until more information becomes available for its use.

COMORBID IMPULSE CONTROL DISORDERS

High rates of comorbid impulse control disorders (intermittent explosive disorder, pathological gambling, kleptomania, pyromania, and trichotillomania) have been reported to co-occur in patients with affective illness (Kmetz, McElroy, & Collins, 1997; McElroy, 1999; McElroy et al., 1992; McElroy et al., 1996). Some authors have suggested that impulse control disorders and bipolar disorder may be related (McElroy et al., 1996). In bipolar disorder, the rates of comorbid impulse control disorder have been reported to range from 13 to 23% (Black, Winokur, Bell, Nasrallah, & Hulbert, 1988; Black, Winokur, Hulbert, & Nasrallah, 1988; Kruger et al., 1996, Table 1; McElroy et al., 1995; Strakowski et al., 1993). One study reports that comorbid impulse control disorder is an antecedent to bipolar disorder in the majority of the cases (Strakowski, Keck, et al., 1995). Another study found no differences in the rates of impulse control disorder between patients with mixed and pure mania (McElroy et al., 1995). Impulse control disorders have been referred to by some authors as part of an obsessive-compulsive spectrum and as a result theoretically would respond to SSRIs (Ravindran, Lapierre, & Anisman, 1999). Kleptomania as well has been reported to respond favorably to SSRIs (Kraus, 1999). Patients with intermittent explosive disorder have been reported to have high rates of lifetime comorbid bipolar disorder and a favorable response of explosive episodes to mood stabilizing drugs such as valproate (McElroy, 1999). Due to the risk of worsening the course of bipolar disorder with antidepressants for patients with intermittent explosive disorder, it is recommended to first consider a trial with divalproex before using the SSRIs.

Attention Deficit Hyperactivity Disorder (ADHD)

Both attention deficit hyperactivity disorder and bipolar disorder in adults may coexist (Stein, Roizen, & Leventhal, 1999; Trollor, 1999). Recent studies have suggested that attention hyperactivity disorder is highly prevalent in adolescent patients with bipolar disorder. In one study, eight (57%) of 14 adolescent bipolar patients who were hospitalized for treatment of acute mania also met criteria for attention deficit hyperactivity disorder (West et al., 1995). Another study examined the cooccurrence of comorbid disorders in hospitalized bipolar adolescents ($n = 10$) compared with unipolar depressed adolescents ($n = 33$), and adolescents with nonaffective psychiatric disorders ($n = 11$). The authors found that attention deficit hyperactivity disorder, as well as conduct disorder, psychosis, and any DSM-III-R psychoactive SUD, were all significantly more common in the bipolar than in the unipolar depressed group.

Many treatments are being tested and have been reported to be useful in attention deficit/hyperactive disorder in adults (Wender, 1998). Methylphenidate and pemoline have been studied in double-blind, placebo-controlled trials and pargyline, selegiline, bupropion, levodopa, phenylalanine, and tyrosine in open label studies. In patients requiring treatment for the comorbid attention deficit disorder, the following guidelines are recommended: (1) if the patient is cycling, manic, or in a mixed episode the focus should be first on stabilizing the mood disorder before the treatment of ADHD is attempted, and (2) if the patient is currently in the depressed phase of bipolar disorder, then the clinician may wish to consider a trial of bupropion, which has been found to be useful in both ADHD and acute major depression of the bipolar type. Bupropion has been reported to be associated with low switch rates into mania when compared with desipramine (Sachs et al., 1994), and may not accelerate cycling. Bupropion would, therefore, permit the treatment of both conditions while minimizing the risk of potential complications. Desipramine, selegiline, and the stimulants may also have a role in both conditions. However, it is important to note that both classes of medications may destabilize the bipolar illness. In addition, many patients with bipolar disorder may also have comorbid SUD and hence, stimulants should be used very cautiously in this population if at all.

Conclusions

Comorbid psychiatric and medical conditions are common in bipolar disorder. Given the magnitude of the problem, there has, unfortunately, been little research to guide the clinician about valid diagnostic and treatment strategies in the presence of comorbid or cooccurring psychiatric disorders with bipolar disorder. Currently, the primary principle of treatment is to take all necessary steps to ensure that mood regulation is maintained, and that the comorbid condition is treated by targeting particular symptoms that cause distress or dysfunction. More research needs to be done with special attention to rigorously controlled study designs and well-defined patient selection. Using treatment algorithms will help standardize treatment approaches while studying their effectiveness and helping identify areas where further research is needed.

References

Akiskal, H. S., & Pinto, O. (1999, September). The evolving bipolar spectrum. *Psychiatric Clinics of North America, 22*(3), 517–534.

Albanese, M. J., Bartel, R. L., Bruno, R. F., Morgenbesser, M. W., & Schatzberg, A. F. (1994). Comparison of measures used to determine substance abuse in an inpatient psychiatric population. *American Journal of Psychiatry, 151,* 1077–1078.

Allgulander, C. (1999). Paroxetine in social anxiety disorder: a randomized placebo-controlled study. *Acta Psychiatrica Scand*inavia, *100,* 193–198.

Ananth, J., Wohl, M., Ranganath, V., & Beshay, M. (1993). Rapid cycling patients: conceptual and etiological factors. *Neuropsychobiology, 27*(4), 193–198.

Anton, R. F., Moak, D. H., Waid, L. R., Latham, P. K., Malcolm, R. J., & Dias, J. K. (1999, November). Naltrexone and cognitive behavioral therapy for the treatment of outpatient alcoholics: Results of a placebo-controlled trial. *American Journal of Psychiatry, 156*(11), 1758–1764.

Appolinario, J. C., Coutinho, W., & Fontenelle, L. (2001). Topiramate for binge-eating disorder. *American Journal of Psychiatry, 158*(6), 967–968.

Baer, L., Minichiello, W. E., & Jenike, M. A. (1985). Behavioral treatment in two cases of obsessive-compulsive disorder with concomitant bipolar affective disorder. *American Journal of Psychiatry, 142,* 358–360.

Baetz, M., & Bowen, R. C. (1998). Efficacy of divalproex sodium in patients with panic disorder and mood instability who have not responded to conventional therapy. *Canadian Journal of Psychiatry, 43,* 73–77.

Black, D. W., Hulbert, J., & Nasrallah, A. (1989). The effect of somatic treatment and comorbidity on immediate outcome in manic patients. *Comprehensive Psychiatry, 30,* 74–79.

Black, D. W., Winokur, G., Bell, S., Nasrallah, A., & Hulbert, J. (1988). Complicated mania: comorbidity and immediate outcome in the treatment of mania. *Archives of General Psychiatry, 45,* 232–236.

Black, D. W., Winokur, J., Hulbert, J., & Nasrallah, A. (1988). Predictors of immediate response in the treatment of mania: the importance of comorbidity. *Biological Psychiatry, 24,* 191–198.

Blacker, D., & Tsuang, M. T. (1992). Contested boundaries of bipolar disorder and the limits of categorical diagnosis in psychiatry. *American Journal of Psychiatry, 149,* 1473–1483.

Bowden, C. L. (1995). Predictors of response to divalproex and lithium. *Journal of Clinical Psychiatry, 56*(Suppl. 3), 25–30.

Boyd, J. H., Burke, J. D., Gruenberg, E., Holzer, C. E., III, Rae, D. S., George, L. K., Karno, M., Stoltzman, T., McEvoy, L., & Nestadt, S. (1984). Exclusion criteria of DSM-III: A study of co-occurrence of hierarchy-free syndromes. *Archives of General Psychiatry, 41,* 983–989.

Brady, K., Casto, S., Lydiard, R., Malcom, R., & Arana, G. (1991). Substance abuse in an inpatient psychiatric sample. *American Journal of Drug & Alcohol Abuse, 17,* 389–397.

Brady, K. T., Sonne, S. C., Anton, R., & Ballenger, J. C. (1995). Valproate in the treatment of acute bipolar affective episodes complicated by substance abuse: A pilot study. *Journal of Clinical Psychiatry, 56,* 118–121.

Calabrese, J. R., Bowden, C. L., McElroy, S. L., Cookson, J., Andersen, J., Keck, P. E., Jr., et al. (1999, July). Spectrum of activity of lamotrigine in treatment-refractory bipolar disorder. *American Journal of Psychiatry, 156*(7), 1019–1023.

Calabrese, J. R., Bowden, C. L., Sachs, G. S., Ascher, J. A., Monaghan, E., & Rudd, G. D. (1999, February). A double-blind placebo-controlled study of lamotrigine monotherapy in outpatients with bipolar I depression. Lamictal 602 Study Group. *Journal of Clinical Psychiatry, 60*(2), 79–88.

Calabrese, J. R., & Delucchi, G. A. (1990). Spectrum efficacy of valproate in 55 patients with rapid-cycling bipolar disorder. *American Journal of Psychiatry, 147,* 431–434.

Chen, Y.-W., & Dilsaver, S. C. (1995). Comorbidity of panic disorder in bipolar illness: Evidence from the Epidemiologic Catchment Area Survey. *American Journal of Psychiatry, 152,* 280–282.

Chengappa, R. K. N., Rathore, D., Levine, J., Atzert, R., Solai, L., Parepally, H., et al. (1999). Topiramate as add-on treatment for patients with bipolar mania. *Bipolar Disorders, 1,* 42–53.

Colom, F., Vieta, E., Benaberra, A., Martinez-Aran, A., Reinares, M., Corbella, B., & Gasto, C. (2001). Topiramate abuse in a bipolar patient with an eating disorder. *Journal of Clinical Psychiatry, 62*(6), 475–476.

Cummings, J. L. (1986). Organic psychoses: Delusional disorders and secondary mania. *Psychiatric Clinics of North Ameria, 9,* 293–311.

DiNardo, P. A., & Barlow, D. H. (1990). Syndrome and symptom co-occurrence in the anxiety disorders. In J. D. Maser & C. R. Cloninger (Eds.), *Comorbidity of mood and anxiety disorders* (pp. 205–230). Washington, DC: American Psychiatric Press.

Eaton, W. W., Dryman, A., & Weismann, M. M. (1991). Panic phobia. In L. N. Robins & D. A. Regier (Eds.), *Psychiatric disorders in America: The epidemiologic catchment area study* (pp. 155–179). New York: Free Press.

Fairburn, C. G., Jones, R., Peveler, R. C., Hope, R. A., & O'Connor, M. (1993). Psychotherapy and bulimia nervosa: Longer-term effects of interpersonal psychotherapy, behavior therapy, and cognitive behavior therapy. *Archives of General Psychiatry, 50,* 419–428.

Feinman, J. A., & Dunner, D. L. (1996). The effect of alcohol and substance abuse on the course of bipolar affective disorder. *Journal of Affective Disorders, 37,* 43–49.

Ferugi, G., Toni, C., & Akiskal, H. S. (1999, September). Anxious-bipolar comorbidity: Diagnosis and treatment. *Psychiatric Clinics of North America, 22*(3), 565–584.

Fluoxetine Bulimia Nervosa Collaborative Study Group. (1992). Fluoxetine in the treatment of bulimia nervosa. *Archives of General Psychiatry, 49,* 139–147.

Frye, M. A., Ketter, T. A., Kimbrell, T. A., Dunn, R. M., Speer, A. M., Osuch, A., et al. (2000, December). A placebo-controlled study of lamotrigine and gabapentin monotherapy in refractory mood disorder. *Journal of Clinical Psychopharmacology, 20*(6), 607–614.

Gawin, F. H., & Kleber, H. D. (1984). Cocaine abuse treatment: Open pilot trial with desipramine and lithium carbonate. *Archives of General Psychiatry, 41,* 903–909.

Geller, B., Cooper, T. B., Sun, K., Zimmerman, B., Frazier, J., Williams, M., et al. (1998). Double blind placebo controlled study of lithium for adolescent bipolar disorders with secondary substance dependency. *Journal of American Academy of Child and Adolescent Psychtiatry, 37,* 171–178.

Goldberg, J. F., Garno, J. L., Leon, A. C., Kocsis, J. H., & Portera, L. (1999). A history of substance abuse complicates remission from acute mania in bipolar disorder. *Journal of Clinical Psychiatry, 60,* 733–740.

Goodwin, F. K., & Jamison, K. R. (1990). *Manic-depressive illness.* New York: Oxford University Press.

Himmelhoch, J. M., Mulla, D., Neil, J. F., Detre, T. P., & Kupfer, D. J. (1976). Incidence and significance of mixed affective states in a bipolar population. *Archives of General Psychiatry, 33,* 1062–1066.

Insel, T. R., Murphy, D. L., Cohen, R. M., Alterman, I., Kitts, C., & Linnoila, M. (1983). Obsessive–compulsive disorder: A double-blind trial of clomipramine and clorgyline. *Archives of General Psychiatry, 40,* 605–612.

Jefferson, J. W., Greist, J. H., Perse, T. L., & Rosenfeld, R. (1991). Fluvoxamine-associated mania/hypomania in patients with obsessive-compulsive disorder. *Journal of Clinical Psychopharmacology, 11,* 391–392.

Kassett, J. A., Gershon, M. E., Maxwell, M. E., Guroff, J. J., Kazuba, D. M., Smith, A. L., et al. (1989). Psychiatric disorders in first-degree relatives of probands with bulimia nervosa. *American Journal of Psychiatry, 146,* 1468–1471.

Keck, P. E., Jr., Lipinski, J. F., & White, K. (1986). An inverse relationship between mania and obsessive-compulsive disorder: a case report. *Journal of Clinical Psychopharmacology, 6,* 123–124.

Keck, P. E., Jr., McElroy, S., Strakowski, S., Bourne, M., & West, S. (1997). Compliance with maintenance treatment in bipolar disorder. *Psychopharmacology Bulletin, 33,* 87–91

Keck, P. E., Jr., McElroy, S. L., Strakowski, S. M., West, S. A., Sax, K. W., Hawkins, J. M., et al. (1998). 12-month outcome of patients with bipolar disorder following hospitalization for a manic or mixed episode. *American Journal of Psychiatry, 155,* 646–652.

Keck, P. E., Jr., McElroy, S. L., Strakowski, S. M., West, S. A., Hawkins, J. M., Huber, T. J., et al. (1995). Outcome and comorbidity in first- compared with multiple-episode mania. *Journal of Nervous and Mental Disorder, 183,* 320–324.

Keller, M. B., Lavori, P. W., Coryell, W., Andreasen, N. C., Endicott, J., Clayton, P. J., et al. (1986). Differential outcome of pure manic, mixed/cycling, and pure depressive episodes in patients with bipolar illness. *Journal of the American Medical Association, 255,* 3138–3142.

Kerbeshian, J., Burd, L., & Klug, M. G. (1995). Comorbid tourette's disorder and bipolar disorder: an etiologic perspective. *American Journal of Psychiatry, 152,* 1646–1651

Kessler, R. C., Crum, R. M., Warner, L. A., Nelson, C. B., Schulenberg, J., & Anthony, J. C. (1997, April). Lifetime co-occurrence of DSM-III-R alcohol abuse and dependence with other psychiatric disorders in the national comorbidity survey. *Archives of General Psychiatry, 54,* 313–321.

Kessler, R. C., McGonagle, K. A., Zhao, S., Nelson, C. B., Hughes, M., Eshleman, S., et al. (1994). Lifetime and 12-month prevalence of DSM-III-R psychiatric disorders in the United States: Results from the national comorbidity survey. *Archives of General Psychiatry, 51,* 8–19.

Kmetz, G. F., McElroy, S. L., & Collins, D. J. (1997). Response of kleptomania and mixed mania to valproate. *American Journal of Psychiatry, 154,* 580–581.

Kraus, J. E. (1999). Treatment of kleptomania with paroxetine. *Journal of Clinical Psychiatry, 60,* 793.

Krauthammer, C., & Klerman, G. L. (1978). Secondary mania: Manic syndromes associated with antecedent physical illness or drugs. *Archives of General Psychiatry, 35,* 1333–1339.

Kruger, S., Shugar, G., & Cooke, R. G. (1996). Comorbidity of binge eating disorder and the partial binge eating syndrome with bipolar disorder. *International Journal of Eating Disorders, 19,* 45–52.

Kusumakar, V., & Yatham, L. N. (1997). An open study of lamotrigine in refractory bipolar depression. *Psychiatry Research, 19,* 145–148.

Kusumakar, V., & Yatham, L. N. (1999, September). Newer anticonvulsants in bipolar disorder. Paper presented at the Canadian Psychiatric Association Annual Meeting, Toronto.

Letterman, L., & Markowitz, J. S. (1999), Gabapentin: A review of published experience in the treatment of bipolar disorder and other psychiatric conditions. *Pharmacotherapy, 19,* 565–572.

Liebowitz, M. R. (1999). Update on the diagnosis and treatment of social anxiety disorder. *Journal of Clinical Psychiatry, 60*(Suppl. 18), 22–26.

Maarbjerg, K., Aagaard, J., & Vestergaard, P. (1988). Adherence to lithium prophylaxis: I. Clinical predictors and patient's reasons for nonadherence. *Pharmacopsychiatry, 21,* 121–125

Maser, J. D., & Cloninger, C. R. (Eds.). (1990). *Comorbidity of mood and anxiety disorders.* Washington, DC: American Psychiatric Press.

Mayer, L. E., & Walsh, B. T. (1998), The use of selective serotonin reuptake-inhibitors in eating disorders. *Journal of Clinical Psychiatry, 59*(Suppl. 15), 28–34.

Mayfield, D., & Coleman, L. L. (1968). Alcohol use and affective disorder. *Disorders of the Nervous System, 29,* 467–474

McElroy, S. L. (1999). Recognition and treatment of DSM-IV intermittent explosive disorder. *J Clin Psychiatry, 60*(Suppl. 15), 12–16.

McElroy, S. L., Hudson, J. I., Pope, H. G., Jr., & Aizley, H. G. (1992). The DSM-III-R impulse control disorders not elsewhere classified: Clinical characteristics and relationship to other psychiatric disorders. *American Journal of Psychiatry, 149,* 318–327.

McElroy, S. L., Phillips, K. A., Keck, P. E., Jr., Hudson, J. I., & Pope, H. G., Jr. (1993). Body dysmorphic disorder: Does it have a psychotic subtype? *Journal of Clinical Psychiatry, 54,* 389–395.

McElroy, S. L., Pope, H. G., Jr., Keck, P. E., Jr., Hudson, J. I., Phillips, K. A., & Strakowski, S. M. (1996). Are impulse-control disorders related to bipolar disorder? *Comprehensive Psychiatry, 37,* 229–240.

McElroy, S. L., Strakowski, S. M., Keck, P. E., Jr., Tugrul, K. L., West, S. A., & Lonczak, H. S. (1995). Differences and similarities in mixed and pure mania. *Comprehensive Psychiatry, 36,* 187–194.

Miklowitz, D. J. (1996). Psychotherapy in combination with drug treatment for bipolar disorder. *Journal of Clinical Psychopharmacology, 16*(Suppl. 1), 56S–66S.

Morrison, J. R. (1974). Bipolar affective disorder and alcoholism. *American Journal of Psychiatry, 131,* 1130–1133.

Mury, M., Verdoux, H., & Bourgeois, M. (1995). Comorbidite trouble bipolaire et trouble des conduites alimentaires. Aspects epidemiologigues et therapeutigues. *Encephale, 21,* 545–553.

Najavits, L., & Weiss, R. (1994). The role of psychotherapy in the treatment of substance use disorders. *Harvard Review of Psychiatry, 2,* 84–96.

Nunes, E. V., McGrath, P. J., Wager, S., & Quitkin, F. M. (1990). Lithium treatment for cocaine abusers with bipolar spectrum disorders. *American Journal of Psychiatry, 147,* 655–657.

O'Connell, R. A., Mayo, J. A., Flatlow, L., Cuthbertson, B., & O'Brien, B. E. (1991). Outcome of bipolar disorder on long-term treatment with lithium. *British Journal of Psychiatry, 159,* 123–129.

Pande, A. C., Crockett, J. G., Janney, C. A., Werth, J. L., & Tsaroucha, G. (2000). Gabapentin in bipolar disorder: A placebo-controlled trial of adjunctive therapy. Gabapentin Bipolar Disorder Study Group. *Bipolar Disorder, 19*(3 pt. 2), 249–255.

Pande, A. C., Davidson, J. R., Jefferson, J. W., Janney, C. A., Katzelnick, D. J., Weisler, et al. (1999). Treatment of social phobia with gabapentin: A placebo-controlled study. *Journal of Clinical Psychopharmacology, 19*(4), 341–348.

Pande, A. C., Pollack, M. H., Crockatt, J., Greiner, M., Chouinard, G., Lydiard, R. B., et al. (2000). Placebo-controlled study of gabapentin treatment of panic disorder. *Journal of Clinical Psychopharmacology, 20*(4), 467–471.

Perugi, G., Toni, C., & Akiskal, H. S. (1999, September). Anxious-bipolar comorbidity: Diagnostic and treatment challenges. *Psychiatric Clinics of North America, 22*(3), 565–583, viii.

Ravindran, A. V., Lapierre, Y. D., & Anisman, H. (1999). Obsessive-compulsive spectrum disorders: Effective treatment with paroxetine. *Canadian Journal of Psychiatry, 44*, 805–807.

Regier, D. A.., Farmer, M. E, Rae, D. S., Locke, B. Z., Keith, S. J., Judd, L. L., et al. (1990). Comorbidity of mental disorders with alcohol and other drug abuse: Results from the Epidemiologic Catchment Area (ECA) study. *Journal of the American Medical Association, 264*, 2511–2518.

Reich, L. H., Davies, R. K., & Himmelhoch, J. M., Jr. (1974). Excessive alcohol use in manic-depressive illness. *American Journal of Psychiatry, 131*, 83–86.

Sachs, G. S., Lafer, B., Stoll, A. L., Banov, M., Thibault, A. B., Tohen, M., et al. (1994, September). A double-blind trial of bupropion versus desipramine for bipolar depression. *Journal of Clinical Psychiatry, 55*(9), 391–393.

Savino, M., Perugi, G., Simonini, E., Soriani, A., Cassano, G. B., & Akiskal, H. S. (1993). Affective comorbidity in panic disorder: Is there a bipolar connection? *Journal of Affective Disorders, 28*, 155–163.

Shapira, N. A., Goldsmith, T. D., & McElroy, S. L. (2000). Treatment of binge-eating disorder with topiramate: A clinical case series. *Journal of Clinical Psychiatry, 61*(5), 368–372.

Sheehan, D. V. (1999). Current concepts in the treatment of panic disorder. *Journal of Clinical Psychiatry, 60*(Suppl. 18), 16–21.

Sheehan, M. F. (1993). Dual diagnosis. *Psychiatry* Quarterly, 64, 107–134.

Shobe, F. O., & Brion, P. (1971). Long term prognosis in manic-depressive illness. *Archives of General Psychiatry, 24*, 334–337.

Sonne, S. C., Brady, K. T., & Morton, W. A. (1994). Substance abuse and bipolar affective disorder. *Journal of Nervous and Mental Disorders, 182*, 349–352.

Stein, M. A., Roizen, N. M., & Leventhal, B. L. (1999). Bipolar disorder and ADHD. *Journal of the American Academy of Child and Adolescent Psychiatry*, 38, 1208–1209.

Strakowski, S. M., McElroy, S. L., Keck, P. E., Jr., & West, S. A. (1994). The co-occurrence of mania with medical and other psychiatric disorders. *International Journal of Psychiatry Medicine, 24*, 305–328.

Strakowski, S. M., Sax, K. W., McElroy, S. L., Keck, P. E., Jr., Hawkins, J. M., & West, S. A. (1998). Course of psychiatric and substance abuse syndromes co-occurring with bipolar disorder after a first psychiatric hospitalization. *Journal of Clinical Psychiatry, 59*, 465–471.

Strakowski, S. M., Tohen, M., Stoll, A. L., Faedda, G. L., & Goodwin, D. C. (1992). Comorbidity in mania at first hospitalization. *American Journal of Psychiatry, 149*, 554–556.

Strakowski, S. M., Tohen, M., Stoll, A. L., Faedda, G. L., Mayer, M. L., Kolbrener, M. L., et al. (1993). Comorbidity in psychosis at first-hospitalization. *American Journal of Psychiatry, 150*, 752–757.

Strakowski, S. M., Keck, P. E., Jr., McElroy, S. L., Lonczak, H. S., & West, S. A. (1995). Chronology of comorbid and principal syndromes in first-episode psychosis. *Comprehensive Psychiatry, 36*, 106–112.

Tohen, M., & Goodwin, F. K. (1995). Epidemiology of bipolar disorder. In M. Tsuang, M. Tohen, & G. Zahner (Eds.), *Textbook in psychiatric epidemiology*. New York: Wiley.

Tohen, M., Stoll, A. L., Strakowski, S. M., Faedda, G. L., Mayer, P. V., Goodwin, D. C., et al. (1992). The McLean first episode psychosis project: Six month recovery and recurrence outcome. *Schizophrenia Bulletin, 18*(2), 172–185.

Tohen, M., Waternaux, C. M., Tsuang, M. T., & Hunt, A. T. (1990). Four-year follow-up of twenty-four first-episode manic patients. *Journal of Affective Disorders, 19,* 79–86.

Tohen, M., Zarate, C. A., Jr., Zarate, S. B., Gebre-Medhin, P., & Pike, S. (1996). The McLean/ Harvard First-Episode Mania Project: Pharmacologic treatment and outcome. *Psychiatry Annals, 26*(Suppl. 7). S444–S448.

Trollor, J. N. (1999). Attention deficit hyperactivity disorder in adults: Conceptual and clinical issues. *Medical Journal of Australia, 171,* 421–425.

Weiss, R., & Najavits, L. (1998). Overview of treatment modalities for dual diagnosis patients: Pharmacotherapy, psychotherapy, twelve-step programs. In H. Kranzler & B. Rounsaville (Eds.), *Dual diagnosis: Substance abuse and comorbid medical and psychiatric disorders* (pp. 87–105). New York: Dekker.

Weiss, R. D., Greenfield, S. F., Najavits, L. M., Soto, J. A., Wyner, D., Tohen, M., et al. (1998). Medical compliance among patients with bipolar disorder and substance use disorder. *Journal of Clinical Psychiatry, 59,* 172–174.

Weiss, R. D., Najavits, L. M., & Greenfield, S. F. (1999). A relapse prevention group for patients with bipolar and substance use disorders. *Journal of Substance Abuse Treatment, 16,* 47–54.

Wender, P. H. (1998). Pharmacotherapy of attention-deficit/hyperactivity disorder in adults. *Journal of Clinical Psychiatry, 59*(Suppl. 7), 76–79.

West, S. A., McElroy, S. L., Strakowski, S. M., Keck, P. E., Jr., & McConville, J. (1995):. Attention deficit hyperactivity disorder in adolescent mania. *American Journal of Psychiatry, 152,* 271–273.

Woodman, C. L., & Noyes, R., Jr. (1994). Panic disorder: treatment with valproate. *Journal of Clinical Psychiatry, 55,* 134–136.

CHAPTER 7

Lithium in the Treatment of Bipolar Disorder

Joseph Levine
Jair C. Soares
K. N. Roy Chengappa
Samuel Gershon

Historical Notes

As with many other psychotropic drugs, lithium was discovered by serendipity. In a short essay entitled, "The History of Lithium," Cade (1949) describes the background against which he made the discovery of lithium's specific effects in bipolar illness, his working hypothesis, as well as the unexpected way in which these effects were found.

Lithium has an erratic history in medicine . . . The alkali itself was discovered by Arfvedson in 1817. . . . Lithium salts were introduced to medicine by A.B. Garrod in 1859 for the treatment of gout. . . . Culbreth in 1927 stated that lithium bromide is the most hypnotic of all bromides. My discovery of the specific antimanic effect of lithium ion was an unexpected but to be retrospectively percipient for a moment, inevitable by-product of experimental work I was doing to test a hypothesis regarding the etiology of manic depressive illness. Could mania be a state analogous to thyrotoxicosis and myxoedema, mania being a state of intoxication by a normal product of the body circulating in excess, whilst melancholia is the corresponding deprivative condition? . . . for this purpose guinea pigs were used and fresh urine (of manic patients) was injected intraperitonealy . . . it soon became evident that some specimens of urine from manic patients were far more toxic than any of control specimens from normal persons. . . . (p. 218)

In an attempt to uncover such a toxic metabolite, Cade examined first the role of creatinine and urea, although he hypothesized that a different, third metabolite may be the toxic one. Cade planned to inject his laboratory animals with an aqueous solution of uric acid. However as uric acid is not soluble in water, Cade used the most soluble urate—an aqueous solution of a lithium salt. While examining the effect of the lithium salt itself on the animals, to his surprise he noticed that *"although fully conscious (the animals), they became extremely lethargic and unresponsive to stimuli . . . it may seem a long way from lethargy in guinea pigs to the control of manic patients but . . . "* and here Cade describes at length his experiments with lithium in manic patients (Cade, 1949, p. 223). Interestingly Cade never found the hypothesized toxic metabolite he was looking for, but he opened the way for what is still considered the "gold standard" treatment of bipolar illness. Cade (1970), in a small series of cases, reported remarkable therapeutic effects for the manic patients, while schizophrenic and chronic depressive patients failed to demonstrate any changes. Thus, Cade was the first to notice a specific effect for lithium in bipolar disorder.

Cade later studied the effect of other related alkali metals such as rubidium and cesium along with cerium, lanthanum, neodymium, strontium and praseodymium. Cade even examined the effect of strontium in three manic, seven acute schizophrenic, two psychotic depressed, and 10 chronic schizophrenic patients. Four of the acute schizophrenic patients showed rapid improvement within a few days, and this was true for two out of the three manic patients. None of the chronic schizophrenic patients or the psychotic depressive patients improved. Cade concludes his historical lecture (Cade 1949) stating:

That lithium, a simple inorganic ion, can reverse a major psychotic reaction (manic episode) must have, quite apart from its substantial therapeutic value, profound theoretical significance in unraveling the mystery of the so-called functional psychoses. It must be regarded as a major research tool. Strontium may also prove to have a similar value for research in this field even if it has only minor therapeutic value. (p. 229)

Cade, using the terminology of his time (i.e. psychotic reaction), was right about the major role of lithium in a host of studies trying to unravel the mechanisms underlying bipolar illness. Strontium, however, raised no interest, and no further research was done with this agent.

Lithium in Acute Mania

The study of lithium in acute mania included several phases, some of them overlapping. The drug was first studied openly in small-scale studies, many of them lacking clear diagnostic criteria and well defined rating scales. After initial positive results were reported, placebo controlled double blind studies followed. As these studies demonstrated evidence for the efficacy of lithium in bipolar mania, a series of controlled studies compared it with traditional antipychotics, and also reported antimanic effects. After a lag of about two decades (the 1970s and the 1980s) the marketing of the new antiepileptic and antipsychotic agents, spurred new double-blind studies comparing lithium to these drugs. In the large majority of studies, lithium was shown to be highly effective in acute mania, although more recent naturalistic studies reported lower improvement rates, and some authors even suggested that the benefit of response is compromised by side effects appearing in the early phases of treatment.

One of the main problems in comparing and assessing the results of various studies is that different diagnostic criteria and rating scales were used. We will present here the results of the first two open studies conducted prior to the publication of the Diagnostic Statistical Manual (DSM) I (American Psychiatric Association, 1952) to be followed by double-blind studies during the DSM-I era, 1952 to 1967 (American Psychiatric Association, 1952); DSM-II era, 1968 to 1979 (American Psychiatric Association, 1968); DSM III era, 1980 to 1986 (American Psychiatric Association, 1980); DSM-III-R era, 1987 to 1993 (American Psychiatric Association, 1987); and DSM-IV era, 1994 to 1999 (American Psychiatric Association, 1994a). While not all the double blind studies used this diagnostic system, and some studies published during a certain period were conducted in a previous one, we felt that such an organization may serve as an appropriate framework enabling follow-up and assessment of response rates over these time periods.

PRE-DSM ERA OPEN STUDIES

Two pioneering open studies were conducted during the pre-DSM era. The first one by Cade (1949) included 10 manic patients, all of whom improved following lithium treatment. No clear diagnostic and assessment criteria were presented. Cade's description of the first case of mania ever to be treated with lithium illustrates the magnitude of the breakthrough associated with this new treatment:

> *[T]his was a little wizened man of 51 who had been in a state of chronic manic excitement for 5 years. He was amiably restless, dirty, destructive, mischievous and interfering. He enjoyed preeminent nuisance value in a back ward for all those years and bid fair to remain there for the rest of his life. He commenced treatment with lithium citrate 1200 mg tid on 29 March 1948. On the fourth day the optimistic therapist thought he saw some change . . . by the fifth day it was clear he was in fact more settled, tidier, less disinhibited and less distractible. From that day on there was a steady improvement. . . . He remained well and left hospital (after housing was arranged) on 9 July, 1948 . . . taking a maintenance dose of lithium carbonate 300 mg bid.* (pp. 223–224)

The second open study was that of Noack and Trautner (1951). These authors studied 30 openly manic patients. Twenty-five patients responded well (83%) to lithium treatment. Both of these pioneering studies reported very high response rates to lithium. When comparing their results to results of more recent studies, one should bear in mind the expectation associated with these investigations, the open design utilized, and the fact that patients were lithium naïve.

Double-blind Studies

Lithium vs. Placebo

1952–1967 (DSM-I): Schou, Juel-Nielsen, Stromgren, and Voldby (1954) studied 38 manic (30 typical and eight atypical) patients in Denmark in a partially open and partially placebo-controlled double-blind design. The dose of lithium used resulted in serum lithium levels of 0.5 to 2.0 meq/L. Clinical response was determined by a three point global severity scale. Fourteen patients showed a positive response (37%), 18 a possible response (47%), and six had no response (16%). Schou (1988) also conducted a large open study in which 91 of 119 (76%) manic patients improved. On the role of Schou in introducing lithium treatment for mania, Cade (1970) wrote: *"The person who has done most to achieve this recognition by validating and extending my original observation has been Mogens Schou in Denmark"* (p. 219).

Maggs (1963) studied 28 acute manic patients. The author was not clear as to the diagnostic criteria used for patient selection. Lithium or placebo was each given for 2 weeks in a cross-over design. Two weeks of no drug elapsed between crossing from one drug to another. The Wittenborn Scale for Manic State and Schizophrenic Excitement was used to assess the results. Ten patients dropped out of the study; eight due to uncooperativeness and two due to lithium toxicity. Lithium was found to be superior to placebo. The strengths of this study were the use of a rating scale and its blindness. Its weakness was the high drop-out rate and the cross-over design, which might have biased its results and the short duration of the treatment period.

1968–1979 (DSM-II): Bunney, Goodwin, Davis, and Fawcett (1968) studied two patients in a longitudinal double blind fashion demonstrating the sensitivity of manic symptoms to short periods of withdrawal from lithium treatment. The rating scale used was a 24 item mania scale measuring the core as well as other symptoms associated with mania. Diagnosis was made by the Mayer Gross definition of mania (Gershon & Shopsin, 1973). This longitudinal follow-up demonstrated the reappearance or increase of manic symptoms within 24 hours of lithium discontinuation.

Goodwin, Murphy, and Bunney (1969) studied 30 manic-depressive patients in a double-blind placebo-controlled fashion. This group included 12 manic patients. Doses of lithium used were 900 to 1800 mg daily. Patients' serum lithium level was above 0.8 and below 1.2meq/L. Nurses rating scales were employed. Eight of the 12 manic patients had a complete response (67%), one had partial response, and three worsened. The symptomatology of the three patients who worsened seemed to correspond more closely with schizoaffective disorder than with bipolar mania.

Stokes, Shamoian, Stoll, and Patton (1971), studied 38 manic patients in a double-blind, placebo-controlled cross-over design. Patients were selected for the study after diagnostic consensus was obtained by three psychiatrists. Lithium was given at 0.5meq/kg/day in four divided doses. Mean serum lithium was 0.93meq/L. Data was analyzed for 98 manic periods (56 on lithium and 42 on placebo), each of 7 to 10 days. Seventy-five percent of the 56 lithium-treated episodes responded to lithium treatment, while only 40.5% of the 42 placebo-treated episodes responded to placebo. However, this study has significant flaws. The period chosen for each period of treatment may be too short to examine lithium antimanic effect. There was no washout period between the placebo and lithium periods that may attenuate a carryover or withdrawal effect, and the rating scale used was not well defined. Nevertheless, this study added to the growing body of studies on lithium efficacy in acute mania.

1980–1993 (DSM-III & DSM-III-R):   The above studies established the role of lithium as the gold standard treatment for acute mania. No placebo-controlled studies of lithium effect in acute mania were performed during these years.

1994–1999 (DSM-IV):   Bowden et al. (1994) conducted a double blind placebo-controlled, randomly assigned prospective parallel group study comparing lithium, valproic acid, and placebo in acute mania. No neuroleptics were used, and rescue medication was lorazepam allowed in the first week of the study. One hundred and seventy-nine patients were treated for 3 weeks with either lithium, divalproex, or placebo in a 1:2:2 ratio. Dosage of lithium was increased if tolerated, resulting in up to 1.5 mmol/L. The primary outcome measure was the Mania Rating Scale derived from the Schedule for Affective Disorders and Schizophrenia (SADS). Intent to treat analysis included 35 patients on lithium, 68 patients on divalproex, and 73 patients on placebo. Thirty-three percent of the lithium treated patients, 30% of the divalproex treated patients, and 51% of the placebo treated patients terminated prematurely due to lack of efficacy. More than 50% improvement was noticed in 49, 48, and 25% of patients on lithium, divalproex, and placebo, respectively.

Lithium vs. Antipsychotic Drugs

1968–1979 (DSM-II):   Johnson, Gershon, and Hekimain (1968) and Johnson, Gershon, Burdock, Floyd, and Herimian (1971) compared the effect of lithium versus chlorpromazine in 21 manic-depressive patients and 13 excited schizoaffective patients. Lithium blood levels were maintained above 1.0 meq/L and medications were given for 14 to 21 days. Rating scales included the Brief Psychiatric Rating Scale, and Clinical Global Impression Scale. Specific features of the manic symptomatology including excitability were more responsive to lithium, while motor activity was more responsive to chlorpromazine, suggesting that lithium treatment may be more specific to mania.

Spring, Schweid, Gray, Steinberg, and Horwitz (1970) studied in a double-blind design 14 acute manic patients randomly assigned to treatment with lithium or chlorpromazine. Lithium treatment in the first week was 1800 mg daily, and could subsequently be raised up to 3000 mg daily. Chlorpromazine dose could be adjusted up to 1600 mg daily. Six of seven patients who started on lithium responded, while only three of the five patients starting with chlorpromazine had a therapeutic response. Interestingly, the two chlorpromazine failures were switched to lithium and also responded. While the results are impressive for such a small study, regrettably these authors did not report how they defined response. Although not statistically significant, lithium was found to be more effective than chlorpromazine for the treatment of typical manic symptoms such as motor hyperactivity, flight of ideas, euphoria, expansiveness, and pressured speech.

Platman (1970) studied 23 manic patients in double-blind fashion. Patients were randomized to either lithium or chlorpromazine treatment, each after 2 weeks of lead-in placebo treatment. Plasma lithium levels were maintained at 0.8 mEq/L. The mean daily dose of lithium was 1800 mg, and for chlorpramazine it was 870 mg. Thirteen patients were treated with lithium and 10 with chlorpromazine. Ten patients dropped out of the study. Clinical change was evaluated blindly with the Psychiatric Evaluation Form. After 3 weeks of treatment, lithium seemed to be superior to chlorpromazine, but statistical significance was not reached.

The Veterans Administration and the National Institute of Mental Health initiated a collaborative project on lithium involving 18 U.S. centers (Prien, Caffey, & Klett, 1972). One of its objectives was to compare the efficacy of lithium and chlorpromazine in the treatment of bipolar manic and schizoaffective patients. After a lead-in period of 3 to 5 days, patients were randomly assigned to lithium or chlorpromazine for 3 weeks. The Brief Psychiatric Rating Scale (BPRS) and Multidimensional Psychiatric Scale were used to evaluate the results; data from 225 patients were analyzed. No major differences between the two drugs were found among study completers; however, a large proportion of the patients treated with lithium terminated prematurely because of lack of cooperativeness, lack of improvement (at least some of it may be attributed to delay in lithium therapeutic effect), or toxicity, while this was true for only 8% of the chlorpromazine-treated patients. Patients defined as highly active were improved by both drugs.

Shopsin, Gershon, Thompson, and Collins (1975) compared lithium, haloperidol, and chlorpromazine in severely ill hospitalized manic patients, in a double-blind study design, with random treatment assignment. All drugs showed similar efficacy on most clinical measures. The authors suggest however, that the scales used were not sensitive enough to measure the manic psychopathlogy, as the majority of lithium treated patients met discharge criteria at the end of the trial, but this was not true for patients receiving antipsychotic drugs. The authors suggested that lithium and haloperidol significantly improved the manic symptoms without sedation, while chlorpromazine, on the other hand, seemed to produce considerable sedation, contributing less to improving the underlying manic symptoms. They also suggested that while haloperidol had rapid impact on behavioral-motor activity, lithium tended to act more evenly on the entire manic clinical picture.

Takahashi, Sakuma, Itoh, Itoh, and Kuriharo (1975) conducted a multicenter trial comparing lithium and chlorpromazine in a double-blind controlled design in a series of 80 Japanese patients with endogenous manic psychosis. The dosages employed were at a ratio of 4:1 (lithium: chlorpromazine). Lithium was found to be superior to chlorpromazine in physicians' overall ratings. The onset of therapeutic effects of lithium in 65% of the patients occurred within 10 days. Lithium, but not chlorpromazine, was found to improve mood and pressured speech.

1980–1986 (DSM-III):   Garfinkel, Stancer, and Persad (1980) studied lithium plus placebo versus haloperidol plus placebo vs. the combination of lithium and haloperidol in a double-blind study with random treatment assignment. Each treatment was administered for 3 weeks, in 21 severely ill manic patients. The subjects on placebo and haloperidol and the subjects on lithium and haloperidol significantly improved after 7 days of treatment in comparison to the lithium and placebo treated group. The authors concluded that haloperidol is superior to lithium in the treatment of acutely severe hospitalized manic patients, and mentioned that the combination of haloperidol and lithium was not superior to haloperidol and placebo.

1987–1993 (DSM-III-R):   No studies comparing lithium and neuroleptics were reported during these years. Such studies had to wait until the development and marketing efforts of the atypical antipsychotics.

1994–1999 (DSM-IV):   Segal, Berk, and Brook (1998) studied 45 inpatients diagnosed by DSM-IV as bipolar manic patients in a randomized, controlled, double-blind study of either six mg daily of risperidone, 10 mg daily of haloperidol, or 800 to 1200 mg daily of lithium. Similar improvement was reported for all the three groups after 4 weeks of treatment as determined by Global Assessment of Functioning (GAF), Clinical Global Impression (CGI), and BPRS (mean BPRS—Brief Psychiatric Rating Scale—improvement scores: lithium = 9, haloperidol = 5, risperidone = 6.5) scales.

Comparison of these various studies is not an easy task, as different time points and rating scales were used. However, since some of the above studies suggested lithium to be superior to neuroleptics, and others suggested the superiority of neuroleptics, while still others found no difference, it seems logical to sum up the reviewed studies by stating that, overall, there are no overwhelming differences between these drugs in the treatment of bipolar mania. It appears, however, that neuroleptics tend to influence primarily the behavioral motor signs (haloperidol) or produce sedation (chlorpromazine), while lithium tends to affect the core manic symptoms in a more even way. This may lead to the observation of Segal et al. (1998) that haloperidol may have an advantage over lithium in the first week of treatment for severe hospitalized manic patients.

Lithium vs. Anticonvulsants

1987–1993 (DSM-III-R):   Lerer, Moore, Meyendorff, Cho, and Gershon (1987) conducted a double-blind study comparing lithium and carbamazepine in acute mania. Fourteen patients were assigned randomly to each group. BPRS, CGI, and Beigel-Murphy Manic State Rating Scales were employed. A more consistent level of improvement across patients was found for lithium compared to a minority of good responders in the carbamazepine group.

   Small et al. (1991) studied 52 hospitalized manic patients who were randomized to either carbamazepine or lithium treatment after 2 weeks of drug withdrawal. The subjects were followed for 8 weeks. No difference was found between the two groups. The researchers had the impression that patients treated with carbamazepine were more manageable than those treated with lithium, while lithium-treated patients remained longer in a follow-up phase. The authors concluded that monotherapy with either drug may not be sufficient for hospitalized manic patients.

   Freeman, Clothier, Pazzaglia, Lesem, and Swann (1992) studied 27 DSM-III-R manic patients in a 3-week randomized, double-blind parallel study comparing the efficacy of valproate and lithium; BPRS, GAF, and SADS-C were used as rating scales. Nine of the 14 (64%) patients treated with valproate and 12 out of the 14 (86%) patients treated with lithium responded favorably, suggesting that both drugs are effective in the treatment of acute mania.

1994–1999 (DSM-IV):   Emilien, Maloteaux, Seghers, and Charles (1996) conducted a meta-analysis comparing the efficacy of lithium, valproic acid and carbamazepine in the treatment of mania. The analysis included only randomized double-blind controlled clinical trials in which the therapeutic plasma level of lithium was 0.4 to 1.5 mmol/L. Effect sizes were measured by the odds ratio using the Mantel-Haenszel method. No significant difference was observed among the three drugs.

   Bowden et al. (1994) conducted a double blind placebo-controlled, randomly assigned study comparing lithium, valproic acid, and placebo in acute mania on 179 patients. The dosage of lithium was increased, if tolerated, to 1.5mmol/L. Bowden analyzed the effect size for the efficacy of each treatment arm in a later publication (Bowden et al., 1997). Effect size for the improvement score in the Manic Syndrome Score was 0.79 for lithium and 1.01 for divalproex, compared with only 0.37 for placebo. Effect size for the improvement score at the Behavior and Ideation Score (BIS) was 0.62 for lithium, and 0.67 for divalproex, compared with only 0.25 for placebo. These results suggest that both drugs are effective in the treatment of mania compared to placebo.

In summary, lithium was demonstrated to be effective in the treatment of mania. Some clinicians treat manic patients with lithium alone, while others may start with combined lithium and antipsychotic treatment, or may add lithium after the first few days of neuroleptic treatment. Alternatively, clinicians may use divalproex or carbamazepine, or in certain cases, combine each one of them with lithium (i.e., lithium and divalproex or lithium and carbamazepine). Additionally, there is evidence demonstrating that other mood stabilizers, such as lamotrigine, etc., given alone or with antipsychotic treatment, may have beneficial effects in the treatment of acute mania.

Lithium in Depressed, Mixed, and Dysphoric Manic Episodes

Although the hallmark of bipolar illness may be its manic episode, this disorder is also characterized by depressive episodes. Six placebo-controlled trials examined lithium efficacy in bipolar depression (F. K. Goodwin & Jamison, 1990). Goodwin et al. (1969) studied the role of lithium in 13 bipolar depressed patients, and reported that in 10 cases there was indication of some response. Stokes et al. (1971) (described above) reported that lithium administration for bipolar depressive episodes of up to 10 days resulted in a significant trend toward response compared with placebo. Eighteen of their 38 patients demonstrated depressive episodes. Eleven patients with 17 depressive episodes were treated with lithium, while 15 patients with 21 depressive episodes were treated with placebo. Fifty-nine percent of the lithium treated episodes improved as compared to 48% of the placebo treated episodes. F. K. Goodwin, Murphy, Dunner, and Bunney (1972) studied 40 bipolar depressed patients, reporting that 80% of these patients responded. Noyes, Dempsey, and Blum (1974) reported that six of six bipolar depressed patients responded to lithium. Baron, Gershon, Rudy, Jonas, and Buchsbaum (1975) studied nine bipolar depressed patients of whom seven responded, and Mendels (1975) reported that nine of 13 bipolar depressed patients responded to lithium treatment. Overall, response rates of bipolar depression to lithium treatment seemed to exceed 70%. All these studies suggested that lithium has antidepressant effects in bipolar depression. Interestingly, some of these studies also reported lithium's effects on unipolar depression, which were lower than in bipolar depression, and in general fell under 50% of response rate. Other studies in depressed individuals compared lithium to the classical tricyclic antidepressants. Fieve, Platman, and Plutchick (1968), Mendels (1975), Watanabe, Ishino, and Otsuki (1975), and Worrall et al. (1979) compared the efficacy of lithium to either imipramine (three studies) or desipramine in samples containing bipolar depressed and unipolar depressed patients. Although the majority of these studies suggested that lithium is at least as effective as the tricyclic antidepressants (see also review by Srisurapanont, Yatham, and Zis, 1995), the study of Fieve et al. (1968)—the only one comparing both lithium and tricyclic drug to placebo—reported only a mild antidepressant effect for lithium. These results, and the fact that lithium seemed to be more effective in the prevention of mania than in the prevention of bipolar depression, suggested that lithium may have a greater role in the treatment of bipolar mania than bipolar depression.

Only a few studies examined the role of lithium in mixed and dysphoric mania. Clothier, Swann, and Freeman (1992) reported that both lithium and valproate were found to be equally effective in the control of depressed mood or anxiety associated with a manic episode. Swann, Bowden, et al. (1997) reported that in a parallel group, placebo controlled, double-blind, multicenter study of lithium and divalproex for mania (Bowden et al., 1994), depressive symptoms were associated with poor antimanic response to lithium and better response to divalproex. Mixed patients were also suggested to have a poor response to lithium treatment varying between 29 and 42% (de Montigny, Grunnberg, Mayer, & Deschenes, 1981; Dilsaver, Swann, Shoaib, Bowers, & Halley, 1993b; Himmelhoch, Mulla, Neil, Detre, & Kupfer, 1976; Prien, 1988; Secunda et al., 1985; Soares & Gershon, 1998; Swann, Secunda, et al., 1986).

Interestingly although the existence of depressive symptoms during mania seems to lower responsivity to lithium, lithium has a role in the treatment of resistant depression and its addition to ongoing antidepressant treatment was suggested to reverse refractoriness to treatment (Heninger, Chamey, & Sternberg, 1983; Prien et al., 1972). It is thus surprising that no trials were done in which lithium was added to bipolar depressed patients not responding to an antidepressant treatment.

In summary, lithium seems to have a modest therapeutic effect in the treatment of bipolar depression. It is also generally less effective in dysphoric and mixed manic states. In such instances, other anticonvulsant mood stabilizers may be more effective.

Lithium Maintenance Therapy of Biopolar Disorder

The issue of long-term prevention or prophylaxis of illness episodes is of utmost importance for this cycling disorder. A variety of studies to be detailed here corroborate the effectiveness of lithium as an important prophylactic agent for this disorder. These studies will be grouped as open versus double-blind, or prospective versus discontinuation studies.

1952–1967 (DSM-I)

Three open studies suggested that lithium may be effective in the prophylaxis of bipolar disorder (Baastrup, 1964; Baastrup & Schou, 1967; Hartigan, 1963).

1968–1979 (DSM-II)

During the 1970s, a series of double-blind studies were conducted to examine the possible efficacy of lithium in the prophylaxis of bipolar disorder. Goodwin (1994) summarized these studies calculating the recurrence rates over a one year period for placebo to be 81%, but only 34% for lithium. These included both prospective and discontinuation studies.

Prospective Trials

Coppen et al. (1971) conducted a parallel group, randomized, prospective trial that included 17 patients on lithium and 21 on placebo, who were followed for 4 to 6 months. The recurrence rates were 18% in the lithium group and 95% in the placebo one.

Prien, Caffey, and Klett (1973a) conducted a parallel group, randomized, prospective trial with patients admitted to hospital for the treatment of a manic episode. One hundred and one patients were on lithium, and 104 patients were on placebo. The duration of the study was 24 months. The recurrence rates were 43% in the lithium group and 80% on placebo. The recurrence rates of manic and depressive episodes were 32% and 16% on lithium, and 68% and 26% on placebo.

Prien, Coffey, and Klett (1973b) conducted a parallel group, randomized, prospective trial in patients admitted for hospitalization due to the occurrence of depressive episodes. Eighteen patients were on lithium, 13 patients on placebo. The duration of the study was 5 to 24 months with a recurrence rate on lithium of 28% and on placebo 77%. Percent recurrence of manic and depressive episodes for lithium was 11 and 22%, for placebo 38 and 62% respectively.

Stallone, Shelley, Mendlewicz, and Fieve (1973) conducted a parallel group, randomized, prospective trial. Twenty-five patients were on lithium, and 27 patients were on placebo, for a study duration of up to 28 months. The recurrence rates on lithium were 44%, and on placebo 93%. The recurrence rates for manic and depressive episodes were 20 and 28% in the lithium group, and 56 and 48% in the placebo group, respectively.

Dunner, Fleiss, and Fieve (1976) conducted a parallel group, randomized, prospective trial in bipolar II patients. Sixteen patients were on lithium and 24 patients on placebo. The study duration was up to 36 months. Recurrence rates for manic and depressive episodes on lithium were 6 and 56%, and on placebo 25 and 50%, respectively.

Fieve, Kumbarachi, and Dunneo (1976) conducted a parallel group, randomized, prospective trial in bipolar patients. Seventeen patients were on lithium and 18 patients on placebo. They were followed for up to 53 months. The recurrence rates for manic and depressive episodes on lithium were 59 and 29%, while on placebo they were 94 and 44%, respectively. Fieve et al. (1976) also studied bipolar II patients. Seven patients were on lithium and 11 patients on placebo, and those were followed for up to 53 months. The recurrence rates for manic and depressive episodes on lithium were 0 and 57%, and on placebo were 9 and 64%, respectively.

Discontinuation Trials

Baastrup, Paulson, Schou, Thomsen, and Amdisen (1970) studied 22 patients on placebo, and 28 patients on lithium. The duration of the study was up to 5 months. The recurrence rates of illness episodes were 0 on lithium and 55 on placebo. The recurrence rates of manic episodes for lithium and placebo were 0 and 27% respectively. The recurrence rates for depressive episodes for lithium and placebo were 0 and 23% respectively.

Melia (1970) studied seven patients on lithium and eight patients on placebo for a period of 24 months. Percent recurrence on lithium was 57 %, and on placebo 78%. Cundall, Brooks, and Murray (1972) studied 12 patients on lithium and 12 patients on placebo, who were followed for 6 months. The recurrence rates on lithium were 33 %, and on placebo 83%. The recurrence rates of manic and depressive episodes in the lithium group were 8 and 25%, and in the placebo group 75 and 42%, respectively.

Hullin, McDonald, and Allsop (1972) studied 18 patients on lithium and 18 patients on placebo, who were followed for 6 months. The recurrence rates were 6% on lithium, and 33% on placebo.

1980–1986 (DSM-III)

Prospective Trials

Coppen, Abou-Saleh, Milln, Bailey, and Wood (1983) studied 72 patients in a prospective double-blind fashion. Patients continued with their ongoing lithium treatment or received a 25 to 50% reduction in their lithium dosage resulting in plasma levels of 0.45 to 0.79mmol/L. The patients on the reduced dose had fewer side effects, including hand tremors, and decreased thyroid stimulating hormone (TSH) blood levels. They also had significantly decreased affective morbidity. The authors suggested that there may be an advantage in keeping maintenance blood lithium levels at about 0.6mml/L.

Prien et al. (1984) studied 117 bipolar patients receiving either lithium, imipramine, or both in a long-term double-blind study. Lithium carbonate and the combination were found superior to imipramine in preventing the manic recurrence, and equally effective to imipramine in preventing depressive episodes.

Discontinuation Studies

Christodoulou and Lykouras (1982) abruptly discontinued prophylactic treatment in a placebo-controlled, double-blind design in 18 manic-depressive patients for a total period of 18 days. Side effects were significantly reduced, no withdrawal symptoms were noted, and three patients relapsed within 4 days.

1987–1993 (DSM-III-R)

Prospective Trials

Luszanat, Murphy, and Nunn (1988) studied the long-term effects of lithium versus carbamazepine in 44 bipolar patients, both initiated during an acute manic phase. There was a high drop-out rate. Both drugs were found to have prophylactic properties, although lithium appeared to be more effective in the treatment of acute mania.

Gelenberg et al. (1989) compared standard and low serum lithium levels in the maintenance treatment of 94 bipolar disorder patients, in a prospective randomized double-blind trial. Standard plasma levels were defined as 0.8 to 1.0 mmol/L, while low levels were defined as 0.4 to 0.6mmol/L. Six of 47 (13%) patients assigned to standard versus 18 of 47 (38%) assigned to low levels relapsed. The authors recommend that standard range of lithium plasma levels rather than low range should be used in maintenance lithium therapy.

Abou-Selah and Coppen (1989) conducted a prospective double blind lithium dose reduction study in patients receiving lithium prophylactic therapy over 1 year. Lithium dose was reduced by up to 50%. No association between lithium dose/level and affective morbidity was found among patients on standard or low lithium levels. Dose reduction was associated with decreased plasma TSH levels, and decreased side effects, including tremor and weight gain. Interestingly, elderly patients had significantly increased affective morbidity in the low versus standard dose group. Coxhead, Silverstone, and Cookson (1992) studied 31 bipolar patients in a double-blind design over 1 year. All patients had previously been stable on lithium. Sixteen patients remained on lithium, and 15 were switched to carbamazepine. Relapse occurred in eight of the patients on lithium and six of those on carbamazepine. Most of the carbamazepine patients relapsed within 1 month of the switch. Such relapse was suggested by the authors to be associated with lithium withdrawal.

Keller et al. (1992) studied bipolar patients demonstrating a subsyndromal clinical picture in a double-blind fashion. Low (0.4–0.6 mmol/L) versus standard (0.8–1.0 mmol/L) lithium levels were compared. Results showed a 2.6 times increased risk for recurrence in the low dose regimen.

1994–1999 (DSM-IV)

Meta-analysis

Dardennes, Even, Bange, and Heim (1995) conducted a meta-analysis to compare the efficacy of lithium and carbamazepine prophylaxis. This meta-analysis included four randomized, double-blind controlled studies demonstrating significant heterogeneity. The analysis could not confirm the equipotency of carbamazepine and lithium in maintenance therapy. The authors concluded that the prophylactic efficacy of carbamazepine remained questionable.

Prospective Trials

Jensen et al (1995) compared prophylactic treatment with lithium given every second day (median dose 800mg/day, plasma level 0.6–0.7 mmol/L) compared with daily dosing (median dose 1200mg/day, plasma level 0.6–0.7 mmol/L) in a double-blind fashion. Fifty bipolar patients were included. The authors found that the risk of relapse increased three times in the "every second day" lithium treatment group compared with daily treatment. Interestingly, Jensen et al. (1996) reported that alternate day dosing schedule with lithium did not result in significant reduction in side-effects.

Maj, Pirozzi, Magliano, and Bartoli (1998) studied prospectively 402 bipolar patients analyzing the long-term outcome of lithium prophylaxis. These authors reported that at the end of 5 years 28% were no longer taking lithium, 23% were taking lithium and had no recurrence, and 38% were taking lithium and had at least one recurrence.

Greil and Kleindienst (1999a) reported in a randomized clinical trial comparing the efficacy of lithium versus carbamazepine—each given for 2.5 years—in 114 patients with bipolar I disorder, that lithium is superior to carbamazepine on several outcome criteria. These authors also used the same study design in 57 patients with bipolar II or bipolar NOS disorders reporting no significant difference between lithium and carbamazepine prophylaxis (Greil & Kleindienst, 1999b).

Kulhara, Basu, Mattoo, Sharan, and Chopra (1999) conducted a retrospective chart review in 118 bipolar patients, who were enlisted between 1989 and 1990) and prospectively followed up until 1995. Mean follow up was approximately 11 years (range 2–27). Patients had mean of 0.43 relapses per year while on lithium, which was significantly less than prelithium episode frequency. About half of the subjects were good responders to lithium. It is of note that other psychotropic medications were also utilized by the patients and this may have affected the results.

In summary, data coming from the above studies suggested that lithium is an effective treatment in the prevention of future bipolar episodes. Recent studies suggest that lithium plasma levels of 0.8 to 1.0 meq/L, if tolerated, are more effective than lower levels. Some authors suggested that there are cases in which the response to lithium prophylaxis decreases with time, while in other instances it may not continue to be effective upon reinstitution of treatment after discontinuation. Some authors even called into question the role of lithium in maintenance therapy of the bipolar illness

(Akhondzadeh, Emanian, Ahmudi-Abhari, Shabestari, & Dadgarnejad, 1999). Recently Grof (1999) suggested that a group of patients with classical bipolar illness have a long-term good prophylactic response to lithium treatment.

Lithium in Rapid Cycling Bipolar Disorder

Rapid cycling bipolar disorder is defined as more than four illness episodes in a year by DSM-IV (American Psychiatric Association, 1994a). These patients generally have lower response to lithium compared to nonrapid cycling bipolar disorder patients (Dunner & Fieve, 1974; Kukopulos et al., 1980). This form of bipolar disorder seems to respond to other mood stabilizers including divalproex (Bowden et al., 1994).

Predictors of Lithium Response in Bipolar Disorder

ACUTE MANIA

Paranoid and Depressive Symptomatology

Murphy and Beigel (1974) suggested that paranoid destructive manic patients respond less well to lithium, however this was not confirmed by Swann, Secunda, et al. (1986) who studied paranoid-irritable manic patients. Cohen et al. (1989) suggested that depressive symptomatology and earlier age of onset may be related to decreased response. However since these authors had small numbers of subjects, their findings should be interpreted with caution. Swann, Secunda, et al. (1986) suggested that more severe forms of mania, high anxiety, and depression may be associated with decreased response to lithium. In addition, patients exhibiting mixed or dysphoric mania seem to respond less to lithium (Dilsaver, Swann, Shoaib, & Bowers, 1993; Dilsaver, Shoaib, Bowers, & Halle, 1993; McElroy, Keck, et al.,1992).

RAPID CYCLING

Approximately 20% of bipolar patients demonstrate rapid cycling. This group of patients responded less well to lithium prophylactic treatment (Post, Kramlinger, Altschuler, Ketter, & Denicoff, 1990). However, Maj (1992) reported that a certain subgroup of these patients may respond more favorably to lithium treatment compared to other subgroups.

ACUTE BIPOLAR DEPRESSION

Bipolar depression compared with unipolar depression seemed to respond well to lithium treatment (Goodwin & Jamison, 1990). Jefferson (1996) suggested that some clinicians reported that bipolar patients with reverse vegetative symptoms such as anergia, increased sleep, and appetite may be more responsive to lithium treatment compared to bipolar patients with anxiety, insomnia, and anorexia.

PROPHYLAXIS

Grof et al. (Grof, Alda, Grof, Fox, & Cameron, 1993; Grof, Hux, Grof, & Arato, 1983; Grof, 1999) suggested that course of illness with periods of euthymia, mania-depression-euthymia course, absence of rapid cycling, positive family history for bipolar disorder, absence of personality disorder, and diagnosis of primary bipolar disorder (i.e., not secondary to organic cause) predicts a good prophylactic response to lithium.

Faedda et al. (1991), in agreement with Grof et al, (Grof, Alda, et al., 1993; Grof, Hux, et al., 1993; Grof, 1999), suggested that the mania-depression-euthymia course is related to good response to lithium prophylaxis, but not the depression-mania-euthymia course. Similarly, to Grof et al (Grof, Alda, et al., 1993; Grof, Hux, et al., 1993; Grof, 1999), family history of mood disorder was suggested to be associated with good response to lithium, as well as positive response to lithium in close relatives (Jefferson, 1996). Aagaard and Vestegaard (1990) suggested that bipolar patients tend to demonstrate decreased response to lithium treatment when they have a lengthy episode, they are young and of female gender. Abu-Saleh and Coppen (1990) suggested that positive prophylactic response to lithium over 6 to 12 months predicts further good response in the future. Patients with dysphoric and mixed mania were suggested to respond less to lithium treatment and some, but not all studies suggest the same for rapid cycling bipolar disorder (Jefferson, 1996). Grof, Alda, et al. (1993) and Goodnick, Fieve, Schlegel, and Baxter (1987) suggested that good level of functioning between episodes predicts good response to lithium prophylaxis.

LITHIUM EFFICACY IN DIFFERENT AGE GROUPS

There is a lack of well-designed controlled studies with lithium in bipolar disorder children and adolescents. Several studies were reported suggesting a role for lithium in acute mania in adolescents and children. Youngerman and Casino (1987) reviewed the available literature, amounting to 211 cases of children and adolescents treated with lithium. In 46 cases there was enough data to assess response. Sixty-five percent responded to lithium treatment. Delong and Aldershot (1987) reported similar response (66%) in 59 children diagnosed with bipolar disorder. Papatheodorou and Kutcher (1996) reviewed this literature, and suggested that lithium was effective in adolescent mania, with a response rate of 50 to 66%. These authors also suggested that adolescent mania often presents itself as mixed or atypical mania, possibly resulting in lower rates of response compared with adult mania. Geller et al. (1998) conducted a double blind controlled study of lithium administered for 6 weeks in adolescents with dual diagnosis of bipolar disorders spectrum and secondary substance dependence. Twenty-five subjects were enrolled and 21 completed the study. Lithium showed superiority for treatment of both bipolar illness spectrum and drug dependence (mainly to alcohol and marijuana). The Children Global Assessment Scale (CGAS) was used to assess the subject's clinical status. Six out of 10 completers on lithium responded with a CGAS score of 65, whereas this was true only for one out of 11 patients treated with placebo. The mean lithium blood level for active responders was 0.9 mEq/L. The results of this study should, however, be taken with caution since the study population was heterogenous and only a global assessment was used for both diagnoses. There seems to be a lack of data on the use of lithium in bipolar depression and prophylaxis. Strober, Morrell, Lampert, and Burroughs (1990) conducted a discontinuation study of lithium in bipolar disorder adolescents. In a follow-up of 18 months, patients treated with lithium had only 37.5% relapses compared with 92.3% of patients whose lithium was discontinued, suggesting that lithium has beneficial effects in the prophylaxis of bipolar disorder in adolescents.

No placebo controlled studies of lithium have been conducted in geriatric mania. Some of the systematic studies of lithium in mania included elderly patients, but in general the age effect has not been extensively studied (Dunn & Rabins, 1996). Chen et al. (1999) retrospectively studied the efficacy of lithium versus valproate in the treatment of mania in 59 hospitalized manic patients, age 55 years and older. A greater proportion of patients improved on lithium versus valproate (67% vs. 38%). Higher lithium plasma levels (≥ 0.8 mmol/L) were associated with increased response. Further analysis showed that the superiority of lithium was associated with classic mania, while no difference between lithium and valproate was noted when mixed mania was analyzed separately. Young and Falk (1989) conducted a study of lithium, which suggested a weak negative effect of age on the response rate of lithium treatment in bipolar illness. However, elderly patients were not specifically included in this study. There is also a lack of data on the therapeutic role of lithium in prophylactic treatment for bipolar disorder in the elderly (Dunn & Rabins 1996).

To summarize, a variety of factors seem to modify the response to lithium treatment and should be considered when deciding upon lithium treatment.

Clinical Decision Making and Lithium Treatment

Several algorithms were published in the 1990s for the treatment of bipolar disorder; however no one specifically addressed the variety of parameters reported to affect response to lithium treatment (American Psychiatric Association, 1994b; Bauer et al., 1999; Frances, Docherty, & Kahn, 1996; Kusumakar & Yatham, 1997). In addition, these algorithms were in general of a dichotomous (each step consisting of yes or no options) qualitative nature making them less useful in complex individual cases in which a variety of patient, illness and drug related parameters have to be considered. The following recommendations in Table 7.1 have tried to address the variety of parameters affecting the response to lithium treatment as well as to provide a guide for the clinician facing a decision as to the use of lithium in an individual patient. In the case of missing data 0.5 point is scored in order to differentiate it from a case where existing data suggests a score of zero or below. No missing data is allowed for diagnosis.

The reader should be aware that by no means is this score accurate; it stands as a recommendation only. The clinician should take into consideration other available data before making a decision upon lithium use, including history of the illness and its response to previous drug therapy, the age and physical condition of the patient, and available data as to side effect profile of lithium treatment and its interaction with other drugs. Also, we did not include in this proposed scoring system the possible use of lithium augmentation in cases of resistant unipolar depression.

General Recommendations as to Indication for Lithium Use[1]

If the sum of scores for diagnosis and course of illness ≥5 (maximal score is 7) and; the sum of scores for family history and previous history of lithium treatment ≥–0.5 (maximal score is 4) then: *lithium treatment is probably indicated.*

---

1. Developed by Joseph Levine, M.D.

TABLE 7.1
Proposed Scoring System as to Indication for Lithium Use

Choose One Most Appropriate Score for Each of the Following Groups (diagnosis, course, family history & treatment history)

Diagnosis
Bipolar Disorder
- Manic episode (5 points)
- Dysphoric mania (2 points)
- Mixed episode (2 points)
- Acute depressive episode (2.5 points)
- In remission (5 points)

Schizoaffective Disorder
- Acute manic episode (4 points)
- Dysphoric mania (1.5 points)
- Mixed episode (1.5 points)
- Acute depressive episode (0 points)
- In remission (3 points)

Unipolar Depression
- Acute depression (1.5 points)
- in remission (0 points)

Schizophrenia (1)
- Acute episode (1 points)
- In remission (0 points)

Course of Illness
- Depressive episodes only (0 points)
- Sequence of Mania—depression—euthymia (2 points)
- Sequence of Depression—mania—euthymia (1.5 points)
- Rapid cycling (−1 points)
- Missing data (0.5 point)
- Other (0 points)

Family History
- With affective disorder (2 points)
- Without affective disorders (−1 points)
- Missing data (0.5 point)

Previous History with Lithium Treatment
- Beneficial effect in acute treatment (1 point)
- Beneficial effect in acute treatment and good quality of remission (2 points)
- Adequate previous acute trial with lithium therapy failed (−3 points)
- Missing data (0.5 point)

If the sum of scores for diagnosis and course of illness ≥ 3 and <5; and the sum of scores for family history and previous history of lithium treatment ≥–0.5 (maximal score is 4) then: *lithium treatment may be initiated.*

If the sum of scores for diagnosis and course of illness ≥3 (maximal score is 7) and the sum of scores for family history and previous history of lithium treatment = –1 then: *lithium treatment is questionable since previous trial with lithium was unfavorable.*

If the sum of scores for diagnosis and course of illness <3 (minimal score is –1); and/or the sum of scores for family history and previous history of lithium treatment <–1 (minimal score is –4) then: *lithium treatment is probably not recommended.*

References

Aagaard, J., & Vestergaard, P. (1990). Predictors of outcome in prophylactic lithium treatment: A two year prospective study. *Journal of Affective Disorders, 18,* 259–266.

Abou-Saleh, M. T., & Coppen, A. J. (1990). Predictors of long term outcome of mood disorder on prophylactic lithium. *Lithium, 1,* 27–35.

Akhondzadeh, S., Emamian, E. S., Ahmadi-Abhari, A., Shabestari, O., & Dadgarnejad, M. (1999). Is it time to have another look at lithium maintenance therapy in bipolar? *Progress in Neuropsychopharmacology and Biological Psychiatry, 23,* 1011–1017.

American Psychiatric Association. (1952), *Diagnostic and statistical manual of mental disorders.* Washington, DC: Author.

American Psychiatric Association. (1968). *Diagnostic and statistical manual of mental disorders* (2nd ed.). Washington, DC: Author.

American Psychiatric Association. (1980). *Diagnostic and statistical manual of mental disorders* (3rd ed.). Washington, DC: Author.

American Psychiatric Association. (1987). *Diagnostic and statistical manual of mental disorders* (3rd, revised ed.). Washington, DC: Author.

American Psychiatric Association. (1994a). *Diagnostic and statistical manual of mental disorders* (4th ed.). Washington, DC: Author.

American Psychiatric Association. (1994b). Practice guidelines for the treatment of patients with bipolar disorder. In *American Psychiatric Association practice guidelines* (pp. 135–208). Washington, DC: Author.

Baastrup, P. C. (1964). The use of lithium in manic depressive psychosis. *Comprehensive Psychiatry, 5,* 396–408.

Baastrup, P. C., Poulsen, J. C., Schou, M., Thomsen, K., & Amdisen, A. (1970). Prophylactic lithium: Double-blind discontinuation in manic-depressive and recurrent-depressive disorders. *Lancet, 2,* 326–330.

Baastrup, P. C., & Schou, M. (1967). Lithium as a prophylactic agent. *Archives of General Psychiatry, 16,* 162–172.

Baron, A., Gershon, E. S., Rudy, V., Jonas, W. Z., & Buchsbaum, M. (1975). Lithium carbonate response in depression: Prediction by unipolar/bipolar illness, average-evoked response, catechol-O-methyl transferase, and family history. *Archives of General Psychiatry, 32,* 1107–1111.

Bauer, M. S., Callahan, A. M., Jampala, C., Petty, F., Sajatovic, M., Schaefer, V., et al. (1999). Clinical practice guidelines for bipolar disorder from the Department of Veterans Affairs. *Journal of Clinical Psychiatry, 60,* 9–21.

Bowden, C. L., Brugger, A. M., Swann, A. C., Calabrese, J. R., Janicak, P. G., Petty, F., et al. (1994). Efficacy of divalproex vs lithium and placebo in the treatment of mania. *Journal of the American Medical Association, 271,* 918–924.

Bowden, C. L., Davis, J., Morris, D., Swann, A., Calabrese, J., Lambert, M., et al. (1997). Effect size of efficacy measures comparing divalproex, lithium and placebo in acute mania. *Depression and Anxiety, 6,* 26–30.

Bunney, W. E., Goodwin, F. K., Davis, J. M., & Fawcett, J. A. (1968). A behavioral-biochemical study of lithium treatment. *American Jounral of Psychiatry, 125,* 499–512.

Cade, J. F. J. (1949). Lithium salts in the treatment of psychotic excitement. *Medical Journal of Australia, 2,* 349–352.

Cade, J. F. J. (1970). The story of lithium. In F. J. Ade & F. B. Blackwell (Eds.). *Discoveries in biological psychiatry* (pp. 218–229). Philadelphia: J. B. Lippincott.

Chen, S. T., Altshuler, L. L., Melnyk, K. A., Erhart, S. M., Miller, E., & Mintz, J. (1999). Efficacy of lithium vs. valproate in the treatment of mania in the elderly: A retrospective study. *Journal of Clinical Psychiatry, 60,* 181–186.

Christodoulou, G. N., & Lykouras, E. P. (1982). Abrupt lithium discontinuation in manic depressive patients. *Acta Psychiatrica Scandinavia, 65,* 310–314.

Clothier, J., Swann, A. C., & Freeman, T. (1992). Dysphoric mania. *Journal of Clinical Psychopharmacology, 12*(Suppl. 1), 13S–16S.

Cohen, S., Khan, A., & Coz, G. (1989). Demographic and clinical features predictive of recovery in acute mania. *Journal of Nervous and Mental Disorders, 177,* 638–642.

Coppen, A., Abou-Saleh, M., Milln, P., Bailey, J., & Wood, K. (1983). Decreasing lithium dosage reduces morbidity and side effects during prophylaxis. *Journal of Affective Disorders, 5,* 353–362.

Coppen, A., Noguera, R., Bailey, J., Burns, B. H., Swani, M. S., Hare, E. H., et al. (1971). Prophylactic lithium in affective disorders: controlled trial. *Lancet, 2,* 275–279.

Coxhead, N., Silverstone, T., & Cookson, J. (1992). Carbamazepine versus lithium in the prophylaxis of bipolar affective disorder. *Acta Psychiatrica Scandanavia, 85,* 114–118.

Cundall, R. L., Brooks, P. W., & Murray, L. G. (1972). A controlled evaluation of lithium prophylaxis in affective disorders. *Psychological Medicine, 2,* 308–311.

Dardennes, R., Even, C., Bange, F., & Heim, A. (1995). Comparison of carbamazepine and lithium in the prophylaxis of bipolar disorder [a meta-analysis]. *British Journal of Psychiatry, 166,* 378–381.

de Montigny, C., Grunberg, F., Mayer, A., & Deschenes, J. P. (1981). Lithium induces rapid relief of depression in tricyclic antidepressant drug non-responders. *British Journal of Psychiatry, 138,* 252–256.

Delong, G. R., & Aldershof, A. L. (1987). Long-term experience with lithium treatment in childhood: Correlation with clinical diagnosis. *Journal of the American Academy of Child and Adolescent Psychiatry, 26,* 389–394.

Dilsaver, S. C., Swann, A. C., Shoaib, A. M., & Bowers, T. C. (1993a). The manic syndrome: Factors which may predict a patient's response to lithium, carbamazepine and valproate. *Journal of Psychiatry and Neuroscience, 18,* 61–66.

Dilsaver, S. C., Swann, A. C., Shoaib, A. M., Bowers, T. C., & Halle, M. T. (1993b). Depressive mania associated with nonresponse to antimanic agents. *American Journal of Psychiatry, 150,* 1548–1551.

Dunn, K. L., & Rabins, P. V. (1996). Mania in old age. In K. I. Shulman, M. Tohen, & S. P. Kutcher (Eds.), *Mood disorders across the life span* (pp 399–406). New York: Wiley.

Dunner, D. L., & Fieve, R. R. (1974). Clinical factors in lithium carbonate prophylaxis failure. *Archives of General Psychiatry, 30,* 229–233.

Dunner, D. L., Fleiss, J. L., & Fieve, R. R. (1976). Lithium carbonate prophylaxis failure. *British Journal of Psychiatry, 129,* 40–44.

Emilien, G., Maloteaux, J. M., Seghers, A., & Charles, G. (1996). Lithium compared to valproic acid and carbamazepine in the treatment of mania: A statistical meta-analysis. *European Neuropsychopharmacology, 6,* 245–252.

Faedda, G. L., Baldessarini, R. J., Tohen, M., Strakowski, S. M., & Waternaux, C. (1991). Episode sequence in bipolar disorder and response to lithium treatment. *American Journal of Psychiatry, 148,* 1237–1239.

Fieve, R. R., Kumbarachi, T., & Dunner, D. L. (1976). Lithium prophylaxis of depression in bipolar I, bipolar II, and unipolar patients. *American Journal of Psychiatry, 133,* 925–929.

Fieve, R. R., Platman, S. R., Plutchick, R. R. (1968). The use of lithium in affective disorders: II. Prophylaxis of depression in chronic recurrent affective disorder. *American Journal of Psychiatry, 125,* 492–498.

Frances, A. J., Docherty, J. P., & Kahn, D. A. (1996). The expert consensus guideline series: Treatment of bipolar disorder. *Journal of Clinical Psychiatry, 57*(Suppl. 12A), 1–88.

Freeman, T. W., Clothier, J. L., Pazzaglia, P., Lesem, M. D., & Swann, A. C. (1992). A double-blind comparison of valproate and lithium in the treatment of acute mania. *American Journal of Psychiatry, 49,* 108–111.

Garfinkel, P. E., Stancer, H. C., & Persad, E. (1980). A comparison of haloperidol, lithium carbonate and their combination in the treatment of mania. *Journal of Affective Disorders, 2,* 279–288.

Gelenberg, A. L., Kane, J. M., Keller, M. B., Lavori, P., Rosenbaum, J. F., Cole, K., et al. (1989). Comparison of standard and low serum levels of lithium for maintenance treatment of bipolar disorder. *New England Journal of Medicine, 321,* 1489–1493.

Geller, B., Cooper, T. B., Sun, K., Zimerman, B., Frazier, J., Williams, M., et al. (1998). Double-blind and placebo-controlled study of lithium for adolescent bipolar disorders with secondary substance dependency. *Journal of the American Academy of Child and Adolescent Psychiatry, 37,* 171–178.

Gershon, S., & Shopsin, B. (1973). *Lithium: Its role in psychiatric research and treatment.* New York: Plenum.

Goodnick, P. J., Fieve, R. R., Schlegel, A., & Baxter, N. (1987). Predictors of interepisode symptoms and relapse in affective disorder patients treated with lithium carbonate. *American Journal of Psychiatry, 144,* 367–369.

Goodwin, F. K., & Jamison, K. R. (1990). *Manic-depressive illness.* New York: Oxford University Press.

Goodwin, F. K., Murphy, D. L., & Bunney, W. E. J. (1969). Lithium-carbonate treatment in depression and mania: a longitudinal double-blind study. *Archives of General Psychiatry, 21,* 486–496.

Goodwin, F. K., Murphy, D. L., Dunner, D. L., & Bunney, W. E. J. (1972). Lithium response in unipolar vs. bipolar depression. *American Journal of Psychiatry, 129,* 44–47.

Goodwin, G. M. (1994). Recurrence of mania after lithium withdrawal. *British Journal of Psychiatry, 164,* 149–152.

Greil, W., & Kleindienst, N. (1999a). The comparative prophylactic efficacy of lithium and carbamazepine in patients with bipolar I disorder. *International Clinical Psychopharmacology, 14,* 277–281.

Greil, W., & Kleindienst, N. (1999b). Lithium versus carbamazepine in the maintenance treatment of bipolar II disorder and bipolar disorder not otherwise specified. *International Clinical Psychopharmacology, 14,* 283–285.

Grof, P. (1999, May). Excellent lithium responders people whose lives have been changed by lithium use. *Proceeding of Symposium "Lithium Lexington 99."* Lexington, KY.

Grof, P., Alda, M., Grof, E., Fox, D., & Cameron, P. (1993). The challenge of predicting response to stabilizing lithium treatment. *British Journal of Psychiatry, 163*(Suppl. 21), 16–19.

Grof, P., Hux, M., Grof, E., & Arato, M. (1983). Prediction of response to stabilizing lithium treatment. *Pharmacopsychiatry, 16,* 195–200.

Hartigan, G. P. (1963). The use of lithium salts in affective disorders. *British Journal of Psychiatry, 109,* 810–814.

Heninger, G. R., Charney, D. S., & Sternberg, D. E. (1983). Lithium carbonate augmentation of antidepressant treatment: An effective prescription for treatment-refractory depression. *Archives of General Psychiatry, 40,* 1335–1342.

Himmelhoch, J. M., Mulla, D., Neil, J. F., Detre, T. P., & Kupfer, D. J. (1976). Incidence and significance of mixed affective states in a bipolar population. *Archives of General Psychiatry, 33,* 1062–1066.

Hullin, R. P., McDonald, R., & Allsopp, M. N. E. (1972). Prophylactic lithium in recurrent affective disorders. *Lancet, 1,* 1044–1046.

Jefferson, J. W. (1996). Lithium. In P. J. Goodnick (Ed.), *Predictors of treatment response in mood disorders* (pp. 95–117). Washington, DC: American Psychiatric Press.

Jensen, H. V., Davidson, K., Tofteraard, L., Mellerup, E. T., Plenge, P., Aggernaes, H., et al. (1996). Double-blind comparison of the side-effect profile of daily versus alternate-day dosing schedules in lithium maintenance treatment of manic-depressive disorder. *Journal of Affective Disorders, 36,* 89–93.

Jensen, H. V., Plenge, P., Mellerup, E.,T., Davidson, K., Tofteraard, L., Aggernaes, H., et al. (1995). Lithium prophylaxis of manic-depressive disorder: Daily dosing schedule versus second day. *Acta Psychiatrica Scandinavia, 92,* 69–74.

Johnson, G., Gershon, S., Burdock, E. I., Floyd, A., & Hekimian, L. (1971). Comparative effects of lithium and chlorpromazine in the treatment of acute manic states. *British Journal of Psychiatry, 119,* 267–276.

Johnson, G. Gershon, S., & Hekimian, L. J. (1968). Controlled evaluation of lithium and chlorpromazine in the treatment of manic states: An interim report. *Comprehensive Psychiatry, 9,* 563–567.

Keller, M. B., Lavori, P. W., Kane, J. M., Gelenberg, A. J., Rosenbaum, J. F., Walzer, E. A., et al. (1992). Subsyndromal symptoms in bipolar disorder: A comparison of standard and low serum levels of lithium. *Archives of General Psychiatry, 49,* 371–376.

Kukopulos, A., Reginaldi, D., Laddomada, P., Floric, G., Serra, G., & Tondo, L. (1980). Course of the manic depressive cycle and changes caused by treatment. *Pharmacopsychiatry, 13,* 156–167.

Kulhara, P., Basu, D., Mattoo, S. K., Sharan, P., & Chopra, R. (1999). Lithium prophylaxis of recurrent bipolar affective disorder: Long-term outcome and its psychosocial correlates. *Journal of Affective Disorders, 54,* 87–96.

Kusumakar, V., & Yatham, L. N. (1997). The treatment of bipolar disorder: Review of the literature, guidelines, and options. *Canadian Journal of Psychiatry, 42*(Suppl. 2), 67S–100S.

Lerer, B., Moore, N., Meyendorff, E., Cho, S. R., & Gershon, S. (1987). Carbamazepine versus lithium in the treatment of mania: A double-blind study. *Journal of Clinical Psychiatry, 48,* 89–93.

Lusznat, R. M., Murphy, D. P., & Nunn, C. M. H. (1988). Carbamazepine vs. lithium in the treatment and prophylaxis of mania. *British Journal of Psychiatry, 153,* 198–204.

Maggs, R. (1963). Treatment of manic illness with lithium carbonate. *British Journal of Psychiatry, 109,* 56–65.

Maj, M. (1992). Clinical prediction of response to lithium prophylaxis in bipolar patients: A critical update. *Lithium, 3,* 15–21.

Maj, M., Pirozzi, R., Magliano, L., & Bartoli, L. (1998). Long term outcome of lithium prophylaxis in bipolar disorder: A 5 year prospective study of 402 patients at a lithium clinic. *American Journal of Psychiatry, 155,* 30–35.

McElroy, S. L., Keck, P. E., Pope, H. G., Hudson, J. I., Faedda, G. L., & Swann, A. C. (1992). Clinical and research implications of the diagnosis of dysphoric or mixed mania or hypomania. *American Journal of Psychiatry, 149,* 1633–1644.

Melia, P. I. (1970). Prophylactic lithium: A double-blind trial in recurrent affective disorders. *British Journal of Psychiatry, 116,* 621–624.

Mendels, J. (1975). Lithium in the acute treatment of depressive states. In F. N. Johnson (Ed.), *Lithium research and therapy* (pp. 43–62). London: Academic.

Murphy, D. L., & Beigel, A. (1974). Depression, elation, and lithium carbonate responses in manic patient sub-groups. *Archives of General Psychiatry, 31,* 643–648.

Noack, C. H., & Trautner, E. M. (1951). The lithium treatment of maniacal psychosis. *Medical Journal of Australia, 38,* 219-222.

Noyes, R. J., Dempsey, G. M., & Blum, A. (1974). Lithium treatment of depression. *Comprehensive Psychiatry, 15,* 187–190.

Papatheodorou, G., & Kutcher, S. P. (1996). Treatment of bipolar in adolescents. In K. I. Shulman, M. Tohen, & S. P. Kutcher (Eds.), *Mood disorders across the life span* (pp. 159–186). New York: Wiley.

Platman, S. R. (1970). A comparison of lithium carbonate and chlorpromazine in mania. *American Journal of Psychiatry, 127,* 351–353.

Post, R. M., Kramlinger, K. G., Altschuler, L. L., Ketter, T. A., & Denicoff, K. (1990). Treatment of rapid cycling bipolar illness. *Psychopharmacology Bulletin, 26,* 37–47.

Prien, R. F. (1988). Maintenance treatment of depressive and manic states. In A. Georgotas & R. Cancro (Eds.), *Depression and mania* (pp. 439–451). New York: Elsevier.

Prien, R. F., Caffey, E. M., & Klett, C. J. (1972). Comparison of lithium carbonate and chlorpromazine in the treatment of mania. *Archives of General Psychiatry, 26,* 146–153.

Prien, R. F., Caffey, E. M., & Klett, C. J. (1973a). Prophylactic efficacy of lithium in manic-depressive illness. *Archives of General Psychiatry, 28,* 337–341.

Prien, R. F., Klett, C. J., & Caffey, E. M. (1973b). Lithium carbonate and imipramine in prevention of affective episodes. *Archives of General Psychiatry, 29,* 420–425.

Prien, R. F., Kupfer, D. J., Mansky, P. A., Small, J. G., Tuason, V. B., & Voss, C. B. (1984). Drug therapy in the prevention of recurrences in unipolar and bipolar affective disorders. *Archives of General Psychiatry, 41,* 1096–1104.

Schou, M. (1988). Lithium in psychiatric therapy and prophylaxis. *Journal of Psychiatric Research, 6,* 67–95.

Schou, M., Juel-Nielsen, N., Stromgren, E., & Voldby, H. (1954). The treatment of manic psychoses by the administration of lithium salts. *Journal of Neurology, Neurosurgery, and Psychiatry, 17,* 250–260.

Secunda, S. K., Katz, M. M., Swann, A., Koslow, S. H., Maas, J. W., Chuang, S., et al. (1985). Mania diagnosis state measurement and prediction of treatment response. *Journal of Affective Disorders, 8,* 113–121.

Segal, J., Berk, M., & Brook, S. (1998). Risperidone compared with both lithium and haloperidol in mania: A double-blind randomized controlled trial. *Clinical Neuropharmacoloyg, 21,* 176–180.

Shopsin, B., Gershon, S., Thompson, H., & Collins, P. (1975). Psychoactive drugs in mania: A controlled comparison of lithium carbonate, chlorpromazine, and haloperidol. *Archives of General Psychiatry, 32,* 34–42.

Small, J. G., Klapper, M. H., Milstein, V., Kellams, J. J., Miller, M. J., Marheke, J. D., et al.

(1991). Carbamazepine compared with lithium in the treatment of mania. *Archives of General Psychiatry, 48,* 915–921.

Soares, J. C., & Gershon, S. (1998). The lithium ion: A foundation for psychopharmacological specificity. *Neuropsychopharmacology, 19,* 167–182.

Spring, G., Schweid, D., Gray, C., Steinberg, J., & Horwitz, M. (1970). A double-blind comparison of lithium and chlorpromazine in the treatment of manic states. *American Journal of Psychiatry, 126,* 1306–1310.

Srisurapanont, M., Yatham, L. N., & Zis, A. P. (1995). Treatment of acute bipolar depression: A review of the literature. *Canadian Journal of Psychiatry, 40,* 533–544.

Stallone, F., Shelley, E., Mendlewicz, J., & Fieve, R. R. (1973). The use of lithium in affective disorders. III: A double-blind study of prophylaxis in bipolar illness. *American Journal of Psychiatry, 130,* 1006–1010.

Stokes, P. E., Shamoian, C. A., Stoll, P. M., & Patton, M. J. (1971). Efficacy of lithium as acute treatment of manic-depressive illness. *Lancet, 1,* 1319–1325.

Strober, M., Morrell, W., Lampert, C., & Burroughs, J. (1990). Relapses following discontinuation of lithium maintenance therapy in adolescents with bipolar I illness: A naturalistic study. *American Journal of Psychiatry, 147,* 457–461.

Swann, A. C., Bowden, C. L., Morris, D., Calabrese, J. R., Petty, F., Small, J., et al. (1997). Depression during mania. Treatment response to lithium or divalproex. *Archives of General Psychiatry, 54,* 37–42.

Swann, A. C., Secunda, S. K., Katz, M. M., Koslow, S. H., Maas, J. W., Chuang, S., et al. (1986). Lithium treatment in mania. Clinical characteristics, specificity of symptom change, and outcome. *Psychiatry Research, 18,* 127–141.

Takahashi, R., Sakuma, A., Itoh, K., Itoh, H., & Kurihara, M. (1975). Comparison of efficacy of lithium carbonate and chlorpromazine in mania. *Archives of General Psychiatry, 32,* 1310–1318.

Watanabe, S., Ishino, H., & Otsuki, S. (1975). Double-blind comparison of lithium carbonate and imipramine in treatment of depression. *Archives of General Psychiatry, 32,* 659–668.

Worrall, E. P., Moody, J. P., Peet, M., Dick, P., Smith, A., Chambers, C., et al. (1979). Controlled studies of the acute antidepressant effects of lithium. *British Journal of Psychiatry, 135,* 255–262.

Young, R. L., & Falk, J. R. (1989). Age, manic psychopathology and treatment response. *International Journal of Geriatric Psychiatry, 4,* 73–78.

Youngerman, J., & Casino, I. A. (1987). Lithium carbonate use in children and adolescents: A survey of the literature. *Archives of General Psychiatry, 35,* 216–224.

CHAPTER 8

The Role of Atypical Neuroleptics in Bipolar Disorder

Roy H. Perlis
A. Eden Evins
Gary S. Sachs

Introduction

The traditionally sharp boundaries between thought and affective disorder, are maintained in modern diagnostic nomenclature primarily for their heuristic value. Similarly, medications are characterized as antidepressants or antipsychotics, anxiolytics or anticonvulsants, though these distinctions may be determined by marketing considerations rather than actual pharmacodynamic properties. Both classification systems assert a specificity of action which can needlessly narrow the therapeutic application of psychotropic medications. In particular, molecules which happen to possess antipsychotic properties may also have independent antidepressant or antimanic effects.

Utilization of neuroleptics for treatment of mood disorders quickly followed the introduction of chlorpromazine, when Delay and Deniker (1952) demonstrated its efficacy for controlling agitation. Subsequently, neuroleptics were shown to control not only agitation but psychotic symptoms as well. Before the advent of lithium, they were the primary means of treating acute manic episodes, and were sometimes used in prophylaxis (Baldessarini, 1985). More recently, the introduction of so-called "atypical" neuroleptics has led to a resurgence of interest in antipsychotics as treatment for bipolar disorder.

This chapter reviews the possible roles for atypical neuroleptics in bipolar disorder and schizoaffective disorder, bipolar type. After emphasizing the importance of treating psychosis in this population, the evidence that typical and atypical neuroleptics may also possess mood stabilizing properties is discussed. The chapter concludes by offering guidelines for neuroleptic use in this population and directions for future investigation.

Psychosis in Affective Illness

Psychotic symptoms are common during the course of bipolar illness. As reviewed by Goodwin and Jamison (1990), 20 studies conducted since 1970 found 48% of manic episodes were associated with delusions and 15% with hallucinations. In these studies, the lifetime incidence of psychotic symptoms averaged 58% and ranged from 47 to 74%.

The presence of psychotic symptoms in bipolar disorder is often associated with earlier age of onset (Rosen, Rosenthal, Van Dusen, Dunner, & Fieve, 1983) and generally indicates a poorer prognosis. For example, Strakowski and colleagues (1998) found that in the year following an initial hospitalization for an affective episode with psychotic features, only 35% of patients achieve symptomatic recovery; functional recovery is equally unlikely. Psychotic symptoms during a manic episode may predict higher vulnerability to recurrence compared to patients with nonpsychotic mania (Tohen, Tsung, & Goodwin, 1992). Tohen and colleagues (1990) also reported a four year follow-up study of first episode manic patients, which showed a significant association between psychotic features and unfavorable outcome.

This effect is not limited to the initial episode. Coryell et al. (1996) found the negative prognostic implications of an index episode with psychotic features extended throughout a 10-year follow-up period. These studies associate psychotic index episodes with greater illness severity, as measured by fewer weeks with minimal symptoms, shorter interepisode duration, and more psychosocial impairment overall. Further, they show that the best predictor of *future* psychotic episodes is the presence of psychotic symptoms in the index episode.

Psychotic symptoms may also interfere with effective pharmacotherapy. Medication noncompliance is a particular concern in bipolar patients; the rate of noncompliance may be as high as 57% following a first affective episode (Cochran, 1984). Psychotic symptoms may exacerbate this problem: Maj, Pirozzi, Magliane, and Bantolic (1998) found patient initiated discontinuation of lithium higher among bipolar patients with psychotic features.

Adequate treatment of psychotic symptoms, then, is clearly as important in affective illness as it is in schizophrenia or schizoaffective disorder. The efficacy of atypical neuroleptics in this regard has been well documented; for an overview, see Marder (1998).

Neuroleptics as Mood Stabilizers

Beyond their antipsychotic effects, some neuroleptics may also be effective mood stabilizers; however, the term *mood stabilizer* itself is applied inconsistently. We propose that a mood stabilizer must demonstrate at least two of the following four criteria: (1) treatment of acute manic/hypomanic episodes; (2) treatment of acute depressive episodes; (3) prophylaxis against manic recurrence or prophylaxis against depressive recurrence; (4) causes neither switch into, nor an exacerbation of, mania/hypomania or depression, and does not increase cycle frequency, with administration during any phase of the illness.

Judged by the above criteria, antidepressants, although effective in treating depressive episodes, do not qualify as mood stabilizers. On the other hand, lithium, valproate, and carbamazepine have documented mood stabilizing properties (Keck, McElroy, & Strakowski, 1998). They treat acute episodes and also likely have utility in maintenance. Unfortunately, these drugs all require ongoing monitoring of blood levels and carry potential toxicities. In addition, many patients will experience affective episodes which are refractory to these agents. Some of the newer anticonvulsants, such as lamotrigine, may also be effective mood stabilizers (Calabrese, Bowden, McElroy, et al., 1999; Calabrese, Bowden, Sachs, et al. 1999); these agents are reviewed elsewhere (see chapter 10).

In considering whether neuroleptics can act as true mood stabilizers, acute and maintenance treatment will be reviewed separately. After establishing that the data for typical neuroleptics is suggestive, but not conclusive, of their mood-stabilizing properties, the chapter will summarize the data for atypical neuroleptics.

Typical Neuroleptics

Multiple controlled trials have demonstrated that typical neuroleptics are superior to placebo in the treatment of acute mania (Chou, 1991; Goodwin & Jamison, 1990). A recent meta-analysis concluded that they are less effective than lithium (Janicak, Newman, & Davis, 1992) overall. However, the largest and most rigorous study (Prien, Caffey, & Klett, 1972) provides the clearest result. In this double-blind, 3-week study, 255 bipolar and schizoaffective patients with manic episodes were treated with lithium or chlorpromazine. Among manic patients without agitation, the efficacy of lithium and chlorpromazine was equivalent. Chlorpromazine was more effective than lithium in treating "hyperactive" mania. Subsequent studies showed similar advantage in efficacy with psychomotor agitation (e.g., Garfinkel, Stancer, & Persad, 1980) and in speed of onset of action.

Interestingly, this benefit may not be attributable to the sedating properties of neuroleptics. While sedation often governs clinician choice of initial neuroleptic treatment, the literature shows no clear evidence to suggest increased efficacy of low potency (more sedating) neuroleptics over high potency ones (reviewed in Tohen et al., 1998). Garfinkel et al. (1980) found that haloperidol was better than lithium in the treatment of mania, and that combined treatment was no more effective than haloperidol alone. There has been no clear difference in antimanic efficacy between specific typical neuroleptics (Chou, 1991).

The value of typical neuroleptics in maintenance therapy is less clear. In one longitudinal study of 434 bipolar patients over periods averaging 17 years, the long-term use of typical neuroleptic agents was associated with a worsening of the course of illness (Kukopulos et al., 1980). Three small open prospective trials with depot flupenthixol gave conflicting results (reviewed in Tohen et al., 1998). In a life-chart study of 18 outpatients comparing their time spent on and off depot neuroleptics, Littlejohn, Leslie, and Cookson (1994) showed some benefit in prophylaxis. While on depot agents, the patients experienced fewer relapses and spent less time in hospital than when receiving treatment with oral medication only.

Conversely, other trials have suggested that neuroleptics may have prodepressant effects. One study (Kukopulos et al., 1980) indicated that bipolar patients on antipsychotics were at increased risk of developing depressive episodes. However, the evidence is inconsistent overall, and not all studies have adequately controlled for the extrapyramidal side effects or sedation, which may be difficult to distinguish from depression.

In clinical practice, typical neuroleptics are widely used in patients with bipolar illness, particularly during manic episodes. Nearly all patients hospitalized for mania receive at least one dose of neuroleptic (Tohen et al., 1998). Despite the relatively poor evidence of their efficacy in prophylaxis, patients often continue to take neuroleptics following discharge. At 6 months posthospitalization, 68% of a cohort of bipolar patients continued to take maintenance neuroleptics (Keck et al., 1995).

Unfortunately, typical neuroleptics have a number of disadvantages, particularly in their use as maintenance therapy. First, they may be poorly tolerated as a result of extrapyramidal symptoms (EPS), including akathisia, stiffness, or dystonic reactions. In addition, over the longer term, they pose the risk of tardive dyskinesia. This risk may be particularly great in patients with primarily affective illness (Kane, 1999; Saltz et al., 1991). These limitations have prompted many clinicians to consider changing from typical to atypical neuroleptics.

Atypical Neuroleptics: Overview

Success with the first atypical neuroleptic, clozapine, led to the development of several other agents with similar properties. The factors which make the newer agents atypical are still disputed (Richelson, 1999). The original definition recognized that newer agents were less likely to increase prolactin levels or cause extrapyramidal side effects than (EPS) typical neuroleptics. However, this distinction is imperfect. Risperidone, for example, may increase prolactin levels at therapeutic doses without causing EPS (Richelson, 1999). More recent definitions focus on the receptor binding properties of these drugs. While the potency of typical neuroleptics is well-correlated with their blockade of the dopamine D_2 receptor, newer agents possess significant serotonin 5-HT_{2A} receptor antagonism as well. Some authors have suggested that the ratio of D_2:5-HT_{2A} blockade may distinguish the atypical agents (Richelson, 1999).

Atypical Neuroleptics in Mania

The impressive efficacy of clozapine as an antipsychotic led to its application in mania. A meta-analysis of retrospective and open-label trials between 1973 and 1995 revealed that manic patients were more likely to respond to clozapine than schizophrenic patients (Tohen et al., 1998). In these studies, manic or mixed patients were more likely to respond than depressed patients. Two small open-label trials with clozapine, which included a total of 42 patients, likewise suggested a role in treatment-refractory mania (Calabrese et al., 1996; Tohen et al., 1998). In an open randomized trial, Suppes and colleagues (1999) found adjunctive treatment with clozapine superior to other treatment options.

Concerns about the risk of agranulocytosis and the availability of newer agents led to a proliferation of open studies with risperidone and olanzapine (reviewed in Ghaemi & Goodwin, 1999); to date, only one case series with quetiapine has appeared (Ghaemi & Katzow, 1999). These studies utilized small numbers of patients and were varied in their use of concurrent medications and assessment of endpoints. Nonetheless, they suggested some efficacy in acute mania, either as monotherapy or adjunctive treatment. A representative study was conducted by Tohen and colleagues (1996), in which 15 patients were treated with risperidone for up to 6 weeks. The eight patients who remained in treatment at 6 weeks showed a 75% improvement on the Brief Psychiatric Rating scale.

Perhaps more significantly, these studies also suggested equal benefit in nonpsychotic affective episodes (Ghaemi, Sachs, Baldassano, & Truman, 1997). That is, the acute benefit of neuroleptic treatment was not limited to treatment of psychosis. On the other hand, there was no consistent evidence, despite early interest in the subject, that these drugs were better for treatment of rapid cycling bipolar disorder (Calabrese, Meltzer, & Markowitz, 1991).

Several case reports also raised the concern that atypical neuroleptics could precipitate a manic switch (Gelenberg, 1996), perhaps because of their interaction with the serotonergic system. For example, a number of case reports suggested induction of mania by risperidone (see, e.g., Koek & Kessler, 1996) and olanzapine (Fitz-gerald et al., 1999). At least one case report suggested that withdrawal from an atypical neuroleptic could induce manic symptoms (Lane & Chang, 1998). However, these results have not been replicated in subsequent trials. Moreover, most of these cases were not on concurrent mood stabilizer treatment, so the switches could have occurred spontaneously. Finally, some of these reports could have misclassified the transient activation or "hypomanic blip" (Aubry, Simon, & Bertschy, 2000) noted by other investigators.

Building on these open trials, randomized controlled trials investigating the efficacy of atypical neuroleptics in the treatment of mania have been completed. In a small parallel group study 45 manic patients were randomized to risperidone (6 mg), haloperidol (10 mg), or lithium (800–1200 mg) treatment for 4 weeks (Segal, Berk, & Brook, 1998). While all groups were rated as improved, at day 28 there was no significant difference between groups on various outcome measures. This study does suggest that risperidone is an effective and well-tolerated treatment for mania. Unfortunately, the small number of patients in each cell ($n = 15$) yielded inadequate power to demonstrate a difference between groups, so it cannot be concluded that these treatments are equally effective. A larger double-blind trial ($n = 158$) (Sachs & Ghaemi, 2000) compared treatment with placebo, haloperidol, or risperidone as adjunctive to mood stabilizer therapy (lithium or divalproex) for patients with manic or mixed episodes. This 3-week study found robust statistically significant advantage, for the groups receiving the mood stabilizer plus antipsychotic as early as the first week of treatment.

Similarly, another double blind study ($n = 150$) that compared the efficacy of risperidone versus placebo add on to mood stabilizers in acute mania reported a significant difference in percentage of responders favoring the risperidone group (Yatham, 2000).

More recently, a multicenter trial (Tohen et al., 1999) randomized 139 manic or mixed patients to 3 weeks of treatment with either olanzapine (at an average dose of 15 mg) or placebo in a double-blind design. The olanzapine treated group showed a significantly greater improvement, as measured by the Young Mania Rating scale, and included a greater number of treatment responders.

A second study (Tohen et al., 2000), comparing olanzapine to placebo, produced similar results to the first except that the difference between active treatment and placebo was statistically significant at the week 1 evaluation. The main difference between the studies is that the second study initiated treatment with a 15 mg dose of olazanpine, while the first study started with 10 mg and did not show significant separation between drug and placebo until week 3.

Olanzapine monotherapy ($n = 125$) was compared with divalproex sodium monotherapy ($n = 123$) in a 3 week acute mania trial. Results showed that olanzapine was superior to divalproex sodium ($p < 0.028$) on the primary efficacy measure of change in YMRS scores from baseline to endpoint (Tohen, Baker, et al., 2001). In another multicentre double-blind study, Tohen, Chengappa, et al. (2002) reported that olanzapine addition ($n = 229$) was significantly more effective than placebo addition ($n = 115$) to the mood stabilizers lithium or valproate in acute mania. In this study, 67% of patients assigned to the olanzapine and mood stabilizer combination responded compared to only 44% in the mood stabilizer alone group when 50% or more decrease in YMRS scores was used as the criterion for response. Furthermore, olanzapine add-on was more effective compared with placebo add-on in treating depressive symptoms as measured by changes in HAM-D 21 item scores.

Ziprasidone ($n = 131$) was compared with placebo ($n = 66$) in acute mania in a 3-week double-trial trial (Keck et al., 2000). Results showed that ziprasidone was significantly more effective than placebo in treating manic symptoms as measured by changes in Mania rating scale scores with differences between the groups emerging at as early as day 2.

In a recent smaller double-blind study, quetiapine add on to valproate was shown to be significantly superior to placebo add on in adolescent mania (DelBello et al., 2001).

Several aspects of these studies are particularly notable. First, atypicals as a group may all be effective in the treatment of acute mania. Second, haloperidol, olanzapine, quetiapine and risperidone were effective in patients without psychosis. Third, improvement was also seen in subjects with a history of rapid cycling, which is generally considered to be more treatment refractory. Finally, drop out rates were substantially lower in patients receiving antipsychotic treatments compared to placebo for olanzapine and compared to mood stabilizer alone, for haloperidol and risperidone.

The studies are somewhat limited by allowing concurrent administration of benzodiazepines, which may have contributed to a significant placebo effect, although treatment groups did not differ significantly in amount of use. As follow-up ended at 3 to 6 weeks, it also could not address the role of antipsychotics in maintenance therapy.

Additional trials will be needed to clarify the role of atypical neuroleptics in the treatment of acute mania. Particularly useful will be comparisons with traditional mood stabilizers or typical neuroleptics, either as monotherapy or in combination with these agents.

Atypical Neuroleptics in Treatment of Depression

Atypical neuroleptics have also been considered for treatment of depressive episodes. Several small case series addressed the use of clozapine in depression with psychotic features (e.g., Parsa, Ramirez, Loula, and Meltzer, 1991). Importantly, in schizophrenic or schizoaffective patients, clozapine has been shown to markedly decrease suicidality (Meltzer & Okayli, 1995); this decrease was associated with improvement in symptoms of depression.

Another suggestive study was a reanalysis of a subgroup of schizoaffective, bipolar patients who participated in a trial of olanzapine versus haloperidol (Tollefson, Bensley, & Tamura, 1997). Of the 52 patients who met criteria for a depressive episode, the olanzapine-treated group showed some improvement on MADRS (Montgomery-Asberg Depression Rating Scale), versus a slight worsening in the haloperidol group. Finally, in one retrospective, blinded comparison of olanzapine with typical neuroleptics ($n = 30$) in depressed patients (Rothschild, Bates, Boehringer, & Sayed, 1999), more of the olanzapine group was rated as much or very much improved.

On the other hand, some studies have shown no effect of atypical neuroleptics on depressive symptoms (Tohen, 1999). At this point, then, there is no strong evidence to support an antidepressant effect of atypical neuroleptics. Including measures of depression in future atypical neuroleptic trials, particularly in well-designed, controlled trials, will be essential to clarifying their role.

Atypical Neuroleptics as MaintenanceTherapy

A true mood stabilizer, by our definition, would also demonstrate the ability to prevent switches from euthymia into mania or depression. Thus far, there are no controlled trials to address this property of atypical neuroleptics. Several investigators have compiled open trials of clozapine as maintenance therapy in bipolar disorder, most recently Suppes et al. (1999). That study randomized 38 patients with bipolar or schizoaffective illness to clozapine add-on therapy or treatment as usual; the clozapine-treated group scored significantly better on a variety of rating scales, though not the Hamilton depression scale.

An earlier open trial (Banov et al., 1994) with 52 bipolar patients and 81 schizoaffective patients showed that clozapine-treated patients improved on multiple outcome measures, including overall level of function, at a mean of 18.7 months follow-up. The two double-blind trials that examined the efficacy of risperidone in acute mania for 3 weeks had a 10 week open label extension phase during which all patients received risperidone in combination with a mood stabilizer (Sachs, 2000; Yatham, 2000). Results showed that manic symptoms continued to improve during this phase in patients. In another study, 527 patients with bipolar disorder in various phases were recruited and treated with a combination of a mood stabilizer and risperidone for six months (Vieta et al., 2001). Results showed that YMRS scores decreased from a baseline score of 30 to 10 by week 4, and to 5 by week 6 indicating a substantial improvement in manic symptoms. More importantly, patients who entered the study in a depressive phase had a mean Hamilton Depression Rating scale (HAM-D) score of 25 which decreased to 13 by week 4 and continued to decrease during the following months. Only a very small number of these patients (less than 10%) were receiving antidepressants both at baseline and at end point. Therefore, although it was an open study and there was no comparator group, the results indicated that risperidone given in combination with mood stabilizers such as lithium or valporate leads to improvement not only in manic symptoms but also in depressive symptoms. Further support for this came from another study (Yatham, 2001), which reported significant reductions in both manic as well as depressive symptoms with risperidone and mood stabilizer combination over a 3-month period. In a smaller study, Ghaemi and Sachs (1997) assessed 12 risperidone-treated patients over 6 months. Over this period, four improved, four dropped out, and four failed to improve.

Patients who participated in a double-blind study of the efficacy of olanzapine for acute mania entered open label treatment ($n = 114$) with olanzapine for 49 weeks (Sanger et al., 2001). Of these, 98 patients had assessments conducted over the 49 week period and 15 dropped out. The mean YMRS scores were 25 at baseline and dropped to 7 by end point. Similarly, the mean HAM-D score at entry was 12 and it dropped to 5 by end point. Forty-one percent of patients received olanzapine monotherapy while the other 59% received mood stabilizers and/or other psychotropic medication add on therapy. Overall, the results of this study provide some indication that olanzapine also likely provides mood stability when given alone or in combination with other medications.

In a recent study, olanzapine add on to mood stabilizers ($n = 51$) was compared with placebo add on to mood stabilizers ($n = 49$) in an 18 month double-blind maintenance treatment study (Tohen, Chengappa, et al., 2001). Olanzapine and mood stabilizer therapy was superior to mood stabilizer plus placebo in time to manic recurrence but not time to recurrence of depression. Although the results of the above studies are promising, longer term double-blind follow up studies which compare these agents with placebo and traditional mood stabilizers will be needed before atypical neuroleptics can be recommended for maintenance therapy for the prophylaxis of bipolar disorder.

Clinical Parameters for Atypical Neuroleptic Use

At present, olanzapine is the only atypical neuroleptic that has received U.S. Food and Drug Administration approval for use in the treatment of mania. Most studies in bipolar disorder have utilized similar dosages to those used in schizophrenia studies, and reported similar side effect profiles. The following text briefly reviews the clinical considerations for atypical neuroleptic use. (For details, Buckley & Meltzer, 1998).

Clozapine dosing parameters vary widely. One common approach uses a starting dose of 25 mg/day, which is increased every other day by 25 mg until a dose of 100 mg/day is reached. The dose is then titrated up by 50 mg/day every other day. The optimal target dosage is unknown, but 300 to 450 mg/day is a common range, with the maximum dose of 900 mg/day. Generally, clozapine is dosed twice daily.

The most critical side effect of clozapine is agranulocytosis which may occur in fewer than 1% of patients. For this reason, patients beginning clozapine require weekly white blood cell count (WBC) monitoring for the first 6 months, and biweekly monitoring thereafter. Other side effects include seizure (a dose-related effect), orthostatic hypotension or tachycardia, sedation and dizziness, and weight gain.

Olanzapine dosing commonly ranges from 5 to 20 mg/day, with a starting dose of 5 to 15 mg; it is given once daily. Common side effects include weight gain, sedation, and orthostasis. Agranulocytosis has not been widely seen, although it was noted in one recent case report (Naumann, Felker, Heilemann, & Reuster, 1999).

Risperidone is generally initiated at 0.5 or 1 mg/day, and titrated upward to between 1 and 6 mg/day. Above 4 to 6 mg, the rate of extrapyramidal symptoms increases significantly. Like typical neuroleptics, risperidone may also produce increased serum prolactin levels.

Quetiapine may be initiated at 50 mg/day, and titrated upward to a target range of 300 to 750mg/day, with twice daily dosing. Its side effect profile resembles that of olanzapine, with sedation and weight gain, although there is no evidence that the weight gain is as marked as with olanzapine.

Finally, although atypical neuroleptics are generally better tolerated than typical agents, several caveats are worth noting. While the atypicals do exhibit a lower incidence of extrapyramidal symptoms, such symptoms may still occur (Miller et al., 1998), particularly with risperidone (Rosebush & Mazurek, 1999). In addition, there are isolated case reports of patients developing tardive dyskinesia with atypical neuroleptic treatment (Buzan, 1996). However, the risk is probably equivalent to the spontaneous risk (0–2%) (Woerner et al., 1991) with clozapine (Kane, Woerner, Pollack, Safferman, & Lieberman, 1993), risperidone (Lemmens, Brecher, & Van Baelen, 1996) and olanzapine (Tollefson et al., 1997).

Future Directions

The role of atypical neuroleptics in the treatment of bipolar disorder will undoubtedly be clarified as more data from controlled trials becomes available. Comparison studies will be needed to discern their value in monotherapy or adjunctive therapy. Similarly, long-term follow-up studies will be particularly important in clarifying the utility of atypicals in maintenance therapy and prophylaxis.

Atypical neuroleptics may also provide important clues to the neurobiology of bipolar disorder. The authors of one recent study (Suppes et al., 1999) suggest that the dosages required for mood stabilization may be lower than those required for antipsychotic effect, which could imply a distinct mechanism of action. Clarifying this mechanism may require a reconsideration of the therapeutic action of these agents. For example, a growing body of evidence suggests that some of clozapine's effects may be mediated by the glutamatergic system (Goff & Wine, 1997). Understanding the relevant properties of the atypical neuroleptics may finally elucidate the neurotransmitter systems involved in switching and maintaining mood states.

References

Aubry, J.-M., Simon, A. E., & Bertschy, G. (2000). Possible induction of mania and hypomania by olanzapine or resperidone: A critical review of reported cases. *Journal of Clinical Psychiatry, 61*(9), 649–655.

Baldessarini, R. J. (1985). *Chemotherapy in psychiatry.* Cambridge, MA: Harvard University Press.

Banov, M. D., Zarate, C. A., Jr., Tohen. M., Scialabba, D., Wines, J. D., Jr., Kolbrener, M., et al. (1994). Clozapine therapy in refractory affective disorders: polarity predicts response in long-term follow-up. *Journal of Clinical Psychiatry, 55,* 295–300.

Buckley, P. F., & Meltzer, H. Y. (1994). Treatment of schizophrenia. In A. F. Schatzbert & C. B. Nemeroff (Eds.), *American Psychiatric Press Textbook of Psychopharmacology* (pp. 615–640). Washington, DC: American Psychiatric Press.

Buzan, R. D. (1996). Risperidone-induced tardive dyskinesia [letter]. *American Journal of Psychiatry, 153,* 734–735.

Calabrese, J. R., Bowden, C. L., McElroy, S. L., Cookson, J., Andersen, J., Keck, P. E., Jr., et al. (1999). Spectrum of activity of lamotrigine in treatment-refractory bipolar disorder. *American Journal of Psychiatry, 156,* 1019–1023.

Calabrese, J. R., Bowden, C. L., Sachs, G. S., Ascher, J. A., Monaghan, E., & Rudd, G. D. (1999). A double-blind placebo-controlled study of lamotrigine monotherapy in outpatients with bipolar I depression. Lamictal 602 Study Group. *Journal of Clinical Psychiatry, 60,* 79–88.

Calabrese, J. R., Kimmel, S. E., Woyshville, M. J., Rapport, D. J., Faust, C. J., Thompson, P. A., et al. (1996). Clozapine for treatment-refractory mania. *American Journal of Psychiatry, 153,* 759–764.

Calabrese, J. R., Meltzer, H. Y., & Markovitz, P. J. (1991). Clozapine prophylaxis in rapid-cycling bipolar disorder. *Journal of Clinical Psychopharmacology, 11,* 396–397.

Chou, J. C. (1991). Recent advances in treatment of acute mania. *Journal of Clinical Psychopharmacology, 11,* 3–21.

Cochran, S. D. (1984). Preventing medical noncompliance in the outpatient treatment of bipolar affective disorders. *Journal of Consulting Clinical Psychology, 52,* 873–878.

Coryell, W., Leon, A., Winokur, G., Endicott, J., Keller, M., Akiskal, H., et al. (1996). Importance of psychotic features to long-term course in major depressive disorder. *American Journal of Psychiatry, 153,* 483–489.

Delay, J., Deniker, P., & Harl, J. (1952). Utilization therapeutique psychiatrique d'une phenothiazine d'action cetrale elective (4560 RP). *Annals of Medico Psychologiques, 110,* 112–117.

DelBello, M. P., Rosenberg, H. L., Hudepohl, A. M., & Strakowski, S. M. (2001). Quetiapine as adjunctive treatment for adolescent mania. *Bipolar Disorders, 3*(Suppl. 1), 33, Abstract 33.

Fitz-gerald, M. J., Pinkofsy, H. B., Brannon, G., Dandridge, E., & Calhoun, A. (1999). Olanzapine induced mania. *American Journal of Psychiatry, 156,* 1114.

Garfinkle, P. E., Stancer, H. G., & Persad, E. (1980). A comparison of haloperidol, lithium carbonate and their combination in the treatment of mania. *Journal of Affective Disorders, 2,* 279–288.

Gelenberg, A. J. (1996). Can risperidone trigger mania? *Biological Therapies in Psychiatry Newsletter, 19,* 18–19.

Ghaemi, S. N., & Goodwin, F. K. (1999). Use of atypical antipsychotic agents in bipolar and schizoaffective disorders: Review of the empirical literature. *Journal Clinical Psychopharmacology, 19,* 354–361.

Ghaemi, S. N, & Katzow, J. J. (1999). The use of quetiapine for treatment-resistant bipolar disorder: A case series. *Annals of Clinical Psychiatry, 11,* 137–140.

Ghaemi, S. N., & Sachs, G. S. (1997). Long-term risperidone treatment in bipolar disorder: 6-month follow up. *International Clinical Psychopharmacology, 12,* 333–338.

Ghaemi, S. N., Sachs, G. S., Baldassano, C., & Truman, C. J. (1997). Acute treatment of bipolar disorder with adjunctive risperidone in outpatients. *Canadian Journal of Psychiatry, 42,* 196–199.

Goff, D. C., & Wine, L. (1997). Glutamate in schizophrenia: Clinical and research implications. *Schizophrenic Research, 27,* 157–168.

Goodwin, F. K., & Jamison, K. R. (1990). *Manic depressive illness.* New York: Oxford University Press.

Janicak, P. G., Newman, R. H., & Davis, J. M. (1992). Advances in the treatment of mania and related disorders: a reappraisal. *Psychiatric Annals, 22,* 92–103.

Kane, J. M. (1999). Tardive dyskinesia in affective disorders. *Journal of Clinical Psychiatry, 60*(Suppl. 5), 43–47.

Kane, J. M., Woerner, M. G., Pollack, S., Safferman, A. Z., & Lieberman, J. A. (1993). Does clozapine cause tardive dyskinesia? *Journal of Clinical Psychiatry, 54,* 327–330.

Keck, P. E., McElroy, S. L., & Strakowski, S. M. (1998). Anticonvulsants and antipsychotics in the treatment of bipolar disorder. *Journal of Clinical Psychiatry, 59,* (Suppl. 6), 74–81.

Keck, P. E., Jr., Wilson, D. R., Strakowski, S. M., McElroy, S. L., Kizer, D. L., Balistreri, T. M., et al. (1995). Clinical predictors of acute risperidone response in schizophrenia, schizoaffective disorder, and psychotic mood disorders. *Journal of Clinical Psychiatry, 56,* 466–470.

Koek, R. J., & Kessler, C. C. (1996). Probable induction of mania by risperidone. *Journal of Clinical Psychiatry, 57,* 174–175.

Kukopulos, A., Reginaldi, D., Laddomada, P., Floris, G., Serra, G., & Tondo, L. (1980). Course of the manic-depressive cycle and changes caused by treatment. *Pharmakopsychiatrie-Neuropsychopharakol, 13,* 156–167.

Lane, H. Y., & Chang, W. H. (1998): Manic and psychotic symptoms following risperidone withdrawal in a schizophrenic patient [Letter to the editor]. *Journal of Clinical Psychiatry, 59,* 620–621.

Lemmens, P., Brecher, M., & Van Baelen, B. (1996, December). Extrapyramidal symptoms in patients treated with risperidone. Paper presented at the American College of Neuropharmacology Annual Meeting, San Juan, Puerto Rico.

Littlejohn, R., Leslie, F., & Cookson, J. (1994). Depot antipsychotics in the prophylaxis of bipolar affective disorder. *British Journal of Psychiatry, 165,* 827–829.

Maj, M., Pirozzi, R., Magliano, L., & Bartoli, L. (1998). Long-term outcome of lithium prophylaxis in bipolar disorder: A 5-year prospective study of 402 patients at a lithium clinic. *American Journal of Psychiatry, 155,* 30–35.

Marder, S. R. (1998). Antipsychotic medications. In A. F. Schatzberg & C. B. Nemeroff (Eds.), *Textbook of psychopharmacology* (2nd ed., pp. 309–322). Washington, DC: American Psychiatric Press.

Meltzer, H. Y., & Okayli, G. (1995). The reduction of suicidality during clozapine treatment in neuroleptic-resistant schizophrenia: Impact on risk-benefit assessment. *American Journal of Psychiatry, 152,* 183–190.

Miller, C. H., Mohr, F., Umbricht, D., Woerner, M., Fleischhacker, W. W., & Lieberman, J. A. (1998, February). The prevalence of acute extrapyramidal signs and symptoms in patients treated with clozapine, risperidone, and conventional antipsychotics. *Journal of Clinical Psychiatry, 59*(2), 69–75

Naumann, R., Felber, W., Heilemann, H., & Reuster, T. (1999). Olanzapine-induced agranulocytosis. *Lancet, 354,* 566–567.

Parsa, M., Ramirez, L. F., Loula, E. C., & Meltzer, H. Y. (1991). Effect of clozapine on psychotic depression and parkinsonism. *Journal of Clinical Psychopharmacology, 11,* 330–331.

Prien, R. F., Caffey, E. M., Jr., & Klett, C. J. (1972). Comparison of lithium carbonate and chlorpromazine in the treatment of mania. *Archives of General Psychiatry, 26,* 146–153.

Richelson, E. (1999). Receptor pharmacology of neuroleptics: Relation to clinical effects. *Journal of Clinical Psychiatry, 60*(Suppl. 10), 5–14.

Rosebush, P. I, & Mazurek, M. F. (1999). Neurologic side effects in neuroleptic-naïve patients treated with haloperidol or risperidone. *Neurology, 52,* 782–785.

Rosen, L. N., Rosenthal, N. E., Van Dusen, P. H., Dunner, D. L., & Fieve, R. R. (1983). Age at onset and number of psychotic symptoms in bipolar I and schizoaffective disorder. *American Journal of Psychiatry, 140,* 1523–1524.

Rothschild, A. J., Bates, K. S., Boehringer, K. L., & Syed, A. (1999). Olanzapine response in psychotic depression. *Journal of Clinical Psychiatry, 60,* 116–118.

Sachs, G., & Ghaemi, S. N. (2000). Safety and efficacy of resperidone versus placebo in combination with lithium or valproate in the treatment of the manic phase of bipolar disorder [Abstract]. *The International Journal of Neuropsychopharmacology, 3*(Suppl. 1), S143.

Saltz, B. L., Woerner, M. G., Kane, J. M., Lieberman, J. A., Alvir, J. M., Bergmann, K. J., et al. (1991). Prospective study of tardive dyskinesia in the elderly. *Journal of the American Medical Association, 266,* 2402–2406.

Sanger, T. M., Grundy, S. L., Gibson, P. J., Namjoshi, M. A., Greaney, M. G., & Tohen, M. F. (2001, April). Long-term olanzapine therapy in the treatment of bipolar I disorder: An open-label continuation study. *Journal of Clinical Psychiatry, 62*(4), 273–281.

Segal, J., Berk, M., & Brook, S. (1998). Risperidone compared with both lithium and haloperidol in mania: A double-blind randomized controlled trial. *Clinical Neuropharmacology, 21,* 176–180.

Strakowski, S. M., Keck, P. E., Jr., McElroy, S. L., West, S. A., Sax, K. W., Hawkins, J. M., et al. (1998). Twelve-month outcome after a first hospitalization for affective psychosis. *Archives of General Psychiatry, 55,* 49–55.

Suppes, T., Webb, A., Paul, B., Carmody, T., Kraemer, H., & Rush, A. J. (1999, August). Clinical outcome in a randomized 1-year trial of clozapine versus treatment as usual for patients with treatment-resistant illness and a history of mania. *American Journal of Psychiatry, 156,* 1164–1169.

Tohen, M., Baker, R. W., Milton, D. R., Risser, R. C., Gilmore, J. A., Davis, A. R., et al. (2001). Olanzapine versus divalproex sodium for the treatment of acute mania. [Abstract 125]. *Bipolar Disorders Abstract Book, 3*(Suppl. 1), 60.

Tohen, M., Chengappa, K. N. R., Suppes, T., Baker, R. W., Risser, R. C., Evans, A. R., et al. (2001). *Olanzapine combined with lithium or valproate in prevention of recurrence in bipolar disorder: An 18-month study.* Paper presented at the American College of Neuropsychopharmacology Meeting, Hawaii.

Tohen, M., Chegappa, K. N., Suppes, T., Zarate, C. A., Jr., Calabrese, J. R., Bowden, C. L., et al. (2002). Efficacy of olanzapine in combination with valproate or lithium in the treatment of mania in patients partially nonresponsive to valproate or lithium monotherapy. *Archives of General Psychiatry, 59*(1), 62–69.

Tohen, M., Jacobs, T. G., Grundy, S. L., McElroy, S. L., Banov, M. C., Janicak, P. G., et al. (2000). Efficacy of olanzapine in acute bipolar mania: A double-blind, placebo-controlled study. The Olanzapine HGGW Study Group. *Archives of General Psychiatry, 57*(9) 841–849.

Tohen, M., Sanger, T. M., McElroy, S. L., Tollefson, G. D., Chengappa, K. N., Daniel, D. G., et al. (1999). Olanzapine versus placebo in the treatment of acute mania. *American Journal of Psychiatry, 156,* 702–709.

Tohen, M., Tsuang, M. T., & Goodwin, D. C. (1992). Prediction of outcome in mania by mood-congruent or mood-incongruent features. *American Journal of Psychiatry, 149,* 1580–1584.

Tohen, M., Waternaux, C. M., & Tsuang, M. T. (1990). Outcome in mania. A 4-year prospective follow-up of 75 patients utilizing survival analysis. *Archives of General Psychiatry, 47*(12), 1006–1111.

Tohen, M., & Zarate, C. A. (1998). Antipsychotic agents and bipolar disorder. *Journal of Clinical Psychiatry, 59*(Suppl. 1), 38–48.

Tohen, M., Zarate, C. A., Centorrino, F., Hegarty, J. I., Froeschl, M., & Zarate, S. B. (1996). Risperidone in the treatment of mania. *Journal of Clinical Psychiatry, 57,* 249–253.

Tollefson, G. D., Beasley, C. M., & Tamura, R. N. (1997). Blind, controlled, long-term study of the comparative incidence of treatment-emergent tardive dyskinesia with olanzapine or haloperidol. *American Journal of Psychiatry, 154,* 1248–1254.

Tollefson, G. D., Beasley, C. M., Tran, P. V., Street, J. S., Krueger, J. A., Tamura, R. N., et al. (1997). Olanzapine versus haloperidol in the treatment of schizophrenia and schizoaffective and schizophreniform disorders: results of an international collaborative trial. *American Journal of Psychiatry, 154,* 457–465.

Vieta, E., Goikolea, J. M., Corbella, B., Benabarre, A., Reinares, M., Martinez, G., et al. (2001). Risperidone safely and efficacy in the treatment of bipolar and schizoaffective disorders: Results from a 6-month, multicenter, open study. *Journal of Clinical Psychiatry, 62*(10), 818–825.

Woerner, M. G., Kane, J. M., Lieberman, J. A., Alvir, J., Bergmann, K. J., Borenstein, M., et al. (1991). The prevalence of tardive dyskinesia. *Journal of Clinical Psychopharmacology, 11,* 34–42.

Yatham, L. N. (2000). Safety and efficacy of risperidone as combination therapy for the manic phase of bipolar disorder: Preliminary findings of a randomised, double-blind study (RIS-INT-46). [Abstract]. *International Journal of Neuropsychopharmacology, 3,* S142.

Yatham, L. N. (2001, July). *Risperidone add-on to mood stabilizers in acute and continuation treatment of mania.* 7th World Congress of Biological Psychiatry, Berlin.

CHAPTER 9

Antidepressants in Bipolar Disorder: A Review of Efficacy

Karen Saperson
L. Trevor Young

Introduction

Bipolar disorder is a chronic, potentially debilitating mental illness affecting 1.2 to 1.6% of the population. It is characterized by both manic and depressive episodes although there is considerable variability in the manifestation, course, and prognosis of illness across patients (Kessler, McConagle, & Zhao, 1994). Bipolar disorder may have a predominantly manic or depressive course, predictable or erratic course, slow, continuous, or rapid cycling (characterized as four or more episodes per year) (Goodwin & Jamison, 1990).

Classification

Accurate classification of bipolar disorder subgroups may have particular relevance for treating episodes, in particular with respect to the use of prescribing antidepressants. Bipolar disorder, or manic depression as it was previously known, was first described by Hippocrates more than 2,000 years ago (although the two ends of the symptom spectrum were termed "Black bile" for mania and "Yellow bile" for melancholia) (Goodwin & Jamison, 1990). The illness came to be described in different terms over the centuries, and at the end of the 19th century, Kraeplin was first responsible for using the term *manic depression*, and went on to further delineate this illness from dementia praecox, now known as schizophrenia (Goodwin & Jamison, 1990). Over time, there have been attempts to classify various components of bipolar disorder to achieve more homogeneity within subgroups; logic dictates that this has very important treatment implications. Angst has further characterized bipolar disorder into four groups: MD (with severe manias and depression), Md (with severe manias and mild depression or dysthymia), mD (with hypomanias and severe depressions), and md (with hypomanias and milder depressions) (Angst, 1978). The mD group closely resembles subjects who have more recently been described as bipolar type II, which may be a more common subtype of bipolar disorder than previously thought (Simpson et al., 1993). In a scholarly review by Akiskal and Pinto (1999), the authors argue for the necessity of a partial return to Kraeplin's broad-based view of manic depressive illness but go on to describe subtypes I to IV (bipolar 1, full blown mania; bipolar 1.5, depression with a protracted hypomania; bipolar 2, depression with hypomania, bipolar 2.5; cyclothymic depressions; bipolar 3, antidepressant associated hypomania; bipolar 3.5, bipolar masked and unmasked by stimulant abuse; bipolar 4, hyperthymic depression). The authors go on to cite compelling reasons for the reclassification, in order to find optimum therapeutic guidelines (Akiskal & Pinton, 1999), most notably the need to exercise caution when prescribing antidepressants in the absence of mood stabilizers. Joffe, Young, and McQueen (1999) hypothesize that "the current notion of bipolar disorder as a discrete disease entity distinct from unipolar illness, may be neither clinically nor theoretically useful and is not wholly supported by the literature" (p. 25). They propose an alternative hypothesis in which bipolar disorder may constitute two separate, but interrelated disorders, depression and mania. In this hypothesis, they argue that depression in bipolar disorder may be a common heterogeneous disorder, no different from the broad range of depressive disorders constituting unipolar depression. They go on to propose that the depressive illness increases vulnerability to and expression of the more rare disorder, mania. This hypothesis, if proven, has significant implications for treatment and the development of treatment guidelines for the depressed phase of bipolar disorder. It is this phase that is most closely associated with chronicity, morbidity, and mortality (Coryell et al., 1998). The hypothesis of Joffe et al. certainly challenges our current understanding as described by Sachs (1996) that while depressive episodes of bipolar disorder may share many phenomenological features of unipolar depression, it seems clear by virtue of the differences in its course, and its response to pharmacotherapy and genetics (Tsuang & Feraone, 1990) that it is a different illness.

In the most comprehensive review of the subject to date, Zornberg and Pope (1993) point out that until now we have based the rationale for treatment of bipolar depression, of necessity, on generalizing data derived from treatment of unipolar depression. Thus we have made the assumption that standard antidepressant medication effective for treating unipolar depression, is also likely to be effective for the depressed phase of bipolar disorder. Zornberg and Pope point out, however, that emerging evidence demands that we consider the limitations of doing so. Much of the research to date has been fraught with methodological challenges, including difficulties surrounding clear definition of mood states, such as mixed states, heterogeneous samples (unipolar/bipolar depression), and inadequate measures of response in studies done prior to 1975, when the usage of research diagnostic criteria (RDC) first came into general use (Feighner et al., 1972). Furthermore, confidence in the assessment of treatment outcome for bipolar depressed patients is further limited by issues such as often defining treatment response on the basis of change in depression rating scales, which can result in mislabeling a clear worsening in a patient's clinical condition as recovery (i.e., mistaking emergent mania for improvement of depression) (Sachs, 1996).

These issues and the resultant lack of clarity present major stumbling blocks in evaluating the effectiveness of various treatment modalities for bipolar depression. The treatment of the depressive phase of bipolar disorder presents considerable challenges and requires great skill on the part of the clinician. With this in mind, this chapter will present an overview of the currently available pharmacotherapeutic options in the class of antidepressant drugs available for individuals with bipolar depression. We will do so by addressing several critical questions, not all of which have definitive answers in the scientific literature to date, including: What is the efficacy of antidepressant agents used to treat the depressed phase of bipolar disorder? Do mood stabilizers moderate the response to treatment and are there clear benefits to combinations of antidepressants and mood stabilizers versus monotherapy with antidepressants alone? What specific issues are important in the rapid cycling phase of bipolar disorder? How does the risk of switching into mania influence the use of antidepressants?

The treatment of depression in bipolar disorder has been covered in several recent reviews (Sachs, 1996; Srisurapanont, Yatham, & Zis, 1995; Yatham et al., 1997; Zornberg et al., 1993). While the authors in these reviews all draw the general conclusion that there are too few randomized, controlled clinical trials with standardized treatments to be useful in establishing practice guidelines, the American Psychiatric Association has published their "Practice Guidelines for Treatment of Patients with Bipolar Disorder (1994). These are similar to those of Goodwin and Jamison in their authoritative text (Goodwin & Jamison, 1990) and can be summarized as follows: (1) optimization of the current mood stabilizer; (2) correction of medical illness and hypothyroidism; (3) addition of antidepressants; (4) change to or addition of another mood stabilizer; (5) electroconvulsive therapy (ECT); (6) addition of other less proven biological strategies. The emphasis in this chapter will be largely on option 3.

Efficacy of Various Classes of Antidepressant Agents

TRICYCLIC ANTIDEPRESSANTS

The treatment of bipolar depression with antidepressants of any class is complicated by the risk of switching (into a manic or hypomanic state). The subject of switching is dealt with more comprehensively below. Results of treatment emergent mania in bipolar disorder patients treated with tricyclic antidepressants alone (in the absence of mood stabilizers) range from 30 to 70 percent (Asberg-Wistedt, 1982; Bunney, 1978; Kupfer, Carpenter, & Frank, 1988b; Prien, Klett, & Caffey, 1973; Wehr & Goodwin, 1987a, b). Some studies, however, are contradictory in this regard (Angst, 1985; Lewis & Winokur, 1982a, b). Tricyclic antidepressants (TCAs) are better than placebo in acute treatment of depression in controlled trials involving more than 5,000 patients (American Psychatric Association, 1994; Goodwin & Jamison, 1990; Zornberg et al., 1993). These studies are largely confined to unipolar depression or to an unspecified mix of unipolar and bipolar depression. The APA Task Force Report (1994) concludes that tricyclic antidepressants are superior to placebo in the treatment of bipolar depression.

Imipramine is the most investigated antidepressant (Srisurapanont et al., 1995). The mean response rate in six double blind studies, having a total of 66 bipolar depressed patients, was 55% for imipramine (range 40–100%) (Baumhachl et al., 1989; Cohn, Collins, Ashbrook, & Wernicke, 1989; Coppen, Whybrow, Noguera, Maggs, & Prange, 1972; Himmelhoch, Thase, Mallinger, & Houck, 1991; Kessell & Holt, 1975; Thase, Mallinger, McKnight, & Himmelhoch, 1992). In two open trial studies the response rate was slightly lower at 44% (Avery & Lubrano, 1979; Kupfer et al., 1988). In the three studies that included both unipolar and bipolar depressed subjects, response rates to acute treatment with imipramine were reported to be similar for the two groups (Baumhachl et al., 1989; Katz et al., 1987; Kupfer et al., 1988a). The results of the NIMH collaborative study (Decarolis, Gilbert, Roccatagliata, Ross, & Vennuti, 1964) suggest no difference in the antidepressant response to acute treatment with either imipramine or ami-triptyline with 85 unipolar and 47 bipolar depressed patients after 2 weeks of placebo washout. In contrast, in an earlier open study of over 200 de-pressed patients, Decarolis reported a lower response to imipramine in 15 bipolar compared with unipolar subjects (Decarolis et al., 1964). Goodwin and Jamison (1990) cite the unpublished findings of Goodwin in 1981 which found only a nonsignificant trend toward less response to tricyclics in bipo-lar depression compared with unipolar depression, although the study de-sign is not known. Zornberg and Pope reviewed seven controlled studies that examined the efficacy of tricyclic antidepressants in the treatment of bipolar depression (Zornberg & Pope, 1993). The conclusions drawn re-main consistent that tricyclic antidepressants are more effective than pla-cebo for patients with bipolar depression. However, their efficacy relative to lithium and other antidepressants, and their utility when combined with mood stabilizers, has not been systematically studied.

MONOAMINE OXIDASE INHIBITORS

Four double blind controlled studies and three open trial studies have ex-amined the efficacy of monoamine oxidase inhibitors (MAOIs) in the treat-ment of bipolar depression. In the benchmark study of Himmelhoch, Detre, Kupfer, Swartzburg, and Byck (1972), the authors demonstrated a 76% re-sponse rate to tranylcypromine in this subpopulation of bipolar depressed patients who were described as "anergic." However, 20 out of 21 patients were receiving lithium as well and thus the improvement cannot be attrib-uted solely to tranylcypromine. In a subsequent study (Himmelhoch, Fuchs, & Symonson, 1982) the authors examined 59 patients with anergic depres-sion (of whom 29 had bipolar depression). Ninety-one percent of patients on tranylcypromine responded compared with 24% to placebo. Two further double blind studies (Himmelhoch, Thase, et al 1991; Thase, Mallinger, McKnight, & Himmelhoch, 1992) compared tranylcypromine to imipramine, in which the former demonstrated clear superiority with response rates of 75 to 81% compared to imipramine (response rates 48 to 50%) in the treat-ment of anergic bipolar depression. Significantly, the tranylcypromine treated group also had a lower number of dropouts as well as a lower incidence of hypomanic switch (11 vs. 19%). Whether or nor similar results would be obtained for "nonanergic" depressed bipolar subjects is unknown. The re-sponse rate of bipolar depressed patients on a variety of MAOIs ranges from 53 to nearly 100%. Most of the studies used tranylcypromine success-fully in the treatment of anergic bipolar depressed patients. Notwithstand-ing the difficulties in making direct comparisons of efficacy due to differences in design, diagnostic impurity, and other factors, tranylcypromine demonstrates the highest response rate (81%) of any drug studied (Thase et al., 1992). In a small open study, Price (Price, Charney, & Heninger, 1985) reported that two bipolar depressed patients previously resistant to the combination of buproprion and lithium, responded to the combination of tranylcypromine and lithium.

With respect to other MAOIs, there have been no double-blind–controlled studies looking at phenelzine, only a series of case reports affirming its effectiveness (Quitkin, McGrath, Liebowitz, Stewart, & Howard, 1981). It is not known if reversible inhibitors of monoamine oxidase (RIMA) are effective. However, in the only double-blind controlled study looking at this class, the response rate of bipolar depressed patients to moclobemide was 53% compared to 60% for imipramine (Baumhachl et al., 1989).

SELECTIVE SEROTONIN REUPTAKE INHIBITORS

In a study by Cohn (Cohn et al., 1998), a double-blind, randomized comparison of fluoxetine, imipramine, and placebo, 18 of 21 subjects on fluoxetine, 12 of 21 on imipramine, and 5 of 13 on placebo improved by more than 50% on depression rating scales. However, only 49% of patients (44) completed the 6-week trial, discontinuing treatment because of side effects or lack of efficacy. Counting the noncompleters of treatment as failures interferes with interpretation of the data, as does the fact that some patients refused lithium.

Newer and atypical antidepressants, including the selective serotonin reuptake inhibitors (SSRIs), have not been well or extensively studied in the treatment of acute bipolar depression. Two double-blind studies involving 68 patients compared SSRIs to tricyclic antidepressants (Asberg-Wistedt, 1982; Cohn et al., 1998) and found that these agents were at least as, and possibly more effective than, imipramine or desipramine in bipolar depression. A review (Srisurapanont et al., 1995) concludes that the response rates to SSRIs appeared to be slightly higher than tricyclics; however, Zornberg and Pope (1993) in their comprehensive review, point out that the short length of treatment time, the lack of control over adjunctive lithium use, and the small number of subjects, make it difficult to draw definitive conclusions from these studies.

In a noncontrolled study by Baldessano, Sachs, Stoll, Lafer, and Truman (1995) of bipolar depressed patients who had failed prior adequate trials of an antidepressant, 65% responded to open treatment with paroxetine while 10% had treatment emergent hypomania or mania. In a case report by Rihmer, Kiss, Kecskes, Pestality, and Gyorgy (1998), the authors report a

42-year-old female with bipolar disorder type I whose dysphoric mania responded rapidly and completely while her manic medications (lithium, carbamazepine, clozapine, haldol, and clonazepam) were supplemented by 20 mg of paroxetine. In an uncontrolled study of fluvoxamine, three of five bipolar depressed subjects responded to fluvoxamine (Saletu, Scherve, Grunberger, Schanda, & Arnold, 1977). In a study by Young, Joffe, Robb, MacQueen, and Marriot (2000) the efficacy of paroxetine in addition to a mood stabilizer was established, as was its more favorable side effect profile, compared with the addition of a second mood stabilizer. Furthermore, the addition of paroxetine was not associated with the emergence of mania or hypomania in a 6-week trial. A double-blind, placebo controlled trial comparing the effect of paroxetine and imipramine in the treatment of bipolar depression found no statistical differences between treatments (Nemeroff et al., 2001).

NEWER ANTIDEPRESSANTS

Venlafaxine

There have been no double-blind, placebo-controlled clinical studies involving venlafaxine. In the personal communication of Nierenberg and Fieghner, as reported in a review by Sachs (1996), they found at least modest improvement in 29% of treatment refractory bipolar patients ($n = 7$) treated openly with venlafaxine. Experienced clinicians might consider that venlafaxine, in view of its noradenergic potential might be more likely to induce switching but thus far this has not been studied in clinical trials. A study by Amsterdam (1998) looking at patients with bipolar disorder, type II, and meeting criteria for major depression, found that venlafaxine treatment may be a safe and effective antidepressant as monotherapy, without the risk of manic switching.

Mirtazapine

There have been no studies regarding the use of mirtazapine in bipolar disorder.

Bupropion

Bupropion has been reported to be useful in treating bipolar disorder patients (Shopsin, 1983). Two open studies investigated the efficacy of bupropion as an augmenting agent in patients with a history of nonresponse to treatment to other drugs (Fogelson, Bustritsky, & Pasnau, 1992; Haykal & Akiskal, 1990). This augmentation strategy converted 60% of nonresponders to responders; none of the patients switched into mania or hypomania.

Sachs et al. (1994) have demonstrated that when combined with mood stabilizers, bupropion is not superior to desipramine in treating bipolar depressed patients (63% vs. 71%). However, the occurrences of hypomania or mania in the bupropion treated group (11%) were considerably lower than the desipramine treated group (30%).

Mixed states, defined by the merging of the elements of manic and depressive syndrome in individuals with bipolar disorder, may represent a particularly virulent form of the disorder, necessitating the development of new strategies for treatment. Sherwood Brown, Dilsauer, Shoabib, and Swann (1994) described the addition of bupropion to four patients in the mixed state, three of whom improved dramatically following this change. This raises the possibility that bupropion may have particular value in the treatment of patients in mixed states who exhibit a remission of mania but have lingering depression. Caution is demanded however, due to the small number of individuals studied, and the absence of information about posthospitalization course of illness. A study by Gardner (1983) suggests some promise for treating bipolar depressed patients with bupropion who are resistant to treatment with other antidepressants.

Electroconvulsive Therapy (ECT)

Electroconvulsive therapy is generally considered to be the most effective antidepressant treatment available, although no study has focused exclusively on the use of ECT in bipolar depression (Janicak et al., 1985). Zornberg and Pope (1993) found seven studies comparing ECT with antidepressant drugs and concluded that ECT was clearly more effective in five of them (Avery & Winokur, 1977; Avery & Lubrano, 1979; Black, Winokur, & Nasrallah, 1987; Bratfos & Haug, 1965; Greenblatt, Grosser, & Wechsler, 1962, 1964; Perris, 1966). There have been no published studies directly comparing ECT with lithium in the treatment of acute bipolar depression nor have there been any studies of electroconvulsive therapy plus an antidepressant and ECT plus lithium. Electroconvulsive therapy-induced switches (to mania/hypomania) are felt by most practicing clinicians, to be milder, more manageable, and to carry less risk of induction of rapid cycling than those induced by antidepressants.

Rapid Cycling and Antidepressant Induced Switching

The major reasons psychiatrists avoid prescribing antidepressants in bipolar disorder are the risks of switching the patient from depression into mania and of shortening the cycle length, thus inducing rapid cycling (Bunney, Murphy, Goodwin, Bethesda, & Borge, 1972; Henry, Chandler, & Rasmussen, 1992; Hon & Preskorn, 1989; Lebuegue, 1987; Lewis & Winokur, 1982; Nakra, Szwabo, & Grossberg, 1989; Settle & Settle, 1984; Wehr & Goodwin, 1979a, 1979b, 1987a, 1987b). Clinical experience and anecdotal evidence support both of these possibilities, but neither has been proved based on placebo-controlled long-term prospective studies (Goodwin et al., 1990; Zornberg & Pope, 1993; American Psychiatric Association, 1994). Furthermore, there is the opposing view that switches into mania and rapid cycling are spontaneous events which are not causally related to the use of antidepressants in bipolar illness. At issue is the need to control for rates of mania in subjects on no antidepressants. Moreover, rates of switching have generally been calculated based on findings from an unspecified mix of unipolar and bipolar depressed subjects (American Psychiatric Association, 1994; Goodwin & Jamison, 1990; Zornberg & Pope, 1993). Depending on the number of previous episodes of depression in a patient, the rates of falsely diagnosing bipolar depression as unipolar in an individual who will subsequently develop mania are relatively high (8 to 28%), complicating the issue even further (Goodwin & Jamison, 1990).

The two opposing views are exemplified by the findings of Lewis and Winokur (1982) and Wehr and Goodwin (1987a, 1987b). In the former study, retrospective chart review revealed that in depressed patients switch to mania occurred in 23% of patients on tricyclics but also in 34% of those who did not. Wehr and Goodwin performed a meta-analysis of data from 12 double-blind placebo controlled studies of tricyclic antidepressant efficacy involving more than 600 patients and found a higher rate of switching into hypomania/mania (seven to nine percent) in those who did receive antidepressants versus those who did not (Wehr & Goodwin, 1987a, b). Similar arguments have been made for and against the induction of rapid cycling by antidepressants.

In a study of 501 patients with bipolar disorder (a heterogeneous group of bipolar I, bipolar II, cyclothymia, and rapid cyclers), Kukopulos et al. (1983) found a rapid cycling course in 118 cases where the previous course could be reliably reconstructed. Thirty-two of these were rapid cyclers from the beginning of the illness while the other 86 had a different course initially, which later changed into rapid cycling. This study was primarily concerned with the acceleration of the course of the disease rather than with the transformation, per se, of a unipolar to a bipolar course. In the majority of cases, the change of the previous course into rapid cycling coincided with antidepressant drug treatments (MAOIs, tricyclic antidepressants, tetracyclic antidepressants). The authors went on to study what they termed *premorbid temperament*, and indicated that patients with a hyperthymic or cyclothymic temperament were more vulnerable to undergo acceleration to rapid cycling under the action of antidepressants. Overall, they found 16% of rapid cyclers among patients with bipolar disorder. The addition of lithium therapy did not appear to change this course.

With regard to other classes of antidepressants besides the tricyclic antidepressants, the meta-analysis of Zornberg and Pope (1993) and also by Peet (1994), found lower rates of induction of hypomania or mania in bipolar depression treated with SSRIs compared with TCs. Indeed, Peet found when combining clinical trial data obtained comparing SSRIs with TCAs and placebo in close to 17,000 patients (including 415 with bipolar disorder) a higher switch rate on TCAs (11%) compared with SSRIs (3.7%). In contrast, Howland (1996) looked at 11 patients who developed mania during treatment with SSRI. The SSRI induced manic episodes were severe with psychotic features requiring patients to be excluded for extreme agitation. However, this group responded completely to antimanic treatment. He emphasizes, however, that the risk of treatment-emergent mania with SSRIs is not trivial. Additional research is needed to compare the actual rate of a drug induced mania with SSRIs and TCAs in patients with different bipolar subtypes. In previous studies comparing tranylcypromine and imipramine, it was observed that switch rates to mania in each group were similar but that switching on the MAOI was more likely to be mild and not require hospitalization (Himmelhoch, Detre, et al., 1972; Himmelhoch, Fuchs, et al., 1982; Himmelhoch, Thase, et al., 1991). Boerlin, Gitlin, Zoellner, and Hammen (1998) examined the response to naturalistic treatment of 29 bipolar I patients experiencing 79 depressive episodes. Treatment consisted primarily of mood stabilizers used alone or in combination with antidepressants. Their findings were that antidepressant treatment combined with mood stabilizer therapy was not associated with higher rates of postdepressive mood elevation than mood stabilizer therapy alone. Subjects treated with TCAs and MAOIs were associated with a higher switch rate than those treated with fluoxetine. Tricyclic antidepresassants were also associated with more intense switches. The authors claim in their conclusion that the frequency and severity of postdepressive mood elevation associated with acute or continuation antidepressant therapy may be reduced by mood stabilizers. The novel antidepressant bupropion may hold promise for treatment of mixed states (Sherwood et al., 1994) and may have considerably lower occurrences of hypomania/mania switching (Sachs et al., 1994).

Hurowitz and Leibowitz (1993) reported six cases of rapid mood cycling induced by antidepressants. These authors point out that the key to effective treatment remains recognition of the pattern of apparent remission, relapse, and antidepressant or stimulant adjustment. They claim that the destabilizing effects of antidepressant drugs were not corrected by the addition of mood stabilizers, necessitating the withdrawal of antidepressant agents. Hurowitz and Liebowitz go on to attempt to define a rational approach and produce some treatment guidelines for this population.

The authors suggest that for medication induced rapid cyclers: (1) that they be taken off antidepressant agents and stimulants as soon as possible (the addition of mood stabilizers may be necessary before attempting this step safely but this remains unclear); (2) if antidepressant treatment is essential then bupropion should be considered because it neither increases hypomania nor rapid cycling; and (3) the use of high-dose T4, with or without the addition of an antidepressant drug, may perform as a mood stabilizer in this population, particularly when discontinuing the antidepressant agent is not appropriate. These guidelines are further tested in another case series by Simpson, Hurowitz, and Leibowitz (1997) in which the guidelines, although not foolproof, were found to be useful.

Altshuler et al. (1995) studied the longitudinal course of 51 patients with treatment refractory bipolar disorder. The goal of the study was to assess possible effects of cyclic antidepressants on occurrence of manic episodes and cycle acceleration. Thirty-five percent of the patients had manic episodes, likely to have been antidepressant induced.

Cycle acceleration was likely to be associated with antidepressant treatment in 26% of patients assessed. Younger age of first treatment was a predictor of vulnerability to antidepressant induced cycle acceleration. Forty-six percent of patients with antidepressant induced mania, as opposed to only 14% of those without, also showed antidepressant induced cycle acceleration at some point in their illness. The authors concluded that in one third of treatment refractory patients, mania is likely to be antidepressant induced and not attributable to the expected course of illness while in one quarter of study patients, rapid cycling is induced. Antidepressant induced mania may be a marker for increased vulnerability to antidepressant induced cycle acceleration. Antidepressant induced cycle acceleration (but not mania) is associated with younger age at first treatment and may be more likely to occur in women and bipolar II patients. Stoll et al. (1994) examined whether antidepressant associated manic states differ in any way, from spontaneous mania. The antidepressant drugs involved included tricyclics, fluoxetine, monoamine oxydase inhibitors (MAOIs), and bupropion. The patients with MAOI and bupropion associated mania had a slightly lower overall rating of severity of psychopathology at admission than the other two subgroups.

They concluded that antidepressant associated mania appears to be a milder and more time-limited syndrome than spontaneous mania and may perhaps represent a distinct clinical entity.

In summary, the treatment of bipolar depression with antidepressants of any class is complicated by the risk of switching, although antidepressant induced mania may be milder and of shorter duration than spontaneous mania (Fogelsen & Sternbach, 1997). It remains controversial whether or not antidepressant induced mania represents a risky adverse effect or an unmasking of underlying vulnerability to bipolar disorder.

Monotherapy Versus Combination Therapy

In planning the treatment protocol for any individual patient in the depressed phase of bipolar disorder, definitive answers to vitally important questions remain elusive. For example, it is unproven whether mood stabilizers in combination with antidepressants prevent switching or cycling, whether antidepressants/mood stabilizer combinations offer definitive advantages over monotherapy, and whether combinations of different mood stabilizers are preferable to mood stabilizer/antidepressant combinations. Quitkin and colleagues (1981) examined 75 bipolar I patients to compare the efficacy of lithium carbonate plus imipramine versus lithium carbonate plus placebo in preventing relapse. There was little evidence that the combination of lithium carbonate and imipramine caused adverse reactions; however, interactions between type of most recent episode, treatment condition, sex, and type of relapse showed that women and mania prone patients treated with imipramine had an increased risk of mania. Life table analysis demonstrated that the overall probability of remaining well was the same for both treatment groups and that two thirds of all relapses occurred in the first 6 months. Prien et al. (1984) examined 117 bipolar patients in a double-blind, long-term follow-up study who were receiving lithium carbonate, imipramine, or both. This group was compared to 150 unipolar patients receiving lithium carbonate, imipramine, both lithium and imipramine, or placebo. With bipolar patients, lithium carbonate and the combination treatment was superior to imipramine in preventing mania recurrences and were as effective as imipramine in preventing depressive episodes. The combination treatment provided no advantage over lithium carbonate alone. The group treated with lithium carbonate had fewer manic episodes than the other groups. Boerlin, Gitlin, Zoellner, and Hammen (1998) found that the frequency and severity of postdepressive mood elevation associated with acute or continuation antidepressant therapy in bipolar patients may be reduced by mood stabilizers. Such elevations may be more likely in patients with a strong history of mania. There remain no definitive answers to these questions although various authors have attempted to provide guidelines (Goodwin & Jamison, 1990; Simpson et al., 1993; Yatham et al., 1997). A treatment approach by one group recommends that mood stabilizers should be considered the first line in view of the fact that the efficacy is at least equal to, if not greater than, antidepressant treatment and that their use is rarely associated with hypomanic switching. If the patient were already on a mood stabilizer, increasing the dose to achieve adequate serum levels and maintaining the dose for 2 to 3 weeks would be the next appropriate step. If this proves ineffective, the addition of a second mood stabilizer or an antidepressant should be the next option, with SSRIs or bupropion being used in preference to tricyclics given their lower propensity to induce switching. In anergic bipolar depressed patients, MAOIs may be the treatment of choice. Electroconvulsive therapy also remains a highly effective treatment choice. Young, Joffe, et al. (2000) compared the addition of paroxetine to a second mood stabilizer and found equivalent efficacy but improved tolerability.

A vitally important question if one considers an antidepressant in combination with mood stabilizer(s) remains the duration of treatment with the antidepressant. While the guidelines are clear for depressive episodes of unipolar depression (Quitkin, Rabkin, et al., 1984) no such guidelines exist for depressive episodes of bipolar disorder. Likewise, questions regarding optimum dosage of antidepressant therapy for bipolar depression have been explored by Frank and Kupfer (1985). The authors of a recent review (Srisurapanont et al., 1995) suggest discontinuing antidepressants within 2 weeks of achieving remission of depressive symptoms in individuals with bipolar disorder. The APA Practice Guidelines (1994) highlight the need for caution in prescribing antidepressants; however, they acknowledge that antidepressants are often necessary in combination with mood stabilizers for both acute and prophylactic treatment. They go on to recommend that these patients should receive the lowest effective dosage for the shortest time necessary without defining these parameters.

The Canadian Network for Mood and Anxiety Treatments (CANMAT), consisting of a group of clinicians and clinical researchers from across Canada, have also provided us with recommendations regarding an approach to the treatment of the depressed phase of bipolar disorder. These recommendations (Yatham & Kusumakar, 1997) are summarized as follows: (1) The mood stabilizer lithium should be the first choice in the treatment of bipolar depression; (2) in depressions with marked suicidality or severe psychosis, ECT should be considered; (3) should antidepressant treatment become necessary, SSRIs and bupropion are preferable to the TCAs because of their lower propensity to induce a mood switch; and (4) should a patient with bipolar depression be responding well to a TCA the robust use of concomitant mood stabilizer such as lithium or divalproex is advisable. The group further indicates that it is inadvisable to use antidepressants without mood stabilizers in bipolar disorder (despite lack of evidence indicating that mood stabilizers are protective). The consensus of the working group is that the antidepressant medication should be gradually reduced and withdrawn completely within 6 to 12 weeks of remission of depressive symptoms.

Conclusions

Antidepressant medications clearly have their place in the treatment of the depressed phase of bipolar disorder. Efficacy of agents from multiple classes is supported by placebo controlled and open trials in addition to clinical experience. The choice of agents needs to be adequately considered because these drugs may differ in their efficacy and their propensity to promote switches into mania and rapid cycling. As reviewed in other chapters in this book, depressive symptoms are frequent, debilitating, and are associated with suicide in this patient group so that a rational approach to their management is essential. In some instances, this involves the judicious use of specific antidepressants. The intensity and length of trial of antidepressants in patients with bipolar disorder is an issue of continued debate but the data suggests brief trials with this agent and withdrawal after symptomatic improvement. The development of new treatments for this phase of bipolar disorder will help clinicians to put these agents in an appropriate context with other effective treatments for bipolar depression.

References

Akiskal, H., & Pinto, O. (1999, September). The evolving bipolar spectrum: prototypes I, II, III, and IV. *The psychiatric clinics of North America, 22*(3), 517–534.

Altshuler, L. L., Keck, P. E., McElroy, S. L., Suppes, T., Brown, E. S., Denicoff, K., et al. (1999). Gabapentin in the acute treatment of refractory bipolar disorder. *Bipolar Disorders, 1*(1), 61–65.

Altshuler, L. L., Post, R. M., Leverich, G. S., Mikalauskas, K., Rosoff, A., & Ackerman, L. (1995, August). Antidepressant-induced mania and cycle acceleration: A controversy revisited. *American Journal of Psychiatry, 152*(8), 1130–1138.

American Psychiatric Association. (1994, December). Practice guidelines for the treatment of patients with bipolar disorder. *American Journal of Psychiatry, 151*(12 Suppl.), 135–208.

Amsterdam, J. (1998, October). Efficacy and safety of venlafaxine in the treatment of bipolar II major depressive episode. *Journal of Clinical Psychopharmacology, 18*(5), 414–417.

Angst, J. (1978). The course of affective disorders: II Typology of bipolar manic depressive illness. *Archives of Psychiatry Nervenkr, 226*, 65–73.

Angst, J. (1985). Switch from depression to mania—A record study over decades between 1992 and 1982. *Psychopathology, 18*, 140–153.

Asberg-Wistedt, A. (1982). Comparison between Zimelidine and desipramine: Endogenous depression. *Acta Psychiatrica Scandinavia, 66,* 129–138.

Avery, D., & Lubrano, L. (1979). Depression treated with imipramine and ECT: The Decarolis study reconsidered. *American Journal of Psychiatry, 136,* 559–562.

Avery, D., & Winokur, G (1977). The efficacy of electroconvulsive therapy and antidepressants in depression. *Biological Psychiatry, 12,* 507–523.

Baldessano, C. F., Sachs, G. S., Stoll, A. L., Lafer, B., & Truman, C. J. (1995). Paroxetine for bipolar depression: outcome in patients failing prior antidepressant trials. *Depression, 3*(4), 182–186.

Baumhachl, U., Biziere, K., Fischbach, R., Geretsegger, C., Hebenstreit, G., Radmayr, E., et al (1989). Efficacy and tolerability of moclobemide compared with imipramine in depressive disorder (DSM-III): An Austrian double-blind multicentre study. *British Journal of Psychiatry, 155*(Suppl. 6), 78S–83S.

Black, D. W., Winokur, G., & Nasrallah, A. (1987). The treatment of depression: Electroconvulsive therapy vs. antidepressants: A naturalistic evaluation of 1,495 patients. *Comprehensive Psychiatry, 28,* 69–82.

Boerlin, H. L., Gitlin, M. J., Zoellner, L. A., & Hammen, C. L. (1998, July). Bipolar depression and antidepressant-induced mania: A naturalistic study. *Journal of Clinical Psychiatry, 59*(7), 374–379.

Bratfos, O., & Haug, J. O. (1965). Electroconvulsive therapy and antidepressant drugs in manic-depressive disease. *Acta Psychiatrica, 41,* 588–596.

Bunney, W. E., Jr., Murphy, D. L., Goodwin, F. K., & Borge, G. F. (1972). The "Switch Process" in manic-depressive illness. *Archives of General Psychiatry, 27,* 295–302.

Bunney, W. E. (1978). Psychopharmacology of the switch process in affective illness. In M. Lipton, A. Dimascio, & K. Killam (Eds.), *Psychopharmacology, a generation of progress* (pp. 1249–1259). New York: Raven Press.

Calabrese, J. R., Bowden, C. L., McElroy, S. L., Codeson, J., Anderson, J., Keck, P. E., Jr., et al. (1999, July). Spectrum of activity of Lamotrigine in treatment refractory bipolar disorder. *American Journal of Psychiatry, 156*(7), 1019–1023.

Calabrese, J. R., Bowden, C. L., Sachs, G. S., Ascher, J. A., Monaghan, E., & Rudd, E. D. (1999, February). A double-blind placebo-controlled study of Lamotrigine monotherapy in outpatients with bipolar I depression. Lamictal 602 study group. *Journal of Clinical Psychiatry, 60*(2), 79–88.

Calabrese, J. R., & Delucchi, G. A. (1990). Spectrum of efficacy of valproate in 55 patients with rapid-cycling bipolar disorder. *American Journal of Psychiatry, 147,* 431–434.

Calabrese, J. R., Markovitz, P. J., Kimmel, S. E., & Wagner, S. C. (1992). Spectrum of efficacy of valproate in 78 rapid-cycling bipolar patients. *Journal of Clinical Psychopharmacology, 12*(Suppl. 1), 53S–56S.

Cohn, J. B., Collins, G., Ashbrook, E., & Wernicke, J. F. (1989). A comparison of fluoxetine, imipramine and placebo in patients with manic depressive disorder. *International Journal of Clinical Psychopharmocology, 4,* 313–322.

Coppen, A., Whybrow, F. C., Noguera, R., Maggs, P., & Prange, A. J., Jr. (1972). The comparative antidepressant value of L-tryptophan and imipramine with and without attempted potentiation by liothyronine. *Archives of General Psychiatry, 26,* 234–241.

Coryell, W., Turvey, C., Endicott, J., Leon, A. L., Mudles, T., Solomon, D., et al. (1998). Bipolar I affective disorder: Predictors of outcome after 15 years. *Journal of Affective Disorders, 50,* 109–116.

Decarolis, V., Gilbert, F., Roccatagliata, G., Ross, R., & Vennuti, G. (1964). Imipramine and ECT in the treatment of depression: A clinical statistical analysis of 437 cases. *Sist-Nerv, 16,* 29–42.

Feighner, J. P., Robins, E., Guze, S. B., Woodruff, R. A., Winokur, G., & Munoz, R. (1972). Diagnostic criteria for use in psychiatric research. *Archives of General Psychiatry, 135,* 552–556.

Fogelsen, D. L., & Sternbach, H. (1997). Lamotrigine treatment of refractory bipolar disorder [Letter to the editor]. *Journal of Clinical Psychiatry, 58,* 271–273.

Fogelson, D. L., Bystritsky, A., & Pasnau, R. (1992). Bupropion in the treatment of bipolar disorders the same old story. *American Journal of Psychiatry, 53,* 443–446.

Frank, E., & Kupfer, D. J. (1985). Maintenance treatment of recurrent unipolar depression: Pharmacology and psychotherapy. *Advances in Biochemical Psychopharmacology, 40,* 139–151.

Gardner, E. A. (1983). Long term preventative care in depression: the use of bupropion in patients intolerant of other antidepressants. *Journal of Clinical Psychiatry, 44,* 157–162.

Goodwin, P. K., & Jamison, K. R. (1990). *Manic depressive illness.* New York: Oxford University Press.

Greenblatt, M., Grosser, G. H., & Wechsler, H. (1962). A comparative study of selected antidepressant medications and ECT. *American Journal of Psychiatry, 119,* 144–153.

Greenblatt, M., Grosser, G. H., & Wechsler, H. (1964). Differential response of hospitalized depressed patients to somatic therapy. *American Journal of Psychiatry, 120,* 936–943.

Haykal, R. F., & Akiskal, H. S. (1990). Bupropion as a promising approach to rapid cycling bipolar II patients. *Journal of Clinical Psychiatry, 51,* 450–455.

Henry, E. W., Chandler, L. P., & Rasmusen, J. G. C. (1992). Assessment of manic reactions during treatment with the SSRI sertraline. Does this afford patient benefit? *Clinical Neuropsychopharmacology, 15*(Suppl.1), 317B.

Himmelhoch, J. M., Detre, T., Kupfer, D. J., Swartzberg, M., & Byck, R. (1972). Treatment of previously intractable depressions with tranylcypromine and lithium. *Journal of Nervous Mental Disorders, 155,* 216–220.

Himmelhoch, J. M., Fuchs, C. Z., & Symons, B. J. (1982). A double-blind study of tranylcypromine treatment of major anergic depression. *Journal of Nervous Mental Disorders, 170,* 628–634.

Himmelhoch, J. M., Thase, M. E., Mallinger, A. G., & Houck, P. (1991). Tranylcypromine versus imipramine in anergic bipolar depression. *American Journal of Psychiatry, 148,* 910–916.

Hon, D., & Preskorn, S. H. (1989). Mania during fluoxetine treatment for recurrent depression. *American Journal of Psychiatry, 146,* 1638–1639.

Howland, R. H. (1996). Induction of mania with serotonin reuptake inhibitors. *Journal of Clinical Psychopharmacology, 16*(6), 425–427.

Hurowitz, G. I., & Liebowitz, M. R. (1993, February). Antidepressant-induced rapid cycling: Six case reports. *Journal of Clinical Psychopharmacology, 13*(1), 52–56.

Janicak, P. G., Davis, J. M., Gibbons, R. D., Ericksen, S., Chang, S., & Gallagher, P. (1985). Efficacy of ECT: A meta-analysis. *American Journal of Psychiatry, 142,* 297–302.

Joffe, R., Young, L. T., & MacQueen, G. M. (1999). A two-illness model of bipolar disorder. *Bipolar Disorders, 1,* 25–30.

Katz, M. M., Koslow, S. H., Maas, J. W., Frazer, A., Bowden, C. L., Casper, R., et al. (1987). The timing specificity and clinical prediction of tricyclic drug effects on depression. *Psychological Medicine, 17,* 297–309.

Kessell, A., & Holt, N. F. (1975). A controlled study of a tetracyclic antidepressant-maprotiline (ludiomil). *Medical Journal of Australia, 1,* 773–776.

Kessler, R. C., McGonagle, K. A., & Zhao, S. (1994). Lifetime and 12 month prevalence of DSM-III-R psychiatric disorders in the United States: Results from the national comorbidity study. *Archives of General Psychiatry, 57,* 8–19.

Kramlinger, K. G., & Post, R. M. (1989). Adding lithium carbonate to carbamazepine: Antimanic efficacy in treatment-resistant mania. *Acta Psychiatrica Scandinavia, 79,* 378–385.

Kukopulos, A., Caliari, B., Tundo, A., Minnai, G., Floris, G., Reginaldi, D., et al. (1983, May/ June). Rapid cyclers, temperament, and antidepressants. *Comprehensive Psychiatry, 24*(3), 249–258.

Kupfer, D. J., Carpenter, L. I., & Frank, E. (1988). Is bipolar II a unique disorder? *Comprehensive Psychiatry, 29,* 228–236.

Kupfer, D. J., Carpenter, L. L., & Frank, E. (1988). Possible role of antidepressants in precipitating manner and hypomania in recurrent depression. *American Journal of Psychiatry, 145,* 804–808.

Lebuegue, B. (1987). Mania precipitated by fluoxetine. *American Journal of Psychiatry, 144,* 1620.

Lewis, J. L., & Winokur, G. (1982). The induction of Mania: a natural history study with controls. *Archives of General Psychiatry, 39*(3), 303–306.

Nakra, B. R. S., Szwabo, P., & Grossberg, G. T. (1989). Mania induced by fluoxetine. *American Journal of Psychiatry, 146,* 1515–1516.

Nemeroff, C. B., Evans, D. L., Gyualia L., Sachs, G. S., Bowden, C. L., Gergel, J. P., et al. (2001). Double-blind, placebo-controlled comparison of imipramine and paroxetine in the treatment of bipolar depression. *American Journal of Psychiatry, 158*(6), 906–912.

Peet, M. (1994). Induction of mania with selective serotonin re-uptake inhibitors and tricyclic antidepressants. *British Journal of Psychiatry, 164,* 549–550.

Perris, C. (1966). A study of bipolar (manic-depressive) and unipolar recurrent depressive psychoses. *Acta Psychiatrica Scandinavia, 42*(Suppl.), 153–194.

Price, L. H., Charney, D. S., & Heninger, G. R. (1985). Efficacy of lithium-tranylcypromine treatment in refractory depression. *American Journal of Psychiatry, 142,* 619–623.

Prien, R. F., Klett, C. J., & Caffey, E. M., Jr. (1973). Lithium carbonate and imipramine—prevention of affective episodes: A comparison in recurrent affective illness. *Archives of General Psychiatry, 29,* 420–425.

Prien, R. F., Kupfer, D. J., Mansky, P. A., Small, J. G., Tuason, V. B., Voss, C. B., et al. (1984, November). Drug therapy in the prevention of recurrences in unipolar and bipolar affective disorders. Report of the NIMH Collaborative Study Group comparing lithium carbonate, imipramine, and a lithium carbonate-imipramine combination. *Archives of General Psychiatry, 41*(11), 1096–1104.

Quitkin, F. M., Kane, J., Rifkin, A., Ramos Lorenzi, J. R., & Nayak, D. V. (1981, August). Prophylactic lithium carbonate with and without imipramine for bipolar I patients. A double-blind study. *Archives of General Psychiatry, 38*(8), 902–907.

Quitkin, F. M., McGrath, P., Liebowitz, M. R., Stewart, J., & Howard, A. (1981). Monoamine oxidase inhibitors in bipolar endogenous depressives. *Journal of Clinical Psychopharmacology, 1,* 70–74.

Quitkin, F. M., Rabkin, J. G., Ross, D., & McGrath, P. J. (1984). Duration of antidepressant drug treatment: what is an adequate trial? *Archives of General Psychiatry, 41,* 238–245.

Rihmer, Z., Kiss, G. H., Kecskes, I., Pestality, P., & Gyorgy, S. (1998, January). SSRI supplementation of anti-manic medication in dysphoric mania. *Pharmacopsychiatry, 31*(1), 30–31.

Sachs, G. S. (1996, June). Treatment-resistant bipolar depression. *The Psychiatric Clinics of North America, 19*(2), 215–236.

Sachs, G. S., Lafer, B., Stoll, A. (1994). A double-blind trial of bupropion versus desipramine for bipolar depression. *Journal of Clinical Psychiatry, 55,* 391–393.

Saletu, B., Scherve, M., Grunberger, J., Schanda, H., & Arnold, O. H. (1977). Fluoxamine and a new serotonin reuptake inhibitor: First clinical and psychometric experiences in depressed patients. *Journal of Neural Transmission, 41,*17–36.

Settle, E. C., & Settle, G. P. (1984). A case of mania associated with fluoxetine. *American Journal of Psychiatry, 141,* 280–281.

Sherwood Brown, E., Dilsaver, C., Shoaib, A. M., & Swann, A. C. (1994). Depressive mania: Response of residual depression to bupropion. *Biological Psychiatry, 35,* 493–494.

Shopsin, B. (1983). Bupropion's prophylactic efficacy in bipolar affective illness. *Journal of Clinical Psychiatry, 44,* 163–169.

Simpson, H. B., Hurowitz, G. I., & Liebowitz, M. R. (1997, December). General principles in the pharmacotherapy of antidepressant-induced rapid cycling: A case series. *Journal of Clinical Psychopharmacology, 17*(6), 460–466.

Simpson, S. G., Folstein, S. E., Meyers, D. A., McMahon, F. J., Brusco, D. M., & DePaolo, J. R., Jr. (1993). Bipolar II: The most common bipolar stereotype. *American Journal of Psychiatry, 150,* 901–903.

Srisurapanont, M. D., Yatham, L. N., & Zis, P. (1995). Treatment of acute bipolar depression: A review of the literature. *Canadian Journal of Psychiatry, 40,* 533–544.

Stoll, A. L., Mayer, P. V., Kolbrener, M., Goldstein, E., Suplit, B., Lucier, J., et al. (1994, November). Antidepressant-associated mania: A controlled comparison with spontaneous mania. *American Journal of Psychiatry, 151*(11), 1642–1645.

Suppes, T., Brown, E. S., McElroy, S. L., Keck, P. E., Jr., Nolen, W., Kupka, R., et al. (1999, April). Lamotrigine for the treatment of bipolar disorder: A clinical case series. *Journal of Affective Disorders, 53*(1), 95–98.

Thase, M. E., Mallinger, A. G., McKnight, D., Himmelhoch, J. M. (1992). Treatment of imipramine-resistant recurrent depression, IV: A double blind crossover study of tranylcypromine for anergic bipolar depression. *American Journal of Psychiatry, 149,* 195–198.

Tsuang, M. T., & Feraone, S. V. (1990). *The genetics of mood disorders.* Baltimore: Johns Hopkins University Press.

Wehr, T. A., & Goodwin, F. K. (1979a). Rapid cycling in manic-depressives induced by tricyclic antidepressants. *Archives of General Psychiatry, 36,* 555–559.

Wehr, T. A., & Goodwin, F. K. (1979b). Rapid cycling between mania and depression caused by maintenance tricyclics. *Psychopharmacology Bulletin, 15,* 17–19.

Wehr, T. A., & Goodwin, F. K. (1987a). Do antidepressants cause mania? *Psychopharmacology Bulletin, 23,* 61–65.

Wehr, T. A., & Goodwin, F. K. (1987b). Can antidepressants cause mania and worsen the course of affective illness? *American Journal of Psychiatry, 144,* 1403–1411.

Yatham, L. N., & Kusumaker, V. (1997). *Lamotrigine in treatment of refractory bipolar depression.* Poster session presented at the Second International Conference on Bipolar Disorder. University of Pittsburgh Medical Centre, Pittsburgh.

Yatham, L. N., Kusumakar, V., Parikh, S. V., Haslam, D. R. S., Matte, R., Sharma, V., et al. (1997). Bipolar depression: Treatment options. *Canadian Journal of Psychiatry, 42*(Suppl. 2) 87S–91S.

Young, L. T., Joffe, R. T., Robb, J., MacQueen, G., & Marriot, M. (2000). A double blind comparison of the addition of a second stabilizer versus an antidepressant to an initial mood stabilizer for treatment of patients with bipolar depression. *American Journal of Psychiatry, 157,* 124–126.

Zornberg, G. L., & Pope, H. G. (1994). Treatment of depression in bipolar disorder: New directives for research. *Journal of Clinical Psychopharmocology, 13,* 397–408.

CHAPTER 10

Anticonvulsants in Treatment of Bipolar Disorder: A Review of Efficacy

Lakshmi N. Yatham
Vivek Kusumakar

Introduction

The first report of the use of an anticonvulsant (i.e., valpromide, the amide prodrug of valproate) for manic depressive illness was published by Lambert and colleagues (1966). Dalby (1971) reported mood altering properties of carbamazepine in patients with epilepsy; Takezaki and Hanaoka (1971) around the same time described the use of cabamazepine in 10 acute manic patients with 7 of these showing marked to moderate improvement in symptoms. Ballenger and Post (1978) conducted and reported the results of the first double blind study that examined the efficacy of an anticonvulsant in bipolar disorder. The interest in studying of anticonvulsants was to some extent fueled by increasing recognition and awareness of the limitations of lithium for treating bipolar disorder.

Since the early 1980s, a number of studies have appeared in the literature supporting the efficacy of both carbamazepine and valproate in the treatment of bipolar disorder. A number of other newer anticonvulsants such as lamotrigine, gabapentin, and topiramate have also been studied for their efficacy in bipolar disorder. In this chapter, we will review the controlled studies that have examined the efficacy of anticonvulsants in acute mania, acute bipolar depression, and prophylaxis of bipolar disorder. Where controlled studies are fewer or not available, we will also review the data from open studies. The efficacy of anticonvulsants in rapid cycling bipolar disorder has been reviewed in the chapter 3. Pharmacokinetics, pharmacodynamics, side effects and the management of side effects, and the dosing strategies of anticonvulsants can be found in chapter 12 in this book.

Carbamazepine

Carbamazepine is an iminostilbene derivative and has a structure that is similar to the tricyclic antidepressant imipramine. It was developed in the late 1950s and its antiepileptic properties were first reported in the early 1960s. It was approved as an antiepileptic in the United States in 1974 and has been used for treatment of generalized and partial complex seizure disorders and paroxysmal pain syndromes. We will provide below an overview of controlled studies of carbamazepine in acute mania, acute bipolar depression, and prophylaxis of bipolar disorder.

ACUTE MANIA

Antimanic efficacy of carbamazepine was examined in 19 double-blind studies. Of these, two compared carbamazepine or oxcarbazepine with placebo in an off-on-off-on design (Emrich, Dose, & von Zerssen, 1985; Post, Ballenger, et al., 1984), five with placebo in a parallel design (Desai et al., 1987; Gonclaves & Stoll, 1985; Klein, Bental, Lerer, & Belmaker, 1984; Moller et al., 1989; Okuma, Yamashita, Takahushi, et al., 1988), six with neuroleptics (Brown, Silverstone, & Cookson, 1989; Emrich, 1990; Grossi et al., 1984; Muller & Stoll, 1984; Okuma, Inanago, et al., 1979; Stoll et al., 1986), and another six with lithium (Emrich, 1990; Lenzi, Luzzerme, Grossi, Massimitti, & Placidi, 1986; Lerer, Moore, Meyendorff, Cho, & Gershon, 1987; Lusznat, Murphy, & Nunn, 1988; Okuma, Yamashita, et al., 1990; Small et al., 1991).

   Both studies that used an off-on-off-on double-blind design did not permit concurrent use of neuroleptics. Carbamazepine led to improvement in symptoms in four out of six patients in one study (Emrich et al., 1985) and 12 out of 19 in the other (Post, Ballenger, et al 1984). Most patients in both studies relapsed with placebo substitution, providing fairly convincing evidence for the antimanic efficacy of carbamazepine. All the studies that compared carbamazepine with antipsychotics reported equal efficacy with two studies reporting fewer side effects with carbamazepine (Brown et al., 1989; Emrich, 1990). Only two out of six studies that compared carbamazepine with lithium did not permit concurrent neuroleptic use (Lerer et al., 1987; Small et al., 1991), and both these studies reported equal efficacy. In the largest study to date (*n* = 100), Okuma, Yamashita, et al. (1990) reported that 62% of the carbamazepine group and 59% of the lithium group responded, again confirming equal efficacy of carbamazepine with lithium.

In the above described 19 double blind studies to date, a total of 825 patients with bipolar disorder were studied and, of these, 355 received carbamazepine, 64 oxcarbazepine, 98 neuroleptics, 146 lithium, and 162 placebo. The data in terms of number of responders for each medication was provided in only some studies. The data is available for 203 patients on carbamazepine, and of these 123 (61%) have been reported to improve with this medication. The improvement rates for neuroleptics and lithium were 57% (51 out of 89) and 55% (49 out of 89) respectively. The available evidence, therefore, clearly supports antimanic efficacy of carbamazepine.

Some studies have reported that several factors associated with nonresponse to lithium might predict response to carbamazepine. These include dysphoric mania, greater severity of mania, a negative family history of bipolar disorder, and those with greater decrements in T4 during treatment (Post, Ballenger, et al., 1984; Post, Uhde, et la., 1986; Post, Uhde, Roy-Byrne, & Joffe, 1987; Roy-Byrne, Toffe, Uhde, & Post, 1984). Although it was initially thought that rapid cycling might predict a response to carbamazepine, more recent data seem to suggest that it predicts poor response to both lithium and carbamazepine, and that in such patients a combination of these two agents might offer better efficacy (Denicoff et al., 1997; Okuma, 1993).

Acute Bipolar Depression

The efficacy of carbamazepine was examined in a total of 40 bipolar depressed patients in three double-blind placebo crossover studies (Ballenger & Post, 1980; Post, Uhde, Ballenger, et al., 1983; Post, Uhde, Roy-Byrne, & Joffe, 1986). Twenty-seven out of 40 (68%) responded while on carbamazepine and 50% relapsed with placebo substitution. In the largest of these three studies, which had a total of 24 bipolar depressed patients (Post, Uhde, Roy-Byrne, et al., 1986), 62% had mild improvement as defined by a reduction of 1 point or more on the Bunney-Hamburg scale with carbamazepine. When a stricter 2-point criterion was used for improvement, about 42% of bipolar depressed patients met criteria for response.

In summary, the available evidence suggests that carbamazepine has at least modest antidepressant properties in bipolar depressed patients.

PROPHYLAXIS OF BIPOLAR DISORDER

In the only double-blind placebo controlled study of prophylaxis to date (carbamazepine $n = 12$, placebo $n = 10$), Okuma, Inanago, et al. (1981) reported that 60% of patients randomized to carbamazepine and 22% randomized to placebo were stable during the one-year study period. A number of other controlled studies compared carbamazepine with lithium and reported that up to two thirds of patients respond to carbamazepine (Bellaire, Demisch, & Stoll, 1988; Coxhead, Silverstone, & Cookson, 1992; Greil, Ludwig-Mayerhofer, et al., 1997; Lusznat et al., 1988; Placidi, Lenzi, Luzzerine, Cassano, & Akiskal, 1986; Simhandle, Denk, & Thau, 1993; Watkins, Callender, Thomas, Tidmarsh, & Shaw, 1987; Wolf, Berky, & Kovacs, 1997).

Greil, Kleindienst, et al. (1998) reported that there was a negative association between hospitalization rate and the number of nonclassical bipolar features in their study population. Furthermore, there was a trend in favour of carbamazepine in the nonclassical bipolar group compared to lithium, in terms of lower hospitalization rates. Simhandl et al. (1993) in their 2-year study that compared carbamazepine with lithium noted that variations in blood levels of carbamazepine had no impact on prophylactic efficacy. Post, Leuerich, Rosoff, & Altshuler (1990) reported that a substantial number of bipolar patients develop tolerance to prophylactic efficacy of carbamazepine. This raises questions about the wisdom of using carbamazepine as a monotherapy for prophylaxis of bipolar disorder.

Valproate

Valproic acid is a simple branched-chain carboxylic acid. It was approved for use as an antiepileptic in the United States in 1978. It is now FDA approved for use as an antimanic agent. It is available in the United States and several other countries in various oral preparations such as valproic acid, sodium valproate, and divalproex sodium.

ACUTE MANIA

Five controlled studies support the efficacy of valproate in acute mania. These studies included a total of 255 acute manic patients, 113 of whom received valproate. Sixty-one of the 113 (54%) patients displayed moderate to marked reduction in acute manic symptoms.

Emrich et al. (1985) were the first to document the evidence for antimanic efficacy of valproate in a controlled study. Using a double-blind placebo crossover A-B-A design, they reported that four out of five manic patients had marked response to valproate. Brennan, Sandyk, and Borsook (1984), using a similar design, found that six out of eight manic patients responded to valproate.

Pope and colleagues (1991) conducted the first double-blind, placebo controlled, parallel group study with valproate in 36 acute manic patients for 1 to 3 weeks. Patients were not allowed to receive any concurrent psychotropic medication with the exception of lorazepam (for agitation/insomnia for the first 10 days). Valproate was significantly superior to placebo on all measures. Nine out of 17 (53%) valproate treated patients and 2 out of 19 (11%) placebo treated patients improved as defined by a 50% or greater reduction in mania rating scale scores. In the largest study to date, Bowden, Brugger, et al. (1994) assessed the efficacy of valproate in 179 acute manic patients in comparison to placebo and lithium. About 48% of patients in the valproate group, 49% in the lithium group, and 25% in the placebo group achieved significant clinical improvement by the end of the study as defined by a reduction in mania rating scale scores of 50% or more. The percentage of responders using 30, 40, or 50% reduction in Mania Rating Scale (MRS) scores was significantly higher in the valproate group compared with the placebo group. Improvement in symptoms was evident by the end of 1 week, particularly in patients that had serum valproate levels of 45 μg/L or greater (Bowden, Janicak, et al., 1996).

In the two studies that compared valproate with lithium (Bowden, Brugger, et al., 1994; Freeman, Clothier, Puzzaglia, Lesem, & Swann, 1992), valproate was found to be as effective as lithium in acute mania. Presence of depressive symptoms predicted better response to valproate in both studies. Response also was seen in 50% of rapid cyclers (Bowden, Brugger, et al., 1994) and the response in manic symptoms was unrelated to previous history of response to lithium.

Valproate oral loading has been reported to be safe and rapidly effective in treating manic symptoms; the speed of response has been reported to be similar to the onset of action with haloperidol (Hirschfeld, Allen, McEvoy, Keck, & Russell, 1999; Keck, McElroy, Tugrul, & Bennett, 1993; McElroy et al., 1996). A recent report suggested that intravenous valproate loading is also well tolerated and led to improvement in six out of seven patients including one patient who was nonresponsive to previous oral loading (Grunze, Erturth, Marcuse, et al., 1999).

ACUTE BIPOLAR DEPRESSION

McElroy, Keck, Pope, and Hudson (1992) reviewed open studies of valproate in bipolar depression and concluded that 30% (58 out of 195) of depressed patients respond to valproate. Since then, Davis et al. (1996) published another open-label prospective study of the efficacy of valproate in major depression and reported that 66% had a response based on intent to treat analysis.

In a pilot double-blind, multicenter, placebo-controlled trial, Sachs et al. (2001) recruited bipolar I or bipolar II depressed patients to examine the efficacy of divalproex monotherapy in comparison to placebo over an 8-week period. The primary efficacy measure was the absence of hypomania (YMRS < 10) with 50% or greater improvement on the HAM-D (26 item). Of the 43 subjects, 9/21 subjects randomized to divalproex met criteria for recovery compared with 6/22 subjects treated with placebo at the final assessment. Although there was a numerical superiority of valproate over placebo, the difference between the two groups was not statistically significant.

PROPHYLAXIS OF BIPOLAR DISORDER

A number of open studies suggest that valproate is effective in reducing the frequency and severity of both manic and depressive episodes (Brennan et al., 1984; Emrich et al., 1985; Hayes, 1989; Lambert, 1984; Lambert & Venaud, 1992; Semadeni, 1967; Vencovsky, Peterova, & Kabes, 1987; Zapletalek, Hayes, & Kindernayova, 1988). However, it appears to have a better efficacy in preventing manic compared to depressive episodes. Lambert and Venaud (1992) randomly assigned 150 patients (121 bipolar and 29 unipolar) to lithium or valproate for a two year maintenance treatment. If a patient did not tolerate the drug, or if the outcome was poor, a switch to an alternative drug was allowed. The number of episodes decreased from 4.12 during 2 years prior to the study to 0.51 during the study period for the valproate group and from 3.92 to 0.61 for the lithium group. This study clearly showed that the efficacy for valproate was similar to lithium. In addition, there were fewer drop-outs in the valproate (10%) group compared to the lithium group (25%).

A multicenter double-blind study that compared the efficacy of valproate with lithium and placebo was published recently (Bowden, Calabrese, McElroy, et al., 2000). In this study, 372 patients who met recovery criteria within 3 months of an index manic episode were randomized to maintenance treatment with divalproex, lithium, or placebo in a 2:1:1 ratio. Psychotropic medications were discontinued before randomization, except for open-label divalproex or lithium, which were gradually tapered over the first 2 weeks of maintenance treatment. The divalproex group did not differ significantly from the placebo group in time to any mood episode, which was the primary outcome measure. Divalproex , however, was superior to placebo in terms of lower rates of discontinuation for either a recurrent mood episode or depressive episode. Divalproex was also superior to lithium in longer duration of successful prophylaxis in the study and less deterioration in depressive symptomatology and GAS scores. Patients in the placebo group in this study had surprisingly good outcomes, which may have been due to the inclusion of patients with milder forms of illness and patients receiving highly supportive care by study personnel during the study. These and other factors led to a lower proportion of manic relapses in the placebo group than projected, yielding inadequate power to test the primary outcome variable; that is, 0.3 rather than the planned power of greater than 0.8.

In summary, the results of open studies suggest efficacy of valproate in prophylaxis of bipolar disorder. Although there was no difference in the primary outcome measure between valproate and placebo groups in the double-blind study, valproate was superior to placebo and lithium on various secondary measures supporting the efficacy of this medication.

Lamotrigine

Lamotrigine (3,5,-diamino-6(2,3-dichlorophenly)-1,2,4-triazine) is a phenyltriazine that acts at voltage sensitive sodium channels and stabilizes neuronal membranes. It is approved for treatment of refractory seizures as adjunctive therapy.

OPEN STUDIES

Acute Mania, Bipolar Depression, and Rapid Cycling

In 19 open studies, a total of 396 patients with various subtypes of bipolar disorder received lamotrigine (please see Table 10.1 for details). The duration of treatment in these studies ranged from 9 days to 3 years. Of these, 84 were treated with lamotrigine monotherapy and the others with lamotrigine in combination with other medications such as mood stabilizers, antidepressants, or neuroleptics. As with other open studies, details about the number of responders were not provided for all the studies. Overall, 71% of patients (264/371) responded when lamotrigine was given as an

TABLE 10.1
Studies of the efficacy of Lamotrigine (Lamictal®) in bipolar disorder

Study	Diagnosis	Patients (n)	Design	Duration	Other Drugs	Lamotrigine Dose Range (mg/day)	Response (ratings)
Weisler et al. (1994)	BP (n = 2) RC (n = 1)	2 D = 2	Open	5 months 7 months	Adjunctive—details not provided	Details not provided	Both patients responded with significant decrease in depressive symptoms. 2/2
Calabrese et al. (1996)	BI & RC (n = 1)	1	Open	11 months	Monotherapy	25–200	1/1 (HAM-D, GAF, SADS-C)
Walden et al. (1996)	BI (n = 1)	1	Open	1 year	VPA, trimipramine	50–300	Patient much improved. (CGI); 1/1
Ferrier (1998)	BP, RC (n = 7),	7	Open	2-3 years	Lithium, VPA, CBZ		Reduction of frequency and severity of episodes shown in 3/7
Fogelson & Sternbach (1997)	BI (n = 6), SA BP (n = 1), RC (n = 4)	7 M = 2 HM = 2 D = 2	Open	8–65 weeks	Lithium, VPA, CBZ et al.	50–400	Moderate to marked improvement in 4/7; 2 of 2 in M, 1 of 2 in HM and 1 of 2 in D
Sporn & Sachs (1997)	BI (n = 13), BII (n = 3), RC (n = 8)	16 M = 1 D = 9 Mixed = 6	Open	2–6 weeks	Lithium, risperidone, NRL, anxiolytic or hypnotic agents	50–250	Positive response in 8/16 (50%) 5/6 in D (CGI, GAF)
Kusumakar & Yatham (1997a)	BI & BII (n = 22), RC (n = 5)	22	Open	4 weeks	VPA	25–50	Response in 16/22 (70%) by week 4 and 50% decline in HAM-D score from baseline
Kusumakar & Yatham (1997b)	BI & BII & RC (n = 7)	7	Open	4 weeks	Monotherapy (n = 6) Combination (n = 1)	50–150	Response in 5/7 by week 4

Study	Diagnosis (n)	Sample size	Design	Duration	Medication	Dose	Outcome
Mandoki (1997)	BP (n = 10)	10	Open	Details not provided	VPA	50–200	10/10 children and adol. improved CGI score.
Fatemi et al. (1997)	BI (n = 1), BII (n = 4), RC (n = 5)	5	Open	226 ± 28 days	Thyroid supplements (n = 4) Lithium, divalproex sodium (n = 1)	150–225	5/5 patients—Only BDI score dropped significantly (BDI, GAF, YMRS)
Labbate & Ruby (1997)	BI & RC (n = 1)	1	Open	6 weeks	Paroxetine, levothyroxine	25–500	1/1
Kotler & Matar (1998)	BI (n = 1), SA (n = 1)	2	Open	6 months 4 months	FLX, buspirone Lithium, perphenazine, FLX	25–100	2/2
Erfurth & Grunze (1998)	BI (n = 1)	1 M = 1	Open	15 days	Monotherapy	50–300	LTG discontinued after 15th day due to skin rash. Improvement in patient observed with lower BRMS score and worsened mania observed after LTG discontinuation.
Erfurth, Walden, & Grunze (1998)	SA (n = 3)	3 M = 3	Open	2–6 months	Monotherapy (n = 3)	125–400	Response in 3/3—improved mood stability when serum concentration is greater than 5 mg/L
Suppes et al. (1999)	BI (n = 9), BII (n = 8) RC (n = 9) BI = 7 BII = 2	17 M = 6 D = 11	Open	14–455 days	Monotherapy (n = 2) Add-on: Lithium (n = 1) Divalproex (n = 6) GBP (n = 2) Clozapine (n = 3) AD (n = 10) BDZ (n = 4) Levothyroxine (n = 2)	25–600	11/17 (65%), M = 5/6 (83%), D = 6/11 (55%), Improvement in 6/9 RC patients (CGI)

Continued

TABLE 10.1
Continued

Study	Diagnosis	Patients (n)	Design	Duration	Other Drugs	Lamotrigine Dose Range (mg/day)	Response (ratings)
Calabrese, Bowden, McElroy, et al. (1999a)	BI (n = 62), BII (n = 11), NOS (n = 2)	75 D = 41 M = 14 HM = 6 Mixed = 11	Open	24 weeks open label; 24 weeks extension	Monotherapy (n = 15) Add-on (n = 60) VPA, antipsychotics, AD, lithium	25–500	54/72 Improvement in 28/41 (68%) of D and 26/31 (84%) of M/HM/mixed (HAM-D, YMRS, CGI, GAF)
Bowden et al. (1999)	BP RC (n = 41), BP non-RC (n = 34)	75	Open	24 weeks open label; 24 weeks extension	Monotherapy (n = 15) Add-on (n = 60) VPA, antipsychotics, AD, lithium	25–500	Marked improvement in the patients based on GAF, YMRS and HAM-D scores
Preda, Fazeli, McKay, Bowers, Jr., & Mazure (1999)	BP (n = 1)	1 M = 1	Open	9 days	Add-on with perphenazine, temazepam, clonazepam, nifedipine	50–400	Positive response with a decrease in the BPRS score
Hoopes (1999)	BI (n = 17), BII (n = 67), NOS (n = 52), Cyclothymic (n = 16), Other (n = 11), MDD (n = 55)	218 D = D	Open	21 months	Monotherapy (n = 57) Use of AD, NRL and anticonvulsants in adjunctive therapy	25–400	Response in 136/196 evaluable patients 32/52 in D 22 dropped out due to adverse effects

Diagnosis: BI = Bipolar I; BII = Bipolar II; BP = Bipolar; NOS = Bipolar Not Otherwise Specified; RC = Rapid Cycling; SA = Schizoaffective; SA BP = Schizoaffective Bipolar; MD = Major Depression

Patients: M = Manic; D = Depressive; HM = Hypomanic

Other Drugs: AD = Anti-Depressants; BDZ = Benzodiazepines; CBZ = Carbamazepine; FLX = Fluoxetine; GBP = Gabapentin; NRL = Neuroleptics; VPA = Valproate

Response: BDI = Beck Depression Inventory; BPRS = Brief Psychiatric Rating Scale; BRMS = Bech-Rafaelsen Mania Scale; CGI-I = Clinical Global Impression scale of Improvement; CGI-S = Clinical Global Impression scale of Severity; GAF = Global Assessment of Functioning scale; HAM-D = Hamilton Rating Scale for Depression; LTG = Lamotrigine; SADS-C = Schedule for Affective Disorders and Schizophrenia, Change version; YMRS = Young Mania Rating Scale

Summary of Results for Lamotrigine in Bipolar Patients

Total Number of Patients: 396

Note: Bowden et al. (1999) uses the same 75 patients as Calabrese, Bowden, Sachs, et al. (1999), hence the same 75 patients are counted once only

Total Number of Patients Data Available for: 371

Percentage Improved: 264/371 = 71.12%

Total Number of Manic/Hypomanic/Mixed Cases: 54
Total Number of Manic/Hypomanic/Mixed Cases Data Available for: 53
Percentage Improved: 40/53 = 75.5%

Total Number of Depressed Cases: 120
Total Number of Depressed Cases Data Available for: 114
Percentage Improved: 74/114 = 64.9%

211

add on or monotherapy. Forty (76%) of 53 had antimanic and 74 (65%) of 114 had antidepressant response when lamotrigine was given to treat manic/hypomanic/mixed symptoms or depressive symptoms respectively. Lamotrigine was noted to be effective in both acute and long-term treatment of bipolar disorder (Bowden, Calabrese, et al., 1999; Calabrese, Fatemi, & Wayshville, 1996; Fatemi, Rapport, Calabrese, & Thurus, 1997; Ferrier, 1998; Hoopes et al., 1999).

Prophylaxis

Two open studies examined the long term efficacy of lamotrigine in the continuation and maintenance treatment of bipolar depression. In the first study, patients who participated in a 7-week double-blind placebo-controlled lamotrigine monotherapy trial for bipolar depression, were enrolled in one year study which consisted of 2 phases (Huffman et al., 2000). During the 3-week double-blind phase (phase 1), patients previously randomized to lamotrigine ($n = 77$) were continued on lamotrigine maintenance treatment while those previously randomized to placebo ($n = 47$) were given escalating doses of lamotrigine. This was followed by a open label treatment phase which lasted for 49 weeks and during this phase, all patients received open label lamotrigine treatment. Fifty-six percent of patients completed the study, 44% withdrew and reasons for withdrawal included adverse events (14%), lack of efficacy (7%), or other reasons (13%), and 10% were lost to follow-up. Patients randomized to lamotrigine during the double-blind phase and continued lamotrigine during the open label phase maintained their improvement in depression during the study period. Those previously randomized to the placebo group during double blind phase and switched to lamotigine during the phase 1 and continued open label lamotiringe during the phase 2 showed significant improvements in HAM-D and MADRS scores and improvement on clinical global impression-improvement scale.

In another study (Bentley et al., 2000), patients who participated in a 10-week double-blind study of lamotrigine vs placebo in bipolar depression, were offered participation in a two-phase one-year continuation study. The first phase consisted of a five-week double-blind treatment during which patients previously randomized to placebo ($n = 63$) were given escalating doses of lamotrigine while those previously randomized to lamotrigine ($n = 64$) continued the same treatment. A 47-week open label phase followed this and during this period, patients were given either lamotrigine monotherapy or add-on therapy to other psychotropic medications. Results indicated that patients previously randomized to lamotrigine during double blind phase maintained their improvement while those previously randomized to placebo and received lamotrigine during the one year study also showed significant improvement.

In summary, the results of these two studies suggest that lamotrigine has efficacy in continuation and maintenance treatment of bipolar depression. This, however, requires confirmation in double-blind studies.

DOUBLE-BLIND STUDIES

Bipolar Depression

One hundred and ninety-five patients with bipolar depression were randomized to receive monotherapy with lamotrigine 50 mg ($n = 66$), lamotrigine 200 mg ($n = 63$), or placebo ($n = 66$) for seven weeks (Calabrese et al., 1999). Patients in the lamotrigine groups received lamotrigine 25 mg at randomization which was increased to 50 mg at the end of 2 weeks. Those in the 200 mg group had the dose increased to 100 mg at the end of week 3 and to 200 mg at the end of week 4. Entry criteria included a score of 18 or more on the 17-item Hamilton Rating Scale for Depression (HAM-D), and the changes in clinical status were assessed using the 31-item HAM-D, Montgomerry Asberg Depression Rating Scale (MADRS), Clinical Global Impression (CGI)-Severity and Improvement scales. The improvement in patients in the lamotrigine 200 mg group was ($p = 0.084$) superior compared to the placebo group as determined by changes in HAM-D scores from baseline using last observation carried forward analysis (LOCF). On MADRS, both the 50 mg and 200 mg groups were significantly better compared to the placebo group using LOCF. The lamotrigine 200 mg group did better on both CGI-Severity and Improvement scales whereas the 50 mg group did better only on the CGI-Severity scale compared to the placebo group. A significantly higher number of patients had a 50% or more decrease in MADRS scores in both the lamotrigine groups compared to the placebo group, but the differences were not significant on HAM-D. Lamotrigine was well tolerated, and headache was the only adverse event that was more common in the lamotrigine groups compared to the placebo group. The incidence of manic episodes was not significantly different between lamotrigine and placebo groups. The results of this study clearly suggest that lamotrigine is effective in treating bipolar depression and that it does not appear to have a propensity to induce a manic switch.

In a second double-blind trial (Bowden, Calabrese, Asher, et al., 2000), the efficacy of lamotrigine ($n = 103$) vs placebo ($n = 103$) was examined in a 10-week study in bipolar I and bipolar II depression. Results showed no significant differences between the groups using LOCF on HAM-D 17 item or MADRS. A subgroup analysis revealed significant differences in favor of lamotrigine on both HAM-D and MADRS in bipolar I and not bipolar II depressed patients. Placebo response was very high (about 50%) in this study which might have obscured the true difference between the groups. As well, it is possible that some of the patients recruited into the study with bipolar II depression might have had unipolar depression as the reliability of diagnosis of hypomania in general is lower than the diagnosis of mania. Manic switch was reported in 1% of patients in both groups in this study.

The selection of primary efficacy measures for studies in bipolar depression have been particularly problematic. HAM-D 17 item scale scores do not capture all the core symptoms of bipolar depression and many researchers now feel that MADRS might be a better alternative. Given a significant difference in favour of lamotrigine on MADRS and a number of secondary efficacy measure in bipolar I depressed patients in both studies, we conclude that lamotrigine monotherapy is effective in treatment of bipolar depression. Furthermore, results of these studies suggest that lamotrigine does not induce manic/hypomanic switch in bipolar patients unlike antidepressant medications.

Acute Mania

Berk (1999) examined the efficacy of lamotrigine monotherapy for acute mania in a double-blind randomized study. Forty-five patients were randomized to lamotrigine ($n = 15$), olanzapine ($n = 15$), or lithium ($n = 15$) for 4 weeks. Patients in the lamotrigine group received 25 mg daily during week 1, 50 mg daily during week 2 and 100 mg daily during weeks 3 and 4. Primary efficacy outcome measures were the MRS, the Brief Psychiatric Rating scale (BPRS), the CGI- scale for Severity and Improvement and Global Assessment of Functioning (GAF) scale. Assessments were completed at baseline and thereafter at weekly intervals. All groups demonstrated significant improvements on all primary outcome measures with no significant differences between the groups. A small sample size and absence of placebo group are the main limitations of this study.

In another double blind study ($n = 16$), patients with mania who had either failed or were intolerant to lithium were randomized to treatment with either lamotrigine or placebo for 8 weeks. Entry criteria included a score of 12 or more on Young Mania Rating Scale (YMRS). Subjects in the lamotrigine group were commenced on 12.5 mg/day and the dose was titrated to a maximum of 200 mg/day. A change in YMRS score of greater than 50% was used to define responders. Five out of eight patients randomized to the lamotrigine group and four out of eight randomized to the placebo group responded with no significant differences between the two groups (Anand, Oren, Berman, Cappliello, & Charney, 1999). The results of this study underscore the necessity to include a placebo arm in double-blind trials.

Two Glaxo-sponsored trials also tested the efficacy of lamotrigine in acute mania. In a 3-week study, lamotrigine monotherapy at a dose of 50 mg/day was compared with placebo monotherapy. In another study of 6 weeks duration, lamotrigine add-on was compared with lithium add-on to anitpsychotics in acute mania. Both studies showed no significant differences on the primary efficacy measure of change in Mania rating scale scores from baseline to endpoint using last observation carried forward analysis between lamotrigine and placebo groups (Bowden, Calabrese, Asher, et al., 2000).

In summary, three out of four double-blind studies failed to show antimanic efficacy of lamotrigine. The design issues complicated the interepretation of the data in the only study that showed positive results. Therefore, the consensus of experts at this point in time is that there is no compelling evidence for the efficacy of lamotrigine in acute mania.

Prophylaxis

The long-term efficacy of lamotrigine was examined in two recent double-blind studies (Bowden, Calabrese, Sachs, Yatham, et al., 2001; Bowden, Calabrese, DeVeaugh-Geiss, et al., 2001) in comparison to placebo and lithium. In the first study (GW#606), patients with bipolar I disorder ($n = 326$) who were or recently had manic or hypomanic episode were recruited while in the second study (GW#605), patients with bipolar I disorder were recruited during a depressive phase ($n = 463$). Patients in both studies were treated with an open label lamotrigine addition to other psychotropic medication for 8 to 16 weeks. Those meeting stabilization criteria were withdrawn from other psychotropic medication and randomized to treatment with lamotrigine ($n = 59$) or lithium ($n = 46$) or palcebo ($n = 70$) upto 18 months in the first study (GW #606) and to lithium ($n = 121$) or placebo ($n = 121$) or lamotrigine 50 mg ($n = 50$) or lamotrigine 200 mg ($n = 124$) or to lamotrigine 400 mg ($n = 47$) for up to 18 months. Preliminary analysis indicated that lamotrigine was significantly superior to placebo on overall survival in the study, time to intervention for any mood episode, time to any bipolar event and time to a depressive episode but not time to intervention for a manic episode in both studies. A sub-analysis in the second study (GW#605) showed that lamotrigine 200 mg group was superior to placebo on all the above measures but not 50 mg or 400 mg which might be due to smaller sample sizes in both these groups. Lithium was superior to placebo on time to intervention for any mood episode, time to any bipolar event and time to manic episode but not depressive episode in both studies. Lamotrigine was well tolerated in both studies.

The results of these studies suggest that lamotrigine has efficacy in longer treatment of bipolar disorder, and in particular in the prevention of bipolar depressive episodes.

Gabapentin

Gabapentin has a chemical structure similar to that of the branched chain amino acids leucine and valine and also the aromatic amino acid phenylalanine. It was developed as a structural analog of the inhibitory neurotransmitter, GABA, and was initially thought to act via GABAergic mechanisms. However, it was found that gabapentin does not interact with GABA receptors, nor does it interfere with GABA uptake or degradation. Gabapentin may increase the GABA content of some brain regions, and unlike carbamazepine, gabapentin does not interact with sodium channels, nor does it appear to have any significant effects on receptors for benzodiazepines, NMDA, catecholamines, or acetylcholine. The mechanism of action of gabapentin remains unknown. It is approved for use as add on therapy in management of refractory epilepsy.

OPEN STUDIES

The efficacy of gabapentin was examined in the majority of studies as an adjunct to other medications (please see Table 10.2 for details). Most, although not all, studies included mainly refractory patients (patients that had failed to respond to previous treatment with mood stabilizers and/or neuroleptics, antidepressants, etc.).

A total of 429 patients with refractory bipolar I, bipolar II, major depression, bipolar disorder NOS, schizoaffective, or rapid cycling received gabapentin add on or monotherapy in 19 uncontrolled studies (Please see Table 10.2 for details). The duration of treatment ranged from as short as 1 week to as long as 36 months. The details in terms of current mood symptoms at the time of commencing gabapentin and the percentage of responders were provided in only a few studies. Overall, about 244 (65%) out of 375 patients responded. About 62 (75%) out of 82 had antimanic response, and 40 (58%) out of 69 had antidepressant response to gabapentin. Seven (39%) out of 18 patients who had initially responded to gabapentin main-

TABLE 10.2

Studies of the efficacy of Gabapentin (Neurontin®) in bipolar disorder

Study	Diagnosis	Patients (n)	Design	Duration	Other Drugs	Gabapentin Dose Range (mg/day)	Response (ratings)	Side Effects
Schaffer & Schaffer (1997) Refractory	BI (n = 10), BII (n = 10), NOS (n = 1), Cyclothymic (n = 7), nonresponders to standard mood stabilizer	28	Open	1–9 months	BDZ, AD, NRL, AED	33(?)–2700	Response in 18 of 28 patients	Oversedation, Overactivation Increased rapid cycling (n = 2)
McElroy et al. (1997) Refractory	BI (n = 7), BII (n = 2), Nonresponsive to at least 1 mood stabilizer; persistent mania or hypomania	9 Mixed = 8 HM = 1	Open	1–7 months	BDZ, AD, NRL, mood stabilizers	300–4800	Moderate to marked response in 7 of 9 (78%)	Sedation (n = 7), ataxia (n = 2), forgetfulness (n = 3)
Marcotte et al. (1997) Refractory	Bipolar with or without concomitant OCD and PD	47	Open, retrospective	6 months	Monotherapy or add-on	600–4800	Improvement in the majority of patients	None clinically relevant

Continued

TABLE 10.2
Continued

Study	Diagnosis	Patients (n)	Design	Duration	Other Drugs	Gabapentin Dose Range (mg/day)	Response (ratings)	Side Effects
Ryback et al. (1997) Refractory	Refractory mood disorders BI (n = 47), BII (n = 24), SA BP (n = 2), RC (n = 41)	73 55 adult, 18 adol. M = 2 D = 28	Open, retrospective	Details not provided	Add-on to other medication; details not provided.	200–3500	Mood stabilization, improved mood, memory and attention in 67 of 73 (91.8%)	6 patients discontinued GBP because of side effects.
Young et al. (1997) Refractory	BI (n = 10), BII (n = 5)	15 D = 15	Open	6 weeks	BDZ, NRL, mood stabilizers	300–2400	Partial to marked in 8 of 15 (53%) (HAM-D, YMRS) 8/15 in D	Gastrointestinal upset, sedation, anxiety, weight gain, neurotoxicity
Bennett et al. (1997) Refractory	BI (n = 3), SA BP (n = 2)	5 M = 1 D = 1 Mixed =1	Open	Details not provided	Lithium, VPA, risperidone, venlafaxine, lorazepam, clonazepam and/or Trifluoperazine	600–2400	Response in 4/5 Marked (n = 3), Moderate (n = 1), 1 of 1 M 1 of 1 D Mild (n =1)	Mild sedation (n = 2)
Stanton et al. (1997) Refractory	BI (n = 1)	1 M = 1	Open	10 days	Monotherapy	900–3600	Improvement with 10 days of therapy	None clinically relevant

Study	Diagnosis	N	Design	Duration	Concomitant medication	Dosage	Outcome	Side effects
Soutullo et al. (1998) Refractory	BI (n = 1)	1 M = 1	Open	1–7 months	CBZ, zolpidem, divalproex	300–1500	Marked improvement in quality of life	Sedation, insomnia, mildly elevated mood, mild circumstantiality, grandiosity
Ghaemi et al. (1998) Refractory	BI (n = 13), BII (n = 19), NOS (n = 8), UP MDD (n = 10) RC (n = 12)	50 M/HM = 3 Mixed = 6 D = 29	Open, retrospective	1–38 weeks	Monotherapy (n = 4), BDZ, AD, lithium, VPA, CBZ	00–5600	Moderate to marked in 15 of 50 (30%) (CGI-I)	Somnolence, ataxia, memory difficulties, anxiety, acne, tremor, reduced appetite, headache, dizziness
Knoll et al. (1998) Refractory	Treatement-resistant mania or hypomania BI (n = 10), BII (n = 1), SA BP (n = 1)	12 PD = 1 Mixed = 2 D = 5	Open	3–60 weeks	BDZ, AD, lithium, VPA, CBZ	900–3300 (Peak dosages)	Response in 8/12. Marked (n = 1), Moderate (n = 7), 2/2 in Mixed 3/5 in D (CGI, GAF)	Sedation, tremor, nausea, weight gain, fatigue, irritability.
Sheldon et al. (1998) Nonrefractory	BI (n = 1)	1 D = 1	Open	2 weeks	Venlafaxine, zopiclone	200–600	Improvement in patient observed	Drowsiness
Erfurth, Kammerer, et al. (1998) Refractory	Acute mania (n = 14)	14 M = 14	Open	21 days	Monotherapy (n = 8) Add-on (n = 6)	1200–4800	Response in 10/12. Add-on 6 of 6 (100%), Monotherapy 4 of 8 (50%) (BRMS)	Fatigue, ataxia, dizziness, gastrointestinal upset

Continued

TABLE 10.2
Continued

Study	Diagnosis	Patients (n)	Design	Duration	Other Drugs	Gabapentin Dose Range (mg/day)	Response (ratings)	Side Effects
Schaffer & Schaffer (1999) Refractory	BI (n = 7), BII (n = 8), Cyclothymic (n = 3)	18	Open	28–36 months (follow-up to 1997 study)	Lithium, flurazepam, venlafaxine, alprazolam, clonazepam, fluoxetine, zolpidem, lorazepam, trazodone	300–2700	Positive in 7 of 18 (39%)	None clinically relevant
Young et al. (1999) Refractory	BI (n = 14), BII (n = 23),	37 M = 7 D = 30	Open	6 months	Monotherapy (n = 5) or add-on (n = 32) with lithium, CBZ or sodium divalproex, NRL	300–3600	Positive in 17 of 30 depressed cases. Improvement shown in manic cases but data not provided	Anxiety, sexual difficulties, daytime drowsiness, insomnia, dry mouth, blurred vision, constipation
Hardoy et al. (1999) Refractory	BP (n = 60)	60	Open	Details not specified	Details not provided	600–1800	Marked to Moderate in 36/60 (60%) Slight in 15%	Oversedation observed that decreased with further treatment

Study	Diagnosis	Design	N	Duration	Concomitant medications	Dose range	Response	Adverse effects
Altshuler et al. (1999) Refractory	BI (n = 23), BII (n = 5)	Open	28 M = 12 HM = 6 D = 5 RC = 5	33.3–274.0 days	Lithium, AD (n = 3) Lithium and DVPX (n = 3) Lithium and CBZ (n = 3) Lithium and verapamil (n = 1) DVPX and anti-psychotics (n = 4) DVPX and BDZ (n = 4)	600–3600	Overall good response in 20/28 patients (72%) 8/12 in M 6/6 in HM 5/5 in D (CGI-I, CGI-S)	Sedation (n = 5) Gastrointestinal upset (n = 4) Ataxia (n = 2) Dizziness (n = 1) Headache (n = 1)
Perugi et al. (1999) Refractory	BI (n = 21)	Open	21 M = 2 D = 12 Mixed = 7	8 weeks	BDZ, AD, NRL, mood stabilizers	300–2000	Response in 10/21 Marked (n = 4), Moderate (n = 6), 5 of 12 D, 1 of 2 M; 4/7 Mixed	Sedation, irritability, ataxia
Cabras et al. (1999) Nonrefractory	BI (n = 16), SA BP (n = 9)	Open	25 M = 9 HM = 16	16 weeks	BDZ, NRL	300–2400	Positive in 19 of 25 (76%) 8 of 9 M (CGI, BPRS)	Oversedation (n = 11)
Hatzimanolis et al. (1999)	Acute Mania (n = 2)	Open	2 M = 2	2 weeks	Monotherapy	600–3600	Improvement in both patients (YMRS)	A few adverse effects after first 2 weeks of treatment when there was no further improvement.

Continued

TABLE 10.2
Continued

Diagnosis: BI = Bipolar I; BII = Bipolar II; MDD = Major Depressive Disorder; NOS = Bipolar Not Otherwise Specified; OCD = Obsessive-Compulsive Disorder; PD = Panic Disorder; UP = Unipolar RC = Rapid Cycling; SA = Schizoaffective; SA BP = Schizoaffective Bipolar

Patients: M = Manic; D = Depressive; HM = Hypomanic

Other Drugs: AD = Anti-Depressants; AED = Anti-Epileptic Drugs; BDZ = Benzodiazepines; CBZ = Carbamazepine; DVPX = Divalproex Sodium; NRL = Neuroleptics; VPA = Valproate

Response: BPRS = Brief Psychiatric Rating Scale; BRMS = Bech-Rafaelsen Mania Scale; CGI-I = Clinical Global Impressions scale of Improvement; CGI-S = Clinical Global Impressions scale of Severity; GAF = Global Assessment of Functioning scale; HAM-D = Hamilton Rating Scale for Depression; LCM = Life Chart Methodology; YMRS = Young Mania Rating Scale

Summary of Results for Gabapentin in Bipolar Disorder Patients

Total Number of Patients: 443

Note: Schaffer et al. (1999) is a follow-up study to Schaffer & Schaffer (1997) using 18 of the original 28 in the study. Hence, they were counted only once

Total Number of Patients Data Available for: 389

Percentage Improved: 250/389 = 64.3%

Total Number of Manic/Hypomanic/Mixed Cases: 101

Total Number of Manic/Hypomanic/Mixed Cases Data Available for: 82

Percentage Improved: 62/82 = 75.6%

Total Number of Depressed Cases: 140

Total Number of Depressed Cases Data Available for: 83

Percentage Improved: 46/83 = 55.4%

tained improvement during the 36-month follow-up period suggesting that gabapentin might offer mood stability for some patients (Schaffer & Schaffer, 1999).

Four out of 19 studies (Hatzimanolis, Lykouras, Oulis, & Christodoulou, 1999; Stanton et al., 1997; Sheldon, Ancill, & Holliday, 1998; Cabras, Hardoy, Hardoy, & Carta, 1999) reported gabapentin use in 29 nonrefractory patients. Of these, 23 (79%) responded. All but one were treated for manic, hypomanic, or mixed episodes. Three of a total of 29 patients in these studies received gabapentin monotherapy and all three responded.

The doses of gabapentin ranged from 300 to 5600 mg/day, and it was in general well tolerated. Sedation, ataxia, or gastrointestinal upset were the most frequently reported side effects in these studies. Reports of gabapentin induced hypomania have also appeared in the literature (Hauck & Bhaumik, 1995; Short & Cooke, 1995).

DOUBLE-BLIND STUDIES

A randomized, double-blind, placebo controlled trial examined the efficacy of gabapentin add-on versus placebo add-on to lithium or valproate in acute mania (Pande, 2000). Patients who met DSM-IV criteria for bipolar manic/ hympomanic/mixed episode and scored 12 or more on YMRS were optimized on either lithium or valproate for 2 weeks. Patients who continued to be symptomatic and scored 12 or more on YMRS were randomized to adjunctive treatment with placebo ($n = 59$) or gabapentin ($n = 58$) for 10 weeks. Both treatment groups had a decrease in YMRS scores from baseline to endpoint but the decrease was significantly greater in the placebo group (-8.9) than the gabapentin group (-5.8) ($p < 0.05$). There were no significant differences between the groups on HAM-D, the Internal States Scale, or National Institute of Mental Health-Life Chart Method (NIMH-LCM) scale scores. The results of this double-blind study suggest that gabapentin is not superior to placebo in treating acute manic symptoms. The results of this study, however, are in contrast to a number of open reports suggesting efficacy of gabapentin as an adjunct in both refractory and nonrefractory bipolar patients.

In another small double-blind randomized trial, patients received gabapentin, lamotrigine, or placebo monotherapy for 6 weeks with two subsequent crossovers so that by the end of the study, each patient would have received all three agents, each for 6 weeks (Frye et al., 2000). The response rates using CGI much or very much improved were 52% (16/31) for lamotrigine, 26% (8/31) for gabapentin, and 23% (7/31) for placebo. Post hoc analysis showed lamotrigine was superior to gabapentin as well as placebo and that gabapentin was not different from placebo. Taken together, the results of two double-blind trials suggest that gabapentin was not effective in treating bipolar disorder.

Topiramate

Topiramate is a sulfamate substitued monosaccharide. This novel anticonvulsant has multiple mechanisms of action, including the potentiation of g-aminobutyric acid (GABA) at GABA receptors, state dependent blockade of voltage sensitive sodium channels, and antagonism of the ability of kainate to activate the kainate/AMPA subtype of glutamate receptor but not NMDA receptor subtype. It is approved for treatment of refractory epilepsy as adjunctive therapy.

OPEN STUDIES

One hundred ninety-two patients with various subtypes of bipolar disorder, including rapid cycling and schizoaffective disorder, received topiramate in eight open studies (see Table 10.3 for details). Topiramate was given as an adjunct to other medications in the majority of patients. Overall, data was available for 181 patients, and of these, 104 (57.5%) had moderate to marked response. Of the 43 patients with manic/mixed/hypomanic symptoms, 22 (51%) responded. Similarly, 24 out of 41 (58.5%) patients that received topiramate for depressive symptoms improved.

In a single-blind trial, McIntyre et al. (2000) reported that topiramate add-on was as effective as bupropion SR add-on in treating depressive symptoms in patients with bipolar depression. The response rate following 8 weeks of treatment was 56% for the topiramate group and 59% for the bupropion SR group.

DOUBLE-BLIND STUDIES

The efficacy of topiramate was examined in a double-blind, randomized, placebo controlled trial. Patients were randomized to placebo, topiramate 256 mg/day or topiramate 512 mg/day. Interim analysis on 36 patients (placebo = 12, topiramate 256 mg/day = 11, topiramate 512 mg/day = 13) showed that the topiramate 512 mg/day group did significantly better on the change in YMRS scores from baseline to endpoint. When the total sample size was increased to 97, the difference was still significant on change in global as-

TABLE 10.3
Studies of the efficacy of Topiramate (Topamax®) on Bipolar Disorder

Study	Diagnosis	Patients (n)	Design	Duration	Other Drugs	Topiramate Dose Range (mg/day)	Response (ratings)	Side Effects
Calabrese et al. (2001)	Severe Mania (n = 11)	11 M = 11	Open-label	28 days	Details not provided	50–1300	Moderate to marked improvement in 5/11 patients. More than 50% improv. (n = 3) 25-49% improv. (n = 2)	Parasthesia, anorexia/weight loss, constipation, nausea.
Marcotte (1998)	RC BI (n = 14), RC BII (n = 6), RC Mixed BP (n = 7), RC BP NOS (n = 7) Cyclothymic (n = 10), SA (n = 9), Dementia (n = 3), Psychosis (n = 2)	58 BP = 53	Open	16 weeks	Monotherapy (n =12)	25–400	30/53 patients with BP showed a positive response	Delirium, parasthesias, sommolence, fatigue, impaired concentration and memory, nausea, diarrhea.

Continued

225

TABLE 10.3
Continued

Study	Diagnosis	Patients (n)	Design	Duration	Other Drugs	Topiramate Dose Range (mg/day)	Response (ratings)	Side Effects
Gordon & Price (1999)	BP RC (n = 1), BP (n=1)	2	Open D = 2	3 months	Bupropion, olanzapine, levothyroxine	200	Positive in 1 of 2 as RC patient had improved	Mood stabilization occurred in the first patient.
				2 months	Bupropion	300	depressive symptoms. The other became increasingly irritable and anxious.	TPM induced a 25 lb weight loss in the responder and a 15 lb loss in the nonresponder as she reported increased anxiety and irritability
Normann et al. (1999)	BP (n = 1)	1 M = 1	Open	30 days	VPA, haloperidol,	25–50	Positive rating with a decreased YMRS score and TPM discontinued on day 15. Recurrence of manic symptoms on discontinuation prompted restarting of TPM on day 19 to day 30.	Sedation, extrapyramidal dyskinesia

Study	Sample	Design	Duration	Treatment	Results	Side effects
Chengappa et al. (1999)	BI (n = 18), SA BP (n = 2), RC (n = 6)	20 Mp = 11 Mnp = 3 HM = 1 Mixed = 5	Open	5 weeks	Add-on with psychotropics (n = 14) GBP (n = 5) VPA (n = 11) Lithium (n = 6) CBZ (n = 4)	25–300	Response in 12/20 (60%) based on decline in YMRS and HAM-D scores. Improvement in 6/11 Mp cases, data for Mnp not provided. (CGI-I, CGI-S)	Mild parasthesia of hands (n = 5), jaws and upper lips (n = 1). Anorexia (n = 5) was observed along with fatigue (n = 3), sedation (n = 2), slowed thinking (n = 3), word-finding difficulty (n = 2), tremor (n = 1) and nausea (n = 1).
McElroy et al. (1998)	BI (n = 28), BII (n = 4), SA (n = 1)	33 M/HM/ Mixed = 22 D = 11 Euthymic = 13	Open	2–237 days	Add on with: VPA (n = 15), lithium (n = 9), LTG (n = 6), thyroxine (n = 6), GBP (n = 6), olanzapine (n = 6) et al.	50–1000	Response in 16/31 patients who completed study. 10/20 in M/HM/ mixed 4/8 in D (YMRS, CGI-I, CGI-S, GAF, IDS)	

Continued

TABLE 10.3
Continued

Study	Diagnosis	Patients (n)	Design	Duration	Other Drugs	Topiramate Dose Range (mg/day)	Response (ratings)	Side Effects
Kusumakar et al. (1999)	BP, RC (n = 27)	27	Open-label	12 weeks	Valproate or lithium	25–400	15/27 who completed the study showed improvement and became euthymic. 4 subjects dropped out.	9/23 subjects lost more than 5% BW, 1/23 gained weight and 12/23 reported no weight change. Discontinuation occurred in 4 patients due to ataxia (n = 1), confusion (n = 2) and drowsiness/dizziness (n =1)
Hussain (1999)	BI (n = 27), BII (n = 18)	45 D = 45	Open-label	1–6 months	Lithium (n = 8), VPA (n = 5), LTG (n = 3), GBP (n = 5), AD (n = 18), BDZ (n = 14)	100–400	31/45 responded, while 14 withdrew. (HAM-D)	Of the 14 patients who withdrew, 9 left due to adverse side effects. Headache (n = 4), tremor (n = 3), dizziness (n = 5), nausea (n = 5), lack of coordination (n = 3), sedation (n = 3), parasthesia (n = 4)

Diagnosis: BP = Bipolar Disorder; BI = Bipolar I; BII = Bipolar II; NOS = Bipolar Not Otherwise Specified; RC = Rapid Cycling; SA = Schizoaffective; SA BP = Schizoaffective Bipolar-type

Patients: D = Depressive; M = Manic; Mp = Manic with psychoses; Mnp = Manic without psychoses

Other Drugs: AD = Anti-Depressants; BDZ = Benzodiazepines; CBZ = Carbamazepine; DVPX = Divalproex Sodium; GBP = Gabapentin; LTG = Lamotrigine; VPA = Valproate

Response: CGI-I = Clinical Global Impressions scale for Improvement; CGI-S = Clinical Global Impressions scale for Severity; GAF = Global Assessment of Functioning Scale; HAM-D = Hamilton Rating Scale for Depression; IDS = Inventory of Depressive Symptoms; TPM = Topiramate; YMRS = Young Mania Rating Scale

Side Effects: BW = Body Weight

Summary of Results for Topiramate in Bipolar Patients

Total Number of Patients: 233
Total Number of Patients Data Available for: 226

Percentage Improved: 126/226 =55.75%

Total Number of Manic/Hypomanic/Mixed Cases: 75
Total Number of Manic/Hypomanic/Mixed Cases Data Available for: 59
Percentage Improved: 43/59= 72.88%

Total Number of Depressed Cases: 60
Total Number of Depressed Cases Data Available for: 46
Percentage Improved: 29/46= 63%

sessment scale score but there was no difference between three groups on change in YMRS scores. In the final sample, about 28 patients had antidepressant induced mania and these patients had very high placebo response rates. An analysis excluding the antidepressant induced manic patients showed that topiramate 512 mg was significantly superior to placebo on change in YMRS scores (Calabrese, 2000).

In summary, the results of open studies and the double-blind study suggest that topiramate probably has antimanic properties and further double-blind studies are underway to confirm this. Open data also suggests that this medication may have antidepressant and mood stabilizing properties, but double-blind studies are clearly needed to verify this.

Clonazepam

Clonazepam is a high potency benzodiazepine anticonvulsant. It is approved for treatment of myoclonic and petit mal seizures. First reports of usefulness of clonazepam for treatment of bipolar disorder appeared in the early 1980s (Chouinard, Annable, Turnier, Holobow, & Szkrumelak, 1983; Lechin & van der Dijs, 1983; Victor, Link, Binder, & Bell, 1984).

ACUTE MANIA

In a 5-day double-blind trial, Edwards, Stephenson, & Flewett (1991) compared the efficacy of clonazepam with placebo for treatment of acute mania ($n = 40$). The group receiving clonazepam was significantly better in their manic symptoms but not in psychotic symptoms compared to the placebo group. Patients, in this study, however, were allowed to receive chlorpromazine on an as needed basis which might have confounded the results.

Clonazepam was also compared with lithium for treatment of acute mania. In a double-blind, crossover design, 12 acutely manic patients, newly admitted from the emergency room, were treated with clonazepam or lithium carbonate (Chouinard, Young, & Annable, 1983). Half the patients (chosen randomly) received 10 days of treatment with clonazepam followed immediately by 10 days of treatment with lithium, while the others received the same treatments in reverse order. Improvement occurred with both treatments and, overall, there was no significant difference on the clinical global impression scale between the two treatments.

Clonazepam was less effective than lorazepam or haloperidol in other double blind trials. Bradwejn, Shriqui, Koszycki, & Meterissian (1990) examined the efficacy of clonazepam versus lorazepam in 24 patients with acute mania using a double-blind randomized design. In the lorazepam group, 61% of patients responded to treatment, with 38.5% achieving remission, as compared to an 18.2% response rate and 0% remission rate in patients treated with clonazepam. In another double-blind trial of 16 acutely agitated psychotic patients with manic/maniclike symptoms who required rapid tranquilization, subjects were randomized to receive intramuscular preparations of clonazepam (1 to 2 mg) or haloperidol (5 to 10 mg) at 0, 0.5, and 1.0 hours (Chouinard et al., 1993). Both medications produced significant reduction of manic symptoms within two hours of initial treatment. Haloperidol, however, produced beneficial results more rapidly than clonazepam. This study concluded that I.M. clonazepam was an effective, safe, but slower acting alternative to I.M. haloperidol for treatment of agitated psychiatric patients.

In summary, clonazepam appears to have some utility at least as an adjunct in treating acute manic symptoms. It should, however, be noted that behavioral disinhibition with clonazepam has also been reported and that clinicians should be wary of this possible complication, especially in manic patients (Amiel, Bryan, & Herjanic, 1987; Binder, 1987; Kubacki, 1987).

ACUTE BIPOLAR DEPRESSION

Clonazepam has also been reported to have antidepressant properties (Alvarez & Freinhar, 1987). Of the 27 patients (major depression = 18, bipolar disorder = 9) treated with 1.5 to 6.0 mg (mean 3.4 mg) of clonazepam, 21 (84%) had marked to moderate improvement (Kishimoto et al., 1988). The onset of the antidepressive effect of clonazepam was noted within one week in the majority of cases who responded to the therapy. Scores on the Hamilton Rating Scale for Depression and the Beck Depression Inventory Scale were significantly reduced after treatment. Side effects occurred in 14 patients, and two dropped out of the study in the early stages. There are no double-blind studies that examined the antidepressant effect of clonazepam in bipolar depression.

PROPHYLAXIS

Aronson, Shukla, and Hirschowitz (1989) examined the efficacy of clonazepam as a substitute to neuroleptics in the maintenance treatment of lithium-refractory bipolar disorder. Five patients who were euthymic on a combination of lithium and neuroleptics were switched from neuroleptics to clonazepam and followed prospectively. All five patients relapsed quickly after taking clonazepam (one within 2 weeks, and the other four within 10–15 weeks) leading to premature termination of the study. Further studies are needed to determine if clonazepam has any utility in the maintenance treatment of bipolar disorder. There are also concerns about the risks of tolerance, abuse, and dependence with this medication.

Tiagabine

Tiagabine is a nipecotic acid linked to an aliphatic chain and a lipophilic anchor. It is a selective inhibitor of GABA uptake and is currently FDA approved as adjunctive treatment for refractory partial seizures. In a case report on three patients, two with bipolar disorder and one with schizoaffective disorder-bipolar type, tiagabine as an adjunct was reported to be effective with few side effects (Kaufman, 1998). In a more recent case report, Schaffer et al. (1999) found a similar positive response to adjunctive tiagabine in two patients with refractory bipolar disorder. However, Grunze et al. (1999) in an open study systematically evaluated the efficacy of tiagabine using the Bech-Rafaelsen Mania rating scale in acute mania. Two patients received tiagabine monotherapy and six others received tiagabine as an adjunct to previously insufficient mood stabilizing medication. None of the patients showed significant improvement over the 2-week study period. Hence, it is currently unknown if tiagabine has any role in treatment of bipolar disorder. Further studies are clearly warranted.

FELBAMATE

There are no published clinical reports regarding felbamate therapy for bipolar disorder. However, like some other anticonvulsants, secondary mania has been noted to result from felbamate treatment (Hill, Stagno, & Tesar, 1995).

Conclusions

It has become increasingly clear that lithium alone, or in combination with antidepressants or neuroleptics, is inadequate for a significant proportion of bipolar patients. The recognition of the efficacy of anticonvulsants in bipolar disorder has offered some new hope for patients with this devastating medical illness. There are still, however, many unanswered questions such as what medication or what combination of medications is best for which patient. This is largely because predictors of response to medications are still unknown and response (or nonresponse) to one anticonvulsant is not predictive of response to another (Calabrese, Markovitz, Kimmel, & Wagner, 1992; Schaff, Fawcett, & Zajecka, 1993). Hence, systematic clinical trials are needed to uncover the optimal treatment algorithm for acute phase of the illness. Trials regarding the prophylactic efficacy of the newer treatments are also required. Unlike the situation 20 years ago when lithium was the sole option, these effective alternatives/adjuncts to lithium are being effectively utilized by clinicians to ameliorate the effects of a debilitating illness.

References

Altshuler, L. L., Keck, P. E. Jr., McElroy, S. L., Suppes, T., Brown, E. S., Denicoff, K., et al. (1999). Gabapentin in the acute treatment of refractory bipolar disorder. *Bipolar Disorders, 1,* 61–65.

Alvarez, W. A., & Freinhar, J. P. (1987). Clonazepam: An antidepressant? [Letter ot the editor]. *American Journal of Psychiatry, 144,* 536–537.

Amiel, M., Bryan, S., & Herjanic, M. (1987). Clonazepam in the treatment of bipolar disorder in patients with non- lithium-induced renal insufficiency [Letter to the editor]. *Journal of Clinical Psychiatry, 48,* 424.

Anand, A., Oren, D., Berman, R., Cappliello, A., & Charney, D. (1999). Lamotrigine treatment of lithium failure outpatient mania-a double blind placebo controlled trial. In J. Soares & S. Gershon (Eds.), *Third International Conference on Bipolar Disorder* (Vol. 1, pp. 23). Pittsburgh, PA: Munksgaard.

Aronson, T. A., Shukla, S., & Hirschowitz, J. (1989). Clonazepam treatment of five lithium-refractory patients with bipolar disorder. *American Journal of Psychiatry, 146,* 77–80.

Ballenger, J. C., & Post, R. M. (1978). Therapeutic effects of carbamazepine in affective illness: A preliminary report. *Communications in Psychopharmacology, 2,* 159–175.

Ballenger, J. C., & Post, R. M. (1980). Carbamazepine in manic depressive illness: A new treatment. *American Journal of Psychiatry, 137,* 782–790.

Bellaire, W., Demisch, K., & Stoll, K. D. (1988). Carbamazepine versus lithium in prophylaxis of recurrent affective disorders. *Psychopharmacology, 96,* 287.

Bennett, J., Goldman, W. T., & Suppes, T. (1997). Gabapentin for treatment of bipolar and schizoaffective disorders. *Journal of Clinical Psychopharmacology, 17,* 141–142.

Bentley, B., Ascher, J., Earl, N., Monaghan, E., Evoniuk, G., & West, S. (2000). A one-year open label study of the safety and efficacy of lamotrigine in the treatment of bipolar depression [Abstract P.16.34]. *The International Journal of Neuropsychopharmacology, 3*(Suppl 1), S340–S341.

Berk, M. (1999), Lamotrigine and the treatment of mania in bipolar disorder. *European Neuropsychopharmacology, 9*(Suppl. 4), S119–123.

Binder, R. L. (1987). Three case reports of behavioral disinhibition with clonazepam. *General Hospital Psychiatry, 9,* 151–153.

Bowden, C., Brugger, A., Swann, A. C., Calabrese, J. R., Janicak, P. G., Petty, F., et al. (1994). Efficacy of divalproex vs lithium and placebo in the treatment of mania. The Depakote Mania Study Group. *Journal of the American Medical Association, 271,* 918–924.

Bowden, C. L., Calabrese, J. R., Ascher, J., DeVeaugh-Geiss, J., Earl, N., Evoniuk, G., et al. (2000). *Spectrum of efficacy of lamotrigine in bipolar disorder: Overview of double-blind, placebo-controlled studies.* Poster session presented at American College of Neuropsychopharmacology Meeting, Puerto Rico.

Bowden, C. L., Calabrese, J. R., DeVeaugh-Geiss, J., Leadbetter, R., Paska, W., & Sachs, G. (2001). *Lamotrigine demonstrates long-term mood stabilizationin bipolar I depression.* Poster presented at American College of Neuropsychopharmacology Meeting, Hawaii.

Bowden, C., Calabrese, J., McElroy, S., Rhodes, L. J., Keck, P. E., Jr., Cookson, J., et al. (1999). The efficacy of lamotrigine in rapid cycling and non-rapid cycling patients with bipolar disorder. *Biological Psychiatry, 45,* 953–958.

Bowden, C., Calabrese, J. R., McElroy, S., Gyulai, L., Wassef, A., Petty, F., et al. (2000). A randomized placebo controlled 12 month trial of divalproex and lithium in the treatment of outpatients with bipolar 1 disorder. *Archives of General Psychiatry, 57,* 481–489.

Bowden, C. L., Calabrese, J. R., Sachs, G. S., Yatham, L. N., Asghar, S. A., Hompland, M., et al. (2001). *A placebo-controlled 18-month trial of lamotrigine and lithium maintenance treatment in recently manic or hypomanic patients with bipolar I disorder.* Manuscript submitted for publication.

Bowden, C. L., Janicak, P. G., Orsulak, P., Swann, A. C., Davis, J. M., Calabrese, J. R., et al. (1996). Relation of serum valproate concentration to response in mania. *American Journal of Psychiatry, 153,* 765–770.

Bradwejn, J., Shriqui, C., Koszycki, D., & Meterissian, G. (1990). Double-blind comparison of the effects of clonazepam and lorazepam in acute mania. *Journal of Clinical Psychopharmacology, 10,* 403–408.

Brennan, M. J. W., Sandyk, R., & Borsook, D. (1984). Use of sodium valproate in the management of affective disorders: Basic and clinical aspects. In H. M. Emrich, T. Okuma, & A. A. Muller (Eds.), *Anticonvulsants in affective disorders* (pp. 56–65). Amsterdam: Excerpta Medica.

Brown, D., Silverstone, T., & Cookson, J. (1989). Carbamazepine compared to haloperidol in acute mania. *International Clinical Psychopharmacology, 4,* 229–238.

Cabras, P. L., Hardoy, M. J., Hardoy, M. C., & Carta, M. G. (1999). Clinical experience with gabapentin in patients with bipolar or schizoaffective disorder: Results of an open-label study. *Journal of Clinical Psychiatry, 60,* 245–248.

Calabrese, J. R. (2000, May). *Update on the use of topiramate in bipolar disorder.* American Psychiatric Association Annual Meeting, Chicago.

Calabrese, J., Markovitz, P., Kimmel, S., & Wagner, S. C. (1992). Spectrum of efficacy of valproate in 78 rapid-cycling bipolar patients. *Journal of Clinical Psychopharmacology, 12,* 53S–56S.

Calabrese, J. R., Bowden, C. L., Sachs, G. S., Ascher, J. A., Monaghan, E., & Rudd, G. D. (1999). A double-blind placebo-controlled study of lamotrigine monotherapy in outpatients with bipolar I depression. Lamictal 602 Study Group. *Journal of Clinical Psychiatry, 60,* 79–88.

Calabrese, J. R., Fatemi, S. H., & Woyshville, M. J. (1996), Antidepressant effects of lamotrigine in rapid cycling bipolar disorder [Letter to the editor]. *American Journal of Psychiatry, 153,* 1236.

Calabrese, J. R., Keck, P. E., Jr., McElroy, S. L., & Shelton, M. D. (2001, June). A pilot study of topiramate as monotherapy in the treatment of acute mania. *Journal of Clinical Psychopharmacology, 21*(3), 340–342.

Chengappa, K. N., Rathore, D., Levine, J., Atzert, R., Solai, L., Perepally, H., et al. (1999, September). Topiramate as add-on treatment for patients with bipolar mania. *Bipolar Disorder, 1*(1), 42–53.

Chouinard, G., Annable, L., Turnier, L., Holobow, N., & Szkrumelak, N. (1993). A double-blind randomized clinical trial of rapid tranquilization with I.M. clonazepam and I.M. haloperidol in agitated psychotic patients with manic symptoms. *Canadian Journal of Psychiatry, 38*(Suppl. 4), S114–S121.

Chouinard, G., Young, S. N., & Annable, L. (1983). Antimanic effect of clonazepam. *Biological Psychiatry, 18,* 451–466.

Coxhead, N., Silverstone, T., & Cookson, J. (1992). Carbamazepine versus lithium in the prophylaxis of bipolar affective disorder. *Acta Psychiatrica Scandinavia, 85,* 114–118.

Dalby, M. A. (1971). Antiepileptic and psychotropic effect of carbamazepine (Tegretol) in the treatment of psychomotor epilepsy. *Epilepsia, 12,* 325–334.

Davis, L. L., Kabel, D., Patel, D., Choate, A. D., Fosliennash, C., Gurguis, G. N. M., Kramer, G. L., & Petty, F. (1996). Valproate as an antidepressant in major depressive disorder. *Psychopharmacology Bulletin, 32,* 647–652.

Denicoff, K. D., Smith-Jackson, E. E., Disney, E. R., Ali, S. O., Leverich, G. S., & Post, R. M. (1997). Comparative prophylactic efficacy of lithium, carbamazepine, and the combination in bipolar disorder. *Journal of Clinical Psychiatry, 58,* 470–478.

Desai, N. G., Gangadhas, B. N., Channabasavanna, S. M., & Shetty, K. T. (1987). Carbamazepine hastens therapeutic action of lithium in mania. In *Proceedings of the International Conference on New Directions in Affective Disorders.* Jerusalem. Abstr. No. 97.

Edwards, R., Stephenson, U., & Flewett, T. (1991). Clonazepam in acute mania: A double blind trial. *Australian and New Zealand Journal of Psychiatry, 25,* 238–242.

Emrich, H. M. (1990). Studies with oxcarbazepine (Trileptal) in acute mania. *International Clinical Psychopharmacology, 5*(Suppl. 1), 83–88.

Emrich, H. M., Dose, M., & von Zerssen, D. (1985), The use of sodium valproate, carbamazepine and oxcarbazepine in patients with affective disorders. *Journal of Affective Disorders, 8,* 243–250.

Erfurth, A., & Grunze, H. (1998). New perspectives in the treatment of acute mania: A single case report. *Progress in Neuro-Psychopharmacology and Biological Psychiatry, 22,* 1053–1059

Erfurth, A., Kammerer, C., Grunze, H., Normann, C., & Walden, J. (1998). An open label study of gabapentin in the treatment of acute mania. *Journal of Psychiatric Research, 32,* 261–264.

Erfurth, A., Walden, J., & Grunze, H. (1998). Lamotrigine in the treatment of schizoaffective disorder. *Neuropsychobiology, 38,* 204–205

Fatemi, S. H., Rapport, D. J., Calabrese, J. R., & Thuras, P. (1997). Lamotrigine in rapid-cycling bipolar disorder. *Journal of Clinical Psychiatry, 58,* 522–527.

Ferrier, I. N. (1998). Lamotrigine and gabapentin: Alternative in the treatment of bipolar disorder. *Neuropsychobiology, 38,* 192–197.

Fogelson, D. L., & Sternbach, H. (1997). Lamotrigine treatment of refractory bipolar disorder (Letter to the editor). *Journal of Clinical Psychiatry, 58*(6), 271–273.

Freeman, T. W., Clothier, J. L., Pazzaglia, P., Lesem, M. D., & Swann, A. C. (1992). A double-blind comparison of valproate and lithium in the treatment of acute mania. *American Journal of Psychiatry, 149,* 108–111.

Frye, M., Ketter, T., Kimbrell, T., Dunn, R. T., Speer, A. M., Osuch, E. A., et al. (2000). A placebo-controlled study of lamotrigine and gabapentin monotherapy in refractory mood disorder *Journal of Clinical Psychopharmacology, 20*(6), 607–614.

Ghaemi, S. N., Katzow, J. J., Desai, S. P., & Goodwin, F. K. (1998). Gabapentin treatment of mood disorders: a preliminary study. *Journal of Clinical Psychiatry, 59,* 426–429.

Gonclaves, N., & Stoll, K. D. (1985). Carbamazepine in manic syndromes. A controlled double-blind study. *Nervenarzt, 56,* 43–47.

Gordon, A., & Price, L. H. (1999). Mood stabilization and weight loss with topiramate (Letter to the editor). *American Journal of Psychiatry, 156*(6), 968–969

Greil, W., Kleindienst, N., Erazo, N., & Muller-Oerlinghausen, B. (1998). Differential response to lithium and carbamazepine in the prophylaxis of bipolar disorder. *Journal of Clinical Psychopharmacology, 18,* 455–460.

Greil, W., Ludwig-Mayerhofer, W., Erazo, N., Schocklin, C., Schmidt, S., Engel, R. R., et al. (1997). Lithium versus carbamazepine in the maintenance treatment of bipolar disorders— A randomised study. *Journal of Affective Disorders, 43,* 151–161.

Grossi, E., Sacchetti, E., Vita, A., Conte, G., Faravelli, C., Hautman, G., et al. (1984). Carbamazepine vs chlorpromazine in mania: A double blind trial. In H. M. Emrich, T. Okuma, & A. A. Muller (Eds.), *Anticonvulsants in affective disorders* (pp. 177–187). Amsterdam: Excerpta Medica.

Grunze, H., Erfurth, A., Amann, B., Giupponi, G., Kammerer, C., & Walden, J. (1999). Intravenous valproate loading in acutely manic and depressed bipolar I patients. *Journal of Clinical Psychopharmacology, 19,* 303–309.

Grunze, H., Erfurth, A., Marcuse, A., Amann, B., Normann, C., & Walden, J. (1999). Tiagabine appears not to be efficacious in the treatment of acute mania. *Journal of Clinical Psychiatry, 60*(11), 759–762

Hardoy, M., Hardoy, M., Carta, M., & Cabras, P. (1999). Gabapentin in the treatment of bipolar disorders. In J. Soares & S. Gershon (Eds.), *Third International Conference on Bipolar Disorder* (Vol 1, p. 34). Pittsburgh, PA: Munksgaard.

Hatzimanolis, J., Lykouras, L., Oulis, P., & Christodoulou, G. N. (1999). Gabapentin as monotherapy in the treatment of acute mania. *European Neuropsychopharmacology, 9,* 257–258.

Hauck, A., & Bhaumik, S. (1995). Hypomania induced by gabapentin [Letter to the editor]. *British Journal of Psychiatry, 167,* 549.

Hayes, S. G. (1989). Long-term use of valproate in primary psychiatric disorders. *Journal of Clinical Psychiatry, 50*(Suppl.), 35–39.

Hill, R. R., Stagno, S. J., & Tesar, G. E. (1995, July–August). Secondary mania associated with the use of felbamate. *Psychosomatics, 36*(4), 404–406.

Hirschfeld, R. M., Allen, M. H., McEvoy, J. P., Keck, P. E., Jr., & Russell, J. M. (1999). Safety and tolerability of oral loading divalproex sodium in acutely manic bipolar patients. *Journal of Clinical Psychiatry, 60,* 815–818.

Hoopes, S. (1999). Lamotrigine in the treatment of bipolar depression and other affective disorders: clinical experience in 218 patients. In J. Soares & S. Gershon (Eds.), *Third International Conference on Bipolar Disorder* (Vol 1, p. 35). Pittsburgh, PA: Munksgaard.

Huffman, R., Rudd, D., Monaghan, E., Ascher, J. A., Womble, G., Bowden, C. L., & Lydiard, B. (2000). *The safety and efficacy of lamotrigine for the long-term treatment of bipolar depression.* Paper presented at the American Psychiatric Association Annual Meeting, Chicago.

Hussain, M. (1999, December). Treatment of bipolar depression with topiramate. Paper presented at the American College of Neuropsychopharmacology Meeting, Acapulco, Mexico.

Kaufman, K. R. (1998). Adjunctive tiagabine treatment of psychiatric disorders: Three cases. *Annals of Clinical Psychiatry, 10,* 181–184.

Keck, P. E., Jr., McElroy, S. L., Tugrul, K. C., & Bennett, J. A. (1993). Valproate oral loading in the treatment of acute mania. *Journal of Clinical Psychiatry, 54,* 305–308.

Kishimoto, A., Kamata, K., Sugihara, T., Ishiguro, S., Hazama, H., Mizukawa, R., et al. (1988). Treatment of depression with clonazepam. *Acta Psychiatrica Scandinavia, 77,* 81–86.

Klein, E., Bental, E., Lerer, B., & Belmaker, R. H. (1984). Carbamazepine and haloperidol v placebo and haloperidol in excited psychoses. A controlled study. *Archives of General Psychiatry, 41,* 165–170.

Knoll, J., Stegman, K., & Suppes, T. (1998). Clinical experience using gabapentin adjunctively in patients with a history of mania or hypomania. *Journal of Affective Disorders, 49,* 229–233.

Kotler, M., & Matar, M. A. (1998). Lamotrigine in the treatment of resistant bipolar disorder. *Clinical Neuropharmacology, 21*(1), 65–77.

Kubacki, A. (1987). Sexual disinhibition on clonazepam [Letter to the editor]. *Canadian Journal of Psychiatry, 32,* 643–645.

Kusumakar, V., & Yatham, L. N. (1997a). An open study of lamotrigine in refractory bipolar depression. *Psychiatry Research, 72,* 145–148.

Kusumakar, V., & Yatham, L. N. (1997b). Lamotrigine treatment of rapid cycling bipolar disorder (Letter to the editor). *American Journal of Psychiatry, 154*(8), 1171–1172.

Kusumakar, V., Yatham, L., O'Donovan, C., & Kutcher, S. (1999). Topiramate in women with refractory rapid cycling bipolar disorder. Paper presented at the American College of Neuropsychopharmacology Meeting, Acapulco, Mexico.

Labbate, L. A., & Rubey, R. N. (1997). Lamotrigine for treatment-refractory bipolar disorder (Letter to the editor). *American Journal of Psychiatry, 154*(9), 1317.

Lambert, P., Cavaz, G., Borselli, S., & Carbel, S. (1966). Action neuropsychotrope d'un nouvel anti-epileptique: le depamide. *Annals of Medical Psychology, 1,* 707–710.

Lambert, P. A. (1984). Acute and prophylactic therapies of patients with affective disorders using valpromide (Dipropylacetamide). In H. M. Emrich, T. Okuma, A. A. Muller (Eds.), *Anticonvulsants in affective disorders* (pp. 33–44). Amsterdam: Excerpta Medica.

Lambert, P. A., & Venaud. G. (1992). Comparative study of valpromide versus Li in treatment of affective disorders. *Nervure, 5*(2), 57–65.

Lechin, F., & van der Dijs, B. (1983). Antimanic effect of clonazepam [Letter to the editor]. *Biological Psychiatry, 18,* 1511.

Lenzi, A., Lazzerine, F., Grossi, E., Massimetti, G., & Placidi, G. F. (1986). Use of carbamazepine in acute psychosis: A controlled study. *Journal of International Medical Research, 14,* 78–84.

Lerer, B., Moore, N., Meyendorff, E., Cho, S. R., & Gershon, S. (1987). Carbamazepine versus lithium in mania: a double-blind study. *Journal of Clinical Psychiatry, 48,* 89–93.

Lusznat, R. M., Murphy, D. P., & Nunn, C. M. H. (1988). Carbamazepine vs. lithium in the treatment and prophylaxis of mania. *British Journal of Psychiatry, 153,* 198–204.

Mandoki, M. (1997), Lamotrigine/valproate in treatment-resistant bipolar disorder in children and adolescents. *Biological Psychiatry, 41,* 93S–94S.

Marcotte, D. (1998). Use of topiramate, a new anti-epileptic as a mood stabilizer. *Journal of Affective Disorders, 50,* 245–251.

Marcotte, D. B., Fogelman, L., & Wolfe, N. (1997). Gabapentin: An effective therapy for patients with bipolar affective disorder. Paper presented at the American Psychiatric Association Meeting, San Diego, CA.

McElroy, S. L., Keck, P. E., Jr., Pope, H. G., Jr., & Hudson, J. I. (1992). Valproate in the treatment of bipolar disorder: Literature review and clinical guidelines. *Journal of Clinical Psychopharmacology, 12,* 42S–52S.

McElroy, S., Keck, P., Stanton, S. P., Tugrul, K. C., Bennett, J. A., & Strakowski, S. (1996). A randomized comparison of divalproex oral loading versus haloperidol in the initial treatment of acute psychotic mania. *Journal of Clinical Psychiatry, 57,* 142–146.

McElroy, S. L., Kmetz, G. F., & Keck, P. E., Jr. (1998). A pilot trial of adjunctive topiramate in the treatment of bipolar disorder. Paper presented at the American Psychiatric Association Meeting, Washington, DC.

McElroy, S. L., Soutullo, C. A., Keck, P. E., Jr., & Kmetz, G. F. (1997). A pilot trial of adjunctive gabapentin in the treatment of bipolar disorder. *Annals of Clinical Psychiatry, 9,* 99–103.

Moller, H. J., Kissling, W., Riehl, T., Bauml, J., Binz, U., & Wendt, G. (1989). Doubleblind evaluation of the antimanic properties of carbamazepine as a comedication to haloperidol. *Progress in Neuropsychopharmacology and Biological Psychiatry, 13,* 127–136.

Muller, A. A., & Stoll, K.-D. (1984). Carbamazepine and oxcarbazepine in the treatment of manic syndromes—Studies in Germany. In H. M. Emrich, T. Okuma, & A. A. Muller (Eds.), *Anticonvulsants in affective disorders* (pp. 139–147). Amsterdam: Excerpta Medica.

Normann, C., Langosch, J., Schaerer, L. O., Grunze, H., & Walden, J. (1999). Treatment of acute mania with topiramate (Letter to the editor). *American Journal of Psychiatry, 156*(12), 2014

Okuma, T. (1993). Effects of carbamazepine and lithium on affective disorders. *Neuropsychobiology, 27,* 138–145.

Okuma, T., Inanaga, K., Otsuki, S., Sarai, K., Takahashi, R., Hazama, H., et al. (1979). Comparison of the antimanic efficacy of carbamazepine and chlorpromazine: A double-blind controlled study. *Psychopharmacology, 66*(3), 211–217.

Okuma, T., Inanaga, K., Otsuki, S., Sarai, K., Takahashi, R., Hazama, H., et al. (1981). A preliminary double-blind study on the efficacy of carbamazepine in prophylaxis of manic-depressive illness. *Psychopharmacology, 73,* 95–96.

Okuma, T., Yamashita, I., Takahashi, R., Itoh, H., Kurihara, M., Otsuki, S., Watanabe, S., Sarai, K., Hazama, H., & Inangana, K. (1988). Double-blind controlled studies on the therapeutic efficacy of carbamazepine in affective and schizophrenic patients. *Psychopharmacology, 96,* 102 (Abstract No. TH18.05).

Okuma, T., Yamashita, I., Takahashi, R., Itoh, H., Otsuki, S., Watanabe, S., et al. (1990, May). Comparison of the antimanic efficacy of carbamazepine and lithium carbonate by double-blind controlled study. *Pharmacopsychiatry, 23,* 143–150.

Pande, A. C., Crockett, J. G., Janney, C. A., Werth, J. L., & Tsaroucha, G. (2000). Gabapentin in bipolar disorder: A placebo-controlled trial of adjunctive therapy. Gabapentin Bipolar Disorder Study Group. *Bipolar Disorder, 2*(3 pt. 2), 249–255.

Perugi, G., Toni, C., Ruffolo, G., Sartini, S., Simonini, E., & Akiskal, H. (1999). Clinical experience using adjunctive gabapentin in treatment-resistant bipolar mixed states. *Pharmacopsychiatry, 32,* 136–141.

Placidi, G. F., Lenzi, A., Lazzerine, F., Cassano, G. B., & Akiskal, H. S. (1986). The comparative efficacy and safety of carbamazepine versus lithium: A randomized, double-blind 3-year trial in 83 patients. *Journal of Clinical Psychiatry, 47,* 490–494.

Pope, H., McElroy, S., Keck, P. E., Jr., & Hudson, J. I. (1991). Valproate in the treatment of acute mania. *Archives of General Psychiatry, 48,* 62–68.

Post, R. M., Ballenger, J. C., Uhde, T. W., & Bunney, W. E., Jr. (1984). Efficacy of carbamazepine in manic depressive illness: Implications for underlying mechanisms. In T. Post & J. Ballanger (Eds.), *Neurobiology of mood disorders* (pp. 777–816). Baltimore: Williams & Wilkens.

Post, R. M., Berrettini, W., Uhde, T. W., & Kellner, C. (1984). Selective response to the anticonvulsant carbamazepine in manic-depressive illness: A case study. *Journal of Clinical Psychopharmacology, 4,* 178–185.

Post, R. M., Leverich, G. S., Rosoff, A. S., & Altshuler, L. L. (1990). Carbamazepine prophylaxis in refractory affective disorders: A focus on long-term follow-up. *Journal of Clinical Psychopharmacology, 10,* 318–327.

Post, R. M., Uhde, T. W., Ballenger, J. C., Chatterji, D. C., Green, R. F., & Bunney, W. E. (1983). Carbamazepine and its 10,11- epoxide metabolite in plasma and CSF: Relationship to antidepressant response. *Archives of General Psychiatry, 40,* 673–676.

Post, R. M., Uhde, T., Kramlinger, K., & Rubinow, D. (1986). Carbamazepine treatment of mania: clinical and biochemical aspects. *Clinical Neuropharmacology, 9,* 547–549.

Post, R. M., Uhde, T. W., Roy-Byrne, P. P., & Joffe, R. T. (1986). Antidepressant effects of carbamazepine. *American Journal of Psychiatry, 143*, 29–34.

Post, R. M., Uhde, T. W., Roy-Byrne, P. P., & Joffe, R. T. (1987). Correlates of antimanic response to carbamazepine. *Psychiatry Research, 21*, 71–83.

Preda, A., Fazeli, A., McKay, B. G., Bowers, M. B., Jr., & Mazure, C. M. (1999). Lamotrigine as prophylaxis against steroid-induced mania (Letter to the editor). *Journal of Clinical Psychiatry, 60*(10): 708–709

Roy-Byrne, P. P., Joffe, R. T., Uhde, T. W., & Post, R. M. (1984). Approaches to the evaluation and treatment of rapid-cycling affective illness. *British Journal of Psychiatry, 145*, 543–550.

Ryback, R., Brodsky, L., & Munasifi, F. (1997). Gabapentin in bipolar disorder [Letter to the editor]. *Journal of Neuropsychiatry and Clinical Neurosciences, 9*, 301.

Schaff, M., Fawcett, J., & Zajecka, J. (1993). Divalproex sodium in the treatment of refractory affective disorders. *Journal of Clinical Psychiatry, 54*, 380–384.

Schaffer, C. B., & Schaffer, L. C. (1997). Gabapentin in the treatment of bipolar disorder [Letter to the editor]. *American Journal of Psychiatry, 154*, 291–292.

Schaffer, C., & Schaffer, L. (1999): Open maintenance of bipolar disorder spectrum patients who responded to gabapentin augmentation in the acute phase of treatment. *Journal of Affective Disorders, 55*, 237–240.

Schaffer, L., Schaffer, C., & Hughes, T. (1999). Tiagabine and the treatment of refractory bipolar disorder. In J. Soares & S. Gershon (Eds.), *Third International Conference on Bipolar Disorder* (Vol. 1, p. 49). Pittsburgh, PA: Munksgaard.

Semadeni, G. W. (1967). Study of the clinical efficacy of dipropylacetamide in mood disorders. *Acta Psychiatrica Belgica, 76*, 458–466.

Sheldon, L. J., Ancill, R. J., & Holliday, S. G. (1998). Gabapentin in feriatric psychiatry patients (Letter to the editor). *Canadian Journal of Psychiatry, 43*(4), 422–423

Short, C., & Cooke, L. (1995). Hypomania induced by gabapentin [Letter to the editor]. *British Journal of Psychiatry, 166*, 679–680.

Simhandl, C. H., Denk, E., & Thau, K. (1993). The comparative efficacy of carbamazepine low and high serum level and lithium carbonate in the prophylaxis of affective disorders. *Journal of Affective Disorders, 28*, 221–231.

Small, J., Klapper, M., Milstein, V., Kellams, J. J., Miller, M. J., Marhenke, J. D., et al. (1991). Carbamazepine compared with lithium in the treatment of mania. *Archives of General Psychiatry, 48*, 915–921.

Soutullo, C. A., Casuto, L. S., & Keck, P. E., Jr. (1998). Gabapentin in the treatment of adolescent mania: A case report. *Journal of Child and Adolescent Psychopharmacology, 8*, 81–85.

Sporn, J., & Sachs, G. (1997). The anticonvulsant lamotrigine in treatment-resistant manic-depressive illness. *Journal of Clinical Psychopharmacology, 17*(3), 185–189.

Stanton, S., Keck, P., & McElroy, S. (1997). Treatment of acute mania with gabapentin (Letter to the editor). *American Journal of Psychiatry, 154*, 287.

Stoll, K. D., Bisson, H. E., Fischer, E., Gammel, G., Goncalves, N., Krober, H. L., et al. (1986, September). Carbamazepine versus haloperidol in manic syndromes—First report of a multicentric study in Germany. In C. Shagass, R. C. Josiassen, W. H. Bridger, K. J. Weiss, D. Stoff, & G. M. Simpson (Eds.), *Biological psychiatry: 1985: Proceedings of the IVth World Congress of Biological Psychiatry* (pp. 332–334). Philadelphia, New York: Elsevier.

Suppes, T., Brown, E. S., McElroy, S. L., Keck, P. E., Jr., Nolen, W., Kupka, R., et al. (1999, April). Lamotrigine for the treatment of bipolar disorder: A clinical case series. *Journal of Affective Disorders, 53*, 95–98.

Takezaki, H., & Hanaoka, M. (1971). The use of carbamazepine (Tegretol) in the control of manic-depressive psychosis and other manic, depressive states. *Seishin-igaku (Clinical Psychiatry), 13,* 173–183.

Vencovsky, E., Peterova, E., & Kabes, J. (1987). Preventive effect of dipropylacetamide in bipolar manic-depressive psychoses. *Psychiatrie Neurologie, and Medizinische Psychologie (Leipz), 39,* 362–364.

Victor, B. S., Link, N. A., Binder, R. L., & Bell, I. R. (1984). Use of clonazepam in mania and schizoaffective disorders. *American Journal of Psychiatry, 141,* 1111–1112.

Walden, J., Hesslinger, B., van Calker, D., & Berger, M. (1996). Addition of lamotrigine to valproate may enhance efficacy in the treatment of bipolar affective disorder. *Pharmacopsychiatry, 29,* 193–195.

Watkins, S. E., Callender, K., Thomas, D. R., Tidmarsh, S. F., & Shaw, D. M. (1987). The effect of carbamazepine and lithium on remission from affective illness. *British Journal of Psychiatry, 150,* 180–182.

Weisler, R. H., Risner, M. E., Ascher, J. A., & Houser, T. L. (1994). Use of lamotrigine in the treatment of bipolar disorder. Paper presented at the American Psychiatric Association Meeting, Philadelphia, PA. (Abstract No. NR 611: 216).

Wolf, C., Berky, M., & Kovacs, G. (1997). Carbamazepine versus lithium in the prophylaxis of bipolar affective disorders: A randomised, double-blind 1-year study in 168 patients (abstract). *European Neuropsychopharmacology, 7*(Suppl. 2), S176.

Young, L. T., Robb, J. C., Hasey, G. M., MacQueen, G. M., Patelis-Siotis, I., Marriott, M., et al. (1999, September). Gabapentin as an adjunctive treatment in bipolar disorder. *Journal of Affective Disorders, 55,* 73–77

Young, L. T., Robb, J. C., Patelis-Siotis, I., MacDonald, C., & Joffe, R. T. (1997). Acute treatment of bipolar depression with gabapentin. *Biological Psychiatry, 42,* 851–853.

Zapletalek, M., Hanus, H., & Kindernayova, H. (1988). Personal experience with the prophylactic effect of dipropylacetamide. *Ceskoslovenska Psychiatric, 84,* 7–10.

CHAPTER 11

Somatic Treatments for Bipolar Disorder

Raymond W. Lam
Anthanasios P. Zis
A. Dooley Goumeniouk

Introduction

The biological revolution in our understanding of psychiatric conditions has produced an unparalleled number of treatments for bipolar disorder. Much of the attention has been focused on psychopharmacology, where the medication armamentarium for treating bipolar disorder grows steadily. However, electroconvulsive therapy (ETC) was among the first somatic treatments used for mental illness, and it remains one of the most effective treatments today.

Since the early 1980s, a large number of studies have shown that other somatic treatments, including light therapy, sleep deprivation, and repetitive transcranial magnetic stimulation, can be effective for treating bipolar disorder and depression. Unfortunately, unlike psychopharmacology, the resources of the pharmaceutical industry do not back research into these somatic treatments. The evidence for these treatments is therefore not as substantial as that for medications because there is scarce funding for large-scale clinical trials. Hence, evaluation of somatic treatments for clinical use often depends on independent replication of small-sample studies. Even when somatic treatments have demonstrated evidence-based efficacy, it remains a challenge to educate busy clinicians about these treatments and to promote their use in clinical settings.

In this chapter, we review the evidence for the use of these somatic treatments for bipolar disorder, and focus on how the clinician can apply these tools as primary or adjunctive treatments for their bipolar patients.

Electroconvulsive Therapy

Electroconvulsive therapy (ECT) is a safe and effective treatment for major depression, including all subtypes such as bipolar depression (American Psychiatric Association Task Force on Electroconvulsive Therapy, 1990).

ECT IN THE TREATMENT OF MANIA

According to the APA Task Force Report of the American Psychiatric Association, ECT is an effective treatment for all subtypes of mania (American Psychiatric Association Task Force on Electroconvulsive Therapy, 1990). The effectiveness of ECT in the treatment of mania is supported by a number of retrospective studies, which were summarized by Mukherjee (1989), and show an immediate overall clinical improvement of approximately 80%.

These findings are supported by the results of two prospective controlled trials comparing ECT to lithium (Small et al., 1988) and comparing real with sham ECT in combination with neuroleptics (Sikdar, Kulhara, Avasthi, & Singh, 1994). Both studies found that the administration of ECT was associated with superior short-term outcome. However for most patients, lithium or anticonvulsants alone, or in combination with neuroleptics, are the first line of treatment for mania, and ECT is usually reserved for the treatment of manic patients refractory to pharmacotherapy or when a rapid clinical response is required (e.g., in cases of manic delirium). There is little or no empirical evidence to support the notion that the treatment of mania requires bilateral electrode placement or a higher number of treatments (Abrams, 1997; Beyer, Weiner, & Glick, 1998) and therefore, the clinician should follow the same principles and guidelines that apply in the treatment of depression (American Psychiatric Association Task Force on Electroconvulsive Therapy, 1990).

ECT TREATMENT EMERGENT HYPOMANIA OR MANIA

There is controversy about the risk of switching into mania during treatment of depression with ECT. Angst, Baruffol, and Meinherz-Surbeck

(1992), based on a large retrospective chart review of patients hospitalized between 1920 and 1981, estimated the risk of switching into hypomania during or following ECT to be approximately 10%. This was approximately 2.5 times higher compared to patients receiving antidepressants or no treatment. In bipolar patients, the incidence of hypomania was reported to be approximately 30%, irrespective of whether the patients received ECT, antidepressant drug treatment, or no treatment.

This study has been criticized on several methodological grounds by Devanand, Pradic, and Sackheim (1992) who argue that ECT-induced mania or hypomania is rare. They attribute the high prevalence rates reported by Angst et al. to the inclusion of episodes occurring well after ECT treatment had ended and when the patients were receiving antidepressants. They also point out that Angst et al. failed to distinguish between true hypomania and "organic euphoria," a syndrome characterized by elation and cognitive impairment (Devanand, Sackheim, Decina, & Prodic, 1988; Fink & Kahn, 1961) which typically resolves within days after the end of ECT treatment. In fact, Abrams (1997) considers the occurrence of such maniclike syndromes as a favorable prognostic sign and an indication to withhold further ECT treatments as, in most cases, they fully resolve within days. Beyer and colleagues (1998) estimate the risk of switching into mania or mixed state for bipolar patients to be about 7%. They contend that the incidence of mania during treatment with ECT is similar to that observed with antidepressant drug treatment and suggest that this switch can be managed by either continuing the ECT course or stopping and administering an antimanic agent for unipolar depressed patients.

In conclusion, treatment emergent mania or hypomania during ECT is rather rare, although it may be more common during treatment of bipolar compared to unipolar depression. Hypomania needs to be distinguished from "organic euphoria," which is associated with the development of a cognitive disturbance. Delaying further ECT treatments and observation of the patient may be the most prudent course of action as these syndromes often resolve within days. If the manic symptoms persist beyond the recovery of cognitive function or the depressive symptoms recur, the clinician has the option of either continuing with ECT or terminating the ECT and beginning pharmacotherapy (American Psychiatric Association Task Force on Electroconvulsive Therapy, 1990).

ECT–DRUG INTERACTIONS DURING TREATMENT OF BIPOLAR DISORDER

Electroconvulsive therapy is usually given to patients who have failed to respond to one or more antidepressant drug trials. Since there is little evidence to support that the administration of antidepressant drugs during a course of ECT will increase its efficacy, there is little justification for the coadministration of ECT and antidepressant agents. Discontinuing lithium or anticonvulsant mood stabilizers in bipolar patients who may need long-term prophylaxis, however, is another matter since it may lead to a manic relapse during ECT or increase the risk for a manic or depressive relapse in the future.

Lithium

The primary concern regarding administration of ECT in patients receiving lithium derives from earlier reports suggesting an increased risk for CNS side effects including confusion, memory loss, and postictal delirium. Mukherjee (1993) has reviewed the literature comprehensively and concluded that these concerns are not fully warranted, and that the combination may be safe. It is, however, recommended that the decision to continue with lithium during a course of ECT should be made on a case-by-case basis, weighing the risk of relapse compared to the potential for increased toxicity. In the case of continuing with lithium prophylaxis during ECT, the dose of lithium should be adjusted to maintain lithium levels at a low or moderate range (0.6–0.8 meq/L).

Concerns about the administration of ECT in patients receiving lithium have also arisen from earlier case reports in the anesthesia literature of prolonged apnea and delayed recovery, as well as animal studies suggesting that lithium potentiates the effect of both depolarizing (succinylcholine) and nondepolarizing neuromuscular relaxants. These studies have been critically reviewed by Martin and Kramer (1982) and Beyer et al. (1998), who conclude that these data are insufficient to prohibit prescribing lithium and ECT.

ANTICONVULSANT MOOD STABILIZERS

Anticonvulsant mood stabilizers are used increasingly as an alternative to lithium treatment and prophylaxis in bipolar patients. It is now widely accepted that the effectiveness of real ECT depends upon the extent to which the stimulus intensity exceeds the seizure threshold (Sackeim et al., 1993). Since anticonvulsants increase the seizure threshold, it is prudent to gradually discontinue or substantively reduce the dose prior to embarking on a course of unilateral ECT as they may interfere with its therapeutic effectiveness (Beyer et al., 1998). Alternatively, the seizure threshold can be estimated at the first treatment and the stimulus intensity of subsequent treatments adjusted accordingly. However, if the initial threshold is too high, the required dose may exceed the capacity of currently available ECT devices. In that case, the anticonvulsants must be reduced or discontinued.

Light Therapy

Light therapy (also called phototherapy) consists of daily exposure to bright fluorescent light (Figure 11.1). Light therapy has been shown to be an effective treatment for seasonal affective disorder (SAD; also known as winter depression), is a syndrome of recurrent major depressive episodes that occur during the fall and winter, with natural remissions occurring during spring and summer (Rosenthal et al., 1984).

Since 1984, dozens of controlled studies have shown that light therapy is effective for SAD, with an overall response rate of about 65%. Major reviews of the literature have summarized these studies (Lam, Kripke, & Gillin, 1989; Rosenthal, 1993; Tam, Lam, & Levitt, 1995), but persistent concerns about the small sample sizes of individual studies (averaging only 10–15 patients per condition) and the difficulty of establishing suitable placebo control conditions limited the confidence of the results.

FIGURE 11.1. Person sitting under a 10,000 lux fluorescent light box.

More recently, these concerns have been addressed by large-sample, randomized controlled trials comparing light therapy against plausible placebo conditions (Eastman, Young, Fogg, Liu, & Menden, 1998; Terman, Terman, & Ross, 1998). Both studies found that the clinical response rates to light therapy were superior to placebo, hence supporting the efficacy of light therapy. Additionally, several meta-analysis studies, where a number of clinical trials are grouped by comparing standardized effect sizes, also confirm that bright light therapy is effective in SAD (Lee & Chan, 1999; Terman et al., 1989). These findings have recently been evaluated through a rigorous, evidence-based consensus process, with published clinical guidelines supporting light therapy as a first-line treatment for SAD (Lam & Levitt, 1999).

The mechanism of action of light therapy for SAD remains unclear (for review, see Lam & Levitan, 2000). There is evidence that bright light corrects dysregulated circadian rhythms in depression, and that light therapy has effects on the serotonergic and catecholaminergic dysfunction found in SAD. It is well recognized that light is the strongest synchronizer of human circadian rhythms, and timed bright light exposure can reliably shift human circadian rhythms in the same predictable manner as in animals. Circadian rhythm dysregulation hypotheses have also been proposed for nonseasonal bipolar disorder (Kripke, Mullaney, Atkinson, & Wolf, 1978; Wirz-Justice, 1995). Light therapy is also useful in treating circadian disorders such as phase-delayed sleep disorder, shift work, and jet lag (Lam, 1998a).

SAD AND BIPOLAR DISORDER

The DSM-IV criteria for seasonal pattern, equivalent to SAD, are set out in Table 11.1. The criteria are based on the pattern of major depressive episodes that must have regular seasonal onset and offset (spontaneous remission). The seasonal pattern qualifier can be applied to major depressive disorder or to bipolar disorder. For patients with bipolar disorder, the offset of depressive episodes may be heralded by hypomanic or manic episodes in the spring.

Initially, SAD was considered to be primarily a bipolar disorder, with clinical reports indicating that up to 95% of patients had hypomanic or manic responses in the springtime (Rosenthal et al., 1984). The atypical depressive features (hypersomnia, hyperphagia, weight gain) found in SAD also seemed consistent with those described in bipolar depression. Subsequent studies, however, have placed the bipolar ratio in SAD to be much lower, in the order of 11 to 15% (Lam, 1998b; White, Lewy, Sack, Blood, & Wesche, 1990), and the investigators of the earlier studies have now agreed that most

TABLE 11.1.
DSM-IV Criteria for Seasonal Pattern Specifier
(Equivalent to Seasonal Affective Disorder)

With Seasonal Pattern

- must meet DSM-IV criteria for major depressive episodes
- can be applied to the pattern of major depressive episodes in bipolar I disorder, bipolar II disorder, or major depressive disorder, recurrent.

A. There has been a regular temporal relationship between the onset of major depressive episodes and a particular time of the year
B. Full remissions (or a change from depression to mania or hypomania) also occur at a characteristic time of the year
C. In the last 2 years, two major depressive episodes have occurred that demonstrate the temporal seasonal relationships defined in criteria A and B, and no nonseasonal major depressive episodes have occurred during that same period
D. Seasonal major depressive episodes (as described above) substantially outnumber the nonseasonal major depressive episodes that may have occurred over the individual's lifetime

patients with SAD are unipolar. The higher rates of bipolar disorder in previous studies were likely related to the use of Research Diagnostic Criteria, which tend to overestimate the prevalence of hypomania compared to DSM criteria.

LIGHT THERAPY FOR BIPOLAR SAD

Many studies of SAD, including treatment studies of light therapy, have included mixed samples of unipolar and bipolar patients. In fact, the first SAD patient to receive light therapy had a bipolar disorder (Lewy, Kern, Rosenthal, & Wehr, 1982). Most of the studies, however, involve drug-free patients, so bipolar II patients are more likely to be included while bipolar I patients are more likely excluded. There are no published controlled studies directly comparing the response rates of unipolar and bipolar SAD patients to light therapy.

In the absence of controlled studies of light therapy for bipolar SAD, the clinical experience from our SAD clinic, where we use a standard method for light therapy, may be informative. In these open studies, we lend patients a commercial light box and instruct them on how to use the light box at home. The light therapy parameters are 10,000 lux fluorescent light (with a filter for ultraviolet wavelengths) with exposure set at about 30 minutes per day, for at least 2 weeks. Patients are rated before and after light therapy using the Structured Interview Guide for the Hamilton Depression Rating scale (SIGH-SAD, Williams, Rosenthal, & Termany, 1988) administered by board-certified psychiatrists. The SIGH-SAD generates a 21-item Ham-D and an 8-item atypical addendum that rates the atypical depressive symptoms that are omitted in the 21-item Ham-D. Clinical response was defined as an improvement in the 29-item SIGH-SAD score of at least 50% from baseline to posttreatment. Only patients who used the lights for at least 5 days each week were included in the analysis.

Figure 11.2 shows the response to this open trial of light therapy for bipolar and unipolar patients. The bipolar patients ($n = 21$) were moderately depressed at baseline, as indicated by their average Ham-29 and Ham-21 scores of 34.1 and 20.1, respectively. Compared to the unipolar patients, the bipolar patients had significantly higher baseline Ham-29 scores ($p < 0.01$), and a trend to higher Ham-21 scores ($p < 0.06$), indicating that they were slightly more depressed. The bipolar patients significantly improved with light treatment in all outcome measures, and there were no significant differences between the bipolar and unipolar patients in their percentage improvement for each subscale score. Although the overall clinical response rate was slightly lower in the bipolar patients (52 vs. 67%), this was not statistically significant ($p > 0.18$). The light therapy was well tolerated by most patients.

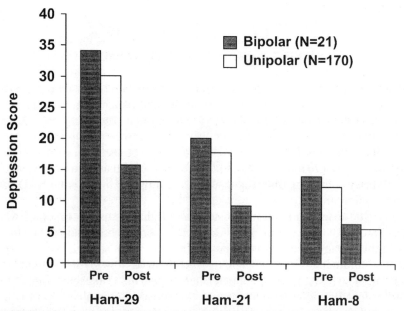

FIGURE 11.2. Clinical response to an open trial of light therapy (10,000 lux, fluorescent light for 30 minutes in the early morning; 2 weeks of treatment) in bipolar and unipolar patients with SAD.

Of course, these results must be interpreted with some caution since this was an open study design. Therefore, any placebo response cannot be separated from the specific effects of the light therapy. However, these response rates are similar to those reported in other centres with open and placebo-controlled studies. These results should also provide an idea of the type of response from light therapy that can be expected in a regular clinical setting. In summary, light therapy appears to be an effective treatment for bipolar patients with SAD when they are depressed during a winter depressive episode.

LIGHT THERAPY FOR NONSEASONAL BIPOLAR DISORDER

Although much of the research on light therapy has been done in SAD, light was first investigated as a treatment for nonseasonal depression (Kripke, 1981). Since then, there have been five controlled studies of light therapy for nonseasonal major depression. Results have been inconsistent, with positive results in three studies (Kripke, Mullaney, Klauner, Risch, & Gillan, 1992; Yamada, Martin-Iverson, Daimon, Tsujimoto, & Takahashi, 1995; Yerevanian, Anderson, Grota, & Bray, 1986) and negative results in two others (Mackert, Volz, Stieglitz, & Muller-Oerlinghausen, 1991; Thalen, Kjellman, Morkrid, Wiborn, & Wetterberg, 1995). These inconsistent results may be due, in part, to the small sample sizes of the individual studies and the short treatment duration (1–2 weeks). Other studies have used light therapy to augment medication use. Ten of 14 unipolar depressed patients who were refractory to medications responded when light therapy was added to their treatment regimen (Levitt, Jaffe, & Kennedy, 1991).

There are a few studies of light therapy for nonseasonal bipolar depression. In one study, bipolar patients had better responses to light therapy than unipolar patients, but the bipolar patients responded to both bright (2500 lux) and dim (400 lux) light (Deltito, Maline, Pollak, Martin, & Maremmani, 1991). In another study, light therapy (10,000 lux for 45 minutes, twice a day for 4 weeks) was used in a small sample of young patients with bipolar disorder who had subsyndromal depressive symptoms during the winter (Papatheodorou & Kutcher, 1995). Moderate or marked response was found in five of the seven patients.

Light therapy has also been used for rapid cycling bipolar disorder. In a detailed case report, a refractory rapid cycling bipolar patient was effectively treated with a combination of sodium valproate, an enforced, extended dark/sleep period of 10 hours, and midday bright light exposure (Wirz-Justice, Quinto, Cajochen, Werth, & Hock, 1999a). The effects of morning, midday, or evening light therapy were studied over a period of 3 months each in nine rapid cycling bipolar patients who were on stable doses of medications, and compared to 3 months without light therapy (Leibenluft et al., 1995). Only midday light exposure had beneficial effects, in three of five patients. In this study, the light therapy was better tolerated when patients discontinued the light treatment on days when they were hypomanic. The morning light exposure also led to significant worsening of symptoms in three patients that required discontinuation of light treatment.

In summary, although the evidence is still limited, there is a suggestion that light therapy is beneficial in nonseasonal bipolar and unipolar depression. Given the mild side effects of light therapy, and the fact that light can be combined with other medications without worrying about drug–drug interactions, some investigators have recommended wider use of light therapy as an adjunctive treatment for nonseasonal depression (Kripke, 1998).

LIGHT THERAPY METHOD

The light therapy protocol used in our clinic is based on the results of controlled studies and on consensus clinical guidelines for SAD (Lam & Levitt, 1999). We use a 10,000 lux fluorescent light box and instruct patients to sit under the light for at least 30 minutes per day, as soon as possible upon arising in the early morning (usually between 7:00 and 8:00 a.m.). The patient does not need to stare at the lights, but can be reading or writing, or eating breakfast under the light box (Figure 11.1). As the intensity of the light is dependent upon the distance to the light source, patients must be careful to be properly positioned to receive the correct "dose" of light exposure.

Commercial light boxes are now readily available at local medical supply stores or by mail order at a cost of between Can$150 to Can$400. We recommend light boxes that: (1) meet government approved electrical safety standards; (2) have an ultraviolet wavelength filter; and (3) have been tested in published clinical trials. Information on reputable light box companies can be found at the Society for Light Treatment and Biological Rhythms (a nonprofit, scientific and professional association) web site at **www.sltbr.org** via the Corporate Members link.

The response to light therapy usually occurs rapidly and is often noticeable within a week of starting light therapy. Many early studies used only 1 week of treatment because statistically and clinically significant results could be demonstrated within that time. Longer duration studies have shown that the response rate increases during the second week, and then tends to plateau over weeks 3 and 4. Thus, an adequate trial of light therapy requires at least 2 weeks.

Relapse of symptoms usually occurs within the same time period, within a week or two, when light therapy is discontinued in the winter. Hence, we recommend that light therapy be continued throughout the winter season, and then discontinued in the spring at the usual time for natural remission.

Side effects to light therapy are relatively mild, with headache, eye-strain, agitation, and nausea the most common effects reported (Labbate, Lafer, Thibault, & Sachs, 1994). Most side effects subside with regular use of light therapy, or can be managed by reducing the "dose" of light, either by reducing the duration of daily exposure or by reducing the intensity (e.g., sitting slightly farther back from the light source).

There are no absolute contraindications to using light therapy. The 10,000 lux light schedule should be safe for most patients, and no adverse retinal effects were found after 5-year follow-up of patients treated with light therapy (Gallin, Termin, Reme, Rafferty, Terman, & Burde, 1995). Routine ophthalmological screening is not necessary before starting light therapy, except for those patients who have ocular risk factors (summarized in Table 11.2). For these higher risk patients, we recommend baseline ophthalmologic assessment and periodic regular monitoring (e.g., annually).

LIGHT THERAPY FOR BIPOLAR DEPRESSION: SPECIAL CONSIDERATIONS

Like other effective antidepressant treatments, light therapy can precipitate hypomanic or manic responses in susceptible patients (Chan, Lam, & Perry,

TABLE 11.2
Ocular Risk Factors for Light Therapy

There are animal data or theoretical concerns about the use of light therapy for patients with the following risk factors. Although none are absolute contraindications to light therapy, baseline ophthalmologic consultation and regular monitoring are recommended for patients with these risk factors.

- Retinal or eye diseases (e.g., retinitis pigmentosa, macular degeneration, glaucoma)
- Systemic diseases that affect the eye, (e.g., diabetes mellitus)
- Elderly patients have a higher risk of macular degeneration
- Photosensitizing medication:
  - Chloroquine (antimalarial)
  - 8-methoxypsoralens (used in ultraviolet phototherapy for psoriasis)
  - Hematoporphyrins (used in photodynamic therapy for cancer)
  - Phenothiazines, e.g., thioridazine (antipsychotics)
  - Lithium
  - St. John's Wort, hypericum (antidepressant)
  - Melatonin (hypnotic)

1994; Kripke, 1991). Feeling agitated or "revved up" can be part of an immediate, energizing effect of bright light exposure, even in normal subjects (Bauer, Kurtz, Rubin, & Marcus, 1994). There has also been some suggestion that bipolar patients are more sensitive to light than unipolar patients or normal subjects (Lewy, Kern, Rosenthal, & Wehr, 1985). In our experience, patients with bipolar disorder, type I (with previous manic episodes) are more likely to experience some agitation with light therapy and usually require dosage adjustment (e.g., reducing the time spent under the lights or sitting farther away from the light source). We also recommend that bipolar I patients be on a mood stabilizer when treated with light therapy.

Medications used to treat bipolar disorder may also require special attention when prescribing light therapy (Table 11.2). Lithium can affect the retina, although clinical studies have not shown any adverse retinal effects of long-term lithium use by ophthalmological examination or by electrophysiological tests of retinal function (Lam, Allain, Sullivan, Beattie, Remick, & Zis, 1997). However, data from animal studies suggest that bright light exposure may potentiate some of the lithium-induced retinal changes (Reme, Rol, Grothmann, Kaase, & Terman, 1996). Similarly, other drugs that may potentially have photosensitizing effects include phenothiazine antipsychotics (e.g., thioridazine), melatonin, and St. John's Wort (hypericum). Ophthalmological consultation prior to light therapy and regular monitoring are recommended for patients taking these medications.

There were several case reports involving bipolar SAD patients that suggest light therapy may induce suicidal ideation or behaviors, particularly in the first week of treatment. However, in a large sample of SAD patients treated with light therapy, we found no evidence for early-onset suicidal ideation (Lam, Tam, Shiah, Yatham, & Zis, 2000). In fact, suicidal ideation was reduced with light therapy in most patients in parallel with improvement. Regardless, it remains clinically prudent to monitor depressed patients carefully during the time when they are beginning to improve, as this is a high-risk time for suicidal behaviors.

Sleep Deprivation

Disturbances in the sleep–wake cycle are cardinal symptoms of bipolar disorder. Patients have reduced need for sleep during manic episodes, while insomnia or hypersomnia is experienced during bipolar depression. It is well recognized that disruption of the sleep–wake cycle can precipitate mania. Hence, manipulation of the sleep–wake cycle has been investigated as a treatment for bipolar disorder.

The most studied sleep manipulation is that of total sleep deprivation

(TSD) for depression. When patients are kept awake all night, they often show an improvement in mood that continues through the next day (Pflug & Tolle, 1971). The mood changes can be dramatic, and many patients feel that their mood returns to baseline. Although it is difficult to design placebo-controlled studies, the fact that TSD is so counterintuitive to patients (most of whom think they will feel better if only they had *more* sleep) makes a placebo response less likely.

Unfortunately, the mood improvement after TSD is not long lived. The majority of patients relapse after a recovery sleep the next day after TSD. Several reviews of sleep deprivation studies found the clinical response rate to TSD averaged about 60%, but 80 to 85% of patients relapsed the next day following recovery sleep (Kuhs & Tolle, 1991; Leibenluft & Wehr, 1992; Wirz-Justice & van den Hoofdakker, 1999b; Wu & Bunney, 1992). Relapse can occur even after brief naps. However, it is intriguing that up to 15% of patients appear to have sustained responses to TSD even after a recovery sleep.

SLEEP DEPRIVATION FOR BIPOLAR DEPRESSION

Although early studies found that diurnal variation predicted response to TSD while unipolar/bipolar diagnoses did not (Elsenga & Van den Hoofdakker, 1987), other studies suggest that bipolar patients have better responses to TSD than unipolar patients (Barbini et al., 1998). Rapid cycling patients had the best responses in a study of 16 patients treated with TSD twice a week for 4 weeks (Papadimitriou, Christodoulou, Katsouyanni, & Stefanis, 1993). Bipolar I patients also had the best responses to late sleep deprivation (sleep time set at 21:00 to 02:00 hr) (Szuba, Baxter, Fairbanks, Guze, & Schwartz, 1991). Bipolar patients do not necessarily switch into hypomania or mania after TSD. The "switch rate" of bipolar patients to TSD was five percent to six percent in a sample of 206 bipolar patients, a switch rate similar to that of antidepressants (Colombo, Benerletti, Barbini, Campori, & Smeraldi, 1999).

The response of bipolar patients to TSD may also be enhanced with concomitant use of light therapy or lithium. In a large study, 115 depressed inpatients with bipolar disorder were randomized to three cycles of TSD in one week, either alone or combined with morning bright light exposure (Colombo et al., 2000). Sixty-six of the patients were medication-free while 49 patients were treated with lithium during the trial. The patients receiving light therapy or ongoing lithium treatment had enhanced subjective mood responses after TSD, but there were no additional benefits when both treatments were combined.

PREVENTING RELAPSE AFTER TSD

A number of studies have investigated ways to maintain the response and prevent the relapse after TSD. Partial sleep deprivation has been examined because it is easier for patients to continue partial sleep deprivation than to continue TSD. Patients can be sleep-deprived during the early part of the usual sleep period (e.g., sleeping from 02:00 to 07:00 hr) or during the later part (e.g., sleeping from 23:00 to 03:00 hr). Some studies found that sleep deprivation in the second half of the usual sleep period was superior to sleep deprivation in the first half. However, a controlled trial of early versus late sleep deprivation in patients refractory to antidepressants found a small but significant effect of both treatments (Leibenluft, Moul, Schwartz, Madden, & Wehr, 1993). Other studies found that advancing the sleep period, i.e., to 17:00 to 24:00 hr, after a TSD resulted in fewer relapses, suggesting there is a "critical" period in the early morning when sleep may be depressogenic (Riemann et al., 1996).

Medication strategies to sustain the response to TSD have also been studied. One strategy attempts to use TSD to reduce the lag time to respond to antidepressant medications. Total sleep deprivation is conducted when starting an antidepressant so that patients have a rapid initial therapeutic response. The TSD is then discontinued once the medication effect begins. In one study five bipolar patients treated with fluoxetine and TSD had faster onset of response than five patients treated with fluoxetine alone (Benedetti et al., 1997). In another study, 41 depressed patients treated with 6 sessions of LSD at 4–5 day intervals plus amitriptyline 150 mg day versus amitriptyline alone. At 4 weeks, but not at 2 weeks, there was superior response to combined treatment in Ham-D but not self-ratings (Kuhs, Farber, Borgstadt, Mrosek, & Tolle, 1996).

Lithium treatment can also maintain the antidepressant response to TSD. Forty depressed bipolar patients were treated with TSD conducted three times over 1 week with a recovery night between TSD sessions. Thirteen of 20 patients responded to lithium plus TSD compared to 2 of 12 patients with TSD alone (Benedetti, Colombo, Barnini, Campori, & Smeraldi, 1999). In 26 unipolar depressed patients, lithium prolonged the effect of a single TSD to a second and third day (Grube & Hartwich, 1990). In a placebo-controlled study, the addition of pindolol (a beta-blocker that in low doses is a specific 5-HT1A autoreceptor antagonist) prevented relapse after three cycles of TSD in 9 days in 40 patients with bipolar depression. Fifteen of 20 patients on pindolol, compared to 3/20 patients on placebo, responded with Ham-D<8. In 65% of the pindolol+TSD cases, lithium alone sustained the response for 6 months (Smeraldi, Benedetti, Barbini, Campori, & Colombo, 1999). Bright light exposure (3000 lux for two hours in the morning and two hours in the evening) can also stabilize the initial antidepressant response to a partial sleep deprivation protocol (sleeping from 21:00 to 01:30 hr) (Neumeister et al., 1996).

CLINICAL USE OF TSD

Given the evidence for the favorable clinical responses to TSD, how can it be used in a clinical setting? In our experience, it is very difficult to conduct TSD as an outpatient without significant help from a family member. Even partial sleep deprivation protocols are difficult to initiate and maintain. We find that TSD is more feasible to conduct in an inpatient setting. Patients can watch television or videos through the night and the hospital staff can periodically monitor patients to ensure that they are awake. Given the current economic climate, any intervention that can improve mood quickly and reduce the number of days in hospital should generate significant interest.

A regimen of three repeated TSD sessions over the course of 1 week is well tolerated by patients who respond to TSD (Table 11.3). On days 1, 3, and 5, patients undergo TSD by staying awake for 36 hours from 07:00 hr to 19:00 hr the next day. On days 2, 4, and 6, patients have a recovery sleep from 19:00 hr to 07:00 hrs the next day (adapted from Smeraldi et al., 1999).

Adding pindolol during TSD is a low-risk procedure that may augment the TSD response. The dose of pindolol (2.5 mg t.i.d.) required for the serotonin autoreceptor antagonism is lower than that for beta-adrenergic blockade and patients have few side effects at that dose. The usual contraindications for using beta-adrenergic blockers (asthma, cardiovascular problems) still apply. Starting or continuing lithium treatment may also augment the TSD response in bipolar patients.

Which bipolar patients could be considered for TSD? We would consider TSD for patients who need a rapid response, (e.g., acutely suicidal patients or patients starting on an antidepressant). Patients with variability

TABLE 11.3
Schedule for 1-Week Repeated Total Sleep Deprivation
(adapted from Smeraldi et al., 1999).

TSD 1	Day 1, 07:00 hr to Day 2, 19:00 hr
Recovery Sleep 1	Day 2, 19:00 hr to Day 3, 07:00 hr
TSD 2	Day 3, 07:00 hr to Day 4, 19:00 hr
Recovery Sleep 2	Day 4, 19:00 hr to Day 5, 07:00 hr
TSD 3	Day 5, 07:00 hr to Day 6, 19:00 hr
Recovery Sleep 2	Day 6, 19:00 hr to Day 7, 07:00 hr

of mood within the day or with melancholic symptoms may be more likely to respond.

If patients respond to the TSD, efforts should focus on maintaining their response. This will likely include medications (lithium or antidepressants), or alternatively bright light exposure. Mood stabilizing medication can be continued while TSD is conducted, especially given the studies showing that lithium can maintain the antidepressant effect of TSD. Unfortunately, there are no data about whether other mood stabilizers also have this effect with TSD.

Transcanal Magnetic Stimulation

Transcranial magnetic stimulation (TMS) is a technique in which a brief, high intensity magnetic field is generated and used to stimulate cortical neurons. The principle of Faraday induction describes the manner by which a magnetic field can induce an electrical current in electrical conductors exposed to a changing magnetic field. In the case of TMS, the cortical neurons are these secondary electrical conductors; the current induced is sufficient to modulate their activity, up to and including depolarization.

While the idea that magnetic fields may influence brain activity is over a century old, it was not until 1985 that Barker and colleagues (Barker, Freeston, Jalinous, & Jarratt, 1985) conducted the first transcranial magnetic stimulation in humans. In this instance, the copper coil responsible for producing the magnetic field was placed on the scalp overlying the motor cortex. The pulse of current was delivered to the coil from the discharge of a large capacitor. The brief magnetic pulse was of sufficient intensity to induce neuronal depolarization and subsequent observable involuntary movement of the contralateral hand and fingers.

The application of TMS to elicit a magnetically evoked potential (MEP) has found a diagnostic role in clinical neurology. When combined with electromyography, for example, measurements of latency of central motor response, such as may be present in multiple sclerosis, can be quantified.

It was not until the mid-1990s that TMS began to be evaluated as a treatment for neuropsychiatric conditions. The earliest, unblinded studies (Hoflich, Kasper, Hufnagel, Ruhrmann, & Moller, 1993; Kolbinger, Hoflich, Hufnagel, Moller, & Kasper, 1995) used single pulses of magnetic energy delivered over the cranial vertex of depressed patients. The results were variable and disappointing, showing at best only mild improvement. Subsequent refinements to Barker's original circular coil saw the development of a figure eight shaped coil able to deliver a more "focused" magnetic field. This permitted experimentation with more specific neuroanatomic coil placement sites. In addition, the nature of the magnetic pulse has been changed from the original single pulse to a "train" of sequential pulses. These multiple magnetic pulse sequences have been termed "repetitive TMS" (*r*TMS) and can be delivered with varying pulse frequencies. "Fast" frequency is distinguished from "slow" when the magnetic pulse frequency is greater than 1 p sec.

With the parameters of the stimulus and the neuroanatomic site of stimulation to manipulate, George et al. (1995) identified the left dorsolateral prefrontal cortex (DLPFC) as a region of interest for *r*TMS in depressed patients. In an open trial, four of six patients refractory to pharmacotherapy improved with *r*TMS (20 Hz, figure eight coil). Pascual-Leone, Rubio, Pallardo, & Catala (1996) replicated this finding with a blinded study of 17 psychotically depressed patients refractory to pharmacotherapy. Patients received *r*TMS (10 Hz, figure eight coil) or sham *r*TMS to the left DLPFC, right DLPFC or vertex. There was a highly significant difference between actual and sham *r*TMS.

Furthermore, the lateralizing finding of the left DLPFC being the site associated with the most improvement in depressive symptoms was also confirmed. Interestingly, the effect of *r*TMS administered to healthy, euthymic individuals also showed a lateralizing effect, however in the opposite direction to that seen in depressed patients. When *r*TMS was applied to the left prefrontal region of the healthy subjects, subjective sadness scores increased. Conversely, *r*TMS applied to the right prefrontal region caused subjective happiness scores to increase.

Since these initial studies, several small to medium scale studies have been conducted by several different investigators assessing the efficacy of *r*TMS in the treatment of depression (for review, see George, Lisanby, & Sackheim, 1999). The parameters of stimulus intensity, frequency, total duration, number of treatments, days of treatments, coil shape, and coil placements have all been varied. While the studies with sham TMS controls (achieved by holding the coil at right angles to the scalp to minimize stimulus) generally support an antidepressant effect of *r*TMS in depression, the clinical utility of *r*TMS and optimization of stimulus parameters have yet to be determined.

rTMS FOR BIPOLAR DISORDER

The role of *r*TMS as a somatic treatment modality in bipolar disorder is, at present, even less certain (Hasey, 2001; Nahas et al., 1999). Of interest is that use of *r*TMS for depression has been associated with induction of hypo-manic or manic responses (Garcia-Toro, 1999; Dolberg, Schreiber, & Grunhaus, 2001).

Few trials have been undertaken of *r*TMS for mania and, in most cases, patients have received *r*TMS and antimanic medications concurrently. Grisaru, Chudakov, Yaroslavsky, and Belmaker (1998) speculated that since there was an apparent benefit of *r*TMS administered to the left prefrontal cortex in depressed patients, and there was a lateralizing effect of *r*TMS in normals, that the effects of left versus right *r*TMS in mania merited investigation. Their study included 18 patients, two of whom dropped out early in the study. Of the 16 who completed the trial, seven were randomized to receive right prefrontal *r*TMS and nine to receive left prefrontal *r*TMS. No changes in clinical pharmacotherapy were made because of study participation. Only one patient in each group was not on a mood stabilizer.

The results, as measured by the Mania Scale, the BPRS mania factor, and Clinical Global Impression (CGI) indicated a significant effect of *r*TMS administration to the right prefrontal cortex. Patients receiving left prefrontal *r*TMS gave the clinical impression that their response was worse than expected, given adequate pharmacotherapy. This observation led the authors to speculate that left prefrontal *r*TMS may actually have worsened their mania. The trial was terminated prematurely as a result of this impression. Another report also suggested that left prefrontal *r*TMS is associated with hypomanic responses (Nedjat & Folkerts, 1999).

Little else has been published in this area. Furthermore, the abstracts published or in press share some of the limitations of this initial study, (e.g., patients were taking concomitant mood stabilizing medication). Erfurth, Michael, Nedjat, Schonauer, and Arolt, (1999) reported on five patients in an open trial, all of whom received right prefrontal stimulation. All five patients had significant reductions in mania scale scores; only one, however, received *r*TMS as monotherapy (Erfurth, Michael, Mostert, & Arolt, 2000).

The role of transcranial magnetic stimulation in the treatment of neuropsychiatric disorders, including bipolar disorder, remains to be clarified. While data is emerging supporting some degree of effectiveness in the treatment of depression, its clinical utility has yet to be established and it cannot be recommended as a routine treatment. While there would appear to be some effect of laterality of stimulation, this and numerous other parameters including intensity, frequency, and duration of pulse trains, intertrain interval, and overall treatment numbers remain to be optimized.

Nonetheless, *r*TMS has many attractions. These include the overall safety, suitability for outpatients, absence of cognitive effects, or need for anesthesia. Such features will undoubtedly fuel further research to determine whether a role exists for TMS in the primary or adjunctive treatment of neuropsychiatric conditions including mania.

References

Abrams, R. (1997). *Electroconvulsive therapy* (3rd ed.). New York: Oxford University Press.

American Psychiatric Association Task Force on Electroconvulsive Therapy (1990). *The practice of electroconvulsive therapy: Recommendations for treatment, training and privileging.* Washington, DC: American Psychiatric Association.

Angst, J., Angst, K., Baruffol, I., & Meinherz-Surbeck, R. (1992). ECT-induced and drug-induced hypomania. *Convulsive Therapy, 8,* 179–185.

Barbini. B., Colombo, C., Benedetti, F., Campori, E., Bellodi, L., & Smeraldi, E. (1998). The unipolar-bipolar dichotomy and the response to sleep deprivation. *Psychiatry Research, 79,* 43–50.

Barker, A. T., Freeston, I. L., Jalinous, R., & Jarratt, J. A. (1985). Non-invasive stimulation of motor pathways within the brain using time-varying magnetic fields. *Electroencephalography & Clinical Neurophysiology, 61* (Suppl. 1), S245.

Bauer, M. S., Kurtz, J. W., Rubin, L. B., & Marcus, J. G. (1994), Mood and behavioral effects of four-week light treatment in winter depressives and controls. *Journal of Psychiatric Research, 28,* 135–145.

Benedetti, F., Barbini, B., Lucca, A., Campori, E., Colombo, C., & Smeraldi, E. (1997). Sleep deprivation hastens the antidepressant action of fluoxetine. *European Archives of Psychiatry and Clinical Neurosciences, 247,* 100–103.

Benedetti, F., Colombo, C., Barbini, B., Campori, E., & Smeraldi, E. (1999). Ongoing lithium treatment prevents relapse after total sleep deprivation. *Journal of Clinical Psychopharmacology, 19,* 240–245.

Beyer, J., Weiner, R. D., & Glick, M. D. (Eds). (1998). *Electroconvulsive therapy. A programmed text.* Washington, DC: American Psychiatric Press.

Chan, P. K., Lam, R. W., & Perry, K. F. (1994). Mania precipitated by light therapy for patients with SAD. *Journal of Clinical Psychiatry, 55,* 454.

Colombo, C., Benedetti, F., Barbini, B., Campori, E., & Smeraldi, E. (1999). Rate of switch from depression into mania after therapeutic sleep deprivation in bipolar depression. *Psychiatry Research, 86,* 267–270.

Colombo, C., Lucca, A., Benedetti, F., Barbini, B., Campori, E., & Smeraldi, E. (2000). Total sleep deprivation combined with lithium and light therapy in the treatment of bipolar depression: Replication of main effects and interaction. *Psychiatry Research, 95,* 43–53

Deltito, J. A., Moline, M., Pollak, C., Martin, L. Y., & Maremmani, I. (1991). Effects of phototherapy on non-seasonal unipolar and bipolar depressive spectrum disorders. *Journal of Affective Disorders, 23,* 231–237.

Devanand, D. P., Prudic, J., & Sackeim, H. (1992). Electroconvulsive therapy-induced hypomania is uncommon. *Convulsive Therapy, 8,* 296–297.

Devanand, D. P., Sackeim, H. A., Decina, P., & Prudic, J. (1988). The development of mania and organic euphoria during ECT. *Journal of Clinical Psychiatry, 49,* 69–71.

Dolberg, O. T., Schreiber, S., & Grunhaus, L. (2001). Transcranial magnetic stimulation-induced switch into mania: a report of two cases. *Biological Psychiatry, 49,* 468–470

Eastman, C. I., Young, M. A., Fogg, L. F., Liu, L., & Meaden, P. M. (1998). Bright light treatment of winter depression: a placebo-controlled trial. *Archives of General Psychiatry, 55,* 883–889.

Elsenga, S., & Van den Hoofdakker, R. H. (1987). Response to total sleep deprivation and clomipramine in endogenous depression. *Journal of Psychiatric Research, 21,* 151–161.

Erfurth, A., Michael, N., Mostert, C., & Arolt, V. (2000). Euphoric mania and rapid transcranial magnetic stimulation. *American Journal of Psychiatry, 157,* 835–836

Erfurth, A., Michael, N., Nedjat, S., Schonauer, K., & Arolt, V. (1999). Treatment of bipolar mania with right prefrontal rapid transcranial magnetic stimulation (rTMS): An open study. *Journal of the European College of Neuropsychopharmacology, 9,* (Suppl. 1), S241.

Fink, M., & Kahn, R. I. (1961). Behavioral patterns in convulsive therapy. *Archives of General Psychiatry, 5,* 30–36.

Gallin, P. F., Terman, M., Reme, C. E., Rafferty, B., Terman, J. S., & Burde, R. M. (1995). Ophthalmologic examination of patients with seasonal affective disorder, before and after bright light therapy. *American Journal of Ophthalmology, 119,* 202–210.

Garcia-Toro, M. (1999). Acute manic symptomatology during repetitive transcranial magnetic stimulation in a patient with bipolar depression. *British Journal of Psychiatry, 175,* 491.

George, M. S., Lisanby, S. H., & Sackeim, H. A. (1999). Transcranial magnetic stimulation: applications in neuropsychiatry. *Archives of General Psychiatry, 56,* 300–311.

George, M. S., Wassermann, E. M., Williams, W. A., Callahan, A., Ketter, T. A., Basser, P., et al. (1995). Daily repetitive transcranial magnetic stimulation (rTMS) improves mood in depression. *Neuroreport, 6,* 1853–1856.

Grisaru, N., Chudakov, B., Yaroslavsky, Y., & Belmaker, R. H. (1988). Transcranial magnetic stimulation in mania: a controlled study. *American Journal of Psychiatry, 155,* 1608–1610.

Grube, M., & Hartwich, P. (1990). Maintenance of antidepressant effect of sleep deprivation with the help of lithium. *European Archives of Psychiatry and Clinical Neurosciences, 240,* 60–61.

Hasey, G. (2001). Transcranial magnetic stimulation in the treatment of mood disorder: A review and comparison with electroconvulsive therapy. *Canadian Journal of Psychiatry, 46,* 720–727.

Hoflich, G., Kasper, S., Hufnagel, A., Ruhrmann, S., & Moller, H. J. (1993). Application of transcranial magnetic stimulation in treatment of drug-resistant major depression: a report of two cases. *Human Psychopharmacology, 8,* 361–365.

Kolbinger, H. M., Hoflich, G., Hufnagel, A., Moller, H. J., & Kasper, S. (1995). Transcranial magnetic stimulation (TMS) in the treatment of major depression: A pilot study. *Human Psychopharmacology, 10,* 305–310.

Kripke, D. F. (1981). Photoperiodic mechanisms for depression and its treatment. In C. Perris, G. Struwe & B. Janson B (Eds.), *Biological psychiatry* (pp. 1248–1252). Amsterdam: Elsevier Press.

Kripke, D. F. (1991). Timing of phototherapy and occurrence of mania. *Biological Psychiatry, 29,* 1156–1157.

Kripke, D. F. (1998). Light treatment for nonseasonal depression: Speed, efficacy, and combined treatment. *Journal of Affective Disorders, 49,* 109–117.

Kripke, D. F., Mullaney, D. J., Atkinson, M. L., & Wolf, S. (1978). Circadian rhythm disorders in manic-depressives. *Biological Psychiatry, 13,* 335–351.

Kripke, D. F., Mullaney, D. J., Klauber, M. R., Risch, S. C., & Gillin, J. C. (1992). Controlled trial of bright light for nonseasonal major depressive disorders. *Biological Psychiatry, 31,* 119–134.

Kuhs, H., Farber, D., Borgstadt, S., Mrosek, S., & Tolle, R. (1996). Amitriptyline in combination with repeated late sleep deprivation versus amitriptyline alone in major depression. A randomised study. *Journal of Affective Disorders, 37,* 31–41.

Kuhs, H., & Tolle, R. (1991). Sleep deprivation therapy. *Biological Psychiatry, 29,* 1129–1148.

Labbate, L. A., Lafer, B., Thibault, A., & Sachs, G. S. (1994). Side effects induced by bright light treatment for seasonal affective disorder. *Journal of Clinical Psychiatry, 55,* 189–191.

Lam, R. W. (Ed.). (1998a). *Seasonal affective disorder and beyond. Light treatment for SAD and non-SAD conditions.* Washington, DC: American Psychiatric Press.

Lam, R. W. (1998b). Seasonal affective disorder. Diagnosis and management. *Primary Care Psychiatry, 4,* 63–74.

Lam, R. W., Allain, S., Sullivan, K., Beattie, C. W., Remick, R. A., & Zis, A. P. (1997). Effects of chronic lithium treatment on retinal electrophysiologic function. *Biological Psychiatry, 41,* 737–742.

Lam, R. W., Kripke, D. F., & Gillin, J. C. (1989). Phototherapy for depressive disorders: A review. *Canadian Journal of Psychiatry, 34,* 140–147.

Lam, R. W., & Levitan, R. D. (2000). Pathophysiology of seasonal affective disorder. *Journal of Psychiatry and Neuroscience, 25*(5), 469–480.

Lam, R. W., & Levitt, A. J. (Eds.). (1999). *Canadian consensus guidelines for the treatment of seasonal affective disorder.* Vancouver: Clinical & Academic Publishing.

Lam, R. W., Tam, E. M., Shiah, I. S., Yatham, L. N., & Zis, A. P. (2000). Effects of light therapy on suicidal ideation in patients with winter depression. *Journal of Clinical Psychiatry, 61,* 30–32.

Lee, T. M., & Chan, C. C. (1999). Dose-response relationship of phototherapy for seasonal affective disorder: A meta-analysis. *Acta Psychiatrica Scandinavia, 99,* 315–323.

Leibenluft, E., Moul, D. E., Schwartz, P. J., Madden, P. A., & Wehr, T. A. (1993). A clinical trial of sleep deprivation in combination with antidepressant medication. *Psychiatry Research, 46,* 213–227.

Leibenluft, E., Turner, E. H., Feldman-Naim, S., Schwartz, P. J., Wehr, T. A., & Rosenthal, N. E. (1995). Light therapy in patients with rapid cycling bipolar disorder: Preliminary results. *Psychopharmacology Bulletin, 31,* 705–710.

Leibenluft, E., & Wehr, T. A. (1992). Is sleep deprivation useful in the treatment of depression? *American Journal of Psychiatry, 149,* 159–168.

Levitt, A. J., Joffe, R. T., & Kennedy, S. H. (1991). Bright light augmentation in antidepressant nonresponders. *Journal of Clinical Psychiatry, 52,* 336–337.

Lewy, A. J., Kern, H. A., Rosenthal, N. E., & Wehr, T. A. (1982). Bright artificial light treatment of a manic-depressive patient with a seasonal mood cycle. *American Journal of Psychiatry, 139,* 1496–1498.

Lewy, A. J., Nurnberger, J. I., Jr., Wehr, T. A., Pack, D., Becker, L. E., Powell, R. L., et al. (1985). Supersensitivity to light: Possible trait marker for manic-depressive illness? *American Journal of Psychiatry, 142,* 725–727.

Mackert, A., Volz, H. P., Stieglitz, R. D., & Muller-Oerlinghausen, B. (1991). Phototherapy in nonseasonal depression. *Biological Psychiatry, 30,* 257–268.

Martin, B. A., & Kramer, P. M. (1982). Clinical significance of the interaction between lithium and a neuromuscular blocker. *American Journal of Psychiatry, 139*(10), 1326–1328.

Mukherjee, S. (1989). Mechanisms of the antimanic effect of electroconvulsive therapy. *Convulsive Therapy, 5,* 227–243.

Mukherjee, S. (1993). Combined ECT and lithium therapy. *Convulsive Therapy, 9,* 274–284.

Nahas, Z., Molloy, M. A., Hughes, P. L., Oliver, N. C., Arana, G. W., Risch, S. C., et al. (1999). Repetitive transcranial magnetic stimulation: Perspectives for application in the treatment of bipolar and unipolar disorders. *Bipolar Disorder, 1,* 73–80.

Nedjat, S., & Folkerts, H. W. (1999). Induction of a reversible state of hypomania by rapid-rate transcranial magnetic stimulation over the left prefrontal lobe. *Journal of Electroconvulsive Therapy, 1,* 73–80.

Neumeister, A., Goessler, R., Lucht, M., Kapitany, T., Bamas, C., & Kasper, S. (1996). Bright light therapy stabilizes the antidepressant effect of partial sleep deprivation. *Biological Psychiatry, 39,* 16–21.

Papadimitriou, G. N., Christodoulou, G. N., Katsouyanni, K., & Stefanis, C. N. (1993). Therapy and prevention of affective illness by total sleep deprivation. *Journal of Affective Disorders, 27,* 107–116.

Papatheodorou, G., & Kutcher, S. (1995). The effect of adjunctive light therapy on ameliorating breakthrough depressive symptoms in adolescent-onset bipolar disorder. *Journal of Psychiatry and Neuroscience, 20,* 226–232.

Pascual-Leone, A., Rubio, B., Pallardo, F., & Catala, M. D. (1996). Rapid-rate transcranial magnetic stimulation of left dorsolateral prefrontal cortex in drug-resistant depression. *Lancet, 348,* 233–237.

Pflug, B., & Tolle, R. (1971). Disturbance of the 24-hour rhythm in endogenous depression and the treatment of endogenous depression by sleep deprivation. *International Pharmacopsychiatry, 6,* 187–196.

Reme, C. E., Rol, P., Grothmann, K., Kaase, H., & Terman, M. (1996). Bright light therapy in focus: lamp emission spectra and ocular safety. *Technology & Health Care, 4,* 403–413.

Riemann, D., Hohagen, F., Konig, A., Schwarz, B., Gomille, J., Voderholzer, U., et al. (1996). Advanced vs. normal sleep timing: Effects on depressed mood after response to sleep deprivation in patients with a major depressive disorder. *Journal of Affective Disorders, 37,* 121–128.

Rosenthal, N. E. (1993). Diagnosis and treatment of seasonal affective disorder. *Journal of the American Medical Association, 270,* 2717–2720.

Rosenthal, N. E., Sack, D. A., Gillin, J. C., Lewy, A. J., Goodwin, F. K., Davenport, Y., et al. (1984). Seasonal affective disorder: A description of the syndrome and preliminary findings with light therapy. *Archives of General Psychiatry, 41,* 72–80.

Sackeim, H. A., Prudic, J., Devanand, D. P., Kiersky, J. E., Fitzsimons, L., Moody, B. J., et al. (1993). Effects of stimulus intensity and electrode placement on the efficacy and cognitive effects of electroconvulsive therapy. *New England Journal of Medicine, 328,* 839–846.

Sikdar, S., Kulhara, P., Avasthi, A., & Singh, H. (1994). Combined Chlorpromazine and Electroconvulsive Therapy in Mania. *British Journal of Psychiatry, 164*(6), 806–810.

Small, J. G., Klapper, M. H., Kellams, J. J., Miller, M. J., Milstein, V., Sharpley, P. H., et al. (1988). Electroconvulsive treatment compared with lithium in the management of manic states. *Archives of General Psychiatry, 45,* 727–732.

Smeraldi, E., Benedetti, F., Barbini, B., Campori, E., & Colombo, C. (1999). Sustained antidepressant effect of sleep deprivation combined with pindolol in bipolar depression. A placebo-controlled trial. *Neuropsychopharmacology, 20,* 380–385.

Szuba, M. P., Baxter, L. R. J., Fairbanks, L. A., Guze, B. H., & Schwartz, J. M. (1991). Effects of partial sleep deprivation on the diurnal variation of mood and motor activity in major depression. *Biological Psychiatry, 30,* 817–829.

Tam, E. M., Lam, R. W., & Levitt, A. J. (1995). Treatment of seasonal affective disorder: A review. *Canadian Journal of Psychiatry, 40,* 457–466.

Terman, M., Terman, J. S., Quitkin, F. M., McGrath, P. J., Stewart, J. W., & Rafferty, B. (1989). Light therapy for seasonal affective disorder. A review of efficacy. *Neuropsychopharmacology, 2,* 1–22.

Terman, M., Terman, J. S., & Ross, D. C. (1998). A controlled trial of timed bright light and negative air ionization for treatment of winter depression. *Archives of General Psychiatry, 55,* 875–882.

Thalen, B. E., Kjellman, B. F., Morkrid, L., Wibom, R., & Wetterberg, L. (1995). Light treatment in seasonal and nonseasonal depression. *Acta Psychiatrica Scandinavia, 91,* 352–360.

White, D. M., Lewy, A. J., Sack, R. L., Blood, M. L., & Wesche, D. L. (1990). Is winter depression a bipolar disorder? *Comprehensive Psychiatry, 31,* 196–204.

Williams, J. B. W., Link, M. J., Rosenthal, N. E., & Terman, M. (1988). *Structured interview guide for the Hamilton Depression Rating scale, Seasonal Affective Disorders Version* (SIGH-SAD). New York: Psychiatric Institute.

Wirz-Justice, A. (1995). Biological rhythms in mood disorders. In F. E. Bloom & D. J. Kupfer

(Eds.), *Psychopharmacology: The fourth generation of progress* (pp. 999–1017). New York: Raven Press.

Wirz-Justice, A., Quinto, C., Cajochen, C., Werth, E., & Hock, C. (1999a). A rapid-cycling bipolar patient treated with long nights, bedrest, and light. *Biological Psychiatry, 45,* 1075–1077.

Wirz-Justice, A., & van den Hoofdakker, R. H. (1999). Sleep deprivation in depression: What do we know, where do we go? *Biological Psychiatry, 46,* 445–453.

Wu, J. C., & Bunney, W. E. (1992). The biological basis of an antidepressant response to sleep derivation and relapse: Review and hypothesis. *American Journal of Psychiatry, 147,* 14–21.

Yamada, N., Martin-Iverson, M. T., Daimon, K., Tsujimoto, T., & Takahashi, S. (1995). Clinical and chronobiological effects of light therapy on nonseasonal affective disorders. *Biological Psychiatry, 37,* 866–873.

Yerevanian, B. I., Anderson, J. L., Grota, L. J., & Bray, M. (1986). Effects of bright incandescent light on seasonal and nonseasonal major depressive disorder. *Psychiatry Research, 18,* 355–364.

CHAPTER 12

Psychotropic Medications in Biopolar Disorder: Pharmacodynamics, Pharmacokinetics, Drug Interactions, Adverse Effects, and Their Management

Terence A. Ketter
Po W. Wang
Xiaohua Li

Introduction

Pharmacotherapy of bipolar disorders is a complex and rapidly evolving field. The development of new treatments has helped refine concepts of illness subtypes and generated important new management options. Although the mood stabilizers lithium, carbamazepine (CBZ), and valproate (VPA) are the primary medications for bipolar disorders, antipsychotics, antidepressants, anxiolytics, and a new generation of anticonvulsants are commonly combined with mood stabilizers in clinical settings. These diverse medications have varying pharmacodynamics, pharmacokinetics, drug–drug interactions, and adverse effects; thus offering not only new therapeutic opportunities, but also a variety of new potential pitfalls. Therefore, clinicians are challenged with integrating the complex data regarding efficacy spectra, described elsewhere in this volume, with the pharmacological properties described in this chapter, in efforts to provide safe, effective, state-of-the-art pharmacotherapy for patients with bipolar disorders.

Mood Stabilizers

The mood stabilizers lithium, carbamazepine, and valproate, have varying structures (Figure 12.1), efficacy spectra, pharmacodynamics, pharmacokinetics, drug-drug interactions, and adverse effects, indicating the need to appreciate both the commonalities and dissociations of these agents. Mood stabilizers are available in suspension, immediate release, and extended release formulations. Unfortunately, intramuscular and depot formulations have not been feasible, as these agents can cause necrosis when in direct contact with muscle tissue. In the last two years, an intravenous valproate formulation has become available.

Baseline evaluation of bipolar disorder patients includes not only psychosocial assessment, but also general medical evaluation, in view of the risk of medical processes, which could confound diagnosis or influence management decisions, and the risk of the adverse effects that may occur with treatment. Assessment commonly includes history, physical examination, complete blood count with differential and platelets, renal, hepatic, and thyroid function, toxicology, and pregnancy tests, as well as other chemistries and electrocardiogram as clinically indicated (American Psychiatric Association, 1994). Such evaluation provides baseline values for param-

LITHIUM   **CARBAMAZEPINE**   **VALPROATE**

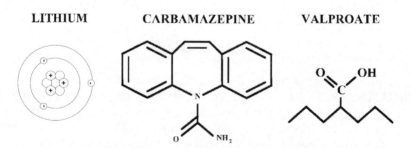

FIGURE 12.1. Mood Stabilizer Structures. The mood stabilizers have dramatically different structures. Lithium (left) is an ion, carbamazapine (center) is a tricyclic molecule with a carbamyl side chain, and valproate (right) is a branched chain fatty acid molecule. Not illustrated to scale, as the lithium ion is much smaller than carbamazapine or valproate.

eters that influence decisions regarding choice of medication and intensity of clinical and laboratory monitoring.

In view of the relative complexity of mood stabilizer therapy, patient education regarding adverse events is crucial. Information sheets or booklets describing clinical monitoring for signs of dehydration and neurotoxicity with lithium, dermatologic, hepatic, and hematologic reactions with carbamazepene, and hepatic and hematologic reactions with VPA can aid in early detection of adverse events to allow assessment and intervention, and enhance safety.

LITHIUM

Lithium is an ion with multiple biochemical effects. Although intracellular signaling (Manji, Potter, & Lenox, 1995) is the most active area of current exploration of lithium mechanisms, this ion also has effects on gamma-aminobutyric acid (GABA), glutamate, calcium, and monoamines. Lithium has impressive efficacy in classic bipolar disorder (euphoric manias, not rapid cycling) (Jefferson, Greist, Ackerman, & Carroll, 1987), but appears less effective in patients with mixed mood states (dysphoric mania), rapid cycling, comorbid substance abuse, severe psychotic or secondary manias, adolescents, and patients who have had three or more prior episodes (Bowden, 1995). In addition, its utility is limited by adverse effects, which can undermine compliance.

Lithium is well absorbed, with a bioavailability close to 100%. It is not bound to plasma proteins and has a moderate volume of distribution of about 1 L/kg, and a half-life of about 24 hr. Lithium is 100% renally excreted with a clearance about one fourth that of creatinine (generally ranging from 10 to 40 mL/min).

In acute settings, such as the inpatient treatment of mania, lithium therapy is commonly initiated at 600 to 1200 mg/day, and increased as necessary and tolerated, by 300 mg/day every 2 to 4 days. However, euthymic or depressed patients tend to tolerate aggressive initiation less well than manic patients. Thus, in less acute situations, such as the initiation of prophylaxis or adjunctive use, lithium can be started at 300 to 600 mg/day, and increased as necessary and tolerated, by 300 mg/day every 4 to 7 days. Target doses are commonly between 900 and 1800 mg/day, yielding plasma levels from 0.6 to 1.2 mEq/L (0.6–1.2 mM/L), with the higher portion of the range used acutely, and lower doses used in prophylaxis or adjunctive therapy.

Brain lithium concentrations measured by magnetic resonance spectroscopy appear to be about one half of plasma lithium concentrations, and may correlate better with serum (r = 0.66) than with red blood cell (r = 0.33) lithium levels (Kato, Shioiri, et al., 1993). Moreover, improvement in manic symptoms appears to correlate with brain lithium concentrations (r = 0.64) and brain/serum lithium ratios (r = 0.60), but not with serum lithium concentrations or lithium dose/weight ratios (Kato, Inubushi, & Takahashi, 1994). Preliminary evidence suggests that brain lithium concentrations may need to be at least 0.2 mEq/L (0.2 mM/L) for adequate therapeutic effects (Kato et al., 1993).

Laboratory monitoring during lithium therapy commonly includes baseline studies and reevaluation of renal and thyroid indices initially at 3 and 6 months, and then every 6 to 12 months (American Psychiatric Association, 1994). Plasma lithium concentrations are typically assessed at steady state, which occurs at about 5 days after a dosage change, and then as indicated by inefficacy or adverse effects.

Due to its renal excretion, lithium has renally mediated rather than hepatically mediated drug–drug interactions (Table 12.1). Lithium excretion is decreased by medications such as thiazides, nonsteroidal anti-inflammatory drugs (NSAIDs), angiotensin converting enzyme (ACE) inhibitors, and physiological states such as dehydration, advanced age, sodium depletion, and renal disease. Due to lithium's poor therapeutic index, these interactions can result in clinical lithium toxicity, unless a dosage adjustment is made. In contrast, lithium clearance is less consistently affected by amiloride, furosemide, acetylsalicylic acid (ASA), and sulindac, and increased with other medications with diuretic effects such as acetazolamide, mannitol, aminophylline, caffeine, and theophylline, as well as during pregnancy. Increases in lithium clearance may yield clinical inefficacy if plasma lithium concentrations fall below the therapeutic range. Pa-

TABLE 12.1
Lithium Clearance

Decreased by	Not changed by	Increased by
Thiazides	Amiloride	Acetazolamide
	Furosemide	Mannitol
NSAIDs	ASA	
	Sulindac	
ACE Inhibitors		Aminophylline
		Caffeine
		Theophylline
Dehydration		Pregnancy
Advanced age		Mania
Sodium Depletion		
Renal Disease		

tients who become manic or hypomanic often have dramatic increases in physical activity which can yield increased cardiac output and renal lithium filtration and excretion, and hence decreased plasma lithium concentrations at the very time when this medication is needed most. Lithium has a rather low therapeutic index with overlapping therapeutic and toxic ranges in some patients. However, at doses of 900 mg per day or less, lithium is usually well tolerated and even with low plasma levels may yield benefit in milder forms of bipolar disorders or when used as an adjunct to other mood stabilizers or antidepressants.

Lithium can cause digestive tract disturbance (Table 12.2), with the lithium citrate solution having more proximal absorption and thus exacerbating upper (nausea and vomiting), or attenuating lower (diarrhea) gastrointestinal adverse effects. The reverse holds for sustained release preparations. Lithium-induced neurotoxicity (sedation, tremor, and cognitive difficulties) is dose-related and can be an important reason for poor adherence. Although lithium is often given in divided doses to decrease peak plasma levels and thus minimize gastrointestinal adverse effects, doses can also be weighted toward bedtime, and patients receiving low to moderate doses may tolerate a single daily dose at bedtime. The latter regimen may aid sleep, attenuate daytime neurotoxicity, and possibly even decrease polyuria. Beta-blocking agents can attenuate lithium-induced tremor.

Although diuretics attenuate polyuria, care must be taken as such agents can influence lithium clearance as described above. Lithium-induced polyuria and polydipsia often resolves with dosage reduction or discontinuing the drug. However, chronic lithium may also yield more long-standing renal complications, apparently most prevalent in cases of repeated lithium toxicity. Clinical and laboratory monitoring may help detect problems early, thus allowing interventions to attenuate adverse effects.

Weight gain with lithium therapy can be another source of compliance

TABLE 12.2
Mood Stabilizer Adverse Effects

Lithium	CBZ	VPA
Gastrointestinal	Gastrointestinal	Gastrointestinal
Weight Gain	Rash	Weight gain
Neurotoxicity	Neurotoxicity	Tremor
Renal	Hepatic	Hepatic
Thyroid	Thyroid	Thrombocytopenia
Hair Loss	Leukopenia	Hair Loss
Cardiac	Cardiac	Pancreatitis
Teratogen	Teratogen	Teratogen
Acne, Psoriasis	Hyponatremia	Polycystic ovary?

problems. Indeed, many of the agents used in treating bipolar disorder patients can yield weight increase as can residual hyperphagia, hypersomnia, and anergy of bipolar depression, or lithium-induced hypothyroidism. Counseling regarding weight gain early in the maintenance phase of treatment may allow early attention to diet and exercise to attenuate this effect. In some cases, early detection of a rising high normal or modestly elevated thyroid stimulating hormone (TSH) can allow crossing over to another mood stabilizer, thus avoiding the need for chronic replacement thyroid hormones which is necessary in more advanced cases of lithium-induced hypothyroidism. Even in some euthyroid patients, addition of thyroid hormones may offer adjunctive antidepressant effects, increasing energy and activity, and thus attenuating weight gain. Another important approach is to minimize the number of concurrent medications that also yield weight gain, thus avoiding potential synergistic weight increases. Classical prescription weight loss agents such as stimulants are generally avoided because they can destabilize mood and result in abuse or dependence. The anticonvulsant topiramate may allow patients to lose about 10% of total body weight without systematically destabilizing mood.

Hair loss, acne, and psoriasis are encountered with lithium. In some patients, symptomatic treatment of dermatological adverse effects can yield enough improvement to allow continuation of therapy, whereas in others switching to or adding another mood stabilizer to allow a decrease in lithium dose is necessary. Lithium, like the other mood stabilizers, is a teratogen, yielding cardiac malformations at a rate of 0.1 to 1.0%. Ultrasound may allow early detection of such malformations. In patients with milder illness, a medication-free interval during pregnancy may be feasible. As rapid discontinuation of lithium may yield rebound episodes (Suppes, Baldessarini, Faedda, & Tohen, 1991), gradual tapering off of medication is a preferable strategy. Some patients have sufficiently severe illness to merit continuing lithium during pregnancy. Frank counseling and discussion of the risks and benefits of this approach is crucial in the management of such cases. Lithium and other mood stabilizers generally ought to be restarted immediately postpartum in view of the risk of relapse. which may be as high as 60% (Cohen, Sichel, Robertson, Hecksher, & Rosenbaum, 1995). As lithium and other mood stabilizers are excreted to varying degrees in breast milk, the most cautious approach is to not breast feed on mood stabilizers.

CARBAMAZEPINE

Carbamazepine (CBZ) has a tricyclic structure, and a wide array of biochemical effects including effects on sodium channels, GABA, glutamate, somatostatin, adenosine, and intracellular signaling (Post, Weiss, Chuangm & Ketter, 1994). Unlike tricyclic antidepressants, CBZ does *not* block reuptake of monoamines. Carbamazepine has an efficacy spectrum similar to VPA, and to some extent complementary to lithium.

Carbamazepine has erratic absorption and a bioavailability of about 80%. It is about 75% bound to plasma proteins and has a moderate volume of distribution of about 1 L/kg. Before autoinduction of the epoxide pathway (presumably via induction of CYP3A3/4), the half-life of CBZ is about 24, and the clearance is about 25 mL/min. However, after autoinduction (2–4 weeks into therapy), the half-life falls to about 8 hr, and clearance rises to about 75 mL/min. This may require dose adjustment to maintain adequate blood levels and therapeutic effects. The active CBZ-10,11-epoxide (CBZ-E) metabolite has a half-life of about 6 hr. Two sustained release CBZ formulations were approved for use in the United States. These formulations given twice a day yield steady state CBZ levels similar to those seen with the immediate release formulation given four times a day (Garnett, Levy, et al., 1998; Thakker, Maugat, Garnett, Levy, & Kochak, 1992).

In acute settings, such as the inpatient treatment of mania, carbamazepine therapy is commonly initiated at 200 to 400 mg/day, and increased as necessary and tolerated, by 200 mg/day every 2 to 4 days. However, euthymic or depressed patients tend to tolerate aggressive initiation less well than manic patients. Thus, in less acute situations, such as the initiation of prophylaxis or adjunctive use, carbamazepine is often started at 100 to 200 mg/day, and increased as necessary and tolerated, by 200 mg/day every four to seven days. Even this gradual initiation may cause adverse effects. Thus, starting with 50 mg (half of a chewable 100 mg tablet) at bedtime and increasing by 50 mg every 4 days can yield a better tolerated initiation. Due to autoinduction, doses after a 2 to 4 weeks of therapy may need to be twice as high as in the first week to yield comparable plasma levels. Target doses are commonly between 600 to 1200 mg/day, yielding plasma levels from 6 to 12 mcg/mL (20 to 60 mM/L), with the higher portion of the range used acutely, and lower doses used in prophylaxis or adjunctive therapy.

Recommended laboratory monitoring during carbamazepine therapy includes baseline studies, and reevaluation of complete blood count, differential, platelets, and hepatic indices initially at 2, 4, 6, and 8 weeks, and then every 3 months (American Psychiatric Association, 1994). Most of the dangerous hematological reactions occur in the first 3 months of therapy (Tohen, Castillo, Baldessarini, Zarate, & Kando, 1995). In clinical practice, somewhat less focus is placed on scheduled monitoring, whereas clinically indicated (e. g., when a patient becomes ill with a fever) monitoring is emphasized. Patients who have abnormal or marginal indices at any point merit fastidious scheduled and clinically indicated monitoring. Plasma CBZ concentrations are typically assessed at steady state, and then as indicated by inefficacy or adverse effects.

The pharmacokinetic properties of CBZ are atypical among medications prescribed by psychiatrists, and necessitate special care when treating patients concurrently with other medications (Ketter, Post, & Worthington, 1991a, 1991b). Carbamazepine is extensively metabolized with only about 3% being excreted unchanged in the urine. The main metabolic pathway of CBZ (to its active 10,11-epoxide, CBZ-E) appears to be mediated primarily by CYP3A3/4 (Figure 12.2), with a minor contribution by CYP2C8 (Kerr et al., 1994). This epoxide pathway accounts for about 40% of CBZ disposition, and even more in patients with induced epoxide pathway metabolism (presumably via CYP3A3/4 induction) (Faigle & Feldmann, 1995). Although a genetic polymorphism has been observed for CYP2C8 (Wrighton & Stevens, 1992), this probably does *not* account for the variability observed in CBZ disposition, in view of the minor role of this isoform. The frequency distribution of CBZ kinetic parameters is unimodal, consistent

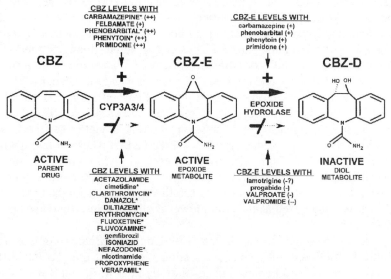

*molecular biochemical evidenxe supports CYP3A3/4

FIGURE 12.2. Carbamazepine Metabolism. Metabolism of carbamazepine (CBZ) and drugs acting on its two major metabolic enzymes. CBZ-E = carbamazepine-10, 11-epoxide. CBZ-D = carbamazepine-10,11-dihydro-dihydroxide. CYP3A3/4 = cytochrome P450 3A3/4. + indicates enzyme induction. − indicates enzyme inhibition. Adapted with permission from (Ketter et al 1991a). *Source:* T.A. Ketter et al.: *Journal of Psychopharmacology* (1991)11, 198–203, 306–313.

with CYP3A3/4 (which lacks genetic polymorphism) being the crucial isoform. With enzyme induction (of the epoxide pathway, presumably via CYP3A3/4 induction), formation of CBZ-E triples, its subsequent transformation to the inactive diol doubles, and thus the CBZ-E/CBZ ratio increases (Eichelbaum, Tomson, Tybring, & Bertilsson, 1985). Other pathways include aromatic hydroxylation (25%), which is apparently mediated by CYP1A2 and not induced concurrently with the epoxide pathway, and glucuronide conjugation of the carbamoyl side chain (15%) by uridine diphosphoglucuronosyltransferase (UGT). These other pathways yield inactive metabolites.

Carbamazepine induces not only CYP3A3/4 and conjugation, but also presumably other cytochrome P450 isoforms (which remain to be characterized). Thus, CBZ decreases the plasma levels of not only CBZ itself (autoinduction), but also many other medications (heteroinduction). Carbamazepine-induced decreases in plasma levels of certain concurrent medications can render them ineffective. Moreover, if CBZ is discontinued, plasma levels of these other medications can rise leading to toxic effects from these agents (Denbow & Fraser, 1990). Also, CBZ metabolism can be inhibited by CYP3A3/4 inhibitors yielding increased plasma CBZ levels and intoxication (Figure 12.2).

The active CBZ-E metabolite can yield therapeutic and adverse effects

TABLE 12.3
CBZ Drug Interactions

	CBZ →↓ Drug	Drug →↑ CBZ
Amitriptyline	Alprazolam (?)	Acetazolamide
Bupropion	BCPs	Cimetidine
Clozapine	Clonazepam	Clarithromycin
Dexamethasone	Cyclosporine (?)	Danazol
Dicumarol (?)	Doxacurium	d-Propoxyphene
Doxepin	Doxycycline	Diltiazem
Ethosuximide	Fentanyl (?)	Erythromycin
Fluphenazine (?)	Haloperidol	Fluoxetine
Methadone	Imipramine	Flurithromycin
Olanzapine	Oxiracetam (?)	Fluvoxamine
Pancuronium	Phenytoin	Gemfibrozil
Prednisolone	Primidone	Isoniazid
Quetiapine (?)	Risperidone	Josamycin
Theophylline (?)	Thiothixene (?)	Nefazodone
Valproate	Vecuronium	Nicotinamide
Warfarin		Ponsinomycin
		Valproate (↑ CBZ-E)
		Verapamil

(?) = The effect is not firmly established.

similar to those of CBZ, but is not detected in conventional CBZ assays. The unwary clinician may misinterpret the significance of therapeutic or adverse effects associated with low or moderate plasma CBZ levels. In addition, valproate (VPA) displaces CBZ from plasma proteins, yielding an increase in free CBZ, which in combination with VPA-induced increases in CBZ-E, can yield toxicity when utilizing CBZ plus VPA combination therapy.

Carbamazepine has a wide variety of drug–drug interactions (Table 12.3), in excess of that seen with lithium or valproate, due to CBZ's constellation of pharmacokinetic properties (Table 12.4). Knowledge of CBZ drug-drug interactions and strategies for treating refractory symptoms is crucial in effective management. CBZ drug–drug interactions are predominantly pharmacokinetic. Recent advances in molecular pharmacology have characterized the specific cytochrome P450 isoforms responsible for metabolism of various medications (Table 12.5) (Ketter, Flockhart, et al., 1995). This may allow clinicians to anticipate and avoid pharmacokinetic drug–drug interactions and thus provide more effective combination pharmacotherapies. The reader interested in detailed reviews of CBZ drug–drug interactions may find these in other articles (Ketter, Post, & Worthington, 1991a, 1991b).

Carbamazepine induces the metabolism of tricyclic antidepressants (TCAs) and bupropion (Ketter, Jenkins, et al., 1995). Theoretical grounds have been stated for concern about combining CBZ with monoamine oxidase inhibitors (MAOIs). However, preliminary data suggest that the addition of phenelzine or tranylcypromine to CBZ may be well tolerated, does not affect CBZ levels, and may provide relief of refractory depressive symptoms in some patients (Ketter, Post, Parekh, & Worthington, 1995). The CYP3A3/4 inhibitors fluoxetine (Grimsley, Jann, Carter, D'Mello, & D'Souza, 1991), fluvoxamine (Fritze, Unsorg, & Lanczik, 1991), and nefazodone (Ashton & Wolin, 1996) have been reported to inhibit CBZ metabolism, yielding increased CBZ levels and toxicity, while paroxetine

TABLE 12.4
Mood Stabilizer Drug Interaction Potential

	Li	CBZ	VPA
Low Therapeutic Index	+	+	±
Long Half-Life	−	−	−
Nonlinear Kinetics	−	±	±
Active Metabolites	−	+	±
Enzyme Inducer	−	++	−
Enzyme Inhibitor	−	−	+
Single Main Elimination Route	+	+	−
CYP Substrate	−	3A3/4	+

(Andersen et al., 1991) and sertraline (Lane, 1994) do not appear to yield clinically significant changes in CBZ levels.

CBZ increases metabolism of haloperidol (Kahn, Schulz, Penel, & Alexander, 1990) and possibly other antipsychotics, such as fluphenazine (Jann, Fidone, Hernandez, Ackemann, & Carroll, 1989) and thiothixene (Ereshefsky, Jann, Saklad, & Davis, 1986). Some patients have improvement in psychiatric status or fewer neuroleptic side effects during combination treatment, while others have deterioration in psychiatric status. Loxapine and the amoxapine plus chlorpromazine combination may increase CBZ-E levels (Pitterle & Collins, 1988). CBZ induces clozapine metabolism (Jerling, Lindstrom, Bondesson, & Bertilsson, 1994), and this combination is not recommended in view of possible (but not proven) synergistic bone marrow suppression. CBZ also increases metabolism of olanzapine and possibly risperidone metabolism (de Leon & Bork, 1997; H. Y. Lane & Chang, 1998). CYP3A4 is crucial in quetiapine (Grimm, Stans, & Bui, 1997), and thus CBZ could induce metabolism of this new antipsychotic. Indeed, the enzyme inducer phenytoin increases quetiapine clearance fivefold.

Carbamazepine may decrease plasma levels of clonazepam (Lai, Levy, & Cutler, 1978), alprazolam (Arana, Epstein, Malloy, & Greenblatt, 1988), and clobazam (Levy, Lane, et al., 1983). The commonly used calcium channel blockers verapamil (Price & DiMarzio, 1988) and diltiazem (Brodie & MacPhee, 1986) can increase CBZ levels and cause clinical toxicity, but this does not occur with the dihydropyridines nifedipine (Brodie & MacPhee, 1986) and nimodipine (Ketter & Post, 1996). Also, enzyme-inducing anticonvulsants like CBZ appear to decrease nimodipine (Tartara, Galimbevti, et al., 1991) and felodipine (Capewell, Freestone, Critchley, Pottage, & Prescott, 1988) levels.

Carbamazepine and lithium are frequently combined in treating bipolar disorder, and may provide additive or synergistic antimanic and antidepressant effects. The combination is generally well tolerated, with merely additive neurotoxicity, which can be minimized by gradual dose escalation. CBZ decreases plasma levothyroxine (T4), free T4 index, and less consistently liothyronine (T3). In contrast, thyroid binding globulin, reverse T3, and basal plasma thyroid stimulating hormone (TSH) levels, and basal metabolic rates are not substantially changed with CBZ therapy.

The CBZ plus VPA combination appears to be not only tolerated, but may show psychotropic synergy (Ketter, Pazzaglia, & Post, 1992). Valproate inhibits epoxide hydrolase, increasing the plasma CBZ-E levels, at times without altering total plasma CBZ levels. These interactions can potentially confound clinicians because patients can have neurotoxicity due to elevated plasma CBZ-E or free CBZ levels in spite of therapeutic plasma total CBZ levels. Thus, in view of increased CBZ-E plasma levels, CBZ plasma levels as low as about one half of those seen without VPA may be required. Carbamazepine decreases plasma VPA levels, and its discontinuation can yield increased plasma VPA levels and toxicity. As a general rule, clinicians should carefully monitor patients on the CBZ plus VPA combination for side effects and consider decreasing the CBZ dose in advance (because of the expected displacement of CBZ from plasma proteins and increase in CBZ-E) and ultimately increasing the VPA dose (because of expected CBZ-induced decrements in VPA).

Drug–drug interactions between CBZ and other (nonpsychotropic) drugs are also of substantial clinical importance. Carbamazepine induces metabolism of diverse medications, raising the possibility of undermining the efficacy of steroids such as hormonal contraceptives, prednisolone, and methylprednisolone; the anticonvulsants primidone, felbamate, lamotrigine, tiagabine, and topiramate; the methylxanthines theophylline and aminophylline; the antibiotic doxycycline; the neuromuscular blockers pancuronium, vecuronium, and doxacurium; and the anticoagulant warfarin, and possibly dicumarol.

Similarly, a variety of medications can increase plasma CBZ levels and yield clinical toxicity, including the antibiotics erythromycin (Steketee et al., 1988), triacetyloleandomycin (Mesdjian, Drauet, Cenraud, & Roger, 1980), clarithromycin (Albani, Riva, & Baruzzi, 1993), and isoniazid (Wright, Stokes, & Sweeney, 1982); and the carbonic anhydrase inhibitor acetazolamide (Forsythe, Owens, & Toothill, 1981). Lamotrigine appears to enhance CBZ neurotoxicity, probably by a pharmacodynamic interaction. In addition, the anticonvulsants phenytoin, phenobarbital, primidone, and felbamate decrease plasma CBZ levels.

Carbamazepine therapy is associated with common, benign, as well as rare, serious, adverse events. Thus, mild leukopenia and rash occur in about 1/10 patients, with the slight possibility that these usually benign phenomena are heralding malignant aplastic anemia and Stevens-Johnson syndrome, seen in about 1/100,000 patients. Hematologic monitoring is intensified in patients with low or marginal leukocyte counts, and CBZ is generally discontinued if the leukocyte count falls below 3,000/μL or the granulocyte count below 1,000/μL. Rash presenting with systemic illness, or involvement of the eyes, mouth, or bladder (dysuria) constitutes a medical emergency and CBZ ought to be immediately discontinued and an emergency assessment made of the patient. For more benign presentations, immediate dermatologic consultation is required to assess the risks of continuing therapy. In selected cases, with the collaboration of dermatology, it may be safe to attempt desensitization by decreasing dose and adding antihistamine or prednisone.

Carbamazepine, like lithium, can cause neurotoxicity (sedation, diplopia, and ataxia). This is particularly the case early in therapy before autoinduction and the development of some tolerance to CBZ's central adverse effects. Gradual initial dosing and careful attention to potential drug–drug interactions can help attenuate this problem.

Carbamazepine, like VPA, can rarely cause hepatic problems, and generally needs to be discontinued if hepatic indices rise above three times the upper limit of normal. Carbamazepine-induced gastrointestinal disturbance can be approached in a fashion similar to that described for lithium. Although CBZ can cause modest TSH increases, frank hypothyroidism is very uncommon. Like other agents with tricyclic structures and sodium blocking properties, CBZ may affect cardiac conduction and should be used with caution in patients with cardiac disorders. A baseline electrocardiogram is worth consideration if there is any indication of cardiac problems.

Carbamazepine appears less likely than lithium or VPA to yield weight gain. For this reason, CBZ may provide an important alternative to other mood stabilizers for patients who struggle with this problem. Carbamazepine-induced hyponatremia is often tolerated in young, physically well individuals, but can yield obtundation and other serious sequelae in frail elderly patients.

Carbamazepine is a teratogen, yielding minor anomalies (craniofacial malformations and digital hypoplasia) in up to 20%, and spina bifida in about 1% of cases. For the latter, folate supplementation may attenuate the risk, and ultrasound may allow early detection. The issue of CBZ therapy in pregnancy can be approached in a fashion similar to that described above for lithium.

VALPROATE

Valproate (VPA) is a fatty acid with a variety of biochemical actions, including effects on sodium channels, gamma-aminobutyric acid (GABA), glutamate, dopamine, and intracellular signaling. Valproate appears to have a wide efficacy spectrum, which includes benefiting bipolar disorder patients who are refractory to lithium (Bowden, Brugger, et al., 1994).

Valproate is well absorbed, with bioavailability close to 100%. It is 80 to 90% bound to plasma proteins. This binding is saturable, so that at higher doses a greater percentage of the drug may be in the free form. Valproate is quite hydrophilic with a low volume of distribution of about 0.1 L/kg. At higher doses, the increased free fraction may remain in the plasma compartment (rather than escaping into the tissues) and thus be cleared by the liver. This may yield "sublinear" kinetics, so that with higher plasma concentrations, greater increases in dose may be required to yield the desired increase in plasma level (Graves, 1995). Binding interactions can occur, so that VPA can increase free diazepam, CBZ, phenytoin, tiagabine, tolbutamide, and warfarin, while ASA and NSAIDs can increase free VPA. In monotherapy VPA has a half-life of about 12 hr, and clearance of about 10 mL/min. Combined with the enzyme inducers such as CBZ, phenytoin, or phenobarbital, VPA's half-life falls 50% to about 6 hr and clearance doubles to about 20 mL/min. Valproate is available as valproic acid and as divalproex sodium, with the latter having better gastrointestinal tolerability. Recently, an extended release formulation of the latter with potentially even better tolerability has been approved for the treatment of migraine in the United States.

In acute settings, such as the inpatient treatment of mania, valproate therapy is commonly initiated at 750 to 2000 mg/day, and increased as necessary and tolerated, by 250 mg/day every one to two days. Recent evidence suggests that valproate initiation at 10 mg/lb (20 mg/kg) is tolerated in acute mania (McElroy et al., 1996). Manic patients may even tolerate loading doses of 30 mg/kg per day for one or two days, followed by 20 mg/kg per day. However, euthymic or depressed patients tend to tolerate aggressive initiation less well than manic patients. Thus, in less acute situations, such as the initiation of prophylaxis or adjunctive use, valproate is often started at 250 to 500 mg/day, and increased as necessary and tolerated, by 250 mg/day every four to seven days. Target doses are commonly between 750 to 2500 mg/day, yielding plasma levels from 50 to 125 mcg/mL (350–850 µM/L) (Bowden, Janicak et al., 1996), with the higher portion of the range used acutely, and lower doses used in prophylaxis or adjunctive therapy. In some cases, all or the majority of the drug can be given at night (Winsberg, DeGolia, Strong, & Ketter, 2001). Laboratory monitoring during valproate therapy commonly includes baseline studies, and re-evaluation of complete blood count, differential, platelets, and hepatic indices every 6 months (American Psychiatric Association, 1994). As with CBZ, most of the concerning hematological reactions occur in the first 3 months of therapy (Tohen et al., 1995). Plasma valproate concentrations are typically assessed at steady state, and then as indicated by inefficacy or adverse effects.

Valproate is extensively metabolized with less than 3% being excreted unchanged in the urine. There are three principal routes of elimination (Figure 12.3). Conjugations to inactive glucuronides and other inactive metabolites account for 50% of VPA disposition. In addition, about 40% undergoes β–oxidation in the mitochondria to several metabolites, including the desaturation product 2-ene-VPA which may contribute to the therapeutic effects of VPA. Preliminary evidence suggests that patients who experience weight gain on VPA may have higher levels of 2-ene-VPA, suggesting

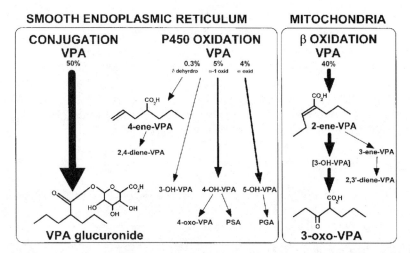

FIGURE 12.3. Valproate Metabolism. Metabolism of valproate (VPA) via microsomes on the smooth endoplasmic reticulum and via mitochondrial –oxidation. The thickness of the arrows and percentage figures roughly indicate the relative proportions going through various pathways. Adapted with permission from (Potter & Ketter, 1993). *Source:* W. Z. Potter & T. A. Ketter (1993, April). *Canadian Journal of Psychiatry, 38,* 551–556.

that dysfunction of the β–oxidation pathway (which metabolizes endogenous lipids) could play a role in this adverse effect (Gidal, Anderson, et al., 1994). About 10% of VPA undergoes cytochrome P450 oxidation reactions to a variety of metabolites including hydroxylation (3-OH-VPA, 4-OH-VPA, 5-OH-VPA), and subsequent ketone (4-oxo-VPA) and dicarboxylic acid {propylsuccinic acid (PSA) and propylglutaric acid (PGA)} products. In addition, the desaturation product, 4-ene-VPA, may be hepatotoxic and teratogenic. Induction of formation of this metabolite by enzyme inducing anticonvulsants could explain why these problems are a greater concern in combination therapies compared to VPA monotherapy.

Valproate has a somewhat more favorable therapeutic index than lithium or CBZ, with a lower incidence of neurotoxicity being an important advantage. This favorable therapeutic index, along with the existence of three principal metabolic pathways (Figure 12.3), may account for the fact that clinical drug–drug interactions yielding toxicity appear less prominent with VPA than with lithium or CBZ (Table 12.4). However, VPA does have some metabolic interactions with other drugs (Table 12.6) (Bourgeois, 1988). Valproate is a weak inhibitor of hepatic metabolism (including some P450 isoforms, epoxide hydrolase, and glucuronyl transferases), and can thus yield increased plasma concentrations of CBZ-E, phenobarbital, phenytoin,

TABLE 12.5
VPA Metabolic Drug Interactions

VPA →↑ DRUG	DRUG →↑ VPA	DRUG →↓ VPA
Amitriptyline	ASA	CBZ
CBZ-E	Cimetidine	± Lamotrigine
Diazepam	Fluoxetine	Mefloquine
Ethosuximide	Felbamate	Phenobarbital
Lamotrigine	Erythromycin	Phenytoin
Lorazepam	Phenothiazines	Rifampin
Nortriptyline		
Phenobarbital		
Phenytoin		
Zidovudine		

ethosuximide, felbamate, lamotrigine, tricyclic antidepressants, benzodiazepines, and zidovudine. In contrast to CBZ, VPA fails to alter bupropion levels (Ketter, Jenkins, et al., 1995). Enzyme inhibitors such as cimetidine (Webster et al., 1984), erythromycin (Redington, Wells, & Petito, 1992), phenothiazines (Ishizaki et al., 1984), fluoxetine (Sovner & Davis, 1991), and felbamate (Wagner et al., 1991) can yield increased VPA levels, while inducers such as CBZ (Levy, Morselli, et al., 1982), phenobarbital and phenytoin (Sackellares, Sato, Dreyfuss, & Penry, 1981), and rifampin (Bachmann & Jauregui, 1993) can yield decreased VPA levels. CBZ appears to induce VPA metabolism by increasing clearance via both the conjugation and cytochrome P450 oxidation routes (Levy, Morselli, et al., 1982). In contrast to the VPA plus CBZ combination, the VPA plus lithium combination lacks clinically significant pharmacokinetic interactions (Granneman, Schneck, Cavanaugh, & Witt, 1996).

Adverse effects with VPA include gastrointestinal disturbance; the divalproex sodium formulation is preferred as it yields this problem less often than valproic acid. Hepatic fatalities are of concern in infants with epilepsy receiving VPA along with enzyme-inducing agents, but rates for patients over 10 years of age are about 1/609,000 with VPA monotherapy, and about 1/28,000 when VPA is given with enzyme inducers (Bryant & Dreifuss, 1996). Valproate, like CBZ, is generally discontinued if hepatic indices rise above three times the upper limit of normal. Valproate-induced pancreatitis may occur in as many as one in 1000 patients, and is detectable by assessing serum amylase in patients with persistent or severe gastrointestinal problems.

Valproate can cause dose-related thrombocytopenia, particularly if plasma levels are above 100 mcg/mL (700 µM/L). Beta blockers can at-

TABLE 12.6
Treatment of Mood Stabilizer Adverse Effects

Adverse Effect	Management Options
General	Decrease/divide dose
	Change mood stabilizer
Gastrointestinal	Give with food
	Change to extended release if nausea or vomiting
	Change to suspension or immediate release if diarrhea
	Symptomatic relief with gastrointestinal agents
Weight Gain	Prior warning; diet; exercise
	Aggressively treat hyperphagic, anergic depression
	(e.g., add bupropion, thyroid)
	Add topiramate
Neurotoxicity	Dose at bedtime
	Gradual initiation (tolerance with Li and CBZ)
Tremor	Add propranolol; atenolol; pindolol
Hair loss	Add selenium 25–100 µg/day, zinc 10–50 mg/day
Polyuria	Single daily dose
	Add thiazide; amiloride; indomethacin
Thyroid	Thyroid replacement
Hepatic	Discontinue CBZ/VPA if hepatic indices > 3 x normal
Rash	Gradual initiation
	Limit other new antigens during initiation
	Dermatology consultation regarding desensitization
	(decrease dose, add antihistamine or prednisone)
Leukopenia	Add lithium
	Discontinue CBZ if WBC < 3000 or neutrophils < 1000
Hyponatremia	Add lithium, demeclocycline, doxycycline?

tenuate VPA-induced tremor. Valproate can cause weight gain, which can be approached in a fashion similar to that described above for lithium (Table 12.6). Limited data suggest that VPA-induced hair loss may be avoided or attenuated by the addition of selenium 25 to 100 mcg/day, or zinc 10 to 50 mg/day, presumably by counteracting VPA-induced depletion of these elements. A possible association between polycystic ovary disease and VPA therapy in epilepsy patients has been reported (Isojarvi, Laatikainen, Pakarinen, Juntuner, & Myllala, 1993). However, clinical observations suggest that polycystic ovary disease with VPA therapy in bipolar disorder patients is rare.

Valproate is a teratogen, yielding spina bifida in about 1% of cases. Folate supplementation may attenuate the risk, and ultrasound may allow early detection. The issue of VPA therapy in pregnancy can be approached in a fashion similar to that described above for lithium.

Antipsychotics

About 50% of patients with mania have psychotic symptoms, and bipolar depression may have psychotic features. Mood stabilizers may fail to provide adequate efficacy in such circumstances. Patients with acute mania with profound agitation may require parenteral medication, and patients with poor adherence may benefit from depot formulations. Unfortunately, mood stabilizers are not available in such formulations. Thus, due to both efficacy and formulation availability limitations of mood stabilizers, adjunctive antipsychotics are commonly used in the treatment of bipolar disorder patients.

TRADITIONAL ANTIPSYCHOTICS

Traditional antipsychotics block D2 dopamine receptors, with the degree of blockade correlating with antipsychotic effects. These agents are effective in the acute (Goodwin & Jamison, 1990) and prophylactic treatment of mania, and are useful adjuncts in the management of psychotic depression (Rothschild, 1996). Severe acute agitation may be treated with parenteral combinations such as haloperidol 0.2 mg/kg i.m., plus lorazepam 2 mg i.m., plus diphenhydramine 50 mg i.m. Lorazepam and diphenhydramine provide additional sedation, with the latter also attenuating the risk of acute extrapyramidal symptoms (EPS). Depot formulations of haloperidol and fluphenazine can prove useful in cases with poor medication compliance.

Traditional antipsychotics are generally well absorbed, with variable (20–80%) bioavailability, high (80–95%) protein binding, and variable volumes of distribution (10–40 L/kg), half-lives (12–24 hours), and clearances (70–600 mL/min). These agents have varying and in some cases complex metabolism, which is susceptible to induction by CBZ, phenobarbital, phenytoin, cigarettes, and rifampin. Several traditional antipsychotics (including haloperidol, perphenazine, and thioridazine) are CYP2D6 substrates, and hence susceptible to inhibition of metabolism. Thus, tricyclics, fluoxetine, beta blockers, and cimetidine can increase traditional antipsychotic blood levels. Some traditional antipsychotics (including haloperidol, fluphenazine, perphenazine, and thioridazine) are themselves CYP2D6 inhibitors, and may thus increase plasma levels of tricyclic antidepressants.

The role of traditional antipsychotics in the management of bipolar disorders is limited due to concerns over acute EPS (Nasrallah, Churchill, & Hamdan-Allan, 1988), tardive dyskinesia (Gelenberg & Jefferson, 1995; Kane & Smith, 1982), and induction of dysphoria (Ahlfors, Baastrup, et al., 1981). Thus, attempts are often made to taper and discontinue these drugs after resolution of acute episodes. Nevertheless, a substantial number of bipolar disorder patients may be maintained on antipsychotics on a chronic basis (Sernyak, Godleski, Griffin, Mazure, & Woods, 1997), during which these neurological adverse effects, as well as sedation and weight gain are major concerns. High potency antipsychotics may offer less sedation but more EPS, while molindone may cause less weight gain (Allison, Mentore et al., 1999). Recently, concerns have been raised around QTc prolongation with agents such as thioridazine and mesoridazine.

ATYPICAL ANTIPSYCHOTICS

Based on the novel efficacy profile, and lack of extrapyramidal symptoms and tardive dyskinesia seen with clozapine, a new generation of "atypical antipsychotics" has been developed. These agents block not only dopamine receptors (like the antimanic traditional antipsychotics) but also 5HT2 receptors (like the antidepressant nefazodone), and thus, depending on the relative size of these as well as other receptor blocking effects, could have antimanic, antidepressant, or even mood stabilizing properties. Clozapine appears effective in treatment-refractory bipolar disorder patients (Suppes et al., 1999), and double-blind placebo-controlled studies found adjunctive risperidone (Sachs & Ghaemi, 2000; Yatham, 2000), olanzapine monotherapy (Tohen et al., 1999; Tohen et al., 2000), and ziprasidone monotherapy (Keck & Ice, 2000) effective in acute mania. Emerging data suggest utility of quetiapine in bipolar disorder patients (Ghaemi & Katzow, 1999).

Clozapine blocks $5HT_{2A}$, $5HT_{1C}$, $5HT_3$, D_4, D_1, D_2, D_3, M_1, $alpha_1$, $alpha_2$, and H_1 receptors. It is well absorbed, with 70% bioavailability, 97% protein binding, a volume of distribution of 5 L/kg, a half-life of 12 hours, and clearance of 750 mL/min. Clozapine is commonly initiated at 25 to 50 mg per day and increased by 25 to 50 mg/day on a daily basis in inpatients, and on a weekly basis in outpatients, targeting final doses of 50 to 900 mg/ day in schizophrenia. In bipolar disorder patients, clozapine is often administered in doses from 50 to 500 mg/day, given all or mostly at bedtime, and commonly in combination with other medications.

Clozapine is a CYP1A2 more than CYP2D6 substrate, and thus its metabolism is decreased with fluoxetine, fluvoxamine, cimetidine, risperidone, and possibly VPA, and increased with cigarettes, CBZ, and phenytoin. The most serious adverse effect is agranulocytosis, which is seen in 1.3% of patients, and requires ongoing hematological monitoring. Seizures occur in 2% of patients on less than 300 mg/day, 4% on 300 to 600 mg/day, and 5% on 600 to 900 mg/day. Thus, combination with an anticonvulsant mood stabilizer could be desirable. Due to concerns regarding potential synergy of marrow toxicity with CBZ, combination with VPA is preferred. Other adverse effects include orthostatic hypotension, sedation, tachycardia, sialorrhea, dizziness, nausea, constipation, headache, fever, and weight gain.

Risperidone blocks $5HT_{2A}$, $5HT_{1A}$, D_1, D_2, alpha$_1$, alpha$_2$, and H_1 receptors. It is well absorbed, with 70% bioavailability, 90% protein binding, a moderate volume of distribution of 1 L/kg, a half-life of 6 hr in extensive CYP2D6 metabolizers, and 24 hr in poor CYP2D6 metabolizers, and clearance of 400 mL/min. Risperidone is commonly initiated at 1 to 2 mg per day and increased by 1 to 2 mg/day on a daily basis in inpatients and a weekly basis in outpatients, targeting final doses of 4 to 16 mg/day in schizophrenia. Double-blind controlled trials suggest the risperidone is an effective monotherapy (Segal, Benic, & Brook, 1998) or add-on therapy (Sachs, Ghaemi, 2000; Yatham, 2000) in mania. In bipolar disorder patients, risperidone is often administered in doses from 0.25 to 2 mg/day, given all or mostly at bedtime, and commonly in combination with other medications.

Risperidone is a CYP2D6 substrate, and thus CYP2D6 inhibitors may decrease its metabolism. Dose-related EPS are particularly evident above 6 mg/day. Seizures occur in 0.3% of patients. Other adverse effects include orthostatic hypotension, sedation, dizziness, rhinitis, constipation, tachycardia, QT prolongation, amenorrhea, galactorrhea, decreased libido and sexual function, and weight gain. Mania induction or exacerbation has been occasionally reported with risperidone, but occurred no more often than with placebo in controlled adjunctive trials (Sachs & Ghaemi, 2000; Yatham, 2000).

Olanzapine blocks $5HT_{2A}$, $5HT_{2C}$, $5HT_3$, $5HT_6$, D_4, D_3, D_1, D_2, M_1-M_5, alpha$_1$, and H_1 receptors, and is a $5HT_{1A}$ agonist. It is well absorbed, with 93% protein binding, a large volume of distribution of 15 L/kg, a half-life of 30 hr, and clearance of 400 mL/min. Olanzapine is commonly initiated at 5 to 20 mg/day and increased to final doses of 5 to 20 mg/day in schizophrenia. Olanzapine monotherapy was effective in mania two double-blind placebo-controlled trials (Tohen et al., 1999; Tohen et al., 2000). In bipolar disorder patients, olanzapine is often administered in similar doses, all or mostly at bedtime, and commonly in combination with other medications. Some nonpsychotic bipolar disorder patients may obtain benefits and require doses as low as 0.625 mg/day (one quarter of a 2.5 mg tablet) (Ketter, Winsberg, Wang, Tate, & String, 1999). Patients who are cutting tablets should be advised to cut only one tablet at a time because cutting accelerates deterioration of the medicine.

Olanzapine is a CYP1A2 substrate, and thus its metabolism is increased with CBZ and cigarettes, and decreased with fluvoxamine. Seizures occur in 0.9% of patients. Other adverse effects include orthostatic hypotension, sedation, dizziness, constipation, transaminase elevation, and weight gain. Exacerbation of agitation or mania has been rarely reported, but occurred no more often than with placebo in controlled trials.

Quetiapine blocks D_1, D_2, $5HT_{2A}$, $5HT_{1A}$, α_1, α_2, H_1, and sigma receptors. It is well absorbed and 100% bioavailable, with 83% protein binding, a large volume of distribution of 10 L/kg, and a short half-life of 6 hr. Quetiapine is commonly initiated at 50 to 100 mg per day in two or three divided doses, and increased to final doses of 50 to 750 mg/day in schizophrenia. There is limited experience with quetiapine in bipolar disorder patients (Sajatovic, Brescan, Perez, Digiovani, & Hattab, 1999), but it tends to be given in lower doses, mostly at bedtime, and in combination with other medications. Some nonpsychotic bipolar disorder patients may obtain benefits and require doses as low as 6.25 mg/day (one quarter of a 25 mg tablet) (T. A. Ketter, personal observation, 2000).

Quetiapine is a CYP3A4 substrate, and its metabolism is increased with phenytoin, thioridazine, and probably CBZ. Quetiapine increases warfarin plasma levels. As expected, quetiapine does not affect plasma lithium levels. Benign leukopenia occurs in three percent of patients. Other adverse effects include sedation, insomnia, agitation, tachycardia, headache, and weight gain. Concern regarding the development of cataracts in animals has led to a recommendation of ophthalmological examinations, but the risk in humans appears to be low (Nasrallah, Dev, Rak, & Raniwalla, 1999).

Ziprasidone blocks $5HT_{2A}$, $5HT_{1A}$, $5HT_{2C}$, $5HT_{1D}$, D_2, alpha$_1$, and H_1 receptors, and is a 5HT and NE reuptake inhibitor. It is metabolized by CYP3A4, and can cause somnolence, headache, dizziness, akathisia, but is apparently not associated with weight gain. Concerns have been raised around the potential of this agent to cause QTc prolongation. A double blind placebo controlled trial found ziprasidone monotherapy effective in the treatment of mania (Keck & Ice, 2000).

Antidepressants

Mood stabilizers offer better antimanic than antidepressant effects and thus adjunctive antidepressant therapy is commonly used in treating bipolar disorder patients. Antidepressants are administered with care, and in many cases for relatively brief periods, as these agents can induce mania, hypomania, mixed states, and cycle acceleration.

SPECIFIC SEROTONIN REUPTAKE INHIBITORS

Specific serotonin reuptake inhibitors (SSRIs) act primarily by blockade of synaptic serotonin uptake, but have a variety of secondary effects which confer these agents with some variability in therapeutic and adverse effects. These drugs have displaced tricyclic antidepressants as first line therapies for depression due to their superior adverse effect profiles, safety in overdose, and in some instances, broader range of therapeutic effects. Serotonin reuptake inhibitors are commonly added to mood stabilizers in the treatment of bipolar depression, although this has only been systematically studied to a limited extent (Cohn, Collins, Ashbrook, & Wernucke, 1989; Simpson & DePaulo, 1991; Nemeroff et al., 2001). SSRIs are generally well absorbed with variable (fluvoxamine 53% to citalopram 80%) bioavailability, high (fluvoxamine 80% to sertraline 98%) protein binding, and variable volumes of distribution (citalopram 12 to fluoxetine up to 45 L/kg), half-lives (fluvoxamine 16 hr to fluoxetine 4 days), metabolite half-lives (norfluoxetine up to seven days), and clearances (fluoxetine 300 to fluvoxamine 1600 mL/min).

Manufacturers have emphasized pharmacokinetic and drug interaction differences among these agents. Serotonin reuptake inhibitors are metabolized by varying CYP450 isoforms, including CYP2D6 (fluoxetine, paroxetine), and CYP3A3/4 (sertraline, citalopram); and they can inhibit CYP2D6 (fluoxetine, paroxetine, sertraline), CYP3A3/4 (fluoxetine, sertraline, fluvoxamine), CYP2C19 (fluoxetine), and CYP1A2 and CYP2C9 (fluvoxamine). Serotonin reuptake inhibitors can thus be targets as well as instigators of CYP450-mediated drug interactions. The most prominent clinical concerns have been raised with agents which inhibit CYP2D6 and CYP3A3/4, thus increasing plasma levels of substrates of these isoforms. Administration of monoamine oxidase inhibitors (MAOIs) and SSRIs within 2 weeks of one another (in the case of fluoxetine a 5-week wait before starting MAOIs) is avoided due to potential fatal pharmacodynamic interactions, possibly related to induction of hyperserotonergic states. Decreased libido and sexual function are common with SSRIs. Various strategies used in treating (unipolar) major depressive disorder patients with these problems may be attempted. Occasional patients treated chronically with these agents can experience weight gain. Serotonin reuptake inhibitors's calming effects may be welcome in anxious patients but may become oversedating in anergic patients. Mania induction can occur, but may be less of an issue than with tricyclic antidepressants (Stoll, Mayer, et al., 1994).

BUPROPION AND ATYPICAL ANTIDEPRESSANTS

A variety of newer antidepressants with diverse mechanisms of action have been introduced. In general, these agents have favorable adverse effect profiles compared to tricyclic antidepressants, and some do not cause the sexual difficulties encountered with SSRIs.

Bupropion has nonserotonergic, presumably dopaminergic/noradrenergic, mechanism(s), is commonly used in treating bipolar depression, and has the advantage of helping with smoking cessation. Bupropion is well absorbed, 85% protein bound, and has a large volume of distribution of 20 L/kg, a half-life of 21 hours, and a clearance of 2300 mL/min. It is metabolized by CYP2B6 and can inhibit CYP2D6. Carbamazepine dramatically decreases bupropion and increases (active) metabolite levels. Administration within 2 weeks of MAOIs should be avoided. Bupropion is generally well tolerated, and lacks the sexual and weight gain problems seen with SSRIs. Its energizing effects may be welcome in anergic patients, but over-stimulating in anxious patients. The sustained release formulation of bupropion is preferred, as given in divided doses up to 300 mg per day, it decreases the risk of seizures to 0.1%. Bupropion may be less likely than tricyclic antidepressants to cause switches into mania (Sachs, Lafer, et al., 1994).

Venlafaxine has dual serotonergic plus noradrenergic mechanisms, and may be effective in treatment refractory depression and bipolar depression (Amsterdam, 1998). Venlafaxine is only 27% protein bound, and has a volume of distribution of 8 L/kg, a half-life of five hours, and a clearance of 1400 mL/min. The extended release formulation is preferred in view of the brief half-life of immediate release venlafaxine. Venlafaxine is metabolized by CYP2D6, and has minimal effects on CYP450 isoforms. Administration within two weeks of MAOIs should be avoided. Venlafaxine has SSRI-like adverse effects as well as the ability to increase blood pressure at higher doses as its noradrenergic effects become more evident. The limited experience with this agent in bipolar depression suggests that mania induction can occur, perhaps at a rate similar to SSRIs and bupropion.

Trazodone blocks $5HT_1$, $5HT_2$, and α_2 receptors, and has more prominent sedative than antidepressant properties, and thus is commonly used as an adjunctive hypnotic agent in (unipolar) major depressive disorder and in bipolar disorder. It is well absorbed, and has 80% bioavailability, 90% protein binding, a moderate volume of distribution of 1 L/kg, a half-life of four hours, and a clearance of 120 to 200 mL/min. Trazodone has few metabolic drug-drug interactions. It is typically given in doses of 50 mg to 200 mg at bedtime. The main adverse effect is sedation. Perhaps due to its modest antidepressant effects, the practice of low dose adjunctive trazodone does not appear clinically to carry much in the way of risk of inducing manic switches, but this issue has not been systematically explored.

Nefazodone blocks $5HT_1$, $5HT_2$, and α_2 receptors and serotonin uptake. There are limited data regarding its use in bipolar disorders. It is well absorbed, has only 20% bioavailability, and 99% protein binding, a low volume of distribution of 0.5 L/kg, a short half-life of 3 hr, and a clearance of 500 to 2000 mL/min. Nefazodone is a CYP3A3/4 substrate and inhibitor, and thus can increase plasma levels of CYP3A3/4 substrates such as alprazolam, triazolam, and CBZ. Nefazodone labeling includes contraindications to combination with terfenadine, astemizole, cisapride, and pimozide out of concern that elevated levels of these CYP3A3/4 substrates will yield potentially fatal cardiac adverse events. It is recommended not to administer nefazodone within 2 weeks of MAOIs. Nefazodone is typically given in doses of 300 to 600 mg, with the bulk of the dose at bedtime. Nefazodone does not cause sexual problems, and its most prominent adverse effects are sedation, dry mouth, and gastrointestinal disturbance. Mania induction has been reported with this drug, but limited experience precludes assessment of this risk relative to other agents.

Mirtazapine blocks α_2, $5HT_2$, $5HT_3$, and H_1 receptors, and there are limited data regarding its use in bipolar disorders. It has only 50% bioavailability, and is 85% protein bound, with a volume of distribution of 4 L/kg, a half-life of 30 hours, and a clearance of 500 mL/min. Mirtazapine is a CYP2D6, more than CYP1A2 or CYP3A4, substrate and is not a clinically significant enzyme inhibitor. Administration within 2 weeks of MAOIs should be avoided. Adverse effects include sedation, dizziness, weight gain, cholesterol increases, 0.1% agranulocytosis, and 2% transaminase elevation above three times the upper limit of normal. Mania induction has been reported, but limited experience precludes assessment of this risk relative to other agents.

MONOAMINE OXIDASE INHIBITORS

Monoamine oxidase inhibitors (MAOIs) block the metabolism of serotonin, norepinephrine, and dopamine. Older agents such as phenelzine, tranylcypromine, and isocarboxazid inhibit both MAO-A and MAO-B irreversibly and are thus called irreversible MAOIs, while newer agents such as moclobemide are reversible inhibitors of monoamine oxidase-A (RIMAs).

Irreversible MAOIs are potent antidepressants, effective in treating refractory depression and bipolar depression (Thase et al., 1992). They have brief half-lives which are not directly related to their clinical effects, presumably due to the irreversible nature of their MAO inhibition, which provides a MAO deficit until a sufficient amount of new enzyme is produced (about 2 weeks). Thus, foods and drugs incompatible with MAOIs must not be ingested within 2 weeks of discontinuing MAOIs. In addition, MAOIs should not be initiated within about 5 (parent or metabolite, which ever is greater) half-lives after discontinuing incompatible medications. For most drugs, this means waiting about 2 weeks. However, after discontinuing drugs with long half-lives, or metabolite half-lives, such as fluoxetine, up to 5 weeks should elapse prior to starting MAOIs. Irreversible MAOIs have complex and incompletely characterized metabolism, which has a "suicide" inhibition component, whereby they are inactivated by covalently bonding to monoamine oxidase. These drugs have serious and potentially fatal interactions with a variety of high tyramine foods such as aged meats, cheese, Chianti wine, and fava beans; and drugs such as SSRIs, clomipramine, venlafaxine, stimulants, decongestants, and opiates. They appear compatible with lithium, VPA, antipsychotics, trazodone, and anxiolytics. Although concerns have been raised around combining these agents with CBZ, limited evidence suggests this may be tolerated and confers benefit in some treatment-refractory bipolar disorder patients (Ketter, Post, et al., 1995). Irreversible MAOIs can cause sedation, sleep fragmentation, orthostasis, gastrointestinal disturbance, urinary retention, decreased libido and sexual function. Irreversible MAOIs, compared to tricyclic antidepressants, may be more effective in bipolar depression and less likely to trigger severe manic switches (Thase, Mallinger, McKnight, & Himmelhoch, 1992).

RIMAs, such as moclobemide, may have more modest antidepressant effects than reversible MAOIs, but have shown utility in bipolar depression (Angst & Stabl, 1992). Moclobemide is a benzamide derivative, which inhibits MAO-A for about 24 hours. It is well absorbed with 90% bioavailability, and has low 50% protein binding, a moderate volume of distribution of 1 L/kg, and a short half-life of two hours, which increases with escalating doses. Moclobemide is a CYP2C19 substrate and inhibits CYP1A2, CYP2C19, and CYP2D6. Unlike irreversible MAOIs, moclobemide lacks serious interactions with high tyramine foods. However, caution is still necessary with respect to some the of drug-drug interactions described for irreversible MAOIs. Coadministration with SSRIs, venlafaxine, or irreversible MAOIs should be avoided. Moclobemide can cause dry mouth, headache, sedation, gastrointestinal disturbance, and sleep fragmentation, but not sexual problems or orthostasis. Mania induction has been reported, but limited experience precludes assessment of this risk relative to other agents.

TRICYCLIC ANTIDEPRESSANTS

Tricyclic antidepressants (TCAs) block reuptake of serotonin and norepinephrine to varying degrees, and in the past were first line agents in the treatment of (unipolar) major depressive disorder. TCAs are generally well absorbed, and have variable (20–70%) bioavailability, high (90%) protein binding, half-lives around 24 hours, and variable volumes of distribution (10 to 30 L/kg), and clearances (300 to 1700 mL/min). Hydroxylation by CYP2D6 is the rate-limiting metabolic step, and thus plasma TCA levels rise with CYP2D6 inhibitors such as fluoxetine, sertraline, paroxetine, haloperidol, methadone, propafenone, and quinidine. TCA plasma levels can also rise with methylphenidate, disulfiram, acute ethanol, hormonal contraceptives, cimetidine, chloramphenicol, and possibly VPA and azole antifungals, although the mechanism(s) of these phenomena are less clear. Tricyclic antidepressants levels fall with CBZ, phenobarbital, phenytoin, chronic ethanol, cigarettes, and possibly rifampin. Administration within two weeks of MAOIs is generally avoided. Tricyclic antidepressant therapy is generally considered a low priority strategy in treating bipolar depression due to adverse effects (sedation, anticholinergic, and orthostasis), danger in overdose, and TCAs being the agents most implicated in causing manic switches (Altshuler et al., 1995).

Benzodiazepines

Benzodiazepines (BZs) modulate $GABA_A$ receptor function, and produce anxiolytic and hypnotic effects. Patients with bipolar disorders commonly have comorbid anxiety disorders, and may need more anxiolytic and sedative effects than those obtained with mood stabilizers. Thus, adjunctive BZs are commonly used in the management of bipolar disorders. These agents are well absorbed, 95% protein bound, have moderate volumes of distribution around 1 L/kg, and have half-lives which are short (less than 6 hr with triazolam, clorazepate, and flurazepam), intermediate (6–20 hr with alprazolam, lorazepam, oxazepam, and temazepam), and long (more than 20 hr with diazepam and clonazepam).

The 2-keto-BZs, clorazepate, diazepam, and flurazepam, are metabolized by CYP2C19 and CYP3A3/4. Plasma levels of these agents are decreased by cigarettes, barbiturates, and rifampin; and increased by fluoxetine, fluvoxamine, disulfiram, hormonal contraceptives, ketoconazole, cimetidine, isoniazid, omeprazole, and propranolol. The triazolo-BZs alprazolam and triazolam are metabolized by CYP3A3/4. Plasma levels of these agents are decreased by CBZ, and increased by fluoxetine, fluvoxamine, nefazodone, diltiazem, hormonal contraceptives, ketoconazole, cimetidine, erythromycin, and propoxyphene. The 7-nitro-BZs, clonazepam and nitrazepam, and the 3-hydroxy-BZs lorazepam, oxazepam, and temazepam are metabolized by robust N-reduction and conjugation reactions, respectively, and are less prone to pharmacokinetic drug interactions.

Although BZs are generally safe in acute treatment, with sedation, memory problems, incoordination, and occasional disinhibition being the main adverse effects, with chronic use concerns around abuse, tolerance, and withdrawal arise. Thus, efforts are made to make BZ exposure brief and to find alternative agents such as trazodone for insomnia, or gabapentin for anxiety. In some patients, very low dose (0.625 mg) olanzapine may allow tapering or discontinuation of BZs (Ketter, Winsberg, et al., 1999). Nevertheless, some patients with comorbid anxiety disorders may need, tolerate, and responsibly use adjunctive BZs on a chronic basis. Benzodiazepines do not commonly trigger manic switches, although concern has been raised around alprazolam at the level of case reports, in view of its putative modest antidepressant effects.

Newer Aniticonvulsants

A series of newer anticonvulsants have been recently marketed (Dichter & Brodie, 1996). Compared to older anticonvulsants, several of the new medications have enhanced tolerability, simpler kinetics, and fewer drug–drug interactions. These drugs have a variety of mechanisms, including enhancing neural inhibition by increasing GABAergic function, and/or decreasing neural excitation by decreasing glutamatergic function (Macdonald & Kelly, 1995). Such agents could yield psychotropic effects as these amino acid neurotransmitters have been implicated in psychiatric disorders (Garland Bunney, Bunney, & Carlsson, 1995; Lloyd, Zivkovic, Scatten, Marselli, & Bartholmi, 1989; Petty, 1995). The psychotropic profiles of these new anticonvulsants have not yet been fully characterized, but important kinetic differences between them have already emerged.

FELBAMATE

The use of felbamate (FBM) is restricted to patients with refractory epilepsy due to its associations with aplastic anemia and fatal hepatitis (Leppik, 1995a; Pennell, Ogaily, & MacDonald, 1995). However, FBM is of considerable theoretical interest in view of its novel mechanisms, pharmacokinetics, and psychiatric effects. Felbamate has a dicarbamate structure similar to meprobamate, and several mechanisms which include sodium channel blockade, modest GABAergic, and more robust antiglutamatergic actions (Palmer & McTavish, 1993). FBM appears to possess a novel stimulantlike psychotropic profile in epilepsy patients (Ketter, Malow, et al., 1996).

GABAPENTIN

Gabapentin (GBP) has a structure similar to gamma-aminobutyric acid (GABA), increases nonsynaptic GABA release from glia, is a substrate and a competitive inhibitor of the large (L) neutral amino acid carrier system, and may modulate (but does not directly block) sodium channels (Taylor, 1995). Gabapentin has an anxiolytic preclinical profile. Emerging data indicate that open GBP augmentation (McElroy, Soutullo, Kecic, & Kmetz, 1997; Marcotte, Fogelman, Wolfe, & Nemine, 1997; Ryback, Brodsky, & Munasifi, 1997; Schaffer & Schaffer, 1997; Young, Robb, Patelis-Siotis, MacDonald, & Joffe, 1997a) is well tolerated and may help some patients with mood disorders. Controlled data suggest efficacy in social phobia (Pande et al., 1999) and panic disorder (Pande, Crockatt, Janney, Weth, & Tsaroucha, 1998), but are less encouraging in acute mania (Pande et al., 2000) and treatment-refractory rapid cycling bipolar disorder (Frye et al., 2000).

Gabapentin has saturable absorption (Stewart, Kugler, Thompson, & Bockbrader, 1993) and a bioavailability of 60%, which declines further if individual doses are greater than 900 mg. Thus, many patients may need to take divided doses of GBP. Like lithium, GBP is not bound to plasma proteins, has moderate volume of distribution of about 1 L/kg, is not metabolized, and is 100% excreted in the urine. Gabapentin has a half-life of about six hours and a clearance similar to that of creatinine (120 mL/min, similar to the glomerular filtration rate), so that increased physical activity may increase GBP clearance (Borchert, 1996) in a fashion similar to lithium. Gabapentin levels could thus fall with the increase in activity seen in hypomania or mania. Gabapentin can be rapidly initiated in epilepsy patients with 300 mg, 600 mg, and 900 mg on the first, second and third days. Final GBP doses usually range between 900 mg/day and an approved maximum of 3600 mg/day in three or four divided doses. Lower doses have been reported to benefit some patients with bipolar disorders (Schaffer & Schaffer, 1997). As GBP is excreted unchanged in the urine and lacks effects on metabolism, it appears to lack hepatically mediated drug–drug interactions (Richens, 1993). Preliminary evidence suggests that GBP also fails to alter lithium kinetics (Frye, Kimbrell, et al., 1998b).

Gabapentin is generally well tolerated, but can cause sedation, dizziness, ataxia, fatigue, and weight gain (Goa & Sorkin, 1993). Some evidence suggests that it can cause behavioral deterioration in some pediatric epilepsy patients who also suffer from cognitive or behavioral disorders (Lee et al., 1996).

LAMOTRIGINE

Lamotrigine (LTG) has a phenyltriazine structure and is a sodium channel and weak $5HT_3$ receptor blocker (this ionotropic receptor gates a cation channel), and decreases glutamate release (Leach, Lees, & Roddall, 1995). Of interest, the latter property is also observed with the mood stabilizing anticonvulsants CBZ and oxcarbazepine (Waldmeier et al., 1995). Moreover, lamotrigine appears to inhibit reuptake of serotonin. Lamotrigine has anxiolytic activity in the Vögel (anticonflict) animal model (Critchley, 1994). In placebo controlled trials, LTG appeared effective in bipolar depression (Calabrese et al., 1999), rapid cycling bipolar disorder (Calabrese et al., 2000), and treatment refractory rapid cycling bipolar disorder (Frye et al., 2000).

Lamotrigine has a bioavailability of about 98%. It is 55% bound to plasma proteins, and has a moderate volume of distribution of about 1 L/kg. In monotherapy its half-life is about 28 hr and clearance is about 40 mL/min. Combined with the enzyme inducer CBZ, LTG's half-life falls 50% to about 14 hours and clearance doubles to about 80 mL/min. Combined with the enzyme inhibitor VPA, LTG's half-life doubles to about 56 hr, and clearance falls 50% to about 20 mL/min.

Dosage is initially titrated *very slowly* in order to decrease the risk of rash. When added to VPA, LTG is started at 12.5 mg/day for 2 weeks, then 25 mg/day for the next 2 weeks, and then increased as necessary and tolerated by 25 mg/day each week with a final dose often around 100 mg/day and, maximum dose of about 200 mg/day in two divided doses. When given without VPA, LTG is started at 25 mg/day for 2 weeks, then 50 mg/day for the next 2 weeks, and then increased as necessary and tolerated by 25 to 50 mg/day each week with final doses often around 200 mg/day, and a maximum dose of 500 mg/day. When given with CBZ, LTG is started at 50 mg/day for 2 weeks, then 100 mg/day for the next 2 weeks, and then increased as necessary and tolerated by 100 mg/day each week with a recommended maximum dose of 500 mg/day.

About 85% of LTG is conjugated to yield inactive glucuronide metabolites, while about 10% is excreted unchanged in the urine. As indicated by the above kinetic data, enzyme inducers such as CBZ can decrease LTG levels, while VPA (Rambeck & Wolf, 1993) and possibly sertraline (Kaufman & Gerner, 1997) can increase LTG levels. These interactions are possibly due to induction and competitive inhibition of glucuronidation, respectively. In addition, LTG may yield modest (25%) decreases in VPA levels, and may exacerbate the neurotoxic effects of CBZ. The latter appears to be a pharmacodynamic interaction, although equivocal evidence suggests that LTG could yield this effect by increasing levels of CBZ-E.

Lamotrigine can cause a rash in 10% of patients, and serious rash in 1/ 1000 patients. Risk factors for rash include rapid initial dose escalation, concurrent VPA, and age less than 16 years. As these rashes are potentially serious, they require discontinuation of the drug. Otherwise, LTG is generally well tolerated, but can cause dizziness, ataxia, headache, sedation, tremor, and nausea. Of potential clinical interest, LTG may be less likely than other anticonvulsants to cause sexual dysfunction (Carwile, Husain, Miller, & Radice, 1997).

TOPIRAMATE

Topiramate (TPM) is a fructopyranose sulfamate which blocks sodium channels (Sombati, Coulter, & DeLorenzo, 1995) and AMPA/kainate gated ion channels (Severt, Coulter, Sombati, & DeLorenzo, 1995). Topiramate also positively modulates $GABA_A$ receptors (Gordey, Delorey, & Olsen, 1995), and inhibits carbonic anhydrase (Shank, Gardocki, et al., 1994). Preliminary open data suggest utility in bipolar disorders (Calabrese, Shelton, et al., 1998; Marcotte, 1998; McElroy, 2000), but at initial double-blind placebo controlled monotherapy study in mania had equivocal results.

Topiramate has a bioavailability of 80%, is 15% bound to plasma proteins, has saturable binding to erythrocytes (which contain carbonic anhydrase) which correlates with hematocrit (Gidal, Lensmeyer, & Pitterle, 1997), and has a moderate volume of distribution of about 0.8 L/kg. Topiramate has a half-life of about 24 hr, and a clearance of about 25 mL/min. TPM is started at 50 mg/day and increased by 50 mg/day each week with a recommended maximum dose of 400 mg/day in two divided doses. In epilepsy studies, doses up to 1000 mg/day did not improve responses compared to those seen with doses of 400 mg/day. During monotherapy, TPM is 70% excreted unchanged in the urine, however, when combined with enzyme inducers, this figure falls to about 50%. Thus, CBZ decreases TPM plasma levels (Gisclon, Curtin, Kravmev, Sachdeo, & Levy, 1994; Sachdeo et al., 1996). The enzyme(s) responsible for the metabolic component of TPM elimination, and the mechanism of CBZ induction of TPM metabolism, remain to be characterized.

Topiramate is generally well tolerated, but can cause sedation, fatigue, and psychomotor slowing. TPM may cause problems with concentration and word finding in 13 to 72% of epilepsy patients, and appears associated with renal calculi in one to two percent of epilepsy patients, presumably due to carbonic anhydrase inhibition (Shorvon, 1996). Depression has been reported in five percent to seventeen percent of epilepsy patients treated with TPM. Topiramate can cause weight loss (McElroy et al., 2000), a potentially useful effect, given that many agents used in the treatment of bipolar disorders cause weight gain.

TIAGABINE

Tiagabine (TGB) is a nipecotic acid derivative, which inhibits GABA reuptake in neurons and glial cells (Suzdak & Jansen, 1995). As TGB was recently marketed, there are few data currently available regarding its psychotropic effects, some suggesting benefit in bipolar disorders (Kaufman, 1998; Schaffer & Schaffer, 1999), and other suggesting lack of efficacy in mania (Grunze et al., 1999). Given the utility of other GABAergic anticonvulsants in mood disorders, and the novel mechanism of action of this agent, it is anticipated that further clinical research of the effects of this drug in mood disorders will soon accumulate.

Tiagabine is well absorbed with a bioavailability of about 90%, and is 96% bound to plasma proteins. In monotherapy TGB has a half-life of about 8 hours and clearance of about 110 mL/min, and with enzyme inducers the half-life falls to about 4 hr and clearance doubles to about 220 mL/min. In patients also taking enzyme inducers, TGB is typically initiated at 4 mg/ day and increased by 4 mg/day each week as tolerated with an approved maximum dose of 56 mg/day in two to four divided doses. Lower doses may be required in patients not taking concurrent enzyme inducers. TGB is a CYP3A substrate. It is extensively transformed into inactive 5-oxo-tiagabine and glucuronide metabolites, with only 2% being excreted unchanged in the urine (Brodie, 1995). The remainder is excreted as metabolites in the feces (65%) and the urine (25%). CBZ decreases plasma TGB concentrations, possibly by induction of CYP3A. In contrast, VPA appears to displace TGB from protein binding sites yielding an increase in free TGB. TGB yields modest (10%) decreases in VPA levels.

Tiagabine appears to be generally well tolerated, but can cause dizziness, fatigue, sedation, tremor, weakness, and gastrointestinal disturbance (Leppik, 1995b). Rapid loading resulted in pronounced adverse effects in two of eight mania patients (nausea and vomiting in one and a generalized tonic–clonic seizure in the other) (Grunze et al., 1999).

OXCARBAZEPINE, LEVETIRACETAM, AND ZONISAMIDE

In 2000 these three new anticonvulsants were marketed in the United States. Their utility in the treatment of bipolar disorders remains to be assessed.

Conclusion

Effective pharmacotherapy of bipolar disorder patients requires not only familiarity with mood stabilizer pharmacodynamics, dosing, pharmacokinetics, drug interactions, adverse effects, and their management, but also similar knowledge of antipsychotics, antidepressants, benzodiazepines, and increasingly the newer anticonvulsants. In the past clinicians have relied on observational drug interaction information, but recent characterization of substrates, inhibitors and inducers of drug metabolism now allows not only the development of mechanistic models, but also enhanced anticipation and avoidance of clinical drug–drug interactions (Table 12.7). These developments promise to yield safer and more effective therapeutics when psychotropics are combined with one another in treatment of patients with bipolar disorders.

TABLE 12.7
Substrates, Inhibitors, and Inducers of Some Important Cytochrome P450 Isoforms

CYP	CYP1A2	CYP2C9/10	CYP2C19[1]	CYP2D6[1]	CYP2E1	CYP3A/4
% of all CYP[2]	13	20 (for all 2C)	20 (for all 2C)	2	7	30 (for all 3A)
S U B S T R A T E S	3° amine TCAs (N-demethylation) clozapine (major) olanzapine caffeine methadone tacrine acetaminophen phenacetin propranolol theophylline	THC NSAIDs phenytoin (major) tolbutamide S-warfarin	citalopram (partly) moclobemide 3° amine TCAs (N-demethylation) diazepam (N-demethylation) hexobarbital mephobarbital lansoprazole omeprazole (5-hydroxylation) rabeprazole (demethylation) phenytoin (minor) S-mephenytoin nelfinavir	fluoxetine (partly) mirtazapine (partly) paroxetine venlafaxine (O-demethylation) 2° & 3° amine TCAs (2,8,10-hyroxylation) trazodone clozapine (minor) haloperidol (reduction) fluphenazine perphenazine risperidone sertindole thioridazine codeine (hydroxylation, O-demethylation) dextromethorphan	ethanol acetaminophen chlorzoxazone halothane isoflurane methoxyflurane sevoflurane	amiodarone disopyramide lidocaine propafenone quinidine erythromycin (macrolides) androgens dexamethasone estrogens (steroids) astemizol loratadine terfenadine lovastatin simvastatin atorvastatin cerivastatin (HMG-CoAR Inhib) carbamazepine alprazolam diazepam (hydroxylation & N-demethylation) midazolam triazolam zolpidem buspirone citalopram (partly) mirtazapine (partly) nefazodone reboxetine sertraline 3° amine TCAs (N-demethylation) sertindole quetiapine ziprasidone

TABLE 12.7
Continued

CYP	CYP1A2	CYP2C9/10	CYP2C19	CYP2D6[1]	CYP2E1	CYP3A3/4
SUBSTRATES				O-demethylation) hydrocodone oxycodone mexiletine propafenone (1C antiarrhythmics) beta blockers donepezil (partly) d- & l- fenfluramine		diltiazem felodipine nimodipine nifedipine nisoldipine nitrendipine verapamil acetaminophen alfentanil codeine (demethylation) fentanyl sufentanil ethosuximide tiagabine cyclophosphamide tamoxifen vincristine vinblastine ifosfamide cyclosporine tacrolimus cisapride donepezil (partly) lovastatin omeprazole / rabeprazole (sulfonation) protease inhibitors sildenafil
INHIBITORS	fluvoxamine moclobemide cimetidine fluoroquinolones	fluvoxamine disulfiram amiodarone	fluoxetine fluvoxamine imipramine moclobemide tranylcypromine	bupropion fluoxetine fluvoxamine (weak) hydroxybupropion paroxetine	diethyldithio- carbamate (disulfiram metabolite)	fluoxetine fluvoxamine nefazodone s ertraline (weak) clarithromycin erythromycin troleandomycin (macrolides)

	INHIBITORS[1]					
	(ciprofloxacin, norfloxacin); naringenin (grapefruit); ticlopidine	azapropazone; d-propoxyphene; fluconazole; fluvastatin; miconazole; phenylbutazone; stiripentol; sulphaphenazole; zafirlukast	diazepam; felbamate; phenytoin; topiramate; cimetidine; omeprazole	sertraline (weak); moclobemide; fluphenazine; haloperidol; perphenazine; thioridazine; amiodarone; cimetidine; methadone; quinidine; ritonavir	diltiazem; verapamil; dexamethasone; gestodene	fluconazole; itraconazole; ketoconazole (azole antifungals); ritonavir; indinavir (protease inhibs); amiodarone; cimetidine; mibefradil; naringenin (grapefruit)
INDUCERS	tobacco; omeprazole	rifampin	rifampin	ethanol; isoniazid	dexamethasone; rifampin; troglitazone	carbamazepine; barbiturates; phenobarbital; phenytoin; St. John's wort

Source: Adapted from T. A. Ketter et al. *Journal of Clinical Psychopharmacology* (1995), 15, 387–398.

[1] clinically significant human polymorphism reported.

[2] CYP %s from Shimada, Yamazaki, Mimura, Inui, & Guengerich (1994).

References

American Psychiatric Association. (1994). Practice guideline for the treatment of patients with bipolar disorder. *American Journal of Psychiatry, 151,* 1–36.

Ahlfors, U. G., Baastrup, P. C., Dencker, S. J., Elgen, K., Lingjaerde, O., Pedersen, V., et al. (1981). Flupenthixol decanoate in recurrent manic-depressive illness: A comparison with lithium. *Acta Psychiatrica Scandinavia, 64,* 226–237.

Albani, F., Riva, R., & Baruzzi, A. (1993). Clarithromycin-carbamazepine interaction: A case report. *Epilepsia, 34,* 161–162.

Allison, D. B., Mentore, J. L., Heo, M., Chandler, L. P., Cappelleri, J. C., Infante, M. C., et al. (1999). Antipsychotic-induced weight gain: A comprehensive research synthesis. *American Journal of Psychiatry, 156,* 1686–1696.

Altshuler, L. L., Post, R. M., Leverich, G. S., Mikalauskas, K., Rosoff, A., & Ackerman, L. (1995). Antidepressant-induced mania and cycle acceleration: a controversy revisited. *American Journal of Psychiatry, 152,* 1130–1138.

Amsterdam, J. (1998). Efficacy and safety of venlafaxine in the treatment of bipolar II major depressive episode. *Journal of Clinical Psychopharmacology, 18,* 414–417.

Andersen, B. B., Mikkelsen, M., Vesterager, A., Dam, M., Kristensen, H. B., Pedersen, B., et al. (1991). No influence of the antidepressant paroxetine on carbamazepine, valproate and phenytoin. *Epilepsy Research, 10,* 201–204.

Angst, J., & Stabl, M. (1992). Efficacy of moclobemide in different patient groups: A meta-analysis of studies. *Psychopharmacology (Berl), 106*(Suppl.), S109–113.

Arana, G. W., Epstein, S., Molloy, M., & Greenblatt, D. J. (1988). Carbamazepine-induced reduction of plasma alprazolam concentrations: A clinical case report. *Journal of Clinical Psychiatry, 49,* 448–449.

Ashton, A. K., & Wolin, R. E. (1996). Nefazodone-induced carbamazepine toxicity [Letter to the editor]. *American Journal of Psychiatry, 153,* 733.

Bachmann, K. A., & Jauregui, L. (1993). Use of single sample clearance estimates of cytochrome P450 substrates to characterize human hepatic CYP status in vivo. *Xenobiotica, 23,* 307–315.

Borchert, L. D. (1996). Exercise-induced exacerbation of partial seizures due to enhanced gabapentin clearance. *Epilepsia, 37*(Suppl. 5), 158. (Abstract 6.26).

Bourgeois, B. F. (1988). Pharmacologic interactions between valproate and other drugs. *American Journal of Medicine, 84,* 29–33.

Bowden, C. L. (1995). Predictors of response to divalproex and lithium. *Journal of Clinical Psychiatry, 56*(Suppl. 3), 25–30.

Bowden, C. L., Brugger, A. M., Swann, A. C., Calabrese, J. R., Janicak, P. G., Petty, F., et al. (1994). Efficacy of divalproex vs. lithium and placebo in the treatment of mania. The Depakote Mania Study Group. *Journal of the American Medical Association, 271,* 918–924.

Bowden, C. L., Janicak, P. G., Orsulak, P., Swann. A. C., Davis, J. M., Calabreses, J. R., et al. (1996): Relation of serum valproate concentration to response in mania. *American Journal of Psychiatry, 153,* 765–770.

Brodie, M. J. (1995). Tiagabine pharmacology in profile. *Epilepsia, 36*(Suppl. 6) S7–S9.

Brodie, M. J., & MacPhee, G. J. (1986). Carbamazepine neurotoxicity precipitated by diltiazem. *British Medical Journal, 292,* 1170–1171.

Bryant, A. E., III, & Dreifuss, F. E. (1996). Valproic acid hepatic fatalities. III. U.S. experience since 1986. *Neurology, 46,* 465–469.

Calabrese, J. R., Bowden, C. L., Sachs, G. S., Ascher, J. A., Monaghan, E., & Rudd, G. D.

(1999). A double-blind placebo-controlled study of lamotrigine monotherapy in outpatients with bipolar I depression. Lamictal 602 Study Group. *Journal of Clinical Psychiatry, 60,* 79–88.

Calabrese, J. R., Shelton, M. D., III, Keck, P. E., Jr., McElroy, S. L., & Werkner, J. E. (1998, May/June). *Topiramate in severe treatment-refractory mania.* Paper presented at the 151st Annual Meeting of the American Psychiatric Association, Toronto. (Abstract No. NR202.)

Calabrese, J. R., Suppes, P., Bowden, C. L., Sachs, G. S., Swann, A. C., McElroy, S. L., et al. (2000). A double-blind, placebo-controlled, prophylaxis study of lamotrigine in rapid cycling bipolar disorder. The Lamictal 614 Study Group. *Journal of Clinical Psychiatry, 61,* 841–850.

Capewell, S., Freestone, S., Critchley, J. A., Pottage, A., & Prescott, L. F. (1988). Reduced felodipine bioavailability in patients taking anticonvulsants. *Lancet, 2,* 480–482.

Carwile, S. T., Husain, A. M., Miller, P. P., & Radtke, R. A. (1997). Lamotrigine and sexual dysfunction in male patients with epilepsy. *Epilepsia, 38*(Suppl. 8), 180. (Abstract No. 5.040).

Cohen, L. S., Sichel, D. A., Robertson, L. M., Heckscher, E., & Rosenbaum, J. F. (1995). Postpartum prophylaxis for women with bipolar disorder. *American Journal of Psychiatry, 152,* 1641–1645.

Cohn, J. B., Collins, G., Ashbrook, E., & Wernicke, J. F. (1989). A comparison of fluoxetine imipramine and placebo in patients with bipolar depressive disorder. *International Clinical Psychopharmacology, 4,* 313–322.

Critchley, M. A. E. (1994). Effects of lamotrigine (Lamictal) in an animal model of anxiety [abstract]. *British Journal of Pharmacology, 111,* 205P.

de Leon, J., & Bork, J. (1997). Risperidone and cytochrome P450 3A [Letter to the editor]. *Journal of Clinical Psychiatry, 58,* 450.

Denbow, C. E., & Fraser, H. S. (1990). Clinically significant hemorrhage due to warfarin-carbamazepine interaction. *Southern Medical Journal, 83,* 981.

Dichter, M. A., & Brodie, M. J. (1996). New antiepileptic drugs. *New England Journal of Medicine, 334,* 1583–1590.

Eichelbaum, M., Tomson, T., Tybring, G., & Bertilsson, L. (1985). Carbamazepine metabolism in man. Induction and pharmacogenetic aspects. *Clinical Pharmacokinetics, 10,* 80–90.

Ereshefsky, L., Jann, M. W., Saklad, S. R., & Davis, C. M. (1986). Bioavailability of psychotropic drugs: Historical perspective and pharmacokinetic overview. *Journal of Clinical Psychiatry, 47,* 6–15.

Faigle, J. W., & Feldmann, K. F. (1995). Carbamazepine: Chemistry and biotransformation. In R. H. Levy, R. H. Mattson, & B. S. Meldrum (Eds.), *Antiepileptic drugs* (4th ed., pp. 499–513). New York: Raven.

Forsythe, W. I., Owens, J. R., & Toothill, C. (1981). Effectiveness of acetazolamide in the treatment of carbamazepine-resistant epilepsy in children. *Developmental Medicine and Child Neurology, 23,* 761–769.

Fritze, J., Unsorg, B., & Lanczik, M. (1991). Interaction between carbamazepine and fluvoxamine. *Acta Psychiatrica Scandinavia, 84,* 583–584.

Frye, M. A., Ketter, T. A., Kimbrell, T. A., Dunn, R. T., Speer, A. M., Osuch, E. A., et al. (2000). A placebo-controlled study of lamotrigine and gabapentin monotherapy in refractory mood disorders. *Journal of Clinical Psychopharmacology, 20,* 607–614.

Frye, M. A., Kimbrell, T. A., Dunn, R. T., Piscitelli, S., Grothe, D., Vanderham, E., et al. (1998). Gabapentin does not alter single-dose lithium pharmacokinetics. *Journal of Clinical Psychopharmacology, 18*(6), 461–464.

Garland, Bunney, B., Bunney, W. E., Jr., & Carlsson, A. (1995). Schizophrenia and glutamate. In

F. E. Bloom, & D. J. Kupfer (Eds.), *Psychopharmacology: The fourth generation of progress* (pp. 1205–1214). New York: Raven.

Garnett, W. R., Levy, B., McLean, A. M., Zhang, Y., Couch, R. A., Rudnic, E. M., et al. (1998). Pharmacokinetic evaluation of twice-daily extended-release carbamazepine (CBZ) and four-times-daily immediate-release CBZ in patients with epilepsy. *Epilepsia, 39,* 274–279.

Gelenberg, A. J., & Jefferson, J. W. (1995). Lithium tremor. *Journal of Clinical Psychiatry, 56,* 283–287.

Ghaemi, S. N., & Katzow, J. J. (1999). The use of quetiapine for treatment-resistant bipolar disorder: A case series. *Annals of Clinical Psychiatry, 11,* 137–140.

Gidal, B. E., Anderson, G. D., Spencer, N. W., Maly, M., Murty, J., Pitterle, M., et al. (1994). *Valproic acid (VPA) associated weight gain in monotherapy patients with epilepsy.* Annual Meeting of the American Epilepsy Society, New Orleans, December 2–8, 1994.

Gidal, B. E., Lensmeyer, G. L., & Pitterle, M. E. (1997). In vitro characterization of topiramate (TPM) binding to erythrocyte (RBCs): Potential impact on therapeutic drug monitoring. *Epilepsia, 38*(Suppl. 8), 98 (Abstract No. 3.036).

Gisclon, L. G., Curtin, C. R., Kramer, L. D., Sachdeo, R. C., & Levy, R. H. (1994). The steady-state (SS) pharmacokinetics of phenytoin (Dilantin) and topiramate (Topamax) in epileptic patients on monotherapy and during combination therapy. *Epilepsia, 35*(Suppl. 8), 54 (Abstract No.2.72).

Goa, K. L., & Sorkin, E. M. (1993). Gabapentin. A review of its pharmacological properties and clinical potential in epilepsy. *Drugs, 46,* 409–427.

Goodwin, F. K., & Jamison, K. R. (1990). *Manic depressive illness.* New York: Oxford University Press.

Gordey, M., Delorey, T. M., & Olsen, R. W. (1995). Topiramate modulates GABA receptor responses in xenopus oocytes expressing several recombinant receptor subunit combinations. *Epilepsia, 36*(Suppl. 4), 48. (Abstract No. 2.55).

Granneman, G. R., Schneck, D. W., Cavanaugh, J. H., & Witt, G. F. (1996). Pharmacokinetic interactions and side effects resulting from concomitant administration of lithium and divalproex sodium. *Journal of Clinical Psychiatry, 57,* 204–206.

Graves, N. M. (1995). Neuropharmacology and drug interactions in clinical practice. *Epilepsia, 36* (Suppl. 2) S27–S33.

Grimm, S. W., Stams, K. R., & Bui, K. (1997, May). *In vitro prediction of potential metabolic drug interactions for quetiapine.* Paper presented at the 150th Annual Meeting of the American Psychiatric Association, San Diego. (Abstract NR251).

Grimsley, S. R., Jann, M. W., Carter, J. G., D'Mello, A. P., & D'Souza, M. J. (1991). Increased carbamazepine plasma concentrations after fluoxetine coadministration. *Clinical Pharmacology and Therapeutics, 50,* 10–15.

Grunze, H., Erfurth, A., Marcuse, A., Amann, B., Normann, C., & Walden, J. (1999). Tiagabine appears not to be efficacious in the treatment of acute mania. *Journal of Clinical Psychiatry, 60,* 759–762.

Ishizaki, T., Chiba, K., Saito, M., Kobayashi, K., & Iizuka, R. (1984). The effects of neuroleptics (haloperidol and chlorpromazine) on the pharmacokinetics of valproic acid in schizophrenic patients. *Journal of Clinical Psychopharmacology, 4,* 254–261.

Isojarvi, J. I., Laatikainen, T. J., Pakarinen, A. J., Juntunen, K. T., & Myllyla, V. V. (1993). Polycystic ovaries and hyperandrogenism in women taking valproate for epilepsy. *New England Journal of Medcine, 329,* 1383–1388.

Jann, M. W., Fidone, G. S., Hernandez, J. M., Amrung, S., & Davis, C. M. (1989). Clinical implications of increased antipsychotic plasma concentrations upon anticonvulsant cessation. *Psychiatry Research, 28,* 153–159.

Jefferson, J. W., Greist, J. H., Ackerman, D. L., & Carroll, J. A. (1987). *Lithium encyclopedia for clinical practice* (2nd ed.). Washington, DC: American Psychiatric Press.

Jerling, M., Lindstrom, L., Bondesson, U., & Bertilsson, L. (1994). Fluvoxamine inhibition and carbamazepine induction of the metabolism of clozapine: Evidence from a therapeutic drug monitoring service. *Therapeutic Drug Monitoring, 16,* 368–374.

Kahn, E. M., Schulz, S. C., Perel, J. M., & Alexander, J. E. (1990). Change in haloperidol level due to carbamazepine—A complicating factor in combined medication for schizophrenia. *Journal of Clin Psychopharmacology, 10,* 54–57.

Kane, J. M., & Smith, J. M. (1982). Tardive dyskinesia: Prevalence and risk factors, 1959 to 1979. *Archives of General Psychiatry, 39,* 473–481.

Kato, T., Inubushi, T., & Takahashi, S. (1994). Relationship of lithium concentrations in the brain measured by lithium-7 magnetic resonance spectroscopy to treatment response in mania. *Journal of Clinical Psychopharmacology, 14,* 330–335.

Kato, T., Shioiri, T., Inubushi, T., & Takahashi, S. (1993). Brain lithium concentrations measured with lithium-7 magnetic resonance spectroscopy in patients with affective disorders: Relationship to erythrocyte and serum concentrations. *Biology of Psychiatry, 33,* 147–152.

Kaufman, K. R. (1998). Adjunctive tiagabine treatment of psychiatric disorders: Three cases. *Annals of Clinical Psychiatry, 10,* 181–184.

Kaufman, K. R., & Gerner, R. (1997). Lamotrigine toxicity secondary to sertraline. *Epilepsia, 38*(Suppl. 8), 100 (Abstract No. 3.047).

Keck, P. E., Jr., & Ice. K. (2000). *A 3-week, double-blind, randomized trial of ziprasidone in the acute treatment of mania.* The Ziprasidone Mania Study Group. 22nd Congress of Collegium Internationale Neuro-Psychopharmacologicum. Brussels, July 9–13. (Abstract: P.16.41). *International Journal of Neuropsychopharmacology, 3,* S342.

Kerr, B. M., Thummel, K. E., Wurden, C. J., Klein, S. M., Kroetz, D. L., Gonzalez, F. J., et al. (1994). Human liver carbamazepine metabolism. Role of CYP3A4 and CYP2C8 in 10,11-epoxide formation. *Biochemical Pharmacology, 47,* 1969–1979.

Ketter, T. A., Flockhart, D. A., Post, R. M., Denicoff, K., Pazzaglia, P. J., Marangell, L. B., et al. (1995a). The emerging role of cytochrome P450 3A in psychopharmacology. *Journal of Clinical Psychopharmacology, 15,* 387–398.

Ketter, T. A., Jenkins, J. B., Schroeder, D. H., Pazzaglia, P. J., Marangell, L. B., George, M. S., et al. (1995b). Carbamazepine but not valproate induces bupropion metabolism. *Journal of Clinical Psychopharmacology, 15,* 327–333.

Ketter, T. A., Malow, B. A., Flamini, R., Ko. D., White, S. R., Stertz, B. E., et al. (1996). Felbamate monotherapy has stimulant-like effects in patients with epilepsy. *Epilepsy Research, 23,* 129–137.

Ketter, T. A., Pazzaglia, P. J., & Post, R. M. (1992). Synergy of carbamazepine and valproic acid in affective illness: Case report and review of the literature. *Journal of Clinical Psychopharmacology, 12,* 276–281.

Ketter, T. A., Post, R. M., Parekh, P. I., & Worthington, K. (1995). Addition of monoamine oxidase inhibitors to carbamazepine: Preliminary evidence of safety and antidepressant efficacy in treatment-resistant depression. *Journal of Clinical Psychiatry, 56,* 471–475.

Ketter, T. A., Post, R. M., & Worthington, K. (1991a). Principles of clinically important drug interactions with carbamazepine. Part I. *Journal of Clinical Psychopharmacology, 11,* 198–203.

Ketter, T. A., Post, R. M., & Worthington, K. (1991b). Principles of clinically important drug interactions with carbamazepine. Part II. *Journal of Clinical Psychopharmacology, 11,* 306–313.

Ketter, T. A., Winsberg, M. E., Wang, P. W., Tate, D. L., & Strong, C. M. (1999, December). *Olanzapine in nonpsychotic bipolar disorders.* Paper presented at 38th Annual Meeting of the American College of Neuropsychopharmacology, Acapulco, Mexico. (Abstract, p. 166).

Lai, A. A., Levy, R. H., & Cutler, R. E. (1978). Time-course of interaction between carbamazepine and clonazepam in normal man. *Clinical Pharmacology and Therapy, 24,* 316–323.

Lane, H. Y., & Chang, W. H. (1998). Risperidone-carbamazepine interactions: Is cytochrome

P450 3A involved? [letter]. *Journal of Clinical Psychiatry, 59,* 430–431.

Lane, R. M. (1994). Carbamazepine and sertraline [Letter to the editor]. *New Zealand Medical Journal, 107,* 209.

Leach, M. J., Lees, G., & Riddall, D. R. (1995). Lamotrigine: Mechanisms of action. In R. H. Levy, R. H. Mattson, & B. S. Meldrum (Eds.), *Antiepileptic drugs* (4th ed., pp. 861–869). New York: Raven.

Lee, D. O., Steingard, R. J., Cesena, M., Helmers, S. L., Riviello, J. J., & Mikati, M. A. (1996). Behavioral side effects of gabapentin in children. *Epilepsia, 37,* 87–90.

Leppik, I. E. (1995a). Felbamate. *Epilepsia, 36*(Suppl. 2), S66–S72.

Leppik, I. E. (1995b). Tiagabine: The safety landscape. *Epilepsia, 36*(Suppl. 6), S10–S13.

Levy, R. H., Lane, E. A., Guyot, M., Brachet-Liermain, A., Cenraud, B., & Loiseau, P. (1983). Analysis of parent drug-metabolite relationship in the presence of an inducer. Application to the carbamazepine-clobazam interaction in normal man. *Drug Metabolism and Disposition: The Biological Fate of Chemicals, 11,* 286–292.

Levy, R. H., Morselli, P. L., Bianchetti, G., Guyot, M., Brachet-Liermain, A., & Loiseau, P. (1982). Interaction between valproic acid and carbamazepine in epileptic patients. In R. H. Levy, W. H. Pitlick, M. Eichelbaum, & J. Meijer (Eds.), *Metabolism of antiepileptic drugs* (pp 45–51). New York: Raven.

Lloyd, K. G., Zivkovic, B., Scatton, B., Morselli, P. L., & Bartholini, G. (1989). The gabaergic hypothesis of depression. *Progress in Neuropsychopharmacology and Biology Psychiatry, 13,* 341–351.

Macdonald, R. L., Kelly, K. M. (1995). Antiepileptic drug mechanisms of action. *Epilepsia, 36*(Suppl. 2), S2–S12.

Manji, H. K., Potter, W. Z., & Lenox, R. H. (1995). Signal transduction pathways. Molecular targets for lithium's actions. *Archives of General Psychiatry, 52,* 531–543.

Marcotte, D. (1998). Use of topiramate, a new anti-epileptic as a mood stabilizer. *Journal of Affective Disorders, 50,* 245–251.

Marcotte, D. B., Fogleman, L., Wolfe, N., & Nemire, R. (1997, May). *Gabapentin: An effective therapy for patients with bipolar affective disorder.* Paper presented at the 150th Annual Meeting of the American Psychiatric Association, San Diego. (Abstract NR261).

McElroy, S. L., Keck, P. E., Stanton, S. P., Tugrul, K. C., Bennett, J. A., & Strakowski, S. M. (1996). A randomized comparison of divalproex oral loading versus haloperidol in the initial treatment of acute psychotic mania. *Journal of Clinical Psychiatry, 57,* 142–146.

McElroy, S. L., Soutullo, C. A., Keck, P. E., Jr., & Kmetz, G. F. (1997). A pilot trial of adjunctive gabapentin in the treatment of bipolar disorder. *Annals of Clinical Psychiatry, 9,* 99.

McElroy, S. L., Suppes, T., Keck, P. E., Frye, M. A., Denicoff, K. D., Altshuler, L. L., et al. (2000, June). Open-label adjunctive topiramate in the treatment of bipolar disorders. *Biological Psychiatry, 47*(12), 1025–1033.

Mesdjian, E., Dravet, C., Cenraud, B., & Roger, J. (1980). Carbamazepine intoxication due to triacetyloleandomycin administration in epileptic patients. *Epilepsia, 21,* 489–496.

Nasrallah, H. A., Churchill, C. M., & Hamdan-Allan, G. A. (1988). Higher frequency of neuroleptic-induced dystonia in mania than in schizophrenia. *American Journal of Psychiatry, 145,* 1455–1456.

Nasrallah, H. A., Dev, V., Rak, I., & Raniwalla, J. (1999, December). *Safety update on quetiapine and lenticular examinations: Experience with 300,000 patients.* Paper presented at the 38th Annual Meeting of the American College of Neuropsychopharmacology, Acapulco, Mexico. (Abstract 109).

Nemeroff, C. B., Evans, D. L., Gyulai, L., Sachs, G. S., Bowden, C. L., Gergel, I. P., et al. (2001). Double-blind, placebo-controlled comparison of imipramine and paroxetine in the treatment of bipolar depression. *American Journal of Psychiatry, 158*(6), 906–912.

Palmer, K. J., & McTavish, D. (1993). Felbamate. A review of its pharmacodynamic and pharmacokinetic properties, and therapeutic efficacy in epilepsy. *Drugs, 45,* 1041–1065.

Pande, A. C., Crockatt, J. G., Janney, C. A., Werth, J. L., & Tsaroucha, G. (2000, September). Gabapentin in bipolar disorder: A placebo-controlled trial of adjunctive therapy. Gabapentin Bipolar Disorder Study Group. *Bipolar Disorder, 2*(3 Pt. 2), 249–255.

Pande, A. C., Pollack, M. H., Crockatt, J., Greiner, M., Chouinard, G., Lydiard, R. B., et al. (2000, August). Placebo-controlled study of gabapentin treatment of panic disorder. *Journal of Clinical Psychopharmacology, 20*(4), 467–471.

Pande, A. C., Davidson, J. R., Jefferson, J. W., Janney, C. A., Katzelnick, D. J., Weisler, R. H., et al. (1999). Treatment of social phobia with gabapentin: A placebo-controlled study. *Journal of Clinical Psychopharmacology, 19,* 341–348.

Pennell, P. B., Ogaily, M. S., & Macdonald, R. L. (1995). Aplastic anemia in a patient receiving felbamate for complex partial seizures. *Neurology, 45,* 456–460.

Petty, F. (1995). GABA and mood disorders: a brief review and hypothesis. *Journal of Affective Disorders, 34,* 275–281.

Pitterle, M. E., & Collins, D. M. (1988). Carbamazepine-10-11-epoxide evaluation associated with coadministration of loxapine or amoxapine [abstract]. *Epilepsia, 29,* 654.

Post, R. M., Weiss, S. R. B., Chuang, D. M., & Ketter, T. A. (1994). Mechanisms of action of carbamazepine in seizure and affective disorders. In R. T. Joffe, & J. R. Calabrese (Eds.), *Anticonvulsants in psychiatry* (pp. 43–92). New York: Marcel Dekker.

Potter, W. Z., & Ketter, T. A. (1993). Pharmacological issues in the treatment of bipolar disorder: Focus on mood-stabilizing compounds. *Canadian Journal of Psychiatry, 38,* S51–S56.

Price, W. A., & DiMarzio, L. R. (1988). Verapamil-carbamazepine neurotoxicity [Letter to the editor]. *Journal of Clinical Psychiatry, 49,* 80.

Rambeck, B., & Wolf, P. (1993). Lamotrigine clinical pharmacokinetics. *Clinical Pharmacokinetics, 25,* 433–443.

Redington, K., Wells, C., & Petito, F. (1992). Erythromycin and valproate interaction [Letter to the editor]. *Annals of Internal Medicine, 116,* 877–878.

Richens, A. (1993). Clinical pharmacokinetics of gabapentin. In D. Chadwick (Ed.), *New trends in epilepsy management: The role of gabapentin* (pp. 41–46). London: Royal Society of Medicine Services.

Rothschild, A. J. (1996). Management of psychotic, treatment-resistant depression. *Psychiatric Clinics of North America, 19,* 237–252.

Ryback, R. S., Brodsky, L., & Munasifi, F. (1997). Gabapentin in bipolar disorder [Letter to the editor]. *Journal of Neuropsychiatry and Clinical Neurosciences, 9,* 301.

Sachdeo, R. C., Sachdeo, S. K., Walker, S. A., Kramer, L. D., Nayak, R. K., & Doose, D. R. (1996). Steady-state pharmacokinetics of topiramate and carbamazepine in patients with epilepsy during monotherapy and concomitant therapy. *Epilepsia, 37,* 774–780.

Sachs, G., & Ghaemi, S. N. (2000). Safety and efficacy of risperidone versus placebo in combination with lithium or valproate in the treatment of the manic phase of bipolar disorder [Abstract P.01.192]. *International Journal of Neuropsychopharmacology, 3,* S143.

Sachs, G. S., Lafer, B., Stoll, A. L., Banov, M., Thibault, A. B., Tohen, M., et al. (1994). A double-blind trial of bupropion versus desipramine for bipolar depression. *Journal of Clinical Psychiatry, 55*(9), 391–393.

Sackellares, J. C., Sato, S., Dreifuss, F. E., & Penry, J. K. (1981). Reduction of steady-state valproate levels by other antiepileptic drugs. *Epilepsia, 22,* 437–441.

Sajatovic, M., Brescan, D. W., Perez, D., Digiovani, S., & Hattab, H. G. (1999, May). *Quetiapine fumarate in neuroleptic-dependent mood disorders.* Paper presented at the 152nd Annual Meeting of the American Psychiatric Association, Washington, DC. (Abstract No. NR456).

Schaffer, C. B., & Schaffer, L. C. (1997). Gabapentin in the treatment of bipolar disorder [Letter to the editor]. *American Journal of Psychiatry, 154,* 291–292.

Schaffer, L. C., & Schaffer, C. B. (1999). Tiagabine and the treatment of refractory bipolar disorder [Letter to the editor]. *American Journal of Psychiatry, 156,* 2014–2015.

Segal, J., Berk, M., & Brook, S. (1998). Risperidone compared with both lithium and haloperidol in mania: A double-blind randomized controlled trial. *Clinical Neuropharmacology, 21,* 176–180.

Sernyak, M. J., Godleski, L. S., Griffin, R. A., Mazure, C. M., & Woods, S. W. (1997). Chronic neuroleptic exposure in bipolar outpatients. *Journal of Clinical Psychiatry, 58,* 193–195.

Severt, L., Coulter, D. A., Sombati, S., & DeLorenzo, R. J. (1995). Topiramate selectively blocks kainate currents in cultured hippocampal neurons. *Epilepsia, 36*(Suppl. 4), 38. (Abstract No. 2.16).

Shank, R. P., Gardocki, J. F., Vaught, J. L., Davis, C. B., Schupsky, J. J., Raffa, R. B., et al. (1994). Topiramate: Preclinical evaluation of structurally novel anticonvulsant. *Epilepsia, 35*(2), 450–460.

Shimada, T., Yamazaki, H., Mimura, M., Inui, Y., & Guengerich, F. P. (1994). Interindividual variations in human liver cytochrome P-450 enzymes involved in the oxidation of drugs, carcinogens and toxic chemicals: studies with liver microsomes of 30 Japanese and 30 Caucasians. *Journal of Pharmacology and Experimental Therapy, 270,* 414–423.

Shorvon, S. D. (1996). Safety of topiramate: adverse events and relationships to dosing. *Epilepsia, 37*(Suppl. 2), S18–S22.

Simpson, S. G., & DePaulo, J. R. (1991). Fluoxetine treatment of bipolar II depression. *Journal of Clinical Psychopharmacology, 11,* 52–54.

Sombati, S., Coulter, D. A., & DeLorenzo, R. J. (1995). Effects of topiramate on sustained repetitive firing and low Mg2+-induced seizure discharges in cultured hippocampal neurons. *Epilepsia, 36*(Suppl. 4), 38. (Abstract No. 2.15).

Sovner, R., & Davis, J. M. (1991). A potential drug interaction between fluoxetine and valproic acid [Letter to the editor]. *Journal of Clinical Psychopharmacology, 11,* 389.

Steketee, R. W., Wassilak, S. G., Adkins, W. N., Jr., Burstyn, D. G., Manclark, C. R., Berg, J., et al. (1988). Evidence for a high attack rate and efficacy of erythromycin prophylaxis in a pertussis outbreak in a facility for the developmentally disabled. *Journal of Infectious Disorders, 157,* 434–440.

Stewart, B. H., Kugler, A. R., Thompson, P. R., & Bockbrader, H. N. (1993). A saturable transport mechanism in the intestinal absorption of gabapentin is the underlying cause of the lack of proportionality between increasing dose and drug levels in plasma. *Pharmaceutical Research, 10,* 276–281.

Stoll, A. L., Mayer, P. V., Kolbrener, M., Goldstein, E., Suplit, B., Lucier, J., et al. (1994). Antidepressant-associated mania: A controlled comparison with spontaneous mania. *American Journal of Psychiatry, 151,* 1642–1645.

Suppes, T., Baldessarini, R. J., Faedda, G. L., & Tohen, M. (1991). Risk of recurrence following discontinuation of lithium treatment in bipolar disorder. *Archives of General Psychiatry, 48,* 1082–1088.

Suppes, T., Webb, A., Paul, B., Carmody, T., Kraemer, H., & Rush, A. J. (1999). Clinical outcome in a randomized 1-year trial of clozapine versus treatment as usual for patients with treatment-resistant illness and a history of mania. *American Journal of Psychiatry, 156,* 1164–1169.

Suzdak, P. D., & Jansen, J. A. (1995). A review of the preclinical pharmacology of tiagabine: A potent and selective anticonvulsant GABA uptake inhibitor. *Epilepsia, 36,* 612–626.

Tartara, A., Galimberti, C. A., Manni, R., Parietti, L., Zucca, C., Baasch, H., et al. (1991). Differential effects of valproic acid and enzyme-inducing anticonvulsants on nimodipine pharmacokinetics in epileptic patients. *British Journal of Clinical Pharmacology, 32,* 335–340.

Taylor, C. P. (1995). Gabapentin: Mechanisms of action. In R. H. Levy, R. H. Mattson, & B. S. Meldrum (Eds.), *Antiepileptic drugs* (4th ed., pp. 829–841). New York: Raven.

Thakker, K. M., Mangat, S., Garnett, W. R., Levy, R. H., & Kochak, G. M. (1992). Comparative bioavailability and steady state fluctuations of Tegretol commercial and carbamazepine OROS tablets in adult and pediatric epileptic patients. *Biopharmacutics and Drug Disposition, 13,* 559–569.

Thase, M. E., Mallinger, A. G., McKnight, D., & Himmelhoch, J. M. (1992). Treatment of imipramine-resistant recurrent depression, IV: A double-blind crossover study of tranylcypromine for anergic bipolar depression. *American Journal of Psychiatry, 149,* 195–198.

Tohen, M., Jacobs, T. G., Grundy, S. L., McElroy, S. L., Banov, M. C., Janicak, P. G., et al. (2000). Efficacy of olanzapine in acute bipolar mania: A double-blind, placebo-controlled study. The Olanzapine HGGW Study Group. *Archives of General Psychiatry, 57*(9) 841-849.

Tohen, M., Castillo, J., Baldessarini, R. J., Zarate, C., Jr., & Kando, J. C. (1995). Blood dyscrasias with carbamazepine and valproate: A pharmacoepidemiological study of 2,228 patients at risk. *American Journal of Psychiatry, 152,* 413–418.

Tohen, M., Sanger, T. M., McElroy, S. L., Tollefson, G. D., Chengappa, K. N., Daniel, D. G., et al. (1999). Olanzapine versus placebo in the treatment of acute mania. Olanzapine HGEH Study Group. *American Journal of Psychiatry, 156,* 702–709.

Wagner, M. L., Graves, N. M., Leppik, I. E., Remmel, R. P., Ward, D. L., & Shumaker, R. C. (1991). Effect of felbamate on valproate disposition [abstract]. *Epilepsia, 32,* 15.

Waldmeier, P. C., Baumann, P. A., Wicki, P., Feldtrauer, J. J., Stierlin, C., & Schmutz, M. (1995). Similar potency of carbamazepine, oxcarbazepine, and lamotrigine in inhibiting the release of glutamate and other neurotransmitters. *Neurology, 45,* 1907–1913.

Webster, L. K., Mihaly, G. W., Jones, D. B., Smallwood, R. A., Phillips, J. A., & Vajda, F. J. (1984). Effect of cimetidine and ranitidine on carbamazepine and sodium valproate pharmacokinetics. *European Journal of Clinical Pharmacology, 27,* 341–343.

Winsberg, M. E., DeGolia, S. G., Strong, C. M., & Ketter, T. A. (2001). Divalproex in medication-naive and mood stabilizer-naive bipolar II depression. *Journal of Affective Disorders, 67,* 207–212.

Wright, J. M., Stokes, E. F., & Sweeney, V. P. (1982). Isoniazid-induced carbamazepine toxicity and vice versa: a double drug interaction. *New England Journal of Medicine, 307,* 1325–1327.

Wrighton, S. A., & Stevens, J. C. (1992). The human hepatic cytochromes P450 involved in drug metabolism. *Critical Review of Toxicology, 22,* 1–21.

Yatham, L. N. (2000). Safety and efficacy of risperidone as combination therapy for the manic phase of bipolar disorder: Preliminary findings of a randomized, double-blind study (RIS-INT-46). *International Journal of Neuropsychopharmacology, 3,* S142.

Young, L. T., Robb, J. C., Patelis-Siotis, I., MacDonald, C., & Joffe, R. T. (1997). Acute treatment of bipolar depression with gabapentin. *Biological Psychiatry, 42,* 851–853.

Index